THE WILD WEST

Help Us Keep This Guide Up to Date

Every effort has been made by the author and editors to make this guide as accurate and useful as possible. However, many things can change after a guide is published—establishments close, phone numbers change, trails are rerouted, facilities come under new management, etc.

We would love to hear from you concerning your experiences with this guide and how you feel it could be made better and be kept up to date. While we may not be able to respond to all comments and suggestions, we'll take them to heart and we'll also make certain to share them with the author. Please send your comments and suggestions to the following address:

The Globe Pequot Press
Reader Response/Editorial Department
P.O. Box 833
Old Saybrook, CT 06475

Or you may e-mail us at:

editorial@globe-pequot.com

Thanks for your input, and happy travels!

TRAVEL
HISTORIC
AMERICA
SERIES

THE
WILD WEST

Second Edition

by
MICHAEL McCOY

A VOYAGER BOOK

The
Globe
Pequot
Press

OLD SAYBROOK, CONNECTICUT

Poem on page 247 by Carole Jarvis

Cover design by Laura Augustine

Cover photos: © 1997 Pete Saloutous/The Stock Market (top); © 1997 D.R. Stoecklein/The Stock Market (inset); © Superstock (bottom)

Interior design by Nancy Freeborn

3·2-98

Library of Congress Cataloging-in-Publication Data

McCoy, Michael, 1951-
    The Wild West : / by Michael McCoy. — 2nd ed.
        p.   cm. — (Travel historic America series)
    "A Voyager book."
    Includes index.
    ISBN 0-7627-0115-3
    1. West (U.S.)—Guidebooks. 2. Historic sites—West (U.S.) —
Guidebooks. I. Title. II. Series.
F590.3.M38 1997
917.804'33—dc21   97-35442
                                               CIP

Manufactured in the United States of America
Second Edition/First Printing

Dedication

For the heroes of my boyhood—Roy Rogers, Spin and Marty, Gene Autry, and Davy Crockett/Fess Parker—who made anything seem possible and who taught me what it means to be a good guy; for the heroes of my adulthood—Chief Joseph, Chief Plenty Coups, Bob Wills, my wife, Nancy, and the rodeoin' Greenoughs of Red Lodge, Montana; and for the trail rider in everyone: Whoopie-ti-yi-yo, git along little dogie! Happy trails to you as you drift along with the tumbling tumbleweed, back in the saddle again, where the water's runnin' free and it's waitin' there for me and you.

Wild West Region

Contents

Photo Credits

All others by the author.

Introduction

For an author, the introduction to a book is a funny thing: What the reader reads first, the writer writes last. Only after the rest of the text is on paper and the subjects have been tossed around in the mind for a spell can an author know what he is introducing.

As I introduce this book, then, I think back to the time when the offer to write it came my way. I came close to refusing, for the thought of its staggering scope nearly bowled me to my knees. We were talking about *eighteen states*. Rather than do the West, which I cherish, an injustice by trying to cover it all in a measly 400 pages, I thought, perhaps I'd better not get involved.

Better sense prevailed, however. "Who's gonna write it if I don't?" I asked.

"Yeah!" I confirmed to myself. I was destined to do it. Like a million kids raised in the nifty fifties, I was weaned on Hopalong Cassidy and the Lone Ranger, and I lived to be a cowboy. Rarely did I go anywhere without packing my pretend Colt .45 Peacemaker, usually with buckskin chaps and a Davy Crockett coonskin cap to top off the outfit. I felt naked without 'em, ma'am. At night I even went to sleep between sheets decorated with pictures of Davy fighting Indians, grizzly bears, and Mexicans. They were the percales that dictated my dreams.

Moreover, I was born in Wyoming, the Cowboy State, which really meant something to me because my family moved from there when I was still an infant, and I grew up in the far tamer reaches of Iowa (but even then in a town originally known as Montana and later renamed Boone, after the son of world-class frontiersman Daniel Boone).

In one of my earliest memories, I recall a family friend from Wheatland, Wyoming, who was visiting us in Iowa. It sounds like nonsense now (but who can explain the workings of a three-year-old's mind?): When I spied his Wyoming license plate, I knew right away that the cowboy adorning it was me.

Whenever I saw a car from the great state of Wyoming after that, I immediately bonded with it, for it gave me a wonderful feeling to see my likeness on its license plate. I can't begin to explain how I felt on my first trip through Wyoming to Yellowstone, when I was still young enough to subscribe to this theory—I was everywhere I looked!

Yes, better sense reigned, and I took on this book project. Now it's completed, but it isn't comprehensive. You're sure to wonder why some attractions or events are included and others are omitted. Here are a couple of reasons: Nearly any western town big enough to have a post office and laundromat has a museum filled with Old West relics and lore. There are simply too many attractions to include them all. Likewise, a book of this size could be written exclusively, say, about the dude ranches of Wyoming—a solitary component of dozens of potential Old West experiences, from just one of the eighteen western states.

In the beginning I thought perhaps the guide should cover only the states that are still part of "the real West," according to my somewhat cock-eyed standards. These are the states west of the Missouri with more cows than people; the states with only one telephone area code. Montana, Wyoming, New Mexico, and a few other states still qualify. Arizona and Oregon obtained their second area codes relatively recently, so they're borderline. California? Well, it claims a dozen at least, so there's no point in arguing. Then I started looking more closely at what there is to see in California and at the amazing things that have unfolded in that state during the past 200 years, and I realized that my theories were bogus (which in my heart I already knew). It became even clearer when I learned that Texas, where the Wild West was practically invented, owns seven or eight area codes.

The Wild West, the arid land of hope and opportunity: For most people the phrase conjures images of tough-talking hombres, shoot-outs in the streets, and, well, John Wayne. That image is partly right, but it's far from a comprehensive view. A late chronicler of the West, Wallace Stegner, who rode out his boyhood on the bucking back end of the days of westward expansion, understood the nineteenth-century West as well as any twentieth-century person ever has or will. "The idea that the West was all cowboys," wrote Stegner, "falsifies the life and societal arrangements I knew, which were more prosaic and ultimately more serious than the myth."

Stegner, paddling upstream against the whitewater of popular thought, underscored his sentiment by arguing that getting along counted for a whole lot more than self-reliance in the untamed West. Those persons who cooperated with others, rather than the rugged individualist, were responsible for taming the broad country west of the 100th meridian.

Important stuff to ruminate on, for it's easy to get roped and tied up in the romance of the Wild West. The region's history has been so stretched and bent out of shape, first by newspapermen and dime-novel authors, later by showmen like Buffalo Bill, and finally by screenwriters, that it's often tough, if not impossible, to separate fact from fiction. This difficulty has led to a skepticism among many as to how much, if any, truth there is to the lion's share of the legends of Wild West lore.

Mostly the West of the nineteenth century was about new people on a frontier who were trying to carve out an existence of some sort. It was an undomesticated, uncivilized country, sparsely peopled and inadequately policed. Individuals with illegal or questionable intentions were drawn toward the wild western horizon, attracted to the opportunities proffered by its lawlessness. Anthropologist Bobbie Ferguson, who in 1988 exhumed several dozen skeletons from an overgrown cemetery at the site of the old Gooding-Loving Cattle Trail town of Seven Rivers, New Mexico, would argue that the violence of the Wild West has not necessarily been embellished upon. "I was stunned," Ferguson said, referring to the findings that ten of the fifteen men who died between the ages of eighteen and forty-five had done so through violent means. "I had always assumed all those tales about the Wild West were exaggerated. But what I think it comes down to is that these peoples' lives were so hard, so full of physical labor, that there just wasn't much time for tenderness or care or warmth."

There's another side to the story, as revealed by a study undertaken a few years back by the University of California, Los Angeles. Dr. Roger D. McGrath found that Bodie, California, one of the bawdiest of the Old West boomtowns, had a robbery rate in the 1880s comparable to that of the proper city of Boston and that a hundred years later, Miami's robbery rate was twenty-five times greater than either! McGrath's study did support the popular idea that homicides were common in the Old West, but it also substantiated that they tended to result from fights between willing participants. Conversely, juvenile offenses and violent crimes like rape were almost unheard of.

The nineteenth-century West wasn't all good guys in white hats, bad guys in black ones, and Indians on the warpath. Like Americans in general, those who populated the West rarely fit within stereotypes. They came from a rich mix of ethnic backgrounds, a fact typically lost on Hollywood interpretations. A lone example from dozens of possibilities: Four of the U.S. Army's Indian-fighting regiments were composed entirely of freed slaves and other blacks, yet how many black cavalry riders did we see gracing the silver screen in those whoop-up-on-the-Indians Westerns of the 1940s, 1950s, and 1960s?

In these relatively enlightened times, in which we've widely agreed that Hollywood's depictions of Native Americans have been way off base, perhaps it's time also to take a closer look at the Indian fighters, as well as every other stereotypical character that populates the Old West of our imaginations.

Consider this partial list of the folks who helped drive the westward expansion of America: the sixteenth-century Spanish explorers, who brought with them the horse, the animal that radically altered the life-ways of the Plains Indians; the Jesuit missionaries, armed with the task of "saving" the Indians; early explorers, including the La Verendrye brothers, who penetrated the Dakotas in 1743, and the Lewis and Clark party; the beaver-trapping mountain men and the buffalo hunters; the Russian and Aleut fur hunters of the West Coast; those people who made fortunes in the 1860s by steamboating goods up the Missouri River to the Montana gold camps; merchants, Mormons, gold seekers, and prospective farm families who pulled up stakes and risked all by striking out along the emigrant trails; the Chinese railroad workers and often-neglected but important early land surveyors; the cowboys responsible for driving hundreds of thousands of longhorn cattle north to range from Texas; rustlers and robbers; the Indian-fighting soldiers who manned the frontier forts and the women who worked the bordellos that inevitably popped up nearby; peacekeepers, including the hanging sheriffs, freelance Texas Rangers, and female judges, the first of whom was elected in South Pass City, Wyoming, in 1869; the desert rats, gamblers, and timber beasts . . . the list goes on.

Today's West is a rapidly changing part of America, but the Old West still exists, for those who care to look for it. You might find it in the rich redolence of sage on the heels of a summer rainstorm in Wyoming's Red Desert, or in the yips and yammers of a coyote pack, hunkering along the flank of Steen's Mountain in southeast Oregon. You may locate the Old West in Medora, North Dakota, where Teddy Roosevelt once lived the Bully Way with frontier cowpokes as *compadres;* at a reenactment of Gen. George Armstrong Custer's Last Stand in Montana's resplendent Crow Country; or on a wagon-train outing along the Oregon Trail in Nebraska. You can even find it in the heart of Denver or Fort Worth, major cities that vie for the title of Capital of the Wild West.

You may find the Wild West at an impromptu, spill-into-the-streets party, such as those that tend to erupt at events like the World Famous Bucking Horse Sale in Miles City, Montana, and the Fourth of July Rodeo in Tensleep, Wyoming. Speaking of the Tensleep Rodeo, I once learned an important lesson there: Never call a cowboy "dude." I did, then had to do some fast talking to keep my front teeth intact. I regarded it a friendly term; the cowboy considered it the ultimate put-down. "I ain't a dude, mister. I'm a hand," he told me, laconically, in no uncertain terms, his lower lip permanently puffed out from the wads of Skoal that obviously had occupied the spot for years. Then he glared at me, hard.

Anyone, incidentally, can be a westerner—a cowboy or cowgirl. It's more a matter of attitude than geography, attire, or livelihood. After all, very few people (other than the Native Americans, who go back at least 10,000 years) have roots in the West that go deeper than a century. All of our famous Wild West characters came to the region from somewhere else and often returned there or went somewhere new after making their mark. Gen. George Custer hailed from Michigan, William Cody from Iowa, Martha "Calamity Jane" Canary and cowboy artist Charlie Russell from Missouri, and mountain man Jim Bridger from Virginia, via Missouri. Even the Sioux and Cheyenne Indians, whom we intimately associate with the western frontier, didn't

migrate out of Minnesota toward the Dakotas and Montana until the late 1600s and early 1700s. Maybe these facts concerning two of our most enduring legends will help to put things in perspective: Bat Masterson left the West in 1902 for New York City, where he became a successful sportswriter; Wyatt Earp, meanwhile, wound up in Los Angeles, selling real estate.

A lot of those individuals you spot wearing cowboy hats in the new West aren't the real thing. The important thing to remember is that you've got to live the cowboy way, and the best way to do that is to get a copy of Gene

Autry's Ten Commandments of a Cowboy and follow them to the letter (examples: A Cowboy Must Never Go Back on His Word; A Cowboy Must Be Gentle with Children, Elderly People, and Animals; and A Cowboy Must Not Possess Racially or Religiously Intolerant Ideas). It's also vitally important to remember never to whine, for whining is the sure mark of a greenhorn dude.

After graduating from high school, like a barnsour horse hurrying home, I traced the Mormon and Oregon trails back to Wyoming. At the state university in Laramie, I studied the archaeology of the Great Plains and the cultures of the Plains Indians, and suddenly all my early idols came crashing down. I began to think that maybe it was the Native American, and not the cowboy, who was the good guy.

Now, having lived in the West for more years than not, I've chewed those old days over a lot and concluded that few individuals were right or wrong, or good or bad. Most everyone was doing what they thought they should do. It was simply the timing of history—who they were when and where. The westward expansion by Anglos and subsequent submission of the Indians and wholesale reduction of the great bison herds were inevitable. All we can do today is learn from our forebears' mistakes and vow to make things better.

A final reminder: A lot of the stories related in the literature of the Old West are exaggerations, if not out-and-out fabrications. Whether or not they ever truly happened, however, is no longer relevant. By now they've been told so many times and in so many ways that they've become fact. I'm certain that I've done my part here to help perpetuate some of those great myths. Here's hoping they're entertaining ones!

By the way, I've known now for many years that I'm not the cowboy gracing the Wyoming license plate. Nope, I'm the one on the cover of this book.

The hours and rates listed in this guidebook were confirmed at press time. We recommend, however, that you call establishments before traveling to obtain current information.

THE PROMISED LAND

▼▼▼

CALIFORNIA
NEVADA
OREGON
WASHINGTON

California

REDWOOD COUNTRY

THE LONELY CORNER

★ Eureka

CENTRAL COAST

GOLD COUNTRY

★ Sacramento

San Francisco ★

N
W   E
S

SAN JOAQUIN VALLEY

SOUTHEAST DESERT COUNTRY

SOUTH COAST

Los Angeles ★

San Diego ★

CALIFORNIA

▼▼▼

C ALIFORNIA is far better known for its wine, earthquakes, and traffic jams than for its Old West heritage, yet ample evidence remains that the West was as wild here as anywhere.

The following narrative leads, in zigzag fashion, from northern to southern California; along the way you'll find reminders of the Native Americans, early Spanish settlers, gold-seeking forty-niners, lumberjacks, and cowboys and *vaqueros*—all of whom helped to ensure that California's formative days were boisterous ones.

Redwood Country

In the 1850s several settlements sprang up around remote Humboldt Bay, serving as shipping and supply hubs for the nearby Trinity River gold mines. **Fort Humboldt State Historic Park,** east of Broadway across from the Bayshore Mall in Eureka, began as a military post, established in 1853 to protect settlers in these towns from Indian attack.

A self-guided trail here leads through one of America's premier exhibits of historic logging paraphernalia, including a fully furnished lumberjack's cabin, a couple of astoundingly large redwood logs, and a "steam donkey," an ingenious machine once used to drag logs through the forest.

The park (707–445–6567) is open from 9:00 A.M. to 5:00 P.M. daily.

Cookhouses, established to appease the voracious appetites of hardworking lumbermen, once were commonplace in the Northwest, but the massive, one-hundred-year-old **Samoa Cookhouse** is the last of its breed still in operation. Be warned: Don't approach the place unless you're hungry!

Adjacent to the dining hall is a museum that celebrates the eatery's vibrant, grub-filled past. The cookhouse, located 4 miles from Eureka across the Samoa Bridge, serves old-fashioned breakfasts, lunches, and dinners seven days a week, at old-fashioned prices. Its phone number is (707) 442–1659.

In 1851 gold was discovered in Yreka—not to be confused with Eureka—where today you can visit a rich display of it at the **Siskiyou County Courthouse,** at 311 Fourth Street. Yreka is situated 200 miles northeast of Eureka on Highways 299 and 3. Along historic Miner Street, a well-preserved late 1800s commercial district, you can sample the home-style cooking at **Grandma's House** (916–842–5300), a restaurant in an 1890s Victorian house. Brochures detailing the Heritage Homes and Historical District tours are available at the visitor center at 117 West Miner Street (916–842–1649).

From Yreka the *Blue Goose* **Excursion Train** passes an old Chinese cemetery before entering the Shasta Valley, where it offers splendid views of 14,162-foot Mount Shasta and sprawling cattle spreads, little changed since the last century. The train turns around in Montague, where passengers can while away their layovers in the **1887 Depot Museum.** The *Blue Goose* leaves Yreka at 10:00 A.M., Wednesday through Sunday, in summer and intermittently in spring and fall. For a detailed schedule call (800) 842–4146.

The Lonely Corner

So you think California is too crowded? Mosey over to Modoc County in northeasternmost California, where you'll encounter an average of two persons per square mile. About 175 miles from Yreka on Interstate 5, Highway 89, and Highway 299, Alturas, steeped in Western lore, is home to the **Modoc County Historical Museum,** with a fine collection of cattle brands and firearms. At the nearby **Niles Hotel and Saloon** cowboy bar, you'll expect at any minute to see a young tough come swaggering in, cruising for a showdown.

Nearby Cedarville claims a number of historic structures, including the town's original 1867 trading post, which now stands in Cedarville Park. The **J. K. Metzker House** B&B was built by William Cressler in 1880 and remained in his family until 1954; in 1992 it was converted into a historically appointed guest house. Three guest rooms await, each with a private bath. For information and reservations call (916) 279–2337.

Surprise Valley/Barrel Springs Back Country Byway

This 93-mile road loop (mostly dirt) begins and ends in Cedarville. Along the way you can spot prehistoric rock art, hot springs, wild horses, and range-riding cowboys.

Gold-seeking forty-niners, following the heavily traveled Applegate-Lassen Trail, were happy, relieved, and, yes, surprised on reaching the relatively verdant Surprise Valley, for they knew the hardest part of their trip, that through the desolate Great Basin, was over.

As pleasant as the valley was, however, few homesteaders moved in until drought drove hundreds from the fertile Central Valley in the early 1860s. By 1865 some 300 people called the Surprise Valley home, and they petitioned the government to send troops to protect them from hostile Indians, which resulted in the establishment of Fort Bidwell. None of the original log fort buildings remains there today, but the historic Fort Bidwell Hotel and Restaurant, and the Fort Bidwell General Store—built in 1874 to withstand Indian attacks, with extraordinarily thick walls and a fireproof roof—still operate.

Just off the Byway from Lake City, on the Fandango Pass Road, wagon ruts can be located along the steep flanks of the Warner Mountains.

For a brochure detailing the Byway, call the Bureau of Land Management's Surprise Resource Area at (916) 279–6101.

Gold Country

En route to Sacramento, detour west on Highway 299 from Interstate 5 to **Shasta State Historic Park** (916–243–8194), once "Queen City of the northern mines." Highway 299 cuts straight through Shasta's well-preserved Gold Rush district, striking for its abundance of red-brick walls and iron shutters. The 1855 Shasta County Courthouse, open Wednesday through Sunday from 10:00 A.M. to 5:00 P.M., serves as the park's museum.

Back at the junction of Highway 299 and Interstate 5, go south on I–5 toward Red Bluff. For three brief weeks in 1846, during the Bear Flag

Revolt, California was an independent nation, ruled by neither Mexico nor America. Two miles northeast of Red Bluff, on Adobe Road, you'll find the **William B. Ide Adobe State Park,** site of the homestead of the man who served as president of the short-lived republic. The monument is situated in a pleasant picnic ground that overlooks the Sacramento River.

The formative days of Sacramento and California's Central Valley are the theme at **Sutter's Fort State Historic Park** (about 130 miles south of Red Bluff). Reconstruction of the fort began in 1891, after the Native Sons of the Golden West donated what remained of it to the state. Now living-history days are conducted at intervals throughout the year, and during the entire month of October, the fort's costumed docents stage a river expedition from Red Bluff to Sacramento. Dressed as 1830s traders and trappers, they establish riverside camps and act out the days when the first mountain men arrived on the scene.

Sutter's Fork State Historic Park, located at 27th and L streets in Sacramento, is open daily from 10:00 A.M. until 5:00 P.M. Call (916) 445–4422 for information.

As many as 300,000 Native Americans occupied California prior to the arrival of Europeans. The **State Indian Museum** (916–324–0971), a block away from Sutter's Fort, is dedicated to those original residents. One display focuses on Ishi, the last of his Yana tribe, who became known throughout America as the Indian who somehow kept himself hidden from 1872 until 1911 amid a burgeoning western civilization. The museum is open daily from 10:00 A.M. to 5:00 P.M.

A stroll along the boardwalks of **Old Sacramento** turns up the largest concentration of nineteenth-century buildings in California. Begin at the 1864 freight depot/Visitor Information Center, at 1104 Front Street. Personnel there will point the way to numerous historic sites; to name a few: the **Big Four Building,** which honors the four most powerful men of western railroading; the **California Citizen-Soldier Museum;** the **California State Railroad Museum,** one of the world's largest storehouses of railroading lore; the **B. F. Hastings Building,** which houses a museum dedicated to early means of communication; the **Discovery Museum,** where you can gaze upon $1 million worth of Mother Lode gold; and the spirited **Pony Express Monument.**

When you need sustenance for additional sightseeing, head to the **Union Restaurant & Bar,** acclaimed for its all-you-can-eat barbecued ribs. If it's simply a rest you need, consider boarding the steam train that departs from the Central Pacific Freight Depot next door to the Visitor Information Center, or hop aboard a riverboat for a cruise on the Sacramento River.

For more information on Old Sacramento, including a long list of B&B possibilities, call the Old Sacramento Visitor Center at (916) 442–7644.

At Coloma (northeast of Sacramento on Highways 50 and 49) is the tranquil spot that started the stampede of forty-niners: **Marshall Gold Discovery State Historic Park.** Here in 1848, when James Marshall was establishing John Sutter's sawmill on the South Fork of the American River, he found gold. Prospectors soon poured in, and Coloma's population mushroomed to 4,000. The town's luster paled nearly as quickly, however, as greater discoveries were made in the hills beyond. Coloma was transformed into an agricultural village; Marshall, who wasn't able to capitalize on his find, died a man of modest means and is buried near his cabin inside the park.

Approximately three quarters of Coloma, present population 200, is within the park. Exhibits and movies in the **Gold Discovery Museum** relate the story of the discovery that so radically altered the course of California's history. Be sure also to take in the full-sized replica of Sutter's Mill and the self-guided trail that leads to the spot where Marshall spotted the gold. The numerous buildings in the park complex are open daily from 10:00 A.M. to 5:00 P.M.; call (916) 622–3470 for more information.

The annual **Wild West Stampede** roars through nearby Auburn (just northwest of Coloma on Highway 49) the third weekend in April. Among the dozens of scheduled events: Professional Rodeo Cowboys Association (PRCA) Pro Rodeo action, cowboy dancing, barbecues, Little Cowboy and Cowgirl contest, Motherlode Quick-Draw Championship, Cowboy Gift Show, and, get this, the Cowboy Classic Golf Tournament, with PRCA cowboys competing in some unusual cowboy-flavored minicompetitions. Call (916) 889–BUCK (2825) to find out more.

A veritable living museum, **Nevada City** (28 miles north of Auburn on Highway 49) is the jewel of renovation on the ring of Gold Country towns. Only four or five years after beginning life as just another tent camp, the town threatened to grow larger than San Francisco. When it reached its maximum population of 10,000, Nevada City was a wild and dangerous place; the notorious Henry Plummer, for instance, began his violent career here. Plummer served for a spell as town marshall, until he murdered the husband of a woman with whom he was having an affair. After a stint in prison, a second murder and another short prison stay (he bribed his way out this time), Plummer hightailed for the golder pastures of Montana, where he eventually was hanged as a gold-robbing road agent.

But today Nevada City is bucolic: Visitors clop along in horse-drawn carriages through winding streets appointed with gaslights and fronted by neatly tended Victorian homes. Two of the town's best-preserved buildings are the granite-and-brick **Firehouse No. 1,** now a museum, and the resplendent **National Hotel** (916–265–4551; 211 Broad Street), opened in 1856 and reportedly the oldest continuously run hotel west of the Rocky Mountains.

Another pair of overnighting possibilities: **Deer Creek Inn** (800–655–0363; 116 Nevada Street), an 1870s Queen Anne–style Victorian situated close to downtown and featuring four suites with private baths, and the **Emma Nevada House** (800–916–3662; 528 East Broad Street), an elegant mansion built in 1856 and named after a popular nine-teenth-century opera singer.

For further information on Nevada City–Grass Valley's many addition-al historic inns and its numerous eateries, antiques shops, and other attrac-tions, call (916) 265–2692 or 273–4667.

By the early 1850s the easily accessible gold was played out, and prospectors were obliged to begin looking for buried quartz veins and "deep gravel," or subterranean dry river beds. The success of this hard-rock mining in California was largely attributable to the thousands of skilled miners who arrived from Cornwall, England, an area with a cen-turies-old tradition of tin and copper mining. **Empire Mine State Historic Park,** in Grass Valley, can be considered a tribute to those Cornish immigrants. Here miners descended daily into tunnels (nearly 400 miles of them web the earth below) to perform their unenviable jobs, via cable-driven "man cars," sort of a cross between a rail train and an elevator.

The mine, open until 1957, was the largest, deepest, and richest of the

Mother Lode mines. Even today the Empire Mine isn't dead; it is only sleeping: Rich gold veins remain, awaiting the day when deep hard-rock mining again becomes profitable. Aboveground remains include the old Mine Office, now a museum, and the carriage house/stable, today a visitor center that offers audiovisual presentations. Living-history days are held several times during the summer. The annual **Miners' Picnic,** held in late July, began in the late 1800s as a fund-raising event to aid the widows and children of deceased miners. Call the park at (916) 273–8522 for more information or to arrange a tour.

Sometimes, rather than descending into the earth, miners simply blew away mountainsides to expose their innards. A vivid example of this tumultuous mining technique can be viewed at **Malakoff Diggins State Historic Park,** 15 miles north of Nevada City. "Hydraulicking," the technique utilized at Malakoff, involved blasting hillsides with a high-pressure stream of water. The muddy effluent flowed through a sluice, where heavier gravels and gold were trapped. Tremendous quantities of water were required, and workers went to great lengths to impound it. Eventually the quantity of earth and water moving downstream was so great that serious silting and flooding occurred; this caused a devastating flood in the town of Marysville, some 40 miles downstream from Malakoff, and resulted in an injunction against further dumping of mine tailings into the streams, effectively ending the hydraulicking era.

The impressive Malakoff mine pit is 7,000 feet long, up to 3,000 feet wide, and as deep as 600 feet. Exhibits at the park museum in North Bloomfield, the town that sprang up near the mine, relate the history of the free-for-all hydraulic-mining era. The buildings are open from 10:00 A.M. to 5:00 P.M. daily in summer, on weekends during autumn, and irregularly in winter. The park has a large campground and three rustic cabins available for rent. The park is open daily from sunrise to sunset; the museum is open only June 1 through September 1. Call (916) 265–2740 for information.

Note: The North Bloomfield Road from Nevada City is unsuitable for motor homes and trailer-pulling rigs. Large vehicles should take the Tyler-Foote Road, which begins 12 miles northwest of Nevada City on Highway 49.

Once a tough, workingman's town where logs met railcars—and where intolerant railroaders and loggers chased out all the Chinese residents in 1886—Truckee (east of Nevada City on Highway 20 and Interstate 80) came into its own as a tourist magnet when the 1960 Olympic Winter Games were held at nearby Squaw Valley. Accommodations in town now

The Donner Party

"Westward fever" was contagious in the East and Midwest during the early 1840s. Formerly rational men closed shop and farm, packed their families and belongings, and lit out for California . . . men like George and Jacob Donner, successful Illinois farmers in their sixties who simply couldn't resist the allure of the land of unlimited opportunity.

In April 1846 the Donner families and the James Reed family trickled into the stream of humanity flowing westward. Things went well until the party crossed Wyoming's South Pass, where they diverted from the beaten path to follow the less-traveled Hastings Cutoff. Several more families joined up here, and the party now consisted of eighty-nine people in twenty wagons.

The alleged shortcut wound up costing three weeks and, ultimately, more than forty lives. After exhausting themselves in the rugged Wasatch Range, the party lost most of its stock while crossing the Great Salt Desert. By the time they arrived at Donner Lake, demoralized, snow was accumulating, portending the vicious winter to come. They became snowbound 6 miles beyond the lake, at Alder Creek.

When rescuers, dispatched from John Sutter's Fort, came to retrieve what remained at the Donner family tents—in April 1847, one year after the spirited party had left Illinois—only one man remained alive: Lewis Keseberg, who had survived by feeding for several days on the body of Tamsen Donner, wife of George.

The survivors from the other camps tried to carry on as originally intended, starting new lives in California—lives forever changed, however, by the terrible ordeal. Lewis Keseberg, for instance, died half crazy, an outcast accused of the grisly murder of Tamsen Donner. (Although there's no question that cannibalism took place, it's not known whether or not any of the dead were killed for food.)

include several B&Bs and the immense, renovated 1868 **Truckee Hotel** (916) 587–4444, built the year the town was founded.

Donner Memorial State Park, near Truckee, memorializes the members of the ill-fated Donner Party. Its **Emigrant Trail Museum** leads visitors along the fascinating path of history in the Truckee Basin, beginning with prehistoric times. The nearby **Pioneer Monument,** erected in 1918, honors those hundreds of travelers who made the arduous journey across the western plains in the 1840s to reach the promised land of California. The base of the monument measures 22 feet high, said to be the depth the snow reached during the Donner Party's captivity in the winter of 1846–47. Camping is available from Memorial Day through Labor Day at the park (916–582–7894).

Bodie State Historic Park, southeast of Bridgeport on Highway 395 and Highway 270, preserves the remains of a town that burgeoned in 1859 during the minirush to the harsh, high desert country of the Sierra's east slope. It was an infamous town—"Goodbye, God, I'm going to Bodie" was an oft-heard phrase—with as many as 10,000 residents by 1879. Today only a fraction of the buildings remain in a state of "arrested decay"; those that do, however, make up one of California's most graphic ghost towns. Still standing, for instance, is the quaint Methodist Church, built in 1882 with donations from businesses that included bordellos, taverns, and opium dens.

The park is open in summer from 9:00 A.M. until 7:00 P.M. and the rest of the year between 8:00 A.M. and 4:00 P.M. For more information call (619) 647–6445.

Gold was struck in 1848 in Tuolumne (to-ALL-uh-me) County, turning it almost overnight from the quiet domain of Miwuk Indians into a progression of bawdy, lawless mining camps, with gold seekers arriving from around the world. This gateway to the Mother Lode, nestled against the west slope of the Sierra Nevada range, is still so crammed full of Gold-Rush lore that it's tough to know where to start touring.

Seventeen miles northeast of Bridgeport on Highway 395 and 75 miles southwest on Highway 108, Sonora's **Tuolumne County Museum and History Center** (209–532–1317) is as good a starting place as any. The museum's Gold Collection, through the use of photographs and artifacts, offers a comprehensive overview of the area's golden past. The Overland Trails to Tuolumne County exhibit relates the years between 1840 and

1860, when scores of wagon trains passed through en route to Oregon. The museum, located in the 1857 county jail at 158 West Bradford Avenue in Sonora, is open year-round (10:00 A.M. to 4:00 P.M. weekdays and 9:00 A.M. to 4:00 P.M. weekends).

In late September historic Sonora hosts the annual **Tuolumne County Wild West Film Fest** (209–533–4420). The event, staged to honor the stars of television and silver-screen Westerns, features cowboy-poetry readings, film showings, panel discussions, Native American dancing, barbecues, and more.

Sonora brims with well-kept Victorian homes, several of which have been transformed into B&Bs. The **Sonora Inn,** though it dates from the Victorian era, is not one of them; rather, it's an 1896 hacienda-style hotel complete with "secret" rooms, a hidden tunnel system, and an opulent lobby of marble and polished wood. The inn (209–532–2400) is located at 106 South Washington Street.

In Jamestown, just southwest of Sonora on Highway 49, chug on down to **Railtown 1897 State Historic Park** and hop aboard for a steam-train ride through foothills that teem with history. The Sierra Railway Company began its short-line operation here in 1897, and its old roundhouse and machine shops are well preserved and open for touring. The park's showpiece is Engine No. 3, built in 1893 and still running. The old trains and Jamestown environs have appeared in numerous Westerns, including the classics *Butch Cassidy and the Sundance Kid* and *High Noon.*

Just north of Sonora, **Columbia State Historic Park** is an authentic Gold Rush country experience waiting to be had. There's live theater, costumed craftspersons and artisans demonstrating mid-1800s skills, horseback riding through historic "diggins," and period saloons and historic hotels and inns.

This "Gem of the Southern Mines" produced more than $1.5 billion worth of gold (in today's dollars) according to the scales at the local Wells Fargo station. At **Hidden Treasure Gold Mine,** you can tour a hard-rock mine discovered in 1879 and still producing. A guide leads clients through some 800 feet of tunnels while explaining the process miners used, and still use, to extract gold. Call (209) 532–9693 for rates and reservations.

Fire destroyed Columbia twice, and today the tenacious town looks much as it did after its third, post-1857 raising. To arrange to view it from

The Tong War of Chinese Camp

Several Tong factions, bringing with them to America age-old rivalries, populated Chinese Camp and other Mother Lode settlements. One day, when workers from two Tongs were mining adjacent claims along the Stanislaus River, a boulder from a hillside dislodged and crashed through the camp below. It hurt no one but caused accusations to fly and tempers to flare.

Formal battle, it was concluded, would be the only honorable way to settle the dispute. White blacksmiths were commissioned to cast proper piercing weapons, and dozens of hoes, rakes, and other metal implements went into the forges.

On September 26, 1856, 900 Yan-Wo Tong members, most of them from Chinese Camp, battled it out with 1,200 of the Sam Yap Tong, predominantly out of nearby Crimea House Camp. The amount of actual fighting and bloodshed, while not insignificant, was far less than the clamor of high-pitched screaming, beating of gongs and cymbals, and banging of fireworks might have indicated. When it was over—after four American lawmen rode in and put a stop to the goings-on—four men were carried to their graves, dead of stab wounds, and some 250 others taken to area jails.

the seat of a horse-drawn stagecoach, call **Columbia Stageline** at (209) 532–0663. Consider holing up while in town at Main Street's historic **City Hotel** (209–532–1479), an antiques-filled inn that boasts an acclaimed restaurant and the Gold Rush–reminiscent **What Cheer Saloon.**

A host of events parades through Columbia's calendar year, including the **Columbia Diggins 1852** celebration in early June, **Victorian Easter,** and **Miner's Christmas,** held during the first two weekends in December.

Note: For information on accommodations other than those specifically mentioned under Sonora, Jamestown, or Columbia, call Gold Country Inns of Tuolumne County at (209) 533–1845.

Chinese Camp, south of Jamestown on Highway 49, is one of the best-preserved nonrenovated mining camps in the Mother Lode. Once the home of 5,000 Chinese immigrants, the place is almost, but not quite, a ghost town today. A few residents hang on.

Hop on down Highway 49 (northwest of Sonora) to the **Calaveras County Fair & Jumping Frog Jubilee,** an event inspired by Mark Twain's story *The Celebrated Jumping Frog of Calaveras County.* Held the third weekend in May at the fairgrounds on Highway 49 south of Angels Camp, the fair offers pig races, arm-wrestling tournaments, and, of course, plenty of frog jumping.

The story goes that Samuel Clemens (Mark Twain), on a trip in 1860 from his nearby cabin to the rollicking gold town of Angels Camp, heard the story of a jumping frog named Dan'l Webster. On returning to his cabin, inspired, he penned the story that later helped establish him as America's premier humorist.

It was not until 1928 that the citizens of Angels Camp began capitalizing on the story by holding their first frog-jump contest. The winner that year: The Pride of San Joaquin, which jumped 3 feet, 9 inches. The current world record is 21 feet, 5 3/4 inches, held by Rosie the Ribiter, "jockied" by Lee Giudici of Santa Clara, California. (Distances are now measured in a straight line from the starting pad to the point where the frog lands on its third jump.)

Thousands of frogs compete annually in the qualifying heats to vie for one of fifty slots in the Grand Finals and for the $5,000 bonus for breaking the world record. Frogs and jockeys arrive from throughout America, as well as from Mexico, China, Africa, Germany, and elsewhere. The antics of the jockeys are what make frog jumping a truly great spectator sport. To find out more, including a listing of frog facts ("Frogs taste better than toads! Ask any dog"), call the organizers at (209) 736–2561.

Starting from **Jensen's Pick & Shovel Ranch,** east of Angels Camp on Highway 4 in Vallecito, visitors head for remote backcountry claims to learn the skills of prospecting. The guided tours are led by experienced prospectors who instruct clients first on how to locate gold, then recover it. Hour-long, daylong, and multiday trips can be arranged. Some of the company's claims are in remote spots accessible only by helicopter or river raft; these ultimate trips must be reserved well in advance by calling (209) 736–0287.

The Central Coast

From Angels Camp go north on Highway 49, then west on Highway 12. In the heart of wine country, visit **Mission San Francisco Solano de Sonoma** on the historic Sonoma Plaza. Established in 1823, it was the last and northernmost of the Golden Chain of twenty-one Spanish Franciscan missions built. Viewing the authentically restored mission today, you'll find it difficult to believe that it was victim of an Indian siege, twice devastated by fire, seriously damaged in the 1906 earthquake, and used through the years as a saloon, hay-storage facility, winery, liquor warehouse, and hennery.

On June 14, 1846, a small group of "foreigners," mostly Americans, captured Sonoma as the first step in their plan to wrest control of Alta California from Mexico and turn it into an independent nation. But the U.S. Navy landed at Monterey on July 7, foiling the rebels' plans, and their Bear Flag flew a mere twenty-two days before the Stars and Stripes supplanted it. (In 1911, however, the Bear Flag was adopted as the flag of the state of California.) The **Bear Flag Monument** now marks the spot where the rebel banner was raised, near the northeast corner of the eight-acre Sonoma Plaza.

The two homes of Mariano Guadalupe Vallejo, the early leader who laid out the plaza in 1835 and was imprisoned in 1846 by the Bear Flaggers, are also situated on the plaza: the 1836 **Casa Grande** adobe and **Lachryma Montis,** a gorgeous Yankee-style house, which Vallejo built in 1852 after embracing the new way of life that arrived with U.S. rule.

Three venerable inns on the tree-lined plaza are evocative of olden times yet refurbished in decidedly upscale fashion: the twenty-seven–room **El Dorado Hotel** (707–996–3030), the **Sonoma Hotel** (707–996–2996), and the **Swiss Hotel** (707–938–2884). The latter was built in the late 1830s by the brother of General Vallejo.

Beyond the plaza visit 800-acre **Jack London State Park,** at 2400 London Ranch Road. You can hike through what Jack London—writer, hobo, war correspondent, horseman, social agitator, sailor, and prospector—called his "Beauty Ranch," where he spent the final days of his forty years. The walls of the stone Wolf House, "designed to remain standing a thousand years," stand as ghostly and ironic reminders of the fire that took

Russians in California

The czarist-owned Russian American Company controlled Russian trade and exploration in North America in the late 1700s and employed many Alaskan Aleut Indians, skilled hunters who traveled in two-man kayaks and used harpoons to hunt sea otters and sea lions.

Determining that it needed to establish a settlement along the northern California coast, the company chose the Fort Ross site because it would be defensible from attack and it offered good soil, timber, water, and grazing. (Although the Spanish had claimed the coast as far north as today's Canadian border, they had built no settlements north of the Presidio in San Francisco.)

Twenty-five Russians and eighty Alaskan natives came ashore at Fort Ross in March 1812. Aided by native Kashaya Pomo Indians, they had constructed two towers and a surrounding wall by year's end. Over the next twelve years, nine houses and the now-famous Russian Orthodox chapel were added, all soundly built of redwood. The population at the active post was a mix of Alaskan and California natives, Russians, Mexican traders, and Creole, the offspring of Russian men and native women.

By the 1830s overhunting had caused the number of fur-bearing sea mammals to dwindle dramatically; simultaneously, the Mexican government was encouraging Americans to settle on the borders of Fort Ross. Rather than recognize the Mexicans' revolutionary government, as he'd been told to do, Czar Nicholas I approved the sale of the now-unprofitable colony. It went to Captain John Sutter in 1841 for $2,000 and a guarantee of $28,000 more to come, a promise on which Sutter never fully delivered. The last of the Russian colonists departed for Sitka, Alaska, on January 1, 1842.

the house just before London and his wife were to move in.

The park is open daily from 9:30 A.M. until sunset. The House of Happy Walls, which features memorabilia from London's adventure-filled life, is open from 10:00 A.M. to 5:00 P.M. Call (707) 938–5216 for more information. (Horseback rides through the park can be arranged through the **Sonoma Cattle Company,** 707–996–8566.)

California is not generally recognized as historic Russian stomping grounds, yet, when established in 1812, **Fort Ross** became that empire's most remote outpost. The state park's **Living History Day,** on the last Saturday of July, is straight out of those times: Interpreters dressed as Russians, Mexicans, Hudson's Bay Company trappers, and Pomo Indians perform their daily tasks, such as candle making, bread baking, tinsmithing, and spinning. Folk dancing, musket and cannon drills, and live Russian liturgical music are also on tap. The park (707–847–3286), 12 miles north of Jenner, which is on the coast northwest of Sonoma, is open daily from 10:00 A.M. until 4:30 P.M.

Reminders of the eighteenth- and nineteenth-century West are abundant in and around legendary San Francisco. For starters: **Mission Dolores** (415–621–8203), at Sixteenth and Dolores streets, which, when established in 1776, was the sixth in the chain of Fransican missions; the **Presidio Army Museum** (415–561–4331; open noon to 4:00 P.M., Wednesday through Sunday; Lincoln Boulevard at Funston on the Presidio Army Base), highlights the important role the military played in the settlement of the region; the **Wells Fargo History Museum** (415–396–2619; open Monday through Friday from 9:00 A.M. to 5:00 P.M.), at 420 Montgomery Street, tells the story of the forty-niners and their wild rush for gold, as well as that of the Wells Fargo Overland Stage; and the **Chinese Historical Society of America** museum (415–391–1188; open 10:00 A.M. to 2:00 P.M., Monday through Friday), at 650 Commercial Street, details the contributions made by Chinese immigrants during the Gold Rush and the building of the railroads.

In San Jose, southeast of San Francisco on Interstate 280, the **Winchester Mystery House** was commissioned by Sarah Winchester, heiress to the $20-million firearms-company fortune, in an attempt to placate the ghosts of those who had died as victims of the model '73 (one of the guns that "won the West") and other Winchester firearms. In order to successfully appease the spirits of these victims, she believed, building on her house had to be continuous, and continuous it was—the bizarre Victorian house was under construction twenty-four hours a day for thirty-eight years. The ceaseless additions resulted in 110 rooms and some extremely odd features, including asymmetrical rooms, narrow passageways, and doors opening into nowhere.

Guided tours of the mansion, located at 525 South Winchester

Boulevard in San Jose, are available daily from 9:00 A.M. to 5:00 P.M. and entail nearly a mile of walking. Call (408) 247–2101 for information.

Hop aboard the **Roaring Camp & Big Trees Narrow-Gauge Railroad** for a ride into history. Turn-of-the-century steam engines haul passengers in antique coach cars along the 6-mile trip to Bear Mountain every day of the year except Christmas.

The ride begins at the re-created 1880s logging town of Roaring Camp, located just east of Felton (north of Santa Cruz on Highway 9). The locomotive gasps up some of the steepest narrow-gauge railway grades in America and chugs through stations with colorful names like Grizzly Flats, Hallelujah Junction, and Shotgun Pass. When its whistle blows in the Welch Grove of protected redwoods, the sound is muted by the impossibly tall, robust trees. Western-style breakfasts and barbecue dinners are served, and conductor-historians relate the rough-and-tumble history of the line, which in the 1880s hauled redwood giants to mill.

For rate information and schedules, which change with the season, call (408) 335–4484. Also request a listing of annual events, which include the **Great Train Robberies** reenactment in April and the **Mountain Man Rendezvous** in November.

Moving southward through the Golden State, beyond the mining and tall-timber country, evidence mounts of the eighteenth- and nineteenth-century Spaniards and Mexicans who settled Alta California. For instance, at **San Juan Bautista State Historic Park,** southeast of Santa Cruz, the largest of California's twenty-one Franciscan missions survives. More than 4,000 Mutsun Indians are buried in the mission cemetery (the tribe is now extinct; the last member died in 1930), and below is an original stretch of El Camino Real (the King's Road), built to link the Golden Chain of California missions.

Numerous living-history days are conducted on the first Saturday of each month at San Juan Bautista, located on Star Route 156, 7 miles west of Hollister. The park is open daily from 10:00 A.M. to 4:30 P.M.; call (408) 623–4881 for more information.

San Joaquin Valley

Between Fresno and Bakersfield, just east off Highway 99, Visalia, in the heart of California's cowboy country, hosts its annual **Spring Round-Up** (209–627–0287) in May. Cowboy poetry, Western music, and exhibits of

Western art and custom cowboying gear are among the highlights. Kernville, southeast of Visalia, conducts its own Wild West fest, **Whiskey Flat Days,** in February. This part of the state had a mini–gold rush in the 1880s, when Kernville was known as Whiskey Flat, and the celebration revives those wild times with gunfights, guided mine tours, and Western melodramas. Rodeo is also on tap; you can call (619) 376–2629 to learn more.

Fort Tejon State Historic Park is situated near Lebec in scenic Grapevine Canyon. The fort, active from 1854 to 1864, was built to protect local settlers and the peaceable Chumash Indians from raiding Paiute, Mojave, and other more aggressive tribes. Throughout the year living-history programs are presented; docents are dressed as dragoons, and civilian volunteers give black-powder and cannon demonstrations. The park (805–248–6692) is located 75 miles north of Los Angeles on Interstate 5.

The South Coast

To take Santa Barbara's Red Tile Tour is to walk through Old California, where Spanish roots run deep. **El Presidio de Santa Barbara State Historic Park** (805–966–9719), at 123 East Cañon Perdido Street, encompasses several buildings from this last of the four presidios built by Spain to protect her holdings in Alta California. The **Historical Society Museum**, at 136 East De la Guerra Street, exhibits the trappings of the Spanish cowboys, or *vaqueros,* along with an impressive collection of Western art. Also of note: **Mission Santa Barbara,** at the upper end of Laguna Street; the **Carriage Museum,** at 129 Castillo Street; and **El Paseo,** at 15 East De la Guerra Street. Known as "the Street in Spain," El Paseo features quaint specialty shops, galleries, and eateries built in and around the 1827 adobe of presidio comandant José De la Guerra and his family. The De la Guerra home served as the epicenter of social activities in Alta California and as the setting for Richard Henry Dana's classic tale *Two Years Before the Mast.*

"Viva la Fiesta!" cry thousands of spectators lining the parade route at the **Old Spanish Days Fiesta,** one of California's largest and oldest celebrations. Since 1924 Santa Barbarans have reveled amid the traditional Spanish and Mexican dancing, concerts, food, and markets. A couple of must-see highlights are the *Competicion de Vaqueros,* featuring trick riding and roping, and *El Desfile Historico,* recognized as the largest annual equestrian-only parade in America. For more information on the early August—and *august*—fiesta, truly one of the grand festivals of the West, call (805) 962–8101.

In the 1820s prospective *rancheros,* many of them ex-soldiers (who had to "be Catholic and of good character") with connections to the Spanish presidios, were granted land in the foothills and inland valleys by the Spanish government. Some holdings grew into vast, feudal-like estates, where Indian men served as *vaqueros* and workers and Indian women as domestic servants. These spreads raised thousands of head of cattle for export to Europe and the East Coast.

In classic busman's-holiday fashion, rodeos and other horse-dependent competitions were central to social gatherings on the *ranchos.* At **Los Rancheros Vistadores** in May, held at the Old Mission Santa Ines in Solvang, hundreds of equestrians from throughout the world gather to honor and emulate the early *vaqueros.* Call (805) 688–0701 to find out more about watching or participating in the gathering of gallopers.

Why would any Old West buff in his or her right mind venture into the concrete wilderness of Los Angeles? For at least two very good reasons, including the **Autry Museum of Western Heritage.** "The West, its mountains, deserts, plains, and particularly its people, has fascinated me since my childhood," said Autry, the famous Singing Cowboy. "To preserve the rich legacy of this special region has been a long-standing dream."

Autry's massive museum, open since 1988, contains two changing exhibits dedicated to the "real" and "mythical" West. Permanent displays include the "Spirit of Discovery Gallery," "Trails West," "Colt: Old West–New Frontier" (featuring a large display of Samuel Colt's firearms and their role in settling the West), and the "Spirit of Cowboy." The history of the Western-movie genre is explored in the Spirit of Imagination, and the grand finale, a special-effects film produced by Walt Disney Imagineering, is presented in the Heritage Theatre.

The museum is found near the Los Angeles Zoo, in Griffith Park, at 4700 Heritage Way. It's open Tuesday through Sunday from 10:00 A.M. until 5:00 P.M.; for more information call (213) 667–2000.

Reason number two: **Will Rogers State Historic Park,** at 14253

Sunset Boulevard in Pacific Palisades. Rogers, known as the Cowboy Philosopher and one of America's best-loved humorists, was born on a ranch in Oklahoma. As a young man he traveled the world with touring rodeos, earning fame as a trick roper, and by the 1930s he had become a smash hit as a radio commentator, newspaper writer, and motion-picture star.

The grounds and ranch house look much as they did when Rogers and his family lived there. The decidedly Western flair of the place, with its polo field, stables, and riding and roping rings, tells a lot about the man. The 186-acre park is open daily from 8:00 A.M. to sunset for hiking and exploring; the ranch house is open from 10:30 A.M. to 4:30 P.M. Call (310) 454–8212 for more information.

In late April and early May, the unique **Ramona Pageant** fills the foothills of Mt. San Jacinto with the sights and sounds of *señoritas,* Indians, and horses. The performances are presented in the Ramona Bowl, a stunning, natural hillside amphitheater on the slopes of the mountain.

Since opening in 1923, the Ramona Pageant has entertained some 2 million visitors and has earned a distinction as the longest-running outdoor drama in America and designation as the California State Outdoor Play. Based on Helen Hunt Jackson's 1884 novel *Ramona,* the story is a Romeo-and-Juliet-flavored tale of ill-fated love in the 1850s between a Mexican *rancho* beauty and an Indian chief. Hunt Jackson wrote the novel in the hope of drawing sympathy to the plight of southern California's mission Indians, but her message became all but lost as the public fell head-over-heels for the love story.

The pageant uses no lighting, recorded music, or artificial sets, and the action leads from the natural backdrop of the bowl to the top of the surrounding hillsides. The cast of 375 and even larger support crew are composed almost entirely of amateurs from the Hemet–San Jacinto area. The gala dancing and colorful costumes, set against a background of drab rock, must be seen to be believed. For information and tickets call (909) 658–3111.

Happy trails are yours at the **Roy Rogers and Dale Evans Museum** in Victorville, located en route to Barstow along Interstate 15. Among the finds at this mecca for fans of the Wild Western are Trigger, Buttermilk, and Bullet the Wonder Dog, all looking nearly as good as ever through the magic of taxidermy. Also on hand are a large array of fancy duds, saddles,

The living ghost town of Calico

boots, and other gear and memorabilia used by America's favorite cow-couple. The museum, open daily from 9:00 A.M. to 5:00 P.M., is found at 15650 Seneca Road; for more information call (619) 243–4547.

Southeast Desert Country

Just east of Barstow and north of Interstate 15, **Calico,** an old silver boom-town near Barstow, was born in 1881, died in 1907, and was resurrected in 1951. It's now a *living* ghost town, with thriving businesses that line the boardwalks of Main Street. The sixty-acre town site, a San Bernardino County regional park, includes an operating restaurant, a saloon, a leather-goods store, a playhouse, a candy shop, and much more. The shops are open daily from 9:00 A.M. to 5:00 P.M., and camping is available. Call (619) 254–2122 for information on Calico's special annual events, which include the Palm Sunday **Calico Hullabaloo** (featuring the World Tobacco Spitting Championships), the **Mother's Day Spring Festival,** October's **Calico Days,** and the Old West art show in November.

Inyo County and the Owens Valley are a world apart from the rest of California—from the rest of the country, actually. Here, within 80 miles of one another, are the lowest point in the contiguous United States (Death Valley's Badwater, at 282 feet below sea level) and the highest (Mt. Whitney, at an elevation of 14,495 feet).

Western-flavored Lone Pine, north of Barstow on Highways 58 and 395, was established in the 1860s as a supply point for miners. Because of its relative proximity to Hollywood and the rugged landscapes surrounding town, Lone Pine began attracting moviemakers in the 1920s, and scores of Westerns have been shot here on location since. (You'll immediately recognize the dramatic terrain of Alabama Canyon, for instance—it's where the Lone Ranger and Tonto "headed 'em off at the pass" on countless occasions.)

The annual **Lone Pine Film Festival,** held in October, pays tribute

"Borax Bill" Parkinson

William T. Coleman's Harmony Borax Works was situated in one of the most forsaken Death Valley locations, and transporting the white salt presented a major hurdle to overcome. Huge wagons were designed and built, each with a ten-ton capacity, front wheels 5 feet in diameter, and rear wheels of 7 feet. Two wagons were hooked together, while a third, carrying 1,200 gallons of water, brought up the rear. When loaded, the three-wagon train weighed thirty-six tons. The trains were pulled by teams of twenty mules over a "road" built by Chinese laborers, who pounded it out with sledgehammers over a sea of 6-inch-high salt spires.

Only the best mule skinners were hired to drive Coleman's twenty-mule-team wagons. Among the best of the best was "Borax Bill" Parkinson, said to have handled his animals with finesse and used his 25-foot whip sparingly. In 1904 Borax Bill and his mule team and three wagons were shipped, via railroad flatbed cars, to the St. Louis World's Fair, where he put the mules through their paces. The Borax Company's publicity stunt became an exceedingly popular attraction.

to John Wayne, Hopalong Cassidy, Errol Flynn, Gail Davis (television's Annie Oakley), Clayton Moore, and dozens of other shoot-'em-up heroes. Movies filmed in the area are shown throughout the weekend, and movie stars march in parades and participate in photograph tours to filming locations. Call (619) 876–4314 for more information and to reserve tickets.

Forty miles east of Lone Pine, en route to Death Valley, take a quick swing into **Darwin,** a ghost town where a scattering of folks still reside. Three-fingered Jack, the notorious California outlaw, met his maker in this Wild West settlement.

Death Valley National Park is huge—half again as big as the state of Delaware—and filled with colorful and foreboding place names: Jubilee Pass, the Funeral Range, Coffin Peak, Devil's Golf Course. Known largely for its unbearably hot temperatures and below-sea-level elevations—fewer than 2 inches of rain fall in an average year and the mercury has climbed as high as 134 degrees F.—Death Valley is less recognized for altitudes reaching as high as 11,049 feet, at Telescope Peak. The park is open year-round, although a midsummer visit is not advised, for the heat is oppressive and services are limited May through October. Call (619) 786–2331 for more information.

If you're in the area in mid-October, check out **Amargosa Days,** in Shoshone, just east of the park. The old-time Western festivities include gunfights, overnight guided hikes, mesquite barbecues, and hard-rock drilling contests. In addition, for four days in November, the **Death Valley 49ers Encampment** celebrates the forty-niners' trek through California's hot spot, with events that include a liar's contest.

Where to Eat

Samoa Cookhouse, Eureka, (707) 442–1659
Grandma's House, Yreka, (916) 842–5300
Union Restaurant & Bar, Sacramento, (916) 448–6466

Where to Stay

J. K. Metzker House, Cedarville, (916) 279–2650
National Hotel, Nevada City, (916) 265–2692

Deer Creek Inn, Nevada City, (800) 655–0363
The Emma Nevada House, Nevada City, (800) 916–3662
Truckee Hotel, Truckee, (916) 587–4444
Sonora Inn, Sonora, (209) 532–2400
City Hotel, Columbia, (209) 532–1479
El Dorado Hotel, Sonoma, (707) 996–3030
Sonoma Hotel, Sonoma, (707) 996–2996
Swiss Hotel, Sonoma, (707) 938–2884

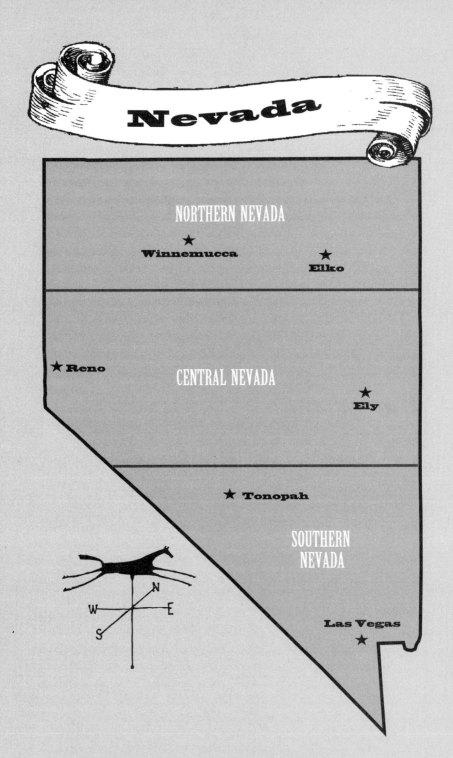

NEVADA

▼▼▼

NEVADA is known more for its glitz, glamour, gambling, and readily accessible marriage proceedings and undoings than for its true grit, but Old West country it is, nevertheless. En route to California, pioneers trekked across these barren lands following the Humboldt Trail, and dozens of mining ghost towns (far too many to include them all in this chapter) litter the state's northern basins and ranges and southern deserts.

One reason Nevada doesn't make as big a deal about its past as it could is because here in the Silver State the West is still wild—in some regards, wilder than it's ever been. Nearly anything goes in Nevada for those with the money and interest to make it happen.

The narrative leading through Nevada begins in the north, appropriately dubbed "Cowboy Country" by the state travel folks; from there it wends down through central Nevada, and ends up in the southern reaches of the state.

Northern Nevada

The farming community of Lovelock graces the banks of the Humboldt River in the area known as Big Meadow to the emigrants, thousands of whom spent a spell here before repairing across the waterless expanse of the 40-Mile Desert.

Joseph Marzen was a German immigrant who, after living his first five years in North America in New York, succumbed to westward fever. For twenty-five years thenceforth he practiced his butchering trade in Sacramento until 1876, when he purchased land in the Lovelock area. His small operation grew into the Big Meadow Ranch, a cattle-growing, farming, and dairy dynasty of regional eminence. Now the local Chamber of Commerce shares Marzen's refurbished home, at the west end of town, with the **Pershing County Museum.** Displays of mining, Native American, and early-day ranching artifacts are featured at the museum, open May through October, Tuesday through Sunday, from 1:30 to 4:00 P.M.; call (702) 273–7213 for information.

Unionville, a town straight out of the 1800s, was born in 1861 when several prospectors from Silver City established claims in the area. Samuel Clemens (Mark Twain) spent a short stint prospecting here during the winter of 1861–62 but quickly gave that up in favor of letting others do the hard work while he traded shares in local mines, including the poetically named Root Hog Or Die.

Mineral production was steady, but still Unionville lost momentum when Winnemucca, a vibrant upstart of a town along the route of the Central Pacific Railroad, stole the county seat in 1872. Today only a few dozen residents endure, and the **Old Pioneer Garden** B&B (702–538–7585) is the town's sole enterprise that caters to visitors. To get to Unionville turn off Interstate 80 at Oreana and proceed 23 miles to the east and north on gravel roads; for a predominantly paved alternative, turn off the interstate instead at Mill City and go 20 miles south.

In September 1900 the bank in Winnemucca, a crossroads town named for a prominent Paiute chief, "contributed" several thousand dollars to Butch Cassidy's Hole in the Wall Gang (which, it seems, was sans Butch at the time). Today's visitor finds the **Buckaroo Hall of Fame and Western Heritage Museum** located, along with the Chamber of Commerce, in the convention center at the corner of Winnemucca Boulevard and Bridge Street. It's open weekdays from 8:00 A.M. to noon and from 1:00 to 5:00 P.M.; call (702) 623–2225 for more information.

This is the heart of America's Basque country—that is, sheep country. Among the many spots in Nevada where a hearty and distinctive Basque meal, served family style, can be sampled is in the 1863 **Winnemucca Hotel,** at 95 Bridge Street. Dinner might include lamb stew, potatoes, hearty soup, and then comes the main course! (The bar here, incidentally, claims a classic backbar straight out of the old days.)

The first-rate **Northeastern Nevada Museum** in bustling Elko, an attractive town backed by the splendid Ruby Mountains, details the colorful

Basques in Nevada

The Basque people, thought to be the oldest ethnic group in Europe, are an enigma of sorts; their language, for instance, is unrelated to any other spoken today, and they've apparently remained culturally distinct since Stone Age times.

Numbering between two and three million, the Basques are native to northern Spain and southwestern France. The first of their people came to the American West infected with gold fever, as '49ers. When the mines in California and Nevada petered out, they turned to sheepherding, a skill they'd practiced for centuries in the Old Country. They thrived in the far and empty reaches of states like Nevada, Idaho, and Wyoming, where the hard work amidst lonely surroundings brought out the best in them.

The high-spirited Basques hold annual festivals in several Nevada towns. Some of them are small affairs only for their people, but others are large-scale, all-comers events where anyone can "Basque" in the revelry. These include the celebrations in Winnemucca (mid-June), Elko (early July), and Ely (July). Parades, dancing, drinking wine from the ever-present *bota*, food, and competitions—including weight lifting and wood chopping—are all part of the fun.

history of this part of the state. In front is an 1860 Pony Express cabin, moved here from Ruby Valley (55 miles southeast) and one of the oldest buildings in the state. The museum (702–738–3418), located at 1515 Idaho Street, is open Monday through Saturday from 9:00 A.M. to 5:00 P.M. and Sunday from 1:00 to 5:00 P.M.

In the nineteenth-century Pioneer Hotel, at 501 Railroad Street, the **Western Folklife Center** features exhibits that celebrate the traditional ways of buckaroos, as cowboys are called in these parts (the word is derived from *vaquero,* the Spanish word for cowboy), and other Western people. At the center's gift shop, cowboy-poetry cassette tapes, hard-to-find books, and more can be purchased. Call (800) 748–4466 for additional information.

Reserve your room early for the Western Folklife Center's annual

Cowboy Poetry Gathering (702–738–7508). This is the one that got the ball rolling for dozens of similar cowpoke-poet fests throughout the West. David Coates, in *Mother Earth News,* wrote, "The Cowboy Poetry Gathering is one of the funnier events on earth. . . . In a world of screaming maniac comedians . . . cowboy poets are oases of subtlety." The *San Francisco Examiner* reported, "It's just like a big family reunion, only everybody likes each other."

The event brings the house down during the fourth weekend in January, typically a leisurely time of year for range riders and fence menders. Cowgirl poets are well represented, too, and a recent gathering included a special show entitled "Real Women Buck Bales." Other events in festival-crazed Elko include the **Silver State Stampede Rodeo and Cowboy Art Fair** in early August, the **National Basque Festival** over the Fourth of July, and the **Cowboy Music Gathering** the fourth weekend in June. For more information on events, accommodations, and other Elko matters, call the Chamber of Commerce at (702) 738–7135 or (800) 428–7143.

Whichever Elko buckaroo fest you're headed to, first stop to get properly duded up at **J. M. Capriola Co.** (702–738–5816), a Western outfitter with a long list of items for sale, including saddles intricately carved and decorated in the tradition of world-renowned saddlemaker G. S. Garcia, who set up shop in Elko in 1896. Garcia's American Eagle saddles have been graced by some of the most famous rear ends in the history of the West, including those of Teddy Roosevelt and Will Rogers. The store is at the corner of Commercial and Fifth and is open daily from 9:00 A.M. to 5:00 P.M.

A pair of outstanding ghost towns lie along various combinations of pavement and dirt roads that wend north from Elko. **Jarbidge,** considered both the most remote ghost town in the state and well worth the long trip, sits in a steep-sided mountain canyon 55 miles north of town on Highway 225, via Adobe Summit, then 47 miles northeast on a dirt road. Ten or twenty residents, along with a small grocery and the **Red Dog Saloon,** await in this town that's said to have hosted the last stagecoach robbery in the United States, in 1916. (Stock up on water and supplies before striking out on this adventure.)

The O'Neil Basin's **Cottonwood Ranch,** run by the Smith family for four generations, offers some of the best in Western hospitality. Out of the seven-room, open-beam guest lodge, which serves a maximum of twenty guests at a time, hands lead dudes into the spectacular Jarbidge Wilderness from June through September. Guests can also participate in seasonal cattle drives; back at the ranch, hayrides, cookouts, singalongs, and cowboy-poetry readings are popular activities. For rates, reservations, and specific directions, call (702) 752–3604.

Wells, 50 miles northeast of Elko on Interstate 80, was established in 1869 as a Union Pacific Railroad station called Humboldt Wells, a name alluding to the nearby springs that partially give rise to the Humboldt River. At the **North American Pony Express Championship Races,** held in Wells in early May, you'll find teams of five riders and horses that run a short circuit through the adjacent desert and come back to town to pass off a mail bag. Call the Chamber of Commerce at (702) 752–3540 for more information.

Central Nevada

Highway 50, the fabled "loneliest road in America," cuts a swath through central Nevada, dubbed Pony Express Country by the state's travel-promotion folks. The road climbs over north-south running range after range, giving travelers graphic evidence of why this is known as basin-and-range country. The showpiece of Ely, located 65 miles northeast of Great Basin National Park, America's newest, is the **Nevada Northern Railway Museum.** The sprawling facility, encompassing the Nevada Northern's large depot and the entire surrounding railyards, is a legacy left by the Kennecott Copper Company when it closed shop here in 1982.

The gem of the abundant railroading lore is the **Ghost Train of Ely,** one of the best-preserved short-line railroads in North America. The tourist train is pulled either by the *Old Number 40* 1910 Baldwin steam engine, the more recently reserviced 1909 *American Locomotive #93,* or the newer diesel *Highliner.* The trains make regular runs on weekends from Memorial Day through Labor Day, with Twilight Special outings, combining rides along both routes, on Saturday nights. The museum and Ghost Train depot (702–289–2085) are located at the north end of Eleventh Street East.

Eureka, 77 miles west of Ely on Highway 50, is proud of being known as "The Loneliest Town on the Loneliest Road in America." Silver was struck here in 1864, and over the next thirty years area mines produced some $40 million in silver and $20 million in gold, along with hundreds of tons of lead. For a short spell during the 1870s, Eureka was Nevada's second-biggest town, with 8,000 people and 100 saloons (apparently each was big enough to hold 80 people!). The **Eureka Sentinel Museum,** built in 1879 as a newspaper office, includes fascinating old newspaper accounts, handbills and posters, and the equipment used to print them. It's open May to September Monday through Saturday from 9:00 A.M. to 5:00 P.M. and Sunday from 10:00 A.M. to 3:00 P.M. The remainder of the year it's closed Sundays and Mondays. The Chamber of Commerce (702–237–5484) is located in the same building.

Kitty-corner from the museum, the **Eureka County Courthouse** has been restored to reflect its original 1879 grandeur, and the elegant, one-hundred-year-old **Parsonage House,** at the corner of Spring and Bateman next to the Methodist Church, welcomes overnighters. Call (702) 237–5756 for reservations.

Seventy miles west of Eureka on Highway 50 is Austin, a frontier mining "untourist" town that sprouted early in Nevada's history. In 1862 a laid-off Pony Express rider, who had settled nearby after the demise of the Express, discovered silver in what he called Pony Canyon (he was looking for his lost horses at the time). By 1865 some 5,000 prospectors were working sixty mining districts. A bonanza of timeworn buildings remain, including a scattering of miners' cabins and a trio of outstanding frontier churches. None is more unusual than **Stokes Castle,** built in 1897 to resemble a Roman villa and to serve as home for a local mine owner. To get there find Castle Road at the south end of town and follow the winding dirt/mud road for about half a mile. The **Pony Express Bed & Make Your Own Breakfast,** a unique overnightery built in the 1860s, offers two bedrooms for rent. It's located at 888 Main Street; call (702) 964–2306 for information and reservations.

Farther along the lonely highway is **Cold Springs,** site of a stop on both the Pony Express and the Overland Stagecoach routes. About a mile from the watering hole here, via a short hiking trail, are the excavated remains of an original Pony Express station. When you reach the irrigated green oasis of Fallon (home, incongruously, to a large Navy base), visit the **Churchill County Museum,** considered one of the top five museums in the state.

Displays interpret the Pony Express and the dreaded crossing by the emigrants of the 40-Mile Desert. The museum, located at 1050 South Maine Street, is open in summer from 10:00 A.M. to 5:00 P.M. Monday through Saturday and Sunday from noon to 5:00 P.M.; it's closed Thursdays the rest of the year. Call (702) 423–3677 for more information. The **All-Indian Stampede Rodeo & Indian Days Pow Wow** (702–423–2544) gets things movin' and keeps 'em going in Fallon in late July.

Continue west on Highway 50 to Silver Springs; then go 9 miles south on Alternate 95 to **Fort Churchill State Historic Park** and the adobe remains of Nevada's first army post. Fort Churchill was established in 1860, in the wake of two bloody skirmishes collectively known as the Pyramid Lake War, in which approximately 75 white militiamen and 150 Paiute Indians died. In addition to serving as a garrison for soldiers who kept sentinel on Overland Trail travelers, Fort Churchill served brief stints as a Pony Express depot, a telegraph station, and a recruitment center for Civil War volunteers. Open daily from 8:00 A.M. to 4:30 P.M., the visitor center features displays on the Pyramid Lake War and the post's eleven years of operation. Call (702) 577–2345 for information.

Nevada in general and Reno in particular have resisted repeated attempts, staged by some of its citizens, to clean up their acts and become respectable. The "sindustry" is, frankly, the state's main income generator. The no-waiting period for marriage (unique in all the states), extremely short residency requirements for divorce, and legalized gambling combine to make Reno and Nevada anachronisms in the new West—wildly successful and popular throwbacks to the past.

Start your tour of Reno, where you'll have no trouble finding a place to feed quarters into one-armed bandits, at the **Reno-Tahoe Visitors Center,** in the old Oddfellows Hall at 135 North Sierra Street. (Call them at 800–367–4766 for information on the celebratory, ten-day **Reno Round-up Rodeo,** held in late June.) The Chamber of Commerce (702–686–3030) is on the third floor of the building, and next door is the huge **Parker's Western Clothing,** which has served Reno residents and visitors since 1919.

From Harold's go to the **Nevada State Historical Society Museum,** located at 1650 North Virginia Street at the north end of the campus of the University of Nevada-Reno, and proceed through 13,000 years of Nevada prehistory and history. Photographs, maps, artifacts, documents, and outstanding exhibits demand hours of browsing. For more information on one

Bob Harmon from Lakeview, Oregon, catches some air in the bareback riding event at the Reno Round-up Rodeo.

of the best museums in the West, call (702) 688–1190.

The **Mackay Museum of Mines,** also on the University of Nevada-Reno campus, in Room 112 of the Mackay Mining School, was named for the Bonanza King of the Comstock, a statue of whom stands outside. Gold, silver, copper, uranium, and other Nevada-mined minerals are displayed, including some out of the Comstock, where it all started. The museum is open from 8:00 A.M. to 5:00 P.M. Monday through Friday; call (702) 784–6988 for information.

For some peace and quiet and some real Basque food—lots of it—try **Louis' Basque Corner,** at 301 East Fourth Street. Dinner is served daily; lunch, Monday through Saturday.

South of Incline Village on Highway 28, along the north shore of Lake Tahoe, is the popular **Ponderosa Ranch,** featuring re-created sets from the ever-popular *Bonanza* television series (the show was filmed on Hollywood soundstages). There's a model of the Cartwrights' ranch house on-site here at the Anderson Ranch and also a complete "Virginia City" Western town with shooting gallery, saloon, sheriff's office, church— where, in line with the Nevada way, you can actually get married—and petting zoo (betcha don't remember that from the television show!). Visitors can dine on pancakes for breakfast or Hossburgers for lunch, then go for a trail ride or a hayride. The theme park is open daily from 9:30 A.M. to 5:00 P.M. April through October (open until 6:00 P.M. in summer); call (702) 831–0691 for information.

By the time Sam Clemens began writing for the *Territorial Enterprise* under the pseudonym Mark Twain, in the early 1860s, some 15,000 luck seekers were living in **Virginia City.** Unlike hundreds of other mining meccas in the West but, coincidentally, very much like the identically named town in Montana, Virginia City has parlayed its past into a thriving tourist magnet.

Lucius Beebe, a newspaper writer from New York City, stoked the dying embers of the town by resurrecting the *Territorial Enterprise* in 1950. Its future as a tourist draw was cinched when the *Bonanza* series premiered and grew tremendously popular, with Pa, Hoss, and the rest of the boys making regular forays into Virginia City. Now hundreds of thousands of people yearly flock from Reno up the serpentine Geiger Grade to walk the boardwalk-lined streets here and to visit the revived Queen of the Comstock.

Virginia City should be nicknamed the "city of museums," for no fewer than ten repositories of things old grace C Street. A sampling: the **Virginia City Visitor Center,** where you can get your bearings; **Mark Twain's Museum of Memories**; the **Nevada Gambling Museum**; the **Wild West Museum;** the **Territorial Prison,** with its electric chair and suffocation chamber; **The Way It Was Museum,** with a fine array of artifacts that interpret the Comstock's gold and silver mining days; and the **Red Light Museum,** found in the basement of the Julia C. Boulette Saloon. This unusual little museum focuses on the sex and drug trade of nineteenth-century Virginia City (and includes some X-rated displays best left unseen by the kids).

To learn about how tough the miners really had it, take in the underground tour of the **Ponderosa Mine,** offered daily, beginning at the back room of the Ponderosa Saloon (702–847–0757). Then, to see how the other half lived—in this case the superintendent of the Empire Mine, Robert Graves—visit **The Castle,** located on B Street. For 125 years one of the most lavish houses in the Silver State, The Castle is open for tours between Memorial Day and Labor Day from 11:00 A.M. to 5:00 P.M. **Majesty's Buckskin & Lace,** also along C Street, serves Cornish pasties, a popular lunch item for early underground miners, and also hawks Victorian and Western collectibles, including books, prints, and art.

The **Delta Saloon and Sawdust Corner,** occupying a renovated tavern on C Street, is one of the best family dining spots in town. The **Gold Hill Hotel,** in nearby Gold Hill, is a good bet for accommodations; in fact, it's Nevada's oldest operational hotel and has recently been restored to its nineteenth-century grandiosity. Call (702) 847–0111 for reservations. In business as drinking establishments, but essentially de facto museums, are the **Bucket of Blood Saloon** and the **Union Brewery,** a microbrewery that serves its frothy product in a building constructed in 1862.

The **Virginia & Truckee Railroad** makes regular round-trip runs on the winding track that links Virginia City and the Gold Hill Depot, a couple of miles south. The steam locomotive chugs out of the siding on F Street Memorial Day through October. The **Comstock Historic Preservation Weekend** in May is a great time to visit Virginia City, with its plays, lectures, tours, and living-history gatherings; funds raised go to support the fine **Fourth Ward School Museum,** found at the south end of town. Call (702) 847–0975 or 847–0311 to find out more.

In Dayton, southeast of Virginia City, visit **Comstock Silversmiths** at 239 Woodlake Circle. The business, more than a century old, manufactures and sells stunning silver belt buckles, conchas, saddle sets, and more.

Carson City was named by town founders Abe Curry and William Ormsby for the ubiquitous Kit Carson, who guided explorer John C. Frémont through the region in 1844. A wonderfully even-tempered place, when compared with the frenetic likes of Reno and Las Vegas, the capital city claims the grand **Nevada State Museum,** housed within the one-time Carson City Mint. Particularly fine exhibits on the Paiute and Washoe Indians grace the upper floor, while below there's a full-blown "ghost town" and mine. Other exhibits detail the process used to turn minerals into currency, a process this place should know about: Between 1870 and 1893 it produced more than fifty million gold and silver coins. Located at 600 North

Carson Street, the museum is open daily from 9:00 A.M. to 5:30 P.M.; call (702) 687–4810 for more information. (If a particular subject at the museum grabs your interest, you can head across the street to the century-old **State Library,** open Monday through Friday from 8:00 A.M. to 5:00 P.M., and read more about it.)

At 106 North Curry, across the street from the **Warren Engine Company Museum** (also an active fire station), poke around in **Comstock Books,** which specializes in volumes on Nevada and the Old West: its railroaders, miners, cowboys, and Indians. At Curry and West King streets is **Wells Fargo & Co.,** an 1876 depot that exhibits the latest in technological widgets and gadgets—the latest in 1876, that is.

A couple of other facilities not to miss include the **Stewart Indian Museum** (702–882–1808), on the campus of the Stewart Indian Boarding School, approximately 3 miles south of downtown on Highway 395, then

Wovoka and the Ghost Dance

The Ghost Dance was key to an emerging Native American religion of the late 1800s, which prophesied the end of westward expansion by the whites and the return of lands and buffalo to the Native Americans. The dance is primarily remembered in association with the Sioux, who performed the multiday ritual, accompanied by hypnotic trances, during the days that led up to the 1890 massacre at Wounded Knee. The "ghost shirts" worn by the Sioux were supposed to protect them from bullets; nevertheless, more than 200 were killed by the 7th Cavalry at Wounded Knee.

Actually the Nevada Paiutes, inspired by their prophet Wovoka, a native of the Yerington area, first practiced the Ghost Dance. Legend has it that a thirty-one-year-old Wovoka, while chopping wood in the Pine Nut Mountains, was visited by God and raised to Heaven. "It was the most beautiful country you can imagine," Wovoka said, "nice and level and green all the time."

God instructed Wovoka to travel the world, carrying the message of peace. He was to tell the people to dance for five nights consecutively and then not dance again for three months. Wovoka's stature as a prophet grew, and the people who visited him spread the word, and the Ghost Dance, throughout the West. He died, still highly revered, in 1932.

a mile east on Snyder Avenue. The school was established in 1897 in an effort to deal with the "problem" of children of captive Indians. The museum is open Monday through Saturday from 9:00 A.M. to 5:30 P.M. and Sunday from 9:00 A.M. to 4:00 P.M. The **Nevada State Railroad Museum,** at the south end of town on Highway 395, features equipment used by the Virginia & Truckee Railroad, a 21-mile line built in 1869 with Chinese labor that connected Carson City with Virginia City. The museum (702–687–6953) is open daily from 8:30 A.M. to 4:30 P.M. (**Hoof Beats'** horse-drawn carriage tours of historic Carson City also originate here.)

Carson City–area celebrations include the **Kit Carson Rendezvous and Wagon Train**—at which mountain men, Indians, and gunfighters convene—and the **Stewart Indian Museum Pow Wow.** Both are slated for June. For information on these events, for a detailed tabloid-sized guide to the city's historical walking tour, and for dining and overnighting information, visit the Chamber of Commerce's trailer at 1191 South Carson Street or call (702) 882–1565.

Head 12 miles south of Carson City to Genoa. The first, and arguably the prettiest, town in Nevada, Genoa was established as the Mormon Station trading post in 1851. The original Mormon fort burned in 1910, but only after being reduced in stature from the town's premier building to a cafe and then a chicken coop. In the late 1940s the state parks department built a replica of the fort, now the showpiece of **Mormon Station State Park** (702–782–2590). The replica houses a museum, open daily from 9:00 A.M. to 5:00 P.M., and the compound grounds are open from 8:00 A.M. to 8:00 P.M. Genoa is also home to many original Victorian dwellings—as well as several dozen new, but made-to-look-old, houses—and to the state's oldest operational house of libation, known as the **Genoa Bar.**

The **Douglas County Historical Museum** (702–782–4325) is housed in the one-time county courthouse that became a school in 1916, when Genoa lost the county seat to Minden. The jam-packed museum includes displays on the Pony Express, Native Americans, and legendary mail carrier Snowshoe Thompson, a Norwegian immigrant who brought the ski to ski country and delivered mail over the Sierra, come hell or high snow bank. The museum is open daily from 10:00 A.M. to 4:30 P.M.

Southern Nevada

Tonopah (230 miles southeast of Carson City) boomed from nothingness in 1900 to a town that claimed 3,000 residents and the county courthouse within five years. Silver production peaked just before World War I, and from that point on Tonopah progressively deteriorated until 1979, when it boomed again, with a resurgence in mining and the addition of an Air Force Test Range. The town's surprisingly large and well-designed **Central Nevada Museum** features collections of mining implements, historic photographs of central Nevada boomtowns, railroading relics, and Shoshone Indian artifacts. It's located off Highway 395 near Logan Field, at the south end of town, and is open daily from 9:00 A.M. to 5:00 P.M. Call (702) 482–9676 for information.

The early history of Tonopah is intertwined with that of a colorful character named Jim Butler, who struck silver here in 1900 and whose life and cantankerous burro are celebrated at the annual **Jim Butler Days,** held over Memorial Day weekend. The festivities include the Nevada state championships in several mining competitions, including mucking and spike driving. The State Liars Contest is also slated for the weekend (no fooling!); call (702) 482–3859 for details.

While in Tonopah, stay at the **Mizpah Hotel B&B** (702–482–6202), at 100 North Main Street, where you can dine in the Jack Dempsey Room or forfeit your vacation funds in the hotel's casino. This National Historic Landmark, extravagantly renovated in the 1970s, has been serving visitors since 1908.

The mostly paved side-trip to **Belmont,** 45 miles northeast of Tonopah, is time and gasoline well invested. The seat of Nye County from 1867 through 1905, boasting 2,000 residents at its zenith, now claims only a handful, and the sometimes-operating tavern is the only active enterprise in town. Belmont is one of the state's best-preserved ghost towns, with its brick court-house, large cemetery, impressive stamp-mill remains, and many original buildings, still standing in the old downtown section. If you're not ghost-towned-out yet, drive over the Toquima Range to Manhattan, 12 miles west of Belmont. From here return to Tonopah on Highways 377 and 376.

South of Tonopah, where silver is and was king, the Great Basin ends and the Mojave Desert begins; you'll know it when suddenly you're surrounded by yucca plants and Joshua trees. In Goldfield, whose name reveals that it was a mineral of a different color that gave rise to the town, Tex Rickard—a name heard often during the Klondike gold rush a few years earlier—promoted a championship prizefight in 1906 that earned him national prominence and many thousands of dollars. Already claiming 10,000 residents at the time, three years later Goldfield had twice that many; it was then, by far, the largest city in the state.

Do as notables such as Virgil Earp and Jack Dempsey did, and swing into the historic **Santa Fe Saloon** to wet your whistle and get your bearings. Then have a look inside the old **Esmeralda County Courthouse** and a glimpse at the outside of the fabulous, once-thriving **Goldfield Hotel,** which cost nearly half a million dollars to build in 1908. It's at the corner of Columbia and Crook streets.

Las Vegas: You love it or hate it; it's either a blight on the Western landscape, the dregs of decadence, or the most fun-filled place on earth. Frankly, Las Vegas is too caught up in its mad rush to nowhere to worry much about its past. The **Old Mormon Fort,** at the corner of Las Vegas Boulevard North and Washington Street, is a quiet, lonely survivor from the past, surrounded by the big, bustling, and new. The adobe was part of the original 1855 mission established when Brigham Young dispatched a Mormon party from Utah, armed with the assignment of converting the Paiute Indians to the Mormon way (the unsuccessful experiment lasted only three years). The fort is open Saturday, Sunday, and Monday during hours that change throughout the year; call (702) 486–3511 to find out more.

Also on your agenda should be the **Nevada State Museum and Historical Society** (702–486–5205), located at 700 Twin Lakes Drive. The museum leads visitors through 10,000 years of prehistory and history and includes displays on the Spanish conquistadors, the building of the railroads, and the development of Nevada's gambling industry. It's open daily from 9:00 A.M. to 5:00 P.M.

Cowboys converge on Las Vegas in early December for the **National Finals Rodeo,** the yearly culmination of Professional Rodeo Cowboys Association (PRCA) action. Call (702) 895–3900 for ticket information. The city also pulls out the stops for its annual **Helldorado Days** (702–870–1221), slated for the last week in May at the Thomas and Mack Center. Bull riding takes center stage at the celebration, which dates from 1935.

The driving loop through scenic **Red Rock Canyon,** a 100-square-mile jumble of geology managed by the BLM (Bureau of Land Management), begins 16 miles west of Las Vegas on Highway 159/West Charleston Boulevard. (A visitor center here is open from 9:00 A.M. to 4:00 P.M.) It's a great place to repair to for a dose of natural-world sanity if you're spending time in Las Vegas. The highlight of a visit is the **Bonnie Springs Ranch,** dating from the 1840s, and the associated **Old Nevada** theme park, with gunfights, street hangings, two museums, nineteenth-century melodrama performances, guided trail rides, and dining and drinking in the dinner house/saloon. The ranch (702–875–4191) is open from 8:00 A.M. to 11:00 P.M. daily for dining; the theme park's hours are 10:00 A.M. to 6:00 P.M.

Also of note: nearby **Spring Mountain Ranch State Park,** a pioneer spread that counts among its numerous owners, since established in 1869, the actress Vera Krupp and billionaire eccentric Howard Hughes. The ranch house/visitor center is open weekends and holidays from 9:00 A.M. to 4:30 P.M.

Near the Las Vegas suburb of Henderson at 1830 South Boulder Highway, visit the **Clark County Heritage Museum,** with its stupefying array of historical artifacts and memorabilia. The museum's historical overview begins with the Anasazi Indians, then progresses through the Mormon pioneers, soldiers, ranchers, and early steamboating and gambling eras, and finally winds up with the construction of Hoover Dam. Outside you'll find a full-blown display on railroading in Nevada and the Heritage Street "town," filled with old houses and business buildings such as the 1890s Print Shop, with displays of old equipment and original copies of early Nevada newspapers. This excellent and regionally comprehensive twenty-five-acre museum complex is open daily from 9:00 A.M. to 4:30 P.M.; call (702) 455–7955 for more information.

One of the earliest white settlements in the region was Overton, 60 miles northeast of Las Vegas on Interstate 15 and Highway 169. The Mormon pioneers who set up shop here, however, were preceded, by several hundred years, by Anasazi settlers, forerunners of today's Pueblo Indians. The main pueblo in this delta region had approximately one hundred rooms, and the **Lost City Museum of Archaeology,** atop a topographical blip just south of Overton, tells all about it, with a high-quality collection of early Southwest artifacts. The small Pueblo Indian residence on the grounds is a replica constructed by the Civilian Conservation Corps in the 1930s. The museum (702–397–2193) is open daily from 8:30 A.M. to 4:30 P.M.

Pioche, 170 miles north of Las Vegas on Interstate 15 and Highway 93, was one of the bawdiest and brawlingest outposts in the nineteenth-century West, rivaling the more famous likes of Tombstone and Dodge City. Around 1870 prospectors poured out of the Comstock to file silver claims here; by 1875 the mines had drawn some 12,000 people, and not a lawman in the bunch, so the story goes—a story that goes on to relate that at least seventy-five men were shot or stabbed to death before anyone there had a chance to die of natural causes. In 1871, during a boisterous Mexican-independence celebration, 300 powder kegs were ignited, basically demolishing the town and killing a dozen people and injuring several dozen more.

Get an overview of this wild-and-woolly Western legend at the **Lincoln County Historical Museum,** on Main Street. A pair of large rooms within brim with minerals and mining paraphernalia, guns, printing equipment, black-and-white photographs, and a lot more. It's open daily from 10:00 A.M. to 4:00 P.M. Call (702) 962–5207 for more information.

Up the street at the high end of Main is the chamber's **Tillie's** (702–962–5205), where you can acquire a map that shows the locations of other historically important structures, such as the **Wells Fargo Building,** the **Thompson Opera House,** an intact miner's cabin, and the **Million Dollar Courthouse,** which was built after the 1871 conflagration. Originally contracted to cost around $26,000, the courthouse wound up costing the city nearly a million dollars by the time it was finally paid off in the late 1930s (in the 1950s it was condemned and auctioned off for $150). Between April and October volunteers are on hand to lead tours through the fabulous structure, which includes a jailhouse and judge's and sheriff's offices.

Where to Eat

Winnemucca Hotel, Winnemucca, (702) 623–2908
Louis' Basque Corner, Reno, (702) 323–7203
Bonnie Springs Ranch, west of Las Vegas, (702) 875–4300

Where to Stay

Old Pioneer Garden Bed & Breakfast, Unionville, (702) 538–7585
Cottonwood Ranch, north of Elko, (702) 752–3604
Parsonage House, Eureka, (702) 237–5756
Pony Express Bed & Make Your Own Breakfast, Austin, (702) 964–2306
Gold Hill Hotel, Virginia City, (702) 847–0111
Mizpah Hotel Bed & Breakfast, Tonopah, (702) 482–6202

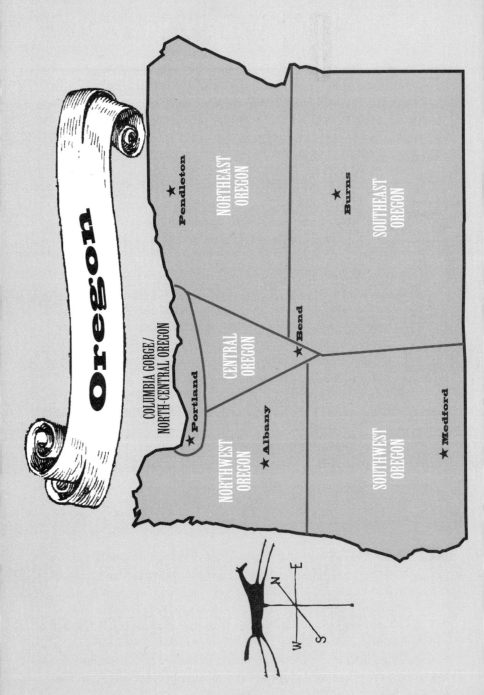

Oregon

COLUMBIA GORGE /
NORTH-CENTRAL OREGON

★ Pendleton

NORTHEAST
OREGON

★ Burns

SOUTHEAST
OREGON

★ Portland

CENTRAL
OREGON

★ Bend

NORTHWEST
OREGON

★ Albany

SOUTHWEST
OREGON

★ Medford

OREGON

▼▼▼

REGON was the end of the line for thousands of 1800s Oregon Trail travelers, after a trip of 2,000 miles that typically took around five months. More than 50,000 emigrants ended up settling in the fertile Willamette Valley in the western part of the state, while others continued north into Washington or south toward the goldfields of California and Nevada. At that time what was called the Oregon Country stretched all the way from the Rocky Mountains to the Pacific.

Oregon is one of the most geographically diverse states in the United States. It leads the country in timber production, providing more than one-fifth of the nation's softwood sawtimber, yet less than half the state is forested. Eastern Oregon, especially, is cow, sheep, sagebrush, and cowpoke country.

The narrative begins in the northwest, and from there leads into the Columbia Gorge area, then through central, northeast, southeast, and, finally, southwest Oregon.

Northwest Oregon

Begin near Astoria at the **Fort Clatsop National Memorial,** 5 miles southeast of town, which claims a detailed replica of the quarters in which the Lewis and Clark party wintered during 1805–06. The visitor center, open year-round, offers audiovisual programs and other exhibits that illuminate the Corps of Discovery's wet winter (it rained 94 of 106 days); in summer buckskin-clad rangers demonstrate the frontier skills that would have been practiced by the party members, such as boat carving, hide tanning, and mapmaking. The memorial is open daily year-round from 8:00 A.M. to 5:00 P.M. Call (503) 861–2471 for more details.

Back in Astoria a replicated blockhouse at the corner of Duane and Fifteenth streets marks the site of **Fort Astoria,** John Jacob Astor's original 1811 Pacific Fur Company outpost, which was abandoned in 1812 and which, apparently, Astor himself never visited. The 1883 **Captain Flavel House Museum,** one of several museums maintained by the Clatsop County Historical Society, is an opulent 1883 Queen Anne mansion filled with reminders of the city's colorful seafaring past. It's located at 441 Eighth Street and is open daily from 10:00 A.M. to 5:00 P.M. for touring. The **Heritage Museum,** found in the old city hall building at 1618 Exchange Street, focuses on Clatsop County's history and the more than two dozen ethnic groups who found their way to Astoria during the days of westward expansion. It's open daily from 10:00 A.M. to 5:00 P.M.; call (503) 325–2203 for more information about either museum.

Near the south end of the seafront Promenade in Seaside, 18 miles south of Astoria, visit the **Lewis and Clark Salt Works** (503–861–2471), site of the salt cairn where the Corps of Discovery boiled seawater. Over a period of two months, they garnered some four bushels of salt, which they used at Fort Clatsop and on their trip back east. In the resort community you can also take in the **Lewis and Clark Historical Pageant,** which dramatizes the expedition's journey to the Pacific. Performances are staged outdoors at Broadway Park from late July through late August.

The **Junction City Historical Museum** explores subjects that range from Oregon Trail wagon trains to the region's first Scandinavian settlers. Located at 655 Holly Street in Junction City (10 miles north of metropolitan Eugene on Highway 99), it opens primarily by appointment; call (541) 998–2924 to make one. **Black Bart's Bed & Breakfast,** named not after a mustachioed bad guy but a champion mammoth donkey, is found at 94125 Love Lake Road. Two guest rooms grace the renovated 1880s farmhouse, out of which mule-drawn rides in turn-of-the-century wagons are a favored pastime. Call (541) 998–1904 for reservations and information.

Brownsville, 18 miles northeast of Junction City, was called Kirk's Ferry when settled in 1846. Here the **Linn County Historical Museum** (541–466–3390), at 101 Park Avenue, encompasses a depot with old train cars and other artifacts. The museum is open daily from 11:00 A.M. to 4:00 P.M. and Sunday from 1:00 to 5:00 P.M. Ask for information on the town's self-guided tour, which takes in the nearby **Moyer House,** a grand structure built in 1882. The venerable **Linn County Pioneer Picnic,** first held in 1857, continues the tradition of Oregon pioneers and their descendants, who gather to share their unique heritage; visitors are welcome, too. For information contact the Linn County Pioneer Association at (503) 466–3390.

Carriage rides, picturesque covered bridges, and Victorian homes define Albany, 30 miles north of Junction City on Highway 99E, which boasts nearly 400 historic houses, shops, and churches. The **Albany Regional Museum** (541–967–6540), at 302 Ferry Street Southwest, displays changing indoor and outdoor exhibits throughout the year and includes a general store, doctor's office, and more. It's open in summer Wednesday through Sunday from noon to 4:00 P.M. The **Monteith House,** at 518 Second Avenue Southwest, is the oldest frame house in town and one of the state's oldest structures, built by the town's founders in 1849. The home represents one of Oregon's most authentic restoration efforts, and costumed docents are on hand to explain the way things were. It opens Wednesday through Sunday from noon to 4:00 P.M. in summer and by appointment at other times.

Call the Albany Visitors Association at (541) 928–0911 for information on self-guided tours, for a listing of the many Victorian- and logging-oriented festivities that fill in the calendar here, and for information on the living-history performances at **Flinn's Top of the Block Theater,** which include the likes of *Reflections of a Pioneer Woman.*

Oregon's origins can be sensed at Salem's **Mission Mill Village,** a living-history gem located 3 blocks from the state capitol at 1313 Mill Street Southeast. Within the Thomas Kay Woolen Mill, docents demonstrate the "fleece to fabric" process followed after the mill was built in the late 1880s. Also within the five-acre park is the Jason Lee House, the oldest frame house in the Pacific Northwest. Lee, the first Protestant missionary into the Oregon Territory, built the place in 1841, before the first Oregon Trail wagon trains arrived at Oregon City. The 1847 John Boon Home and 1858 Pleasant Grove Presbyterian Church are also on the grounds. The large, seductive Museum Store, situated on the first floor of the mill building, features a first-class selection of Northwest books and blankets, quilts, and other handcrafted goods. Theme cafes and boutiques are also situated within the complex, open Tuesday through Saturday year-round from 10:00 A.M. to 4:30 P.M. Call (503) 585–7012 for further information. The **Marion County Historical County Museum** (503–364–2128), located at the northwest corner of Mission Mill Village, includes a dugout canoe and other Kalapuyan Indian and pioneer artifacts. Its doors open between 9:30 A.M. and 4:30 P.M. Monday through Saturday.

Molalla, 30 miles northeast of Salem, hosts the annual **Molalla**

Buckaroo, which celebrates the cowboy way with top contenders from throughout the Northwest competing in traditional rodeo events. The bucking begins during the first week in July; for information call the *Molalla Pioneer* newspaper at (503) 829–2301 or 829–6941.

The **Old Aurora Colony Museum** is a five-building complex that details the compelling history of William Keil's Aurora Colony, Oregon's first religious commune. Previously Keil, a preacher and physician, had left Pennsylvania and founded the town of Bethel, Missouri, near the eastern terminus of the Oregon Trail. In 1855 he led a group of his followers along that trail to here; the peaceful community, named after Keil's daughter and home to as many as 600 residents, ran smoothly until his death in 1877, when it disbanded.

The museum proper, housed in the renovated 1862 ox barn, includes outstanding displays of old quilts and other handcrafted items. Additional structures on the grounds include an 1865 farmhouse and a hand-hewn log cabin. During summer the colony complex is open Tuesday through Saturday from 10:00 A.M. to 4:30 P.M. (It's closed Tuesdays the rest of the year and closed all of January.) Call (503) 678–5754 for additional information.

Champoeg State Park (pronounced sham-POO-ee), west of Interstate 5 off Highway 219, is where Willamette Valley settlers and French-Canadian trappers voted in 1843 to establish the first provisional government in the Northwest, setting the stage for the establishment of the Oregon Territory. The Pioneer Mother's Museum is a replica of an 1850s settler's home, and the barnlike visitor center brims with pioneer artifacts and interpretations of their lives. It's open weekdays from 8:00 A.M. to 4:00 P.M. and weekends from 9:00 A.M. to 5:30 P.M. The outdoor amphitheater rumbles Tuesday through Saturday evenings at 7:30 in July and August, as the park presents *Champoeg: The Story of Oregon,* a reenactment that summarizes the state's formative years. September's **Indian Summer Folk Life Festival** features a fur-traders' encampment, with associated mountain-man and mountain-woman competitions and festivities. Call (503) 678–1251 or 678–1649 for more information.

Near Yamhill (20 miles northwest of St. Paul) the **Flying M Ranch** and its 17,000-square-foot log lodge command a setting at the base of Trask Mountain, along the historic Tillamook-to-Yamhill stagecoach route. The lodge's impressive 30-foot-long, six-ton bar is hewn from a solid Douglas fir log. Barbecues, horseshoe contests, live entertainment, and trail rides— either on horseback or via stagecoach—can all be enjoyed at the getaway.

The Flying M's acclaimed eatery is open Monday through Thursday from 8:00 A.M. to 9:00 P.M. and Friday through Sunday from 8:00 A.M. to 10:00 P.M. Both cabin rentals and campsites are available at the ranch, located 10 miles west of Yamhill at 23029 Northwest Flying M Road; call (503) 662–3222 for further information.

Columbia Gorge / North-Central Oregon

Oregon City is where it all began, or ended, depending on how one looks at it. It was the first incorporated town west of the Rockies and the original capital of the Oregon Territory. Oregon City boasted the first published newspaper and the first minted currency west of the Missouri River. The **End of the Oregon Trail Interpretive Center** (503–657–9336), at 500 Washington Street, displays artifacts left behind by early emigrants and focuses on the years during which more than 300,000 pioneers made the 2,000-mile trek to here from Independence, Missouri. The center is open Monday through Saturday from 9:00 A.M. to 5:00 P.M. and Sunday from 11:00 A.M. to 5:00 P.M.

The **Clackamas County Historical Museum** (503–655–5574) displays the colorful history of Clackamas County in one of Oregon's best small-town museums. The Windows of History exhibit presents a time line of the region's history, from the Native Americans through the fur traders, pioneers, and beyond. The museum includes the society's research library and photograph archives; information on numerous historic homes open for touring can be obtained here, as well. It's located at 211 Tumwater Drive and is open Monday through Friday from 10:00 A.M. to 5:00 P.M. and weekends from 1:00 to 4:00 P.M.

The **McLoughlin House National Historic Site** (503–656–5146), at 713 Center Street, was built in 1846 by the "Father of Oregon." Dr. John McLoughlin, a British-born Canadian and chief factor of the Hudson's Bay Company, laid out the town of Oregon City in 1841 and retired here in 1845 after being forced out of the British-owned Hudson's Bay Company for his pro-American sentiments. The house includes many original furnishings, some of which were shipped around Cape Horn to get here, and a four-poster bed previously owned by Meriwether Lewis. It's open for touring Tuesday through Saturday from 10:00 A.M. to 4:00 P.M. and Sunday from 1:00 to 4:00 P.M. Adjacent to the McLoughlin house is the 1850 **Barclay House,** also included in the tour.

The *Oregon Trail Pageant,* performed at the Clackamas Community College amphitheater south of Oregon City in July and August, is a musical saga that dramatizes the trek of the pioneers. For schedules and reservations, call (503) 657–9336.

In Portland at 1230 Southwest Park, the Oregon Historical Society maintains the superlative **Oregon History Center,** with its regional research library and numerous permanent and revolving exhibits. Displays focus on subjects that include the trails of Oregon and life at sea in the eighteenth century; an outstanding gallery of Western art is also featured. The museum is open Tuesday through Saturday from 10:00 A.M. to 5:00 P.M. and Sunday from noon to 5:00 P.M. Call (503) 222–1741 for more information.

The **Cowboys Then and Now Museum,** at 729 Northeast Oregon Street in Portland's Oregon Square, is a must for individuals intrigued by the Old West. On entering, visitors are immediately immersed in a realistic cattle-drive camp, complete with campfire, chuckwagon, sagebrush, and Zack, the camp cook. The animated old-timer spins tales about the nine-teenth-century cowboying life, speaking both of the beauty and loneliness of life on the prairie. Other displays highlight the lesser-known roles played by women and blacks in the Old West, whereas the tack room gives young and old alike the chance to handle gear like that which cowboys used to accomplish their tasks. Spurs, horse collars, saddles, and hobbles hang from the walls of century-old barnwood. The museum features a reference library, with more than 600 volumes that illuminate the cowboy way, some boast-ing copyrights as early as 1886. Call (503) 731–3333 for more information on this one-of-a-kind attraction.

The *Coming of the White Man* sculpture, in Washington Park (west of downtown on Burnside), depicts the arrival of the first whites from a seldom-expressed perspective: A stoic Multnomah chief, arms folded, stands, emotionless, watching over the Columbia River. A brave by his side points toward the river at the ghosts of the Lewis and Clark expedition, floating by. Sculptor Herman MacNeil created this historic landmark in 1904.

The **Washington County Museum** (503–645–5353) interprets the diverse history of both the county and state, from the early days of the Tualatin Indians through white settlement. The museum, overflowing with artifacts and memorabilia, is located on the Rock Creek Campus of Portland Community College. It's open Monday through Saturday from 10:00 A.M. to 4:30 P.M. The Oregon Historical Society's **Bybee House & Howell Territorial Park** is located on Sauvie Island, 10 miles northwest of Portland off Highway 30. The park features a seventy-five-acre homestead, complete with an 1858 clapboard house, an agricultural museum, and living-history presentations. It's open Wednesday through Sunday between June and Labor Day from noon to 5:00 P.M.

East of Portland on Interstate 84, the town of Cascade Locks is named for the locks completed in 1896 (but begun in 1874!) to move ships safely past what once was a treacherous stretch of rapids. The **Cascade Locks Historical Museum** (541–374–8535), at Marine Park, houses Native American artifacts, Oregon pioneer memorabilia, and photographs of the settlers' portage road and other historical subjects. It's open daily May through September from noon to 5:00 P.M. Monday through Thursday and from 10:00 A.M. to 5:00 P.M. Friday through Sunday. In summer visitors cruise in nineteenth-century fashion aboard the sternwheeler *Columbia Gorge,* which makes two-hour runs three times daily from Marine Park to the Bonneville Dam. Call (503) 223–3928 for tickets and for information on **Sternwheeler Days,** which celebrate an earlier day on the mighty Columbia.

Hood River, in addition to its claim as Sailboarding Capital of the World, boasts the **Hood River County Historical Museum** (541–386–6772), located at Port Marin (off Interstate 84 at exit 64). The museum, holding Oregon Trail artifacts and re-creations is open between April and October on Monday through Saturday from 10:00 A.M. to 4:00 P.M. and on Sunday from noon to 4:00 P.M.

Option number one for an overnight in town: the historic, lavish, and expensive **Columbia Gorge Hotel**—nicknamed "Waldorf of the West" and located at 4000 Westcliff—with breathtaking views of the Columbia and a restaurant rated among the finest in Oregon. Call (800) 345–1921 for reservations. Option number two: the recently restored 1913 **Hood River Hotel** (503–386–1900), at 102 Oak Street, featuring vintage riverview rooms.

The *Fruit Blossom Special* chugs out of the refurbished, 1911 Mount Hood Railroad Depot, hauling rail buffs and others on narrated history trips. The tracks, laid in 1906, link Hood River with the foothills of snow-capped Mount Hood, known as "Wy'east" to the region's Native Americans, who believed it to be a spirit in and of itself. Two rides are offered; the longer,

44-mile round trip to Parkdale, from which point outstanding views of Mount Hood are gained, is suggested. Still "go" and not just for show, the *Fruit Blossom Special* takes on cargoes of lumber from the mountains and pears from the foothills. So authentic is the excursion that outlaws occasionally have been known to capture the railcars and hold passengers at gunpoint. Call (541) 386–3556 for more information.

History is palpable in The Dalles, whose name (derived from the French word *dalle*, which means slab) was used by the French-Canadian voyageurs to describe the river rapids that flow swiftly through a narrow channel over flat rocks. Lewis and Clark camped at a point here, which they named Rock Fort, in October 1805. Kit Carson passed through here with Captain Frémont in 1843, en route to California, and The Dalles was the end of the land route for Oregon Trail travelers until the Barlow Road was hacked out of the side of 11,235-foot Mount Hood in 1845.

After the Cayuse Indians' Whitman Mission Massacre near present Walla Walla in 1847, a volunteer regiment from the Willamette Valley built a stockade here, and in 1850 the army formalized Fort Drum (the name was changed to Fort Dalles in 1853). The **Fort Dalles Museum** is located in the fort's old surgeon's quarters at Fifteenth and Garrison, the last building that remains from the original fort and an attractive example of the "picturesque" or "Prairie Gothic" style of architecture. It's open between March and October on weekdays from 10:30 A.M. to 5:00 P.M. and on weekends from 10:00 A.M. to 5:00 P.M.; during the remainder of the year, it is open Wednesday through Friday from noon to 4:00 P.M. and on weekends from 10:00 A.M. to 4:00 P.M. Call (541) 296–4547 or 296–6616 for information.

Also of note in The Dalles: the old **Wasco County Courthouse** (541–296–4798), which served as headquarters for the largest county ever created in the United States—Wasco County, 130,000 square miles in area and ranging from Oregon into what are now Idaho, Montana, and Wyoming. The courthouse is located on West Second Street, next to the Chamber of Commerce office, and is open Tuesday through Saturday from 10:00 A.M. to 5:00 P.M. Historic walking tours, beginning at the Chamber, take in numerous sites, including the nearby **Lewis and Clark Memorial,** at Second and Mount Hood streets.

Fort Dalles Days, with its Rough-n-Wild Rodeo main event, kicks up the Columbia River silt in mid-July every year. Also on tap are Western art exhibits, dances, and a parade. For overnight accommodations, check into the **Williams House Inn** (541–296–2889), a B&B listed on the National Register of Historic Places and situated at 608 West Sixth Street. Finally, in Old Town check out the **Baldwin Saloon,** at First and Court streets, opened first in 1876 then again in 1991. Turn-of-the-century oil paintings decorate the building's 18-inch-thick brick walls. It opens daily, except Sunday, at 11:00 A.M. as a bar and restaurant that serves homemade foods and a selection of the microbrews Oregon has become famous for in beer-drinking circles. For information on this and other area attractions, call The Dalles Chamber of Commerce at (541) 296–2231 and request the brochure entitled *Discover the Oregon Trail*.

Timberline Lodge, 5 miles up the hill from Government Camp on the shoulder of stunning Mount Hood, is a commanding rock-and-timber National Historic Landmark built by the CCC (Civilian Conservation Corps) in the 1930s, with construction directed by the WPA (Works Progress Administration). Symbolic of the structure's massiveness are its 750-pound brass-and-bronze weather vane and half-ton front door. The base for almost year-round winter sports, the lodge can be toured with Forest Service personnel daily. The grand structure is appointed with handcrafted furnishings and with artifacts and artworks that make it a veritable museum—a mix of early ski, Native American, and Old West. Call (800) 547–1406 for information on rooms and dining facilities.

The HBC, the West's Original Float-Trip Outfitters

The earliest emigrants to travel the Oregon Trail were forced to descend the treacherous Columbia River in order to reach the fecund Willamette Valley. Some lost possessions, even their lives, when their rafts ripped apart or their overloaded canoes capsized. The Hudson's Bay Company offered transport in their boats, at $50 a wagon and $10 a person, but few emigrants could afford the cost. The toll seemed outrageous, but not if you grasped the incredible toil demanded of the HBC's voyageurs to get the boats back upstream through the boiling rapids.

Central Oregon

The **Tygh Valley Rodeo** (541–544–3371), held in mid-May in Tygh Valley (30 miles south of the Dalles on Highway 197), is an all-Indian buck-out held in conjunction with a Western dance and other festivities. Shaniko, 30 miles southeast of Tygh Valley, claims the historic **Shaniko Hotel,** a Wild West relic. From the wide-planked porch that wraps the two-story, red-brick hotel, you can enjoy a view of the streets of Shaniko, now almost a ghost town but once a vibrant center for the wool trade, where cowboys, sheepherders, and

The Barlow Road

Instead of tackling the Columbia River on arriving at The Dalles in 1845, Samuel K. Barlow and Joel Palmer pointed their wagon train southwest. From present Tygh Valley they began exploring the way for a route over the Cascades to the Willamette Valley. The challenges were daunting—thick forests, steep and rocky pitches, year-round snowfields, and the unknown: From the Cascade crest, what if the mountains simply dropped into precipitous, impassable canyons?

Daily, crews pushed ahead with axes to hack a route through the forest. Palmer climbed high onto Mount Hood, above timberline, where he spotted Summit Meadows and a potential pass. In late October, with snow threatening, the remaining wagons and two guards were left at Fort Deposit, while the rest rushed over the pass to reach the Willamette Valley before winter closed the way.

Shortly thereafter Barlow appeared before the Provisional Legislature to petition for a franchise to open a road between The Dalles and Oregon City. He promised to clear and maintain the road if he could collect tolls. The franchise was granted, and the toll road operated from 1846 until 1919, during which time thousands traveled it.

For tour brochures that lead the way along this historic route and even pinpoint several locations where you can walk in ruts carved by wagons, call the Mount Hood National Forest at (503) 352–6002 or 622–3191 and request *The Barlow Road* and *Where to Find Oregon Trail Wagon Ruts on the Mt. Hood National Forest.*

steam locomotives kept things boisterous. Rooms at the hotel evoke images of the frontier days, and the dining room serves hearty home-cooked fare daily from 7:00 A.M. to 8:00 P.M. Call (541) 489–3441 for reservations; also ask about **Shaniko Days,** slated for the first Saturday in August, when fiddlers, barbecues, and arts and crafts draw a crowd to town.

Fifty miles southwest of Shaniko is Warm Springs. Here's what the Confederated Tribes of the Warm Springs Reservation say about their **Museum at Warm Springs:** "This is a place of illumination. A legacy of the past and a hope for the future. A place created so that Native Americans, and newer Americans, can see and touch and hear and feel and know not just how life was, but why."

With displays and performances—singing and drumming, storytelling, crafts, historic photographs, rare documents, traditional dwellings, and full-scale dioramas of tribal life—the Confederated Tribes have created a masterpiece; all in all, it is one of the country's premier collections of Native American artifacts and historical exhibits. Designed to resemble a traditional encampment, the museum grows out of a cottonwood grove along the Deschutes River. The complex, including its outstanding museum shop, is located at 2189 Highway 26 and is open daily from 10:00 A.M. to 5:00 P.M. Call (541) 553–3331 for additional information.

The **Native America Salmon Bake** at Kah-Nee-Ta Resort, also in Warm Springs, is among Oregon's most traditional and tasty culinary possibilities. Visitors are welcomed by tribal members, outfitted in ceremonial dress, as they bake fresh-caught salmon, skewered on cedar sticks, slowly over aromatic alder embers, in the tradition of the Paiute, Wasco, and Warm Springs Indians. Ceremonial dances and traditional stories follow the meal, served Saturdays only, from Memorial Day to Labor Day; call (541) 553–1112 to learn more.

Saddle up in Sisters (60 miles southwest of Warm Springs), a Western-flavored settlement whose downtown stores sport false fronts and where llamas have become more popular than horses for hauling gear into the surrounding Cascade backcountry. The wild and well-known PRCA-sanctioned **Sisters Rodeo** is held during the second weekend in June; call the Chamber of Commerce at (541) 549–0251 for schedules and other information. (PRCA stands for Professional Rodeo Cowboys Association.) When in town, enjoy a chuckwagon dinner at the **Gallery Restaurant,** at 230 West Cascade, a restaurant filled with paintings of and artifacts from the Old West.

Bend's indoor-outdoor 150-acre **High Desert Museum,** among the finest facilities in the Northwest, interprets the legends and lore of cowboys and miners, as well as the natural history of the region. The Settler's Cabin brims with early artifacts—handmade quilts, flour sacks, washtubs, and biscuit pans—whereas the Earle A. Chiles Center's "Spirit of the West" exhibit offers a convincing stroll through an earlier time. Interactive exhibits, living-history presentations, a superb museum store, and history- and nature-oriented field excursions into the surrounding countryside are among the other finds at the complex, located at 59800 South Highway 97. It's open daily year-round from 9:00 A.M. to 5:00 P.M. Call (541) 382–4754 for further information.

A. R. Bowman Memorial Museum and **Wright Cabin & Ranchers' Memorial** (503–447–3715), at 246 North Main Street in Prineville (40 miles east of Sisters), documents area history via photographs and artifacts. It's open Tuesday through Friday from 10:00 A.M. to 5:00 P.M. and Saturday from 11:00 A.M. to 4:00 P.M. (closed January and February). The community's **Crooked River Round-Up,** held in mid-July, is central Oregon's biggest rodeo. On tap in addition to the traditional buck-fest competitions are horse racing, dancing, and a parade. Call the Chamber of Commerce at (541) 447–4479 for further details.

Proceed northeastward through Mitchell and Fossil, through classic Western sagebrush-and-butte country that offers few human-devised attractions but a wealth of sightseeing opportunities. In Condon check out the **Gilliam County Historical Society's Depot Museum,** just north of town adjacent to the fairgrounds. Here you'll find a 1905 railroad depot, a renovated 1884 log cabin, and several other buildings. The complex is open Wednesday through Sunday from 1:00 to 5:00 P.M. May through September. Call (541) 384–4233 for information. (**Pete's Barber Shop Museum,** also in tiny Condon, displays cowboy tack and Indian artifacts.)

Northeast Oregon

You can't book a room too early for the four-day **Pendleton Round-Up,** one of the nation's two top rodeos (the other is Cheyenne Frontier Days in Wyoming). The gathering has been attracting the world's top cowboys and cowgirls since 1910. There's an associated Native American encampment and **Happy Canyon Dance and Pageant,** which kicks off by dramatizing the first meeting between the emigrants and the region's Umatilla Indians. Time rolls on, and the early days in a Wild West town are re-created. Following the show spectators are invited into the Happy Canyon Dance Hall to become part of the action and dance to live music, gamble, and partake of their favorite beverages.

For information on the early-September celebration and Western revelry —which also include barbecues, Western breakfasts, an American Indian beauty pageant, and cowboy shows—call the Pendleton Round-Up Association at (541) 276–2553 or (800) 45–RODEO (76336). Also, whether in town for the round-up or at another time during the summer, be sure to visit the **Round-Up Hall of Fame,** which commemorates successful bronc busters *and* bucking stock. It's located under the south grandstand area of the Pendleton Round-Up Grounds, at Thirteenth and Southwest Court, and is open weekdays from 1:00 to 4:00 P.M.

The **Umatilla County Historical Society Museum,** housed in a renovated 1909 railroad depot on Fourth Street, features an array of Umatilla County artifacts and historic photographs. The society's heartfelt mission is to document and preserve the region's rich legacy and its long list of inhabitants: Native Americans, mountain men, missionaries, soldiers, farmers, cattlemen, sheepherders, and loggers. The museum (541–276–0012), located at 108 Southwest Frazier, is open Tuesday through Saturday from 10:00 A.M. to 4:00 P.M. While out and about, also take the **Pendleton Underground** tour, originating at the corner of First and Emigrant. The tour takes in both the aboveground Miss Stella's bordello and tunnels leading through former Chinese opium dens and living quarters. (The Chinese dug some 70 miles of tunnels here between 1870 and 1930.) Tours are conducted Monday through Saturday between 9:00 A.M. and 5:00 P.M.; call (541) 276–0730 for details.

Hamley's Saddlery, located at 30 Southeast Court, is one of the oldest saddleries in the West, doing business here since 1883. What the Hamley family began back in Wisconsin in 1852, current proprietor Monte Beckman continues today—the slow, deliberate art of crafting world-famous saddles, sporting the Circle H brand. From design through the laminating, squeezing, scraping, polishing, and curing process of the bullhide-and-wood saddles, Beckman does it all himself. Visitors can watch him in action weekdays between 9:00 A.M. and 5:30 P.M. The second floor of the enterprise features a gallery filled with Native American art.

Thirty miles east of Pendleton along the North Fork of the Umatilla River is **Baker's Bar M Ranch,** one of Oregon's foremost ride-and-relax dude ranches, where the likes of Teddy Roosevelt have bunked. The place began life as a stage stop; the main ranch house was built in 1864, its logs cut and hewn even as the War Between the States raged. Outstanding baked goods and other foods are highlights there today, as is the crystal-clear warm-springs pool. Guests, staying in either the eight-room main lodge or in one of the cabins beyond, are assigned a horse for their week-long stay; fishing, hiking, and bird-watching are other popular diversions. For information on this very special Western getaway, call (541) 566–3381.

The **Frazier Farmstead Museum,** at 1403 Chestnut Street in Milton-Freewater (30 miles northeast of Pendleton), is a thriving operation suggestive of the late 1800s, with a restored 1892 farmhouse and outbuildings, and flower, herb, and vegetable gardens. William Samuel Frazier and his large family departed from their home in Texas in 1867 and wound up here, claiming 320 acres of land. Now chiseled down to six acres, the farmstead, lying adjacent to the Walla Walla River, is open to visitors April through December on Thursday, Friday, and Saturday from 11:00 A.M. to 4:00 P.M. and on Sunday from 1:00 to 4:00 P.M. The popular harvest festival is held the first Saturday each October. Call (541) 938–4636 or 938–3480 for more information.

Unpretentious Joseph, beautifully situated at the base of the sawtoothed Wallowa Mountains and typically a rather quiet burg, explodes in summer at 1:00 P.M. on Wednesdays, Fridays, and Saturdays, when desperadoes ride into town and hold up the First Bank of Joseph (now housing the **Wallowa County Museum**). The robbery is a reenactment of an actual bank hoist that occurred in 1896, following which one of the perpetrators became the bank's vice president—after doing suitable time in prison! Learn about this and other Joseph-area history at the museum (541–432–9482), found on Main Street at the south end of town. Exhibited are historical relics, including ones from the Nez Perce culture. It is open daily from 10:00 A.M. to 5:00 P.M. Memorial Day through late September.

Chief Joseph Days, held in late July in Joseph, is among northeast Oregon's largest Indian-and-cowboy fests. Included are several rodeos and parades and an Indian encampment occupied by Nez Perce and Umatilla Indians. Call (541) 426–4622 or 432–1015 for information. While in town try out **Cactus Jack's Cowboy Bar,** which dishes up Western grub in an ancient red-brick building at Main and McCully streets. Hours are Monday through Thursday from 5:00 to 9:00 P.M., Friday and Saturday from 5:00 to 10:00 P.M., and Sunday from noon to 9:00 P.M.

Minam Lodge is a dude ranch of proud tradition, nestled deep in the Eagle Cap Wilderness and accessible only by small plane (charter flights are available) or a long horseback ride. A stay at this rustic ranch, which started out as a pack station in the 1930s, is like going back to a time before there were cars, telephones, and electricity, when the West was young. Guests stay in rustic, riverside log cabins, built of timber felled on the ranch, each with fireplace, hot shower, and kerosene lanterns. Pack trips, fishing, dining on outstanding home-cooked meals, seasonal hunting (for deer, elk, bear, cougar, and bighorn sheep), trail riding, and simply relaxing in a wild setting are the preferred activities. For more information call (541) 432–9171.

Baker City, 115 miles southwest of Joseph, was known simply as Baker from shortly after the turn of the century until the 1980s, when citizens voted to reclaim the name the town was given in the mid-1860s, after Col. J. S. Ruckel built his gold-stamp mill along the banks of the Powder River. Outside town, the Bureau of Land Management's new $10 million **National Historic Oregon Trail Interpretive Center,** on Flagstaff Hill, was developed in celebration of the Oregon Trail 1993 Sesquicentennial. The facility resurrects the heyday of the emigrant trail and the lives of those who traveled it, with living-history presentations, multimedia exhibits, and 150-year-old wagon ruts. The most striking feature is a 100-foot-long pioneer train—its wagons loaded with gear and people (mannequins)—pulled by stuffed oxen and mules. Permanent and changing exhibits, indoor and outdoor theaters, a pioneer encampment, and an interpretive trail system grace the center, open daily from 9:00 A.M. to 6:00 P.M. May 1 through September 30 and from 9:00 A.M. to 4:00 P.M. the rest of the year. Call (541) 523–1843 for more information.

Check out the **Oregon Trail Regional Museum,** at the corner of Campbell and Grove, where you can learn about Baker City's early days of gold mining, timbering, and cowboying and pick up information on a walking tour of town. (Be sure also to swing into the U.S. Bank at 2000 Main Street to have a gander at the 80.4-ounce nugget found during the gold rush of the 1860s.) The museum (541–523–9308) is open daily from 9:00 A.M. to 4:30 P.M. from the second weekend in May through the third weekend in September. The **Miners' Jubilee,** slated for Baker in mid-July, includes gold-panning contests, an old-time fiddler's competition, and a lot more. Call the Chamber of Commerce at (541) 523–5855 for additional information.

Southwest of Baker City on Highway 7, Sumpter, an Old West settlement revived nearly from the dead, is home to a new state park that encompasses the **Sumpter Valley Railroad,** whose *Stumpdodger* locomotive puffs its way along a narrow-gauge line that winds through ample evidence of past gold-dredging operations. Beginning in 1891, the line ran between Baker City and Prairie City, hauling mining equipment and supplies into the mining district and taking timber and gold out. Open-air cars today provide passengers with great views of the verdant, mountain-embraced Sumpter Valley,

Living-history volunteers stage an outdoor wagon encampment at BLM's National Historic Oregon Trail Interpretive Center.

There's Never Been Anything Like It

The sign at the entrance to the Oregon Trail Interpretive Center reads:

No one has ever seen anything quite like it before. More than 300,000 men, women, and children crossed the trail. They sensed that they were making history. While heroic, they were an imperfect people. Intolerant, prone to violence, exploitive, and sometimes ill-tempered, they carried mixed baggage. Despite some tragic consequences, the story of the Oregon Trail is an epic of human endurance and reminds us of those who came as empire builders.

where wildlife is abundant: deer, muskrat, waterfowl, beaver—and mock train robbers. For information call Sumpter Valley Railroad Restoration, Inc., at (541) 894–2268 or 523–5855.

Highway 30, the old Oregon Trail Highway, leads to Haines and the **Eastern Oregon Museum** (541–856–3233), at Third and School streets, with its array of mining, pioneer, household, and farming artifacts. It's open daily from 9:00 A.M. to 5:00 P.M. between April 15 and October 15. The **Haines Steak House,** one of eastern Oregon's best and best-known eateries, serves the finest in Western cuisine, steeped in a true Western ambience, with a mix of cowboy memorabilia on display.

In Prairie City the old Sumpter Valley Railroad Depot houses the **DeWitt Museum,** open summers Thursday through Saturday from 10:00 A.M. to 3:00 P.M. John Day's **Kam Wah Chung Company Museum,** meanwhile, sheds light on a common but seldom-mentioned Old West enterprise: that of the Chinese herbal healer, who doctored mine workers and others. The store, built as a trading post in 1866 and purchased in 1887 by Ing Hay and Lung On, served the Chinese and white communities into the 1940s. After Hay died in 1948, the place was locked up by his heirs for two decades, after which it was presented to the city. Apparently, nothing had been touched since the place was abandoned—and what a booty the citizens of John Day had on their hands! Firecrackers, bootleg whiskey, herbs and teas, and $25,000 in uncashed checks were among the amazing array of items found. The museum is located at 250 Northwest Canton Street and is open Monday through Thursday from 9:00 A.M. to noon and weekends from 1:00 to 5:00 P.M. Call (541) 575–0028 to learn more.

Southeast Oregon

This portion of the Beaver State, largely sagebrush-covered steppe and marsh-land, is short on people but big on cattle spreads, wildlife preserves, and classic Western vistas. If you prefer authentic to upscale, spend a few days at the **Ponderosa Cattle Company Guest Ranch,** situated between John Day and Burns off Highway 395. Boasting a true Old West experience—with "no seafood Alfredo, no swimming pool, and no suite with room service"—the immense, 120,000-acre cattle ranch has employed real cowboys since day one, in 1860. Guests ride alongside the cowpokes, herding, roping, and branding calves. Each of eight rustic log cabins houses three units, every one of which includes a bedroom and full bath; meals are served in the main lodge. For information, reservations, and directions, call (541) 542–2403.

The **Harney County Historical Museum,** at 18 West D Street in Burns—the 3,000-person metropolis of Oregon's Big Empty—displays photographs and relics that bring to life earlier times in this vast and sparsely settled land. It's open from mid-April through September, Tuesday through Saturday from 9:00 A.M. to 5:00 P.M.; call (541) 573–5618 for further details.

Frenchglen, 65 miles south of Burns (that's "just up the road" in this large-scale country), holds the **French Glen Hotel** (541–493–2825). Now operated by the state, the place was built to serve as a stage stop. Eight compact rooms and superb family-style meals are available at the hotel March 1 through November 15. Frenchglen is the kick-off point for a 66-mile outing along the **Steens Mountain National Backcountry Byway.** Generally passable July through October, the byway traverses some of the most dramatic terrain in the state, first crossing 4 miles of the Malheur National Wildlife Refuge, and then arriving at the base of the 30-mile-long escarpment known as Steens Mountain. Golden eagles and wild mustangs are among the wildlife you'll likely see, and wildflowers bloom in profusion in midsummer. A high-clearance-vehicle is recommended; for more information call the BLM in Hines at (541) 573–4402.

Southwest Oregon

In Klamath Falls visit the outstanding **Favell Museum** (541–882–9996), at 125 West Main Street, with pioneer memorabilia displays, Western art, an unusual collection of miniature firearms, and an exceedingly large exhibit of arrowheads and spearpoints. It's open Monday through Saturday from 9:30 A.M. to 5:30 P.M. The **Baldwin Hotel Museum,** at 31 Main Street, is a four-story brick structure, built in 1906 and still appointed with some of its original furnishings. The museum is open between June and September on Tuesday through Saturday from 10:00 A.M. to 4:00 P.M. From here in summer you can catch a trolley to the Klamath County Museum's other facility, located at 1451 Main Street.

Coyote the Trickster

For many Native American groups, the coyote was Trickster, a tough and cunning yet gullible humanlike mythical character who possessed an innate capacity for both good and evil. Most of the early whites' opinions of the coyote were more like those of Mark Twain, who traveled west in 1861 and saw his first of many coyotes near Fort Kearney, Nebraska. Later Twain wrote:

The coyote is a long, slim, sick and sorry-looking skeleton, with a gray wolfskin stretched over it . . . [he is] a living, breathing allegory of Want. He is always hungry. . . . He is so spiritless and cowardly that even while his exposed teeth are pretending a threat, the rest of his face is apologizing for it.

Today it's not uncommon in southeast Oregon, and elsewhere in the West, to see a dead "song dog" strung, limp, over the top strand of a barbed-wire fence. Indeed, a lot of thought and effort have gone into killing coyotes: steel traps, high-powered rifles, "coyote getter" cyanide guns, and even strychnine-laced suet.

The biology of this amazing animal adapts, however: It seems that Trickster multiplies at a rate inversely proportionate to how hard cattlemen and sheep growers try to eradicate him. In an area where coyotes aren't heavily hunted, it's estimated that between 15 and 20 percent of the yearlings will typically breed, but in areas where they're "intensively controlled" (a euphemism for mass-murdered), that figure can go up to 80 percent, and their average litter size actually increases at the same time.

The **Fort Klamath Museum,** 42 miles north of Klamath Falls on Highway 62, details the history of the military fort established in 1863, including that of the Modoc Indian War. The museum is open daily in summer from 10:00 A.M. to 6:00 P.M. The recently renovated **Prospect Historical Hotel** (541–560–3664), at 391 Mill Creek Drive in Prospect (west and south of Klamath on Highway 62), offers meals and overnights in a structure that first served as an 1892 stage stop and hostelry and where the likes of Zane Grey, Jack London, and Teddy Roosevelt took advantage of the offer of a roof over their heads.

In Eagle Point, farther southwest on Highway 62, head straight to the **Butte Creek Mill & Museum,** at 402 Royal Avenue North, where a creek-driven flour mill has been doing duty since 1872. The twin, 1,400-pound imported millstones were quarried in France, milled in Illinois, shipped around Cape Horn to Crescent City, California, then hauled here over the Coast Range by wagon. The mill and the adjacent store—with its old-fashioned peanut butter, fresh-ground flours, meals of corn, rye, and wheat, raw honey, and bulk spices—are open year-round Monday through Saturday from 9:00 A.M. to 5:00 P.M. Call (541) 826–3531 for more information.

Seventy-five miles northwest of Klamath Falls on Highway 140 is Medford. Its **Southern Oregon History Center,** at 106 North Central Avenue, features permanent and changing exhibits, including one of the state's best collections of vintage photographs. The Southern Oregon Historical Society's research library and history store are also located on the premises, and the lower-level museum store sells old-fashioned toys, artwork, and other odds and ends. It's open Monday through Friday from 9:00 A.M. to 5:00 P.M. and Saturday 10:00 A.M. to 5:00 P.M. Call (541) 773–6536 for more information.

Medford grew up around the railroad that pushed into the Rogue River valley in the 1800s. **Railroad Park,** at Table Rock Road and Berrydale Avenue, serves as a reminder of that important legacy, with artifact displays and rides on a one-twelfth-scale steam train, available on the second and fourth Sunday of the month (April through October) between 11:00 A.M. and 3:00 P.M. Call (541) 779–7979 for information.

Jacksonville, which burgeoned along with the gold boom of 1851, is one of a handful of entire towns designated as National Historic Landmarks in the United States. The nineteenth-century atmosphere here is tangible, with several dozen venerable structures that house restaurants, bakeries, and specialty shops. At the Visitors Information Center in the 1891 **Rogue River Valley Railway Depot,** at the corner of Fifth and C streets, you can pick up information on "A Walk Through Time," a stroll that takes in the 1883 Jackson County Courthouse, at 206 North Fifth Street, which now houses the impressive **Museum of Southern Oregon History.** Exhibits at one of the best small-town museums in the state include works by nineteenth-century photographer Peter Britt, whose pioneering shots of Crater Lake helped to ensure that feature's designation as a national park. Other displays focus on early Rogue Valley gold miners, homesteaders, and railroaders. Your ticket will also get you into the adjacent **Children's Museum,** where kids from four to ninety-four can enjoy hands-on exhibits that illustrate the pioneer era. Both museums, operated by the Southern Oregon Historical Society, are open from 10:00 A.M. to 5:00 P.M. daily in summer and daily except Monday the rest of the year. Call (541) 773–6536 for information.

Also worthy of inspection in historic Jacksonville: the 1863 **Beekman Bank,** at 101 West California (open daily from 9:00 A.M. to 4:30 P.M. in summer), and the **Beekman House,** at East California and Laurelwood streets, where docents play the parts of the pioneer banker's employees and family. Call (541) 773–6536 for information on tours of the house, offered on a regular basis.

Stay a night or a week at the **Jacksonville Inn** (541–899–1900), at 175 East California, an 1861 brick mercantile that also boasts one of the best restaurants in Oregon. Call the Chamber of Commerce at (541) 899–8118 for information on additional B&B opportunities and details on mine tours, historic-home tours, gift shops, other eateries, and the mid-June **Pioneer Days** celebration.

Gin Lin, a nineteenth-century Chinese miner, reportedly removed some $2 million in gold through "hydraulicking" his Applegate Valley claims, and results of this destructive mining mode can be viewed along the **Gin Lin Trail.** To reach the trailhead, which is located near the south side of the Flumet Flat Campground, travel south from Jacksonville to the Upper Applegate Road, following signs to the campground.

In Grants Pass, 28 miles northwest of Medford on Interstate 5, stop by the Visitors & Convention Bureau (541–476–5510), at Sixth and Midland streets, to obtain information on a historic walking tour of town. The

Josephine County Historical Society (541–479–7827), housed in the historic Schmidt House at the corner of Fifth and I streets, displays books, photographs, maps, and original furnishings; it's open Tuesday through Friday from 10:00 A.M. to 4:00 P.M. Try to hit town during the frontier-fun-packed **Jedediah Smith Mountain Man Rendezvous and Buffalo Barbecue,** with its free-trapper encampment, black-powder-shooting competitions, and more. It's held during late August/early September; call (541) 476–2040 for dates and details.

    Wolf Creek Tavern, west off Interstate 5 and 20 miles north of Grants Pass, is a Classic Revival inn built as a stop along the California and Oregon Stagecoach Line way back in 1857. Renovated by the state in 1979, the hostelry is open to visitors again today. Home-cooked meals (three per day) are the house specialty, served in the dining room year-round. Call (541) 866–2474 for reservations and information.

    Roseburg's **Douglas County Museum of History** (541–440–4507) is located off Interstate 5 at exit 123, next to the fairgrounds. From Native Americans and fur trappers to early pioneers and cowboys, professionally prepared displays depict 8,000 years worth of Umpqua River valley history and prehistory. Especially intriguing is a full-scale "log pen," representative of some of the first shelters built by early settlers. The museum is open daily 9:00 A.M. to 5:00 P.M. For information on the town's historic walking tour, the numerous B&B possibilities in town, and the annual **Buckaroo Round Up,** call the Visitor and Convention Bureau at (541) 672–9731.

    The historic timbering town of Sutherlin, 12 miles north of Roseburg, offers free covered-wagon tours through its historic, antiques-shop-lined streets, and during the third weekend in July the community celebrates its heritage at the **Douglas County Timber Days** (541–459–5829). Nearby Oakland, a National Historic Landmark, is a town lined with brick store-fronts and which grew up around a grist mill. The **Oakland Museum** (541–459–4531), at 136 Locust, displays old photographs, implements, clothing, furniture, and other reminders of Oakland's boom times. It's open daily from 1:00 to 4:00 P.M. The **Oakland Gaslight Players** serve up classic melodrama in the renovated Washington School. Call (541) 459–3776 for schedule and ticket information. Four miles west of Oakland is the **Stephens Community Historic District,** the only rural designated historic district in Douglas County. The intriguing cluster of buildings sits on the Donation Land Claim of Ebenezer Stephens, along Calapooya Creek.

Call (541) 440–4507 for further information.

Outside Cottage Grove, 35 miles north of Oakland on Interstate 5, tour the compelling high-mountain remains of the **Bohemia Mining District,** but only after stopping by the Chamber of Commerce at 710 Row River Road to pick up a copy of the brochure *Tour of the Golden Past*. Also ask about gold-panning opportunities in the area, where mining boomed between 1890 and 1910 and where large-scale gold mining has resumed recently. The nearby re-created **Bohemia City** is venue for the mid-July **Bohemia Mining Days;** call the Chamber of Commerce at (541) 942–2411 for further information.

Where to Eat

Flying M Ranch, Yamhill, (503) 662–3222
Timberline Lodge, Government Camp, (800) 547–1406 or (503) 272–3724
Gallery Restaurant, Sisters, (541) 549–2631
Cactus Jack's Cowboy Bar, Joseph, (541) 432–5225
Haines Steak House, Haines, (541) 856–3639
Wolf Creek Tavern, north of Grants Pass, (541) 866–2610

Where to Stay

Black Bart's Bed & Breakfast, Junction City, (541) 998–1904
Flying M Ranch, Yamhill, (503) 662–3222
Columbia Gorge Hotel, Hood River, (800) 345–1921
Hood River Hotel, Hood River, (541) 386–1900
Timberline Lodge, outside Government Camp, (800) 547–1406
Shaniko Hotel, Tygh Valley, (541) 489–3441
Baker's Bar M Ranch, Pendleton, (541) 566–3381
Minam Lodge, outside Joseph, (541) 432–9171
Ponderosa Cattle Company Guest Ranch, outside Burns, (541) 542–2403
French Glen Hotel, Frenchglen, (541) 493–2825
Prospect Historical Hotel, north of Klamath Falls, (541) 560–3664
Jacksonville Inn, Jacksonville, (541) 899–1900
Wolf Creek Tavern, north of Grants Pass, (541) 866–2474

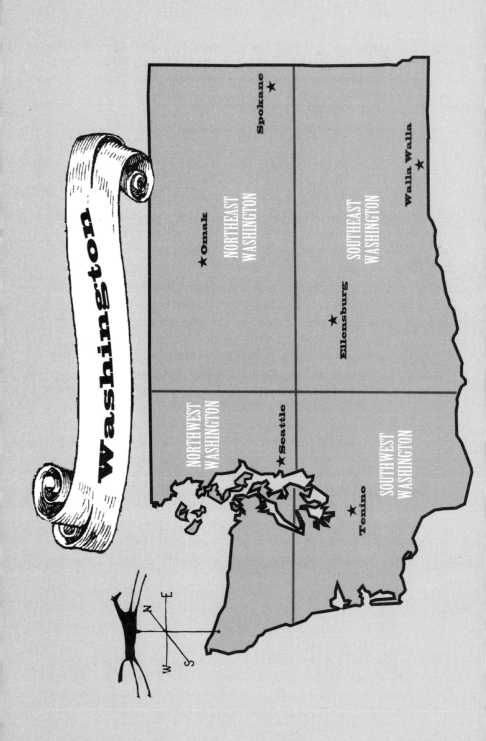

WASHINGTON

▼▼▼

HE WASHINGTON Territory came into its own in 1853, when it was split from the Oregon Territory. The big boom here, which was not in gold or silver but in timber, came relatively late: The industry exploded when the railroads finally webbed into Puget Sound around 1890. Today the state is a bit of an anomaly in the West, in that farming and fruit growing take center stage over big-spread cattle ranching. (An incredibly tough winter in 1881 precipitated the switch from open grazing to grain growing.) Especially in the western portions, the theme tends to go with the sea, so what we consider the traditional Old West isn't as celebrated as it is in most states west of the Mississippi.

Not to say there's nothing for the Wild West aficionado in Washington; there is, particularly east of the Cascade Range. The narrative begins in northwest Washington and from there leads into the southwest, southeast, and, finally, northeast part of the Evergreen State.

Northwest Washington

Pioneer Park, at Ferndale Road and Cherry in Ferndale, claims the state's largest collection of nineteenth-century log buildings. The sound structures, hewn from massive cedars similar to those that blanketed large portions of the Northwest at one time, are open for touring May 1 through September 30 daily from noon to 5:00 P.M.

Hop on a Washington State Ferry at Anacortes, 15 miles west of Interstate 5 on Highway 20, for the scenic trip out to pastoral San Juan Island. Strife between Americans and the British, resulting from the long-standing dispute coming out of the 1846 border "agreement," came to a head here when a

British pig belonging to the Hudson's Bay Company was caught grubbing around in an American farmer's potato garden. The ensuing "Pig War" saw the co-occupation of the island by both countries for thirteen years, from 1859 to 1872. **San Juan Island National Historic Park** encompasses both American Camp, found 5 miles from Friday Harbor on the southeast corner of the island, and English Camp, located on the opposite side about 7 miles northwest of Friday Harbor. National Park Service rangers are on duty daily in summer to interpret those days, which actually saw soldiers from the two "warring" encampments partying with one another. American Camp includes a small visitor center and a couple of old buildings, whereas English Camp features a museum, barracks, blockhouse, and small cemetery. Call (360) 378–2240 for more information.

Fort Casey State Park, 30 miles south of Anacortes on Highway 20 and 3 miles south of Coupeville near the Keystone ferry landing (where you catch the ferry to Port Townsend), includes one of three forts collectively known as the Iron Triangle or Triangle of Fire. The forts (the other two are Fort Worden and Fort Flagler, both near Port Townsend and also encompassed by state parks) were built in the late 1800s and early 1900s to guard Puget Sound in case of enemy attack. The Fort Casey Interpretive Center (360–678–4519) is open Thursday through Sunday from 11:00 A.M. to 5:00 P.M. from early May through late September. (A special dividend earned by visiting: The views of the Olympic Mountains to the west from here are incomparable.)

For historic accommodations in the area, consider the **Colonel Crockett Farm,** located at 1012 South Fort Casey Road. This 1855 farmhouse, built by one of the area's first white settlers, looks out over Admiralty Bay and features five bedrooms. Call (360) 678–3711 for information and reservations.

Five miles north of sunny Sequim (pronounced skwim), a west-slope anomaly where only 17 inches of rain fall in an average year, visit the **Olympic Game Farm** (360–683–4295). Here at the Hollywood Hilton of game farms, operated by Walt Disney Studios, you might spot grizzlies— including the one and only Gentle Ben—bison, timber wolves, and other "actors" that have appeared in more than eighty wildlife films. Guided walking tours of the preserve run daily June through September.

At the northwest corner of the Olympic Peninsula on Highway 101, Forks, the ultimate logging and logger's town, has been badly stung in the wake of the spotted-owl controversy. Learn about the days when there were few, if any, restrictions on the logging companies and how they removed the monster trees in the days before chain saws, at the **Forks Timber Museum** (360-374-9663). The museum, open May through October at changing hours, offers a comprehensive look at the culture and economy of early logging, with displays that include a scaled-down logging camp, historical photographs, and dioramas. The community's Fourth of July celebration revives many of the old logging skills through competitions and demonstrations; call the Forks Chamber of Commerce at (800) 443-6757 for more information.

Back on the east side of the Olympic Peninsula, pass through historic Port Gamble; then cross the Hood Canal Bridge and proceed to the Port Madison Indian Reservation's **Suquamish Museum,** just south off Highway 305. The heritage of the Suquamish people, including information on their great leader Chief Sealth, or Seattle (who is buried nearby), are at the forefront. A walk-through longhouse leads to a theater that runs the *Waterborne: Gift of the Indian Canoe* multimedia presentation, which highlights the tribe's canoe-building traditions and their present-day efforts at restoring salmon habitat. The museum is open from 10:00 A.M. to 5:00 P.M. daily in summer and from 11:00 A.M. to 4:00 P.M. Friday through Sunday the rest of the year. Call (360) 598-3311 for further information.

In Seattle's early timbering days of the 1870s and 1880s, logs were skidded down a steep incline, greased with dogfish oil, to penny-pinching Henry Yesler's steam-driven sawmill on Elliott Bay, around which grew Pioneer Square. The street—the original Skid Road, or Skid Row—came to be called Yesler Way.

Other than the frenetic logging activity, the biggest boom experienced in Seattle was one that actually set the stage for a gold rush at a far-off location, in another country. Learn about it at Seattle's contribution to the **Klondike Gold Rush National Historic Park,** at 117 South Main Street in Pioneer Square. (The other component is in Skagway, Alaska.) When prospectors arrived at Skagway, Canadian Mounties were there, checking to see that the prospectors carried the requisite year's worth of food and gear. Knowing this, Erastus Brainerd convinced city fathers to transform Seattle into *the* place for prospectors to be outfitted with their great quantities of necessities. The year was 1897, eight years after the immense Seattle Fire consumed the entire downtown area of some sixty city blocks, and the town was still rebuilding. The scheme was wildly successful, and it pulled Seattle out of its doldrums: Soon everything from "Klondike underwear" to "Klondike milk" was selling like Klondike hotcakes, and Seattle zoomed ahead of other would-be outfitting centers, such as Portland and Tacoma. In fact, Seattle businessmen generally made out like bandits, compared with the thousands of prospectors who set out from here, only to find the best Klondike claims already staked. The interpretive center opens daily from 9:00 A.M. to 5:00 P.M.; call (206) 553–7220 for more information.

For information on the abundant, historic overnight possibilities in and around Seattle, call the **Pacific Bed & Breakfast Agency** at (206) 784–0539.

Southwest Washington

Tacoma's world-class Point Defiance Park includes the original granary and factor's house from **Fort Nisqually** (206–591–5339), an 1833 Hudson's Bay Company trading post that represented the first hub of Anglo settlement on Puget Sound. (The buildings were moved to here in the 1930s from their original location, southwest of Tacoma near present DuPont.) **Camp Six,** also in the park, exhibits structures and steam-driven timbering equipment, rescued from moldy and rusty deaths deep in the Washington woods. The **Washington State Historical Society Museum** (206–272–3500) is also located in Tacoma, at 315 North Stadium Way, and is open from 10:00 A.M. to 5:00 P.M. Tuesday through Sunday year-round. The museum recaps the story of the Evergreen State in a nutshell.

West of Interstate 5 at exit 129, Steilacoom, the oldest incorporated town in the Washington Territory, retains some three dozen buildings listed on the National Register of Historic Places. You can sip a soda in historic fashion at **Bair Drug and Hardware,** located at 1617 Lafayette Street and open daily at 9:00 A.M., an 1895 store and pharmacy that was restored in 1976 by the Steilacoom Historical Museum Association. Part thriving enterprise and part museum, the store is chock-full of traditional implements and turn-of-the-century medicines. The memorabilia-packed **Steilacoom Historical Museum** (206–584–4133), situated in the basement of the town hall at the corner of Lafayette and Main, is open from 1:00 to 4:00 P.M. Tuesday through Sunday. The *Guide to Historic Steilacoom* walking-tour brochure can be obtained here.

The **Steilacoom Tribal Cultural Center** (206–584–6308), in the old

Seattle's Frontier Cupid

Seattle was a wild-eyed frontier town in 1864, when Asa Mercer, president and sole instructor at the fledging territorial university, conceived a plot to solve one of the blossoming region's primary problems: a severe lack in numbers of the fairer sex. The Civil War, meantime, was creating a surplus of willing widows back East, so Mercer went there to recruit some of them. He set sail back for Seattle from Boston, with a modest load of eight women, arriving in Puget Sound on May 16. All the women were quickly married.

Momentum gained, Mercer, now somewhat of a hero, headed east again in 1865, hoping for help from President Lincoln. The timing was poor, however, for Lincoln was assassinated the night before Mercer landed in New York. He found support when he contacted Gen. Ulysses S. Grant, the Civil War hero who earlier had been stationed at Fort Vancouver and remembered well the loneliness of life on the forested frontier. Grant proffered a steamboat for Mercer's use, and the Continental sailed from New York on January 6, 1866, with a cargo of more than 300 would-be wives.

En route, Mercer himself fell in love with one of the lovely ladies, who rebuked his affections, but his odds were unbeatable, and he immediately fell for another, who was more receptive to his advances. They married soon after arriving at Seattle, as did nearly all the other women aboard. Mercer, however, was badly in debt and was banished from the local social scene, so he moved on; nevertheless, he remains in spirit, as symbolic of the undying optimism that was abundant on the new frontier.

Congregational Church at 1515 Lafayette Street, encompasses three galleries, with exhibits that include "Visions of the Past: Legends of the Steilacoom Tribe." It is open daily, except Monday, from 10:00 A.M. to 4:00 P.M. Northeast of town the remains of historic **Fort Steilacoom** include several houses built in the 1850s, as well as the old post cemetery.

Travel 25 miles south from Tacoma to Eatonville and then 3 miles west from Eatonville to the **Pioneer Farm Museum and Ohop Indian Village,** at 7716 Ohop Valley Road East. Visitors can grind wheat, run the blacksmith's forge and woodworker's tools, or even milk a cow. Native crafts are demonstrated in the Nisqually longhouse, and the vital importance of

. A. Woodard Memorial Li

salmon to the region's various cultures, native and white alike, is explored at the hatchery on the Mashel River. The gift shop, which occupies an 1887 trading post/cabin, offers an abundance of old-fashioned goodies that range from candy to rabbit skins. Tours leave between 11:00 A.M. and 4:00 P.M. daily in summer and on weekends only during spring and fall; call (360) 832–6300 for more information.

The steam-powered **Mount Rainier Scenic Railroad** chugs the 14 miles from Elbe to Mineral Lake, en route across the Nisqually River and offers stupendous views of the looming, snow-covered mountain called Tahoma by some of the region's Native Americans. The excursion, which includes entertainers on board who relate railroading songs and lore, leaves three times daily from June 15 through Labor Day and weekends from Memorial Day through mid-June and from Labor Day to the end of September. The special four-hour Cascade Dinner Train runs Sunday afternoons spring and fall and Saturday evenings during summer and features an unforgettable five-course prime rib dinner. Call (360) 569–2588 to request more information.

Sing the call of the wild with wolves at a **Wolf Haven** howl-in. This privately owned refuge, located north of Tenino (35 miles northwest of Eatonville) at 3111 Offutt Lake Road, provides foster care for wolves and other animals that, for one reason or another, can't be returned to their native habitats. The howl-ins, at which visitors harmonize with caged wolves, sound off from 7:00 to 10:00 P.M. Friday and Saturday nights during summer. Wolf Haven is open for touring from 10:00 A.M. to 5:00 P.M. daily May through September and from 10:00 A.M. to 4:00 P.M. Wednesday through Sunday the rest of the year. Call (800) 448–WOLF (9653) for more information.

The **Lewis & Clark Interpretive Center,** on Cape Disappointment at Fort Canby State Park (2 1/2 miles southwest of Ilwaco), includes displays on Lewis and Clark's 1805 approach to the mouth of the Columbia; audiovisual displays, artifacts, and journal entries resurrect the long-ago expedition. Also in the park is the Northwest's oldest sea beacon, the Cape Disappointment Lighthouse. Although it was scheduled to be built in 1853, construction didn't happen until 1856 because the ship that was carrying the original building supplies wrecked on a shoal as the captain steered it toward land, and it went down. (He could have used a lighthouse!) Call (360) 642–3078 for more information on the park.

To see a bit of moving history, leave Interstate 5 at Woodland (exit 21) and head east for 10 miles along Northeast Hayes Road/Cedar Creek Road and Grist Mill Road. The rough-hewn **Cedar Creek Grist Mill,** built in 1876, served both the nutritional and social needs (parties and dances were common here) of generations of area residents. The Friends of the Cedar Creek Grist Mill began restoring the run-down mill in the early 1980s, and today it grinds again, with water diverted from Cedar Creek running the turbine that drives the millstones. The fascinating attraction is open Saturday from 1:00 to 4:00 P.M. and Sunday from 2:00 to 4:00 P.M.

Just north over the Columbia River from Portland, Oregon, **Fort Vancouver National Historic Site,** at 1501 East Evergreen in bustling Vancouver, focuses on the Hudson's Bay Company's early fur-trading activities, with ample exhibits and living-history demonstrations that interpret the post's colorful past. Archaeological excavations, begun in the late 1940s, led to the reconstruction of several of the crucial fort's original buildings, including the three-story bastion, a trading post, and the splendid home of chief factor John McLoughlin, the man who became known as "the Father of Oregon" (see Oregon City, Oregon, p. 57). The fort (360–696–7655) is open daily year-round. For information on **Fort Vancouver Days,** held annually in late June and early July, call (360) 693–1313.

The **Officers' Row National Historic District** is a proud parade of twenty-one immaculately restored Victorians that at one time were home to U.S. Army brass, including Ulysses S. Grant and George C. Marshall, stationed at Fort Vancouver. The Grant House (360–699–1213), located at 1101 Officers' Row, today houses a first-class, black-tie restaurant featuring American regional cuisine and serves as the staging area for horse-drawn carriage rides through historic Vancouver.

Pioneer rivermen stopped along the banks of the Columbia near present-day Stevenson long enough to chop and load cord wood to fire their steamships' boilers. Learn more about this and a lot more at the **Columbia Gorge Interpretive Center** (509–427–8211), where the region's past is interpreted via elegantly displayed photographs and artifacts. The museum, open daily from 10:00 A.M. to 5:00 P.M., is located in the basement of the courthouse annex on Vancouver Avenue.

Southeast Washington

The **Flying L Ranch** is a BYOH (bring your own horse) getaway, tucked into a scenic valley outside Glenwood. The main lodge includes six guest

Grant House at Fort Vancouver National Historic Site

rooms, and a two-story guest house and a two-room cabin can bunk another fifteen or so; rooms are named for famous Western characters like Charlie Russell and Will Rogers. Guests either prepare their own meals or dine at eateries in nearby Glenwood. The Flying L is open year-round, with cross-country skiing on groomed trails among the winter possibilities. The address is 25 Flying L Lane; call (509) 364–3488 for reservations and directions.

Toppenish—"Where the West Still Lives!"—boasts a string of false-fronted buildings in its downtown area, along with a bevy of striking outdoor murals that depict the Native American and Old West heritages of the area. The town is located 20 miles southeast of Yakima off Interstate 82 at exit 50. The **Toppenish Historical Museum** (509–865–4510), open Tuesday through Saturday from 2:00 to 5:00 P.M., is located at One South Elm Street, and the newer **Yakima Valley Rail and Steam Museum** is found in the immaculately restored old Toppenish Depot. Grab a bite and then some at the **Cattlemen's Restaurant and Muddy Creek Lounge**, adjacent to Pioneer Park at Two South Division, where you can't go wrong by ordering the house specialty, mesquite-broiled steak.

Fort Vancouver

The English and Americans, unable to determine how the Oregon Territory should be divided, agreed in 1818 to share the region until a final settlement could be forged. In 1825 the British Hudson's Bay Company moved its headquarters to the present site of Vancouver from Fort George, which was situated about a hundred miles west at the mouth of the Columbia (present-day Astoria, Oregon). The Brits hoped this move would tighten their grip on the region; indeed, the fort became the epicenter of a fur-trading dynasty that oversaw some two dozen forts and five smaller trading stations scattered throughout the Northwest.

Thousands of Americans came into the country off the Oregon Trail during the late 1830s and 1840s, however, leading to the 1846 decision to establish the international boundary along the 49th parallel. This put Fort Vancouver smack in the middle of American lands, and by 1860 it was entirely in the hands of the U.S. Army. The Hudson's Bay Company moved north, and Fort Vancouver became an important American frontier military post.

Renting a tipi for the night and dining on Native American cuisine are only a pair of the many possibilities at the **Yakima Nation Cultural Heritage Center,** found along Highway 97 at the southwest edge of Toppenish. Within are the Heritage Inn Restaurant, serving traditional buffalo stews and alder-smoked salmon, and the Yakima Nation Museum. The museum highlights the traditions and history of the Yakima people, through movies and live dramatic presentations, dioramas, traditional lodgings, and skin-covered sweat lodges. The museum is open daily from 10:00 A.M. to 5:00 P.M.; call (509) 865–2800 for more information.

The **Toppenish Pow-Wow and Rodeo** takes center stage in these parts the first weekend in July. It's a great opportunity to observe and absorb the Native American and cowboying cultures at a single bash. Call the Toppenish Chamber of Commerce at (509) 865–3262 for details.

The **Fort Simcoe State Park Heritage Site** is located 25 miles west of the tribal complex, 7 miles southwest of White Swan (venue for powerful summer powwows). Several original buildings, including a barracks and a pair of blockhouses, have been reconstructed at the fort, which was built in 1856 in response to growing tensions between the Yakimas and whites. The interpretive center is open Wednesday through Sunday from April 1 to September 30 and the rest of the year by appointment; call (509) 874–2372 to make one.

Fifteen miles west of Union Gap (which is just south of Yakima) is the **Ahtanum Mission,** or St. Joseph's Mission, bucolicly situated beside a gurgling creek and ancient apple orchard. The mission, among the first in the region, was established in the late 1840s, then burned in 1855 by U.S. Army volunteers, who found a keg of gunpowder on the grounds. The soldiers wrongly assumed that the French Oblate missionaries who ran the place were supporting the local Indians in their strife with the whites, which had come to a head after Yakima warriors killed several miners they'd caught trespassing on their lands. Today the grounds and the log-cabin church, built in 1870, are still owned and used by the Catholic Church.

Originally known as Robber's Roost, Ellensburg, 30 miles north of Yakima, is Washington's foremost cowtown. It might also be the capital of the state today, had Yakima not joined in the 1889 race, thereby splitting the popular vote three ways: Together, Yakima and Ellensburg got more than 50 percent of the votes, but Olympia, already the territorial capital, garnered more votes than either of the other towns did individually. Ellensburg's historic walking tour, maps for which are available at the Chamber of Commerce (509–925–3137) at 436 North Sprague Street, takes in nearly twenty distinctive old buildings. One of them is the 1901 Ramsey Building, at 416 North Pearl, which houses the **Clymer Museum and Gallery,** displaying Western art, including that of the celebrated local historical painter John Clymer. The gallery is open Monday through Friday from 10:00 A.M. to 5:00 P.M. and weekends from noon to 5:00 P.M.; call (509) 962–6416 for information.

A prime photographic opportunity in town is the ready-for-action gunslinger sculpture that guards the corner of Fifth and Pearl. The city's cowboying roots go deep, and they're proudly displayed at the **National Western Art Show & Auction** (509–962–2934), held the third weekend in May, and at the **Ellensburg Rodeo** (800–637–2444), The Greatest Show on Dirt and one of the nation's foremost rodeos. The rodeo screams through Labor Day weekend in conjunction with the Kittitas County Fair.

On a bluff overlooking Interstate 90, at a point northeast of and high above the Columbia River and the settlement of Vantage, the *Grandfather Cuts Loose the Ponies* sculpture is missed by a lot of highway travelers. Those who don't miss it usually do a double-take, for from afar the ponies truly look like wild mustangs, galloping over the arid central Washington landscape. For information on this unusual vision, still under development, call the Thundering Hooves Sculpture Committee at (509) 459–0388.

Cle Elum's **Hidden Valley Guest Ranch** is the state's oldest dude getaway. Situated in the Swauk Valley in the foothills of the Wenatchee Mountains, the ranch has been running since Hollywood cowboy Tom Whited opened it in 1947, by transforming the remains of an 1887 homestead. The homestead cabin and other old buildings, in fact, still form the core of the place, which is situated 8 miles northeast of Cle Elum. Cabins, well-tempered horses, chuckwagon barbecues, and great family-style Western dining in the cookhouse all are part of the deal. "Western fantasy" weekends, gold panning, and overnight wagon trips are additional possibilities that can be arranged. Call (509) 857–2344 for information and reservations.

Sixty miles north of Ellensburg, Cashmere's **Chelan County Historical Museum** (509–782–3230), at 5698 Museum Drive, features one of the best restored Old West towns in the Northwest. A blacksmith shop, mission, and gold mine are among the finds at the facility, open from 9:30 A.M. to 5:00 P.M. Tuesday through Sunday from March through October. Similarly, the two-part **Grant County Museum and Pioneer Village** (509–754–3334), at 742 Basin in Ephrata (60 miles east of Cashmere on Highways 2 and 28), includes an eighteen-structure re-created town, with homestead, one-room schoolhouse, church, saloons, and several shops. It is open from May to mid-September on Monday through Saturday from 10:00 A.M. to 5:00 P.M. and on Sunday from 1:00 to 4:00 P.M. (closed Wednesdays). The Living Museum gathering, slated for the last weekend in June, celebrates the past with old-time craft and skills demonstrations.

Sacajawea State Park (509–545–2361) sits at the confluence of the Snake and Columbia rivers, a couple of miles east of Pasco. The interpretive center here, where Lewis and Clark camped on their way west, includes displays on the Corps of Discovery and the region's Native Americans. It is open from 6:30 A.M. to dusk Wednesday through Sunday from mid-May to mid-September.

Now, read carefully, because this gets confusing: The original Fort Walla Walla evolved from a trading post established in 1816 by the North West Company's Donald McKenzie. The post initially was called Fort Nez Perces, a misnomer, for it was Cayuse and not Nez Perce Indians who inhabited the area. The fort became central to early mountain-man activities in a network that branched out as far east as Wyoming and Montana and south to the Gulf of California. The fort, the site of which today is signed with a roadside marker along Highway 12 near Wallula, was operated during its later years by the Hudson's Bay Company. It ran until 1855, the year before a second Fort Walla Walla came into existence, this one established by the U.S. Army. The **Fort Walla Walla Museum Complex** is located 30 miles east of Wallula in Walla Walla, at Fort Walla Walla Park on Myra Road (go west from downtown on Rose Street). The museum features a frontier village with fourteen log buildings, both originals and re-creations, brimming with early furnishings and implements. It's open from 10:00 A.M. to 5:00 P.M. Tuesday through Sunday May to September and on weekends in October. Call (509) 525–7703 for more information.

Six miles west of Walla Walla on Highway 12, the **Whitman Mission National Historic Site** commemorates the early Oregon Trail mission established by Dr. Marcus and Narcissa Whitman. Museum displays relate life in the Walla Walla Valley from the late 1830s, when hordes of emigrants began filtering in, through 1847, the year that the aloof Dr. Whitman and his wife, neither of whom ever really cared for the Indians, and several boys under their care were slaughtered by Cayuse Indians. The Cayuse were seeking revenge for the scourge of measles (which proved deadly to the Indians) delivered by white travelers. The visitor center is open daily from 8:00 A.M. to 4:30 P.M. in summer and from 8:00 A.M. to 4:30 P.M. in winter. For more information call (509) 522–6360.

Northeast Washington

Spokane's second life began in the late 1870s, following a fifty-year hiatus that started when the Hudson's Bay Company moved its post from the Spokane River to the upper Columbia River country. It was very early on, in 1810, that Jaco Finley, of the Canadian-run North West Company, built Spokane House, the state's first trading post. Two other companies, the American-owned Pacific Fur Company and the British Hudson's Bay Company, operated posts at the site during the ensuing decade. Northwest of Spokane in Riverside State Park, the **Spokane House Interpretive Center** sits where the original post was built, at the point where the Little Spokane empties into the Spokane River. The center (509–456–3964) is open May 1 through Labor Day by appointment.

Patsy Clark's Mansion Restaurant (509–838–8300) is opulent evidence left behind by a man, born in Ireland in 1850, who garnered great wealth by investing in northeast Washington's mining industry. Patrick ("Patsy") Clark commissioned the city's foremost architect, Kirtland Cutter, to design his dream house, first sending him abroad to absorb inspiration and gather furnishings. The restaurant/mansion, located at West 2208 Second Avenue, dishes out elegant lunches and dinners and also offers tours. Across the side street is the **Fotheringham House** B&B (509–838–1891), built in 1891 by Clark to serve as temporary housing for his family while their grander residence was being planned and built.

Molson, lying just below the Canadian border northwest of Republic (120 miles northwest of Spokane on Highways 395 and 20), is almost a ghost town; maybe twenty-five people live there year-round. The town sprang up in 1900 when George Molson, of the Canadian brewing family, invested about $75,000 to create a center of enterprise 4 miles from the Poland China Gold Mine. An insensitive J. H. McDonald later threw a wrench in the community works when he filed for a 160-acre homestead that encompassed the entire town; angry citizens retaliated by building "New Molson" a quarter of a mile to the north. Today the quaint settlement and its pair of museums draw several thousand visitors per year. The **Molson School,** open daily from 10:00 A.M. to 5:00 P.M. Memorial Day through Labor Day, features three floors that are well stocked with local memorabilia; the **Old Molson Outdoor Museum,** open daily April through December, includes timeworn cabins, a shingle mill, and more.

The **Hidden Hills Guest Ranch** is nestled between Tonasket and Omak, at 144 Fish Lake Road. The Old West–style inn promises "an 1890s experience with 1990s convenience." Delicious dinners and bounteous breakfasts are served at the ranch, where active outdoor opportunities beckon. It's located 6 miles west off Highway 20 on Pine Creek Road, from a point approximately 5 miles north of Riverside. Call (800) 468–1890 for information and reservations.

The anachronistic **Omak Stampede and World Famous Suicide Race** pits teams of horses and riders against one another in a race down a precipitous slope and across the Okanogan River. A Western art show, parade, and professional rodeo are also slated for the affair, which takes place the second weekend in August. For more information call (800) 933–6625 or (509) 826–1002. When in the area, visit the **Okanogan County Historical Museum,** at 1410 Second Street North in nearby Okanogan, which boasts a scaled-down Old West town and a rifle that formerly belonged to the great Chief Joseph of the Nez Perce. It's open daily year-round from 10:00 A.M. to 4:00 P.M.; call (509) 422–4272 for information.

About 50 miles west of Omak, hitch your horse to a rail along the board sidewalks of **Winthrop,** an 1890s mining boomtown said to have provided inspiration for some of the events in Owen Wister's 1890s classic *The Virginian.* Winthrop has converted itself into an irresistible Old West theme town, with false-front stores, restaurants, and hotels. The **Schafer Museum** is housed in an 1897 log house built by town founder Guy Waring and located on Castle Avenue a block above downtown. Waring's Methow Trading Post, also established in 1897, is today occupied by an enterprise known as the **Last Trading Post.** (Waring was a Harvard classmate of both Teddy Roosevelt and Owen Wister, and his settling here brought Wister to town for a visit.) The museum is open daily from 10:00 A.M. to 5:00 P.M. Memorial Day through Labor Day. For lodging in Winthrop settle into a log cabin at the **Virginian** (509–996–2535), and for some Wild West fun and libation, head to **3 Fingered Jack's Saloon,** in the center of downtown.

The **Colville Tribal Cultural Museum** in Coulee Dam, 50 miles southeast of Omak on Highway 155, reflects on earlier tribal life, when salmon swam the Columbia River, unhindered by dams. Included among the displays are fishing scenes, re-created lodgings, and traditional crafts. The well-outfitted gift shop specializes in artwork, ceramics, and blankets. The museum, located at 516 Birch Street, is open in summer from 10:00 A.M. to 6:00 P.M. Monday through Saturday and from noon to 5:00 P.M. Sunday. Call (509) 633–0751 for further details. Also ask for directions to the grave (situated on a hillside near Nespelem) of Chief Joseph, who lived out the years following his surrender at Montana's Bears Paw Mountains here on the Colville Indian Reservation.

Lewis and Clark battle the rapids, and Columbia River waves become galloping horses in an amazing laser show that relates the history of the Columbia Basin, with the world-famous dam's own backside serving as the silver screen. The forty-minute show, which spectators watch from riverside bleachers, runs nightly at 10:00 P.M. Memorial Day through July, at 9:30 P.M. in August, and at 8:30 P.M. in September. Call (509) 633–9503 for more information.

The site of old Fort Spokane, built at the confluence of the Spokane and Columbia rivers as Washington's last frontier post, can be found within the boundaries of the Coulee Dam National Recreation Area. The fort was established in 1880, after the Indian Wars were over; its primary function was to ensure that peace continued between new settlers and the still semi-nomadic Indian tribes. The post's potential military might was never employed, although drills were regularly carried out just to remind both the Indians and the whites that the Army was there. The **Fort Spokane Museum,** occupying the original guardhouse, features displays that interpret the soldiering life at the post. The facilities are just off Highway 25, a mile south of the Columbia River (23 miles north of Davenport), and are open daily from 9:30 A.M. to 5:30 P.M. Call (509) 725–2715 for more information.

Where to Eat

The Grant House, Fort Vancouver, (360) 699–1213
Cattlemen's Restaurant, Toppenish, (509) 865–5885
Patsy Clark's Mansion, Spokane, (509) 838–8300

Where to Stay

Colonel Crockett Farm, Coupeville, (360) 678–3711
Flying L Ranch, Glenwood, (509) 364–3488
Hidden Valley Guest Ranch, outside Cle Elum, (509) 857–2344
Fotheringham House Bed & Breakfast, Spokane, (509) 838–1891
Hidden Hills Guest Ranch, between Tonasket and Omak, (800) 468–1890
The Virginian, Winthrop, (509) 996–2535

LAND OF
THE MOUNTAIN MEN

▼▼▼

IDAHO
MONTANA
WYOMING

Idaho

NORTH
IDAHO

★ Wallace

★ Lewiston

NORTH
CENTRAL
IDAHO

CENTRAL
IDAHO

Ketchum
★

★
Boise

★
Idaho
Falls

SOUTHWEST
IDAHO

SOUTHEAST
IDAHO

N
W E
S

IDAHO

▼▼▼

IDAHO was the last state visited by non–Native Americans, when the Lewis and Clark Expedition fought its way through the twisted, timbered northern part of the state in 1805. Although the state hasn't yet capitalized on the past to the extent that many Western states have, Idaho offers a bounty of opportunities to view country largely unchanged since the 1800s—experiences far more vivid in some instances than a visit to any museum or theme park.

The narrative begins in the north and winds southward down the Highway 95–Highway 55 corridor. From just north of Boise, it traces a clockwise loop through the mining country of the central mountains, the Teton-Yellowstone region, the Mormon stronghold of the southeast corner, and along the Oregon Trail corridor back to Boise.

North Idaho

Coeur d'Alene, north Idaho's largest city, sprouted as a frontier military post and grew into a supply hub for the timber and mining industries; today it has blossomed into a world-class, cosmopolitan tourist destination. The **Museum of North Idaho,** detailing the region's early days, is split between two locations. The Fort Sherman Branch, situated on the campus of North Idaho College, features a museum housed in the fort's 1877 powder house; it's open Tuesday through Saturday from 1:00 to 4:45 P.M. from May 1 through September 30. The Park Branch, located at 115 Northwest Boulevard, details the vital role that steamboats played in the settling of this big-timber and big-lake country. The Park Branch is open Tuesday through Saturday from 11:00 A.M. to 5:00 P.M. from April 1 through October 31. Call (208) 683–3400 for information on both branches.

Silverwood theme park presents an interesting mix of old and new; you can ride on a pony or a steam locomotive, for instance, or on the Corkscrew roller coaster or in a biplane. The popular train ride passes through an "Indian encampment" and includes a hold-up and shoot-out on board. Cafes with turn-of-the-century flair, a theater, a saloon, and curio shops line the boardwalks of the rural airport-turned-re-created frontier town. It's located 15 miles north of Coeur d'Alene on Highway 95 and is open June through Labor Day from 11:00 A.M. to 8:00 P.M. Call (208) 683–3400 for information.

The **Cataldo Mission of the Sacred Heart,** 25 miles east of Coeur d'Alene on Interstate 90, is the oldest standing building in Idaho. Built in 1850 by Coeur d'Alene Indians under the direction of the Jesuit, or "Black Robe," Father Ravalli, the mission is held together with wooden pegs and features foot-thick walls of willow sticks, grass, and mud. Cataldo's **Historic Skills Fair** takes place in July, with spinning, quilting, black-powder shooting, and more. The **Coeur d'Alene Indian Pilgrimage** in mid-August, open to the public, features the Coming of the Black Robes pageant. The mission and surrounding eighteen-acre park are open daily from 8:00 A.M. to 6:00 P.M. Call (208) 682–3814 for information.

Just east of Cataldo is a string of historic silver-, lead-, and zinc-mining towns. The area was relentlessly clear-cut and poisoned with tailings during the first half of this century; it's beginning to recover, but the bare slopes and off-color stream banks are still ghastly, compared with what once was surely a gracious, timbered landscape. For an overview hop aboard a recent addition to the area, the **World's Longest Gondola.** It runs winter and summer, originating beside Interstate 90 in Kellogg and ending 3 miles away, at the top of the Silver Mountain ski area.

Until the early 1990s all Interstate 90 traffic filtered through downtown Wallace, where for years it encountered the lone remaining stoplight on the entire length of the highway. The "last red light" was poetically appropriate, for in Wallace the Wild West continued well into the twentieth century, and until very recently the town boasted a thriving red-light district.

A third of Wallace burned in the infamous fire of 1910, which torched some three million acres of north Idaho and northwest Montana timberland. Much of the town survived, however, and a rich legacy of 1800s architecture remains. Highlights include the **Northern Pacific Depot Railroad Museum** (208–752–0111), which was recently moved to make way for the invasive interstate highway. The depot, built of 15,000 Roman-style bricks imported from China and cement made from mine tailings, is open daily in summer from 9:00 A.M. to 7:00 P.M., in spring and fall from 9:00 A.M. to 5:00 P.M., and Tuesday through Saturday during winter from 10:00 A.M. to 3:00 P.M. Horse-drawn carriage rides, offered by **Pony Creek Carriage** (208–682–4597), originate daily at the museum, weather willing.

Across the street the **Sixth Street Melodrama** stages live hiss-and-boo productions May through August. Call (208) 752–8871 for information on tickets and schedules. The **Coeur d'Alene District Mining Museum** (208–753–7151), at Sixth and Pine streets, features photographs, artifacts, and a slide show that focus on the area's rich past. Just west of the museum, you can commence a tour that includes a trolley-car ride and a visit to the **Sierra Silver Mine** (208–752–5151). Tours of the depleted mine, which stretches beneath several blocks of Wallace, leave every thirty minutes between 9:00 A.M. and 4:00 P.M. daily mid-May through October. (In July and August they continue until 6:00 P.M.) Meet at 420 Fifth Street. (No children under 4 are permitted.) The Chamber of Commerce (208–753–7151) can provide information on the tour and on a driving loop that takes in the once-roaring towns of Murray, Prichard, and Burke.

The third floor of the historic **Jameson House,** at 304 Sixth Street, has been refurbished into a bed and breakfast. Downstairs the mirror-backed bar is evocative of the old days, and so are the hearty meals dished up in the chandelier-appointed dining room. Call (208) 752–1252 for information (rooms available Thursday through Sunday only).

From Wallace intrepid backcountry explorers should travel southeast on Forest Service roads to Avery, then west along the St. Joe River to the timber town of St. Maries. The less adventurous can backtrack to Cataldo and follow Highway 3, the **White Pine Scenic Byway,** south to St. Maries. South of St. Maries, take Highway 6 to Potlatch, where you'll emerge from timber country and into the Palouse region.

North Central Idaho

Like the thousands of acres of lentils and wheat surrounding it, Moscow sprouts from the rolling Palouse. The Appaloosa, beloved horse of the Nez Perce—called "a Palouse Horse" or "Appaloosey" by early white settlers—is celebrated at the **Appaloosa Museum and Heritage Center** at 5070 Highway 8 West. Here you'll learn about the evolution of the strong and agreeable breed, which originated in China. Artifacts, a map tracing the 1877 freedom flight of the Nez Perce, saddles, and Western art round out the museum's displays. It's open from 8:00 A.M. to 5:00 P.M. Monday through Friday; call (208) 882–5578 for information.

Lewiston, Idaho's original capital, is the only port in Idaho, with ocean-going grain barges traveling up the Columbia and Snake rivers to retrieve the harvest of the plains. An interesting stop along the Lewiston Levee Parkway is the **Lewis and Clark Interpretive Center,** at the confluence of the Snake and Clearwater rivers. President Jefferson's exploratory party came out of the Clearwater country and into the Snake River drainage here on October 10, 1805. (Lewiston's sister city, just across the Washington border, not coincidentally, is named Clarkston.)

In 1861 Lewiston was a hell-roaring tent camp, where prospectors gathered before heading to the higher ground of the Pierce gold fields. The **Luna House Museum,** at Third and C streets, illuminates the area's compelling history, including that of steamboats on the Snake River. It's open from 10:00 A.M. to 4:00 P.M. Tuesday through Saturday; call (208) 743–2535 for information. The place has calmed down some since the 1800s, but the **Lewiston Roundup** (208–743–3531), held in early September, like most major stops on the PRCA (Professional Rodeo Cowboys Association) circuit, is far from sedate.

Nez Perce National Historic Park is as much a concept as it is real estate. To visit all twenty-four of its sites takes several days and nearly 500 miles of driving through a tangle of the wildest country in the Northwest. The thread that binds the park is the route followed by Chief Joseph and his "non-treaty" Nez Perce Indians during their epic, four-month-long flight from Oregon to north-central Montana in 1877.

At the park visitor center and **Museum of Nez Perce Culture** (208–843–2261; open daily 8:00 A.M. to 5:30 P.M.), located 10 miles east of

Lewiston at Spalding, you can pick up a brochure that details the drive. Among the two-dozen sites:

- **St. Joseph's Mission** at Slickpoo, built in 1874 by Father Joseph Cataldo;

- **White Bird Battlefield,** where the first of the Nez Perce battles was fought (thirty-four U.S. soldiers and no Indians were killed);

- East Kamiah (KAM-e-eye), location of the geologic feature known as **Heart of the Monster,** the place of creation in Nez Perce mythology;

- **Canoe Camp,** where Lewis and Clark's men hollowed out logs to float their final stretch to the Pacific Ocean;

- **Pierce,** site of Idaho's first major gold strike, where today a historical museum resides in the first courthouse built in Idaho;

- **The Lolo Trail,** a rough-and-tumble road hacked out of the convoluted wilderness by the Civilian Conservation Corps in the 1930s. It roughly

The Smoking Place

On their return trip east in 1806, Lewis and Clark's Nez Perce guides asked to stop by a certain rock cairn to smoke a pipe. William Clark wrote in his journal on June 27:

From this place we had an extensive view of these stupendous mountains principally covered with snow like that on which we stood; we were entirely surrounded by those mountains from which to one unacquainted with them it would have seemed impossible ever to have escaped; in short, without the assistance of our guides I doubt much whether we who had once passed them could find our way to Travellers rest [today the location of Lolo, Montana] in their present situation.

The Smoking Place is marked with an interpretive sign along the Lolo Trail.

follows both the Nez Perce and Lewis and Clark trails and is signed with interpretive markers.

In Kamiah the **Chief Lookingglass Days** (208–935–2525), held the third weekend in August, include a traditional powwow organized by descendants of the respected Nez Perce chief. In nearby Orofino the mid-September Clearwater County Fair includes **Lumberjack Days** (208–476–4335), which draws loggers from afar to participate in woodsy competitions.

From 10 miles east of Grangeville on Highway 13, consider making the 100-mile round-trip to Elk City, one of Idaho's many end-of-the-road, modern Old West towns. The truly adventurous may opt to travel either in or out on the **Elk City Wagon Road,** which originated as part of the ancient trail used by the Nez Perce to get to and from Montana's Bitterroot Valley. The route, unsuitable for large or low-clearance vehicles, is detailed in a brochure, available by calling the Elk City Ranger District at (208) 842–2245 or the Clearwater office at (208) 983–0696.

When passing through Grangeville, current and wannabe cowboys and packers should swing into **Ray Holes Saddle Company,** at 213 West Main, to smell the luscious leather and look over the top-notch tack made there. Since 1936 the Holes's stamped-flower-design saddles have been in big demand. South of Grangeville, Highway 95 rapidly loses nearly 3,000 vertical feet as it drops to the Salmon River level at White Bird. In Riggins, where the Salmon turns hard north after flowing westward for more than 100 miles through the wilderness heart of Idaho, you can sign up for a river float into that wilderness (call 208–628–3778 for a listing of outfitters).

The summer and winter resort town of McCall is the jumping-off point for several remote-country drives. One of these—leading first to **Burgdorf Hot Springs,** a rustic resort listed on the National Register of Historic Places, then to the outpost of Warren—can be accompanied by a historical-narrative cassette tape, available from the McCall Ranger District (208–634–0750). Another drive leads to Yellow Pine and Big Creek, at the fringe of the River of No Return Wilderness Area. The Forest Service maintains a small landing strip at Big Creek if you'd rather not drive the long, winding, and often dusty roads. Call the McCall Chamber of Commerce at (208) 634–7631 for more information.

Central Idaho

At Banks, 53 miles south of Donnelly, turn east and travel 10 miles to Garden Valley; from there head south on improved gravel roads to the restored ghost town of Idaho City. The **Boise Basin Historical Museum** (208–392–4550), at Montgomery and Wall streets, relates the rich story of the mining town's early days, when it reportedly was the largest community in the Northwest. The museum opens daily Memorial Day through Labor Day from 10:00 A.M. to 4:00 P.M. The **Basin of Gold Days & Pioneer Picnic,** celebrating those golden days of yore, is held in early August. For information on this and on gold-panning opportunities and other area activities and attractions, call the Chamber of Commerce at (208) 392–4290.

Stanley, gateway to the Sawtooth National Recreation Area, sits amid arguably the most dramatic scenery in the state. It's also one of Idaho's wildest outposts, where the streets are still of dirt and cowboys ride horses for a living. The **Stanley Museum** (208–774–3517), housed in the old Stanley Ranger Station and open daily during summer, focuses on the area's ranching and cowboying heritage. Sawtooth trails, traversing hillsides covered in sage and aspen, beg for the clop of a horse's hooves and the strain of a Sons of the Pioneers tune. You can rent a gentle saddle pony at the **Redfish Lake Corrals** (208–774–3311), on Redfish Lake (5 miles south of Stanley), but you'll have to take it upon yourself to hum "Back in the Saddle Again."

The **Idaho Rocky Mountain Ranch,** which started life in the 1930s as the Idaho Rocky Mountain Club—a private, by-invitation-only getaway—oozes Western ambience. The rustic main lodge has four rooms and is surrounded by nine log cabins; all are appointed with handmade log furniture. The ranch, east off Highway 75 from 10 miles south of Stanley, is open full-gallop June through September, then slows to a canter in winter, when two cabins are available for skiing escapes. (Know this: When the sun is shining on the Sawtooth Valley in winter, there's probably not a prettier spot on earth.) Call (208) 774–3544 for information and reservations.

South of Galena Summit you'll enter the rich-and-famous world of Sun Valley. A "new" resort developed by Averill Harriman in the 1930s, Sun Valley lies just east of Ketchum, a no-holds-barred lead-and-silver mining camp in the late nineteenth century. Both the **Ore Wagon Museum** in Ketchum and the **Blaine County Historical Museum** in nearby Hailey should be on your itinerary. Ketchum's **Pioneer Saloon** is a great place for a burger and a beer in the best of Western tradition, and the **Ketchum Wagon Days Celebration,** in late August, claims the title of "largest non-motorized parade in the West." Call the Chamber of Commerce at (800) 634–3347 for more information.

Drive to Arco, then northwest into the valley of the Big Lost River. From Challis, founded in 1876 as a supply hub for the Salmon River mining country, follow the **Custer Motorway Adventure Road.** When built in 1879 to link Challis and Bonanza, the toll road cost $8.00 to traverse, and the trip took about nine hours by stagecoach.

The 40-plus-mile drive through the historic Yankee Fork Mining District begins at the west end of Main Street. Points of interest include the huge old Yankee Fork gold dredge in Bonanza and the nearby ghost town of Custer City, epicenter of the historic district, with its museum, boot hill cemetery, and numerous interpretive displays. The tour is detailed in a brochure, available by calling (208) 879–5244 or 879–4321; the dredge is open daily for tours between July 1 and Labor Day from 10:00 A.M. to 5:00 P.M. The road, generally free of snow from June through October, is not recommended for motor homes or low-clearance autos.

Traverse Highway 93 from Challis to Salmon, if for no other reason than to enjoy one of the classic drives of the West. Arid foothills rise toward timbered peaks, the delicious scent of sage permeates the air, and low-slung buttes and pocked cliffs rise above the Salmon River; timeworn ranch outbuildings, sun-dried, lean with the prevailing winds. Keep an eye out for coyotes, hawks, and antelope. Forty miles north of Challis (18 miles south of Salmon), you'll spot the left-hand turn to **Twin Peaks Ranch** (208–894–2290), one of Idaho's oldest dude hangouts. The Old West flavor is palpable: Picture a stately old lodge with a rock fireplace, an open-beam ceiling, and knotty-pine walls appointed with bearskin rugs and mounted trophies. Time stands still here, and it's a good time. There are hiking, horseback riding, superb fishing, horseshoes, a shooting range, campouts for kids,

The 1832 Rendezvous

More than 200 mountain men, along with several hundred Nez Perce and Flathead Indians, convened in the remote Teton Valley in July 1832, about a mile from present-day Driggs. It was the Super Bowl of mountain-man gatherings: Bill Sublette was there, and so were Jim Bridger, Captain Bonneville, and Nathaniel Wyeth, to name just a few. Working from the written accounts of Captain Bonneville, Washington Irving penned this description:

> In this valley was congregated the motley populace connected with the fur trade. Here two rival companies [the Rocky Mountain Fur Company and Astor's American Fur Company] had their encampments, with their retainers of all kinds: traders, trappers, hunters, and half-breeds, assembled from all quarters, awaiting their yearly supplies, and their orders to start off in new directions. . . . There was, moreover, a band of fifteen free trappers, commanded by a gallant leader from Arkansas, named Sinclair, who held their encampment a little apart from the rest. Such was the wild and heterogeneous assemblage, amounting to several hundred men, civilized and savage, distributed in tents and lodges in the several camps.

As two brigades from the Rocky Mountain Fur Company, headed by Milton Sublette and Henry Fraeb, left the rendezvous and were headed south toward Utah, they encountered a party of 200 Blackfeet—the Indians most feared by the mountain men—coming down off Teton Pass, near today's Victor. The ensuing Battle of Pierre's Hole resulted in the deaths of four trappers, six "friendly" Indians (Nez Perce), and nine Blackfeet.

The white man responsible for the fracas, Antoine Godin, had a particular hatred of the Blackfeet, since his father had fallen victim to them a couple of years earlier. Like father, it turned out, like son: A few years later, when Godin was trading with a group of Indians near Fort Hall, a Blackfoot shot him and scalped him alive. The Indian carved the initials NJW—those of Godin's employer, Nathaniel J. Wyeth—into his forehead, then rode off.

and much more. The place is nestled up a picturesque side canyon 2 miles off the highway.

Southeast Idaho

In Rexburg (160 miles southeast of Salmon on Highways 28 and 33) the **Upper Snake River Valley Historical Museum** (208–356–9101; open Monday through Friday from 11:00 A.M. to 4:00 P.M.), at 51 Center Street, displays artifacts from prehistoric through pioneer times. As you travel eastward from here, the mighty Teton Range appears. From this side, not from the "back side" in Wyoming's Jackson Hole, early French trappers first viewed the mountains and named them, perhaps induced by a touch of homesickness, Les Trois Tétons (the three breasts).

The Henry's Fork–Teton Valley region was vital to the mountain men and early trapping industry from the 1820s until 1840, when European hat makers turned to using silk, rather than beaver, for their products. Rendezvous afforded the solitary trappers rare opportunities to socialize, and some of the biggest and bawdiest of the get-togethers were held in the Teton Valley, or Pierre's Hole (named in honor of Iroquois trapper Pierre Tevanitagon).

In Victor (at the head of Teton Valley, 8 miles south of Driggs on Highway 33) at **Pierre's Playhouse** (208–787–2249), the Teton Valley Players stage rip-roaring melodramas between June and September. Pierre's famous Dutch-oven chicken dinners are part of the deal.

Pretty Idaho Falls, southeastern Idaho's major city, is home to the **Bonneville Museum** (208–522–1400; open 10:00 A.M. to 5:00 P.M. weekdays and 1:00 to 5:00 P.M. Saturday), located in the 1916 Carnegie Library at 200 North Eastern Avenue. Featured are displays on the area's Native Americans, explorers, and pioneer settlers. The city's Fourth of July **Snake River Settlers Festival** is a step back into the 1800s, and the **War Bonnet Round-Up,** held in August, is the region's premier rodeo. A recent addition to the town is a re-creation of the old Eagle Rock Bridge, spanning the Snake River. Call the Chamber of Commerce at (800) 634–3246 for information.

At Fort Hall, between Blackfoot and Pocatello, Idaho's most populous Native American tribe celebrates its heritage at the **Shoshone-Bannock**

The Oregon Trail in Idaho

The numerous branches of the Oregon Trail spin a web of some 1,700 miles throughout southern Idaho, and from Blackfoot to Boise you're never far from it. During the 1840s and 1850s, more than 300,000 emigrants—with visions of gold, verdant farmlands, or simply a better life—traveled the trail, stretching from Independence, Missouri, to Oregon City, Oregon.

The going was rigorous, with tough terrain, equipment failures, sickness, bad weather, and occasional Indian attacks. More than 20,000 died along the "longest cemetery in America," or an average of more than one person every one-tenth of a mile.

Ruts carved by the hundreds of passing wagons can be seen in many southern Idaho locales; in all, nearly 600 miles of remnants endure. Often, where the trail isn't visible, it's only because highways and main streets were laid out following the routes blazed by our intrepid predecessors.

Indian Festival and Rodeo in mid-August. Included are Indian games, dancing, Indian Pony relay races, and the All-Indian Old Timers Rodeo. If you can't make the festival, do visit the **Shoshone-Bannock Tribal Museum** (208–237–9791) in the Trading Post Complex, where you'll also find **Melina's**, a Mexican-food restaurant.

Located in Pocatello's expansive Ross Park, between Second and Fifth avenues, is a full-scale replica of **Old Fort Hall,** a fur-trading post built in 1834 by Nathaniel Wyeth for the Rocky Mountain Fur Company. In 1837 Wyeth sold out to the Hudson's Bay Company (also known as HBC, or "Here Before Christ"); later the fort became a vital layover for Oregon Trail emigrants. Among the finds within the massive gates are the **Wood River Restaurant & Saloon** and a log-house museum. The fort is open daily throughout most of the year, at varying hours. Call (208) 234–6238 for more information.

Immediately across the street visit the **Bannock County Historical**

Turn-of-the-century tourists breaking the rules at Lava Hot Springs

Museum. Its eclectic collection features fur-trading, pioneering, and rail-roading artifacts, including the mounted head of a moose that in 1911 had a run-in with the *Yellowstone Special* locomotive.

Lava Hot Springs, a great place for a relaxing soak, hosts its **Mountain Man Rendezvous** and associated **Pioneer Days** celebration in late July (call 208–776–5221 for information). The **South Bannock County Historical Center,** located on East Main and open from noon to 5:00 P.M. daily, features displays on "trails, trappers, trains, and travelers." While in town, travel down to the **Lazy "A" Ranch** and take in the Old West music, cowboy poetry, and chuckwagon barbecue. The log-cabin eatery opens Thursday through Saturday at 7:00 P.M., and the dinner bell clangs at 7:30. The Lazy "A" is located a quarter-mile west of town on Highway 30, on an operating cattle ranch. Call (208) 776–5035 for reservations.

Of those people who came to southeastern Idaho and put down roots, most were Mormons. A few miles east of Lava Hot Springs on Highway 30, at Lund, turn north and go 15 miles to the deserted but well-preserved Mormon settlement of **Chesterfield**. The place was named by Chester Call, not for himself, but for his hometown of Chesterfield, England. Call and the others who left Utah to settle here eventually moved on.

From Soda Springs, where Oregon Trail emigrants stopped to enjoy the naturally carbonated spring water that erupted from the earth, follow the **Bear Lake–Caribou Scenic Byway** to Montpelier. In 1896 Butch Cassidy and two companions made an unauthorized $7,000 withdrawal from the bank in this town, where today you'll find the **Daughters of Utah Pioneers Museum** and the **Rails and Trails Museum of the Oregon Trail**. Montpelier's annual **Peg Leg Smith Oregon Trail Rendezvous,** held in late July, celebrates the mountain men who came to trap in this beaver-abundant country. Costumed reenactments and hatchet-throwing contests are included. For Bear Lake–area visitor information, call (800) 448–2327.

In nearby Paris have a look at the resplendent **Bear Lake Stake Mormon Tabernacle,** built in 1889 of striking red standstone, sledded over the snow from a quarry along the east shore of Bear Lake, nearly 20 miles distant. Guided tours of the tabernacle, which features stone carvings and intricate woodworking, are available Memorial Day through Labor Day.

Three miles northwest of Preston (a half-mile north of the Bear River Bridge) a marker commemorates the **Battle of Bear River,** where between 300 and 400 Northern Shoshone men, women, and children were killed by Colonel Patrick Connor and members of his 3rd California Infantry. The bloodiest Indian massacre of the 1800s, the battle, ironically, remains cloaked in relative obscurity. Records at the Logan (Utah) Stake of the Mormon Church read: "We, the people of Cache Valley, looked upon the movement of Colonel Connor as intervention of the Almighty, as the

Indians had been a source of great annoyance to us for a long time, causing us to stand guard over our stock and other property the most of the time since our first settlement."

Franklin, 7 miles south of Preston, was the first official town in Idaho . . . sort of. It was incorporated in 1869 by the Utah legislature. A precise survey done in 1872, however, revealed that Franklin was not in Utah, after all. You can learn more at the **Pioneer Relic Hall,** located on Main Street in an old stone general store that once served simultaneously as a Mormon tithing house.

From American Falls head west for 10 miles along Interstate 86 to **Massacre Rocks State Park.** In 1862 several Oregon Trail travelers were killed by Shoshone Indians a few miles east of here, in the area known as Devils Gate. (The present name came about in the 1920s, in an enterprising move to attract more tourists to the American Falls area.) Deep wagon ruts remain, and 3 miles downstream from the park headquarters is **Register Rock,** where dozens of emigrants carved their names in stone.

In early June another of the region's plentiful tributes to the wild mountain men of the early 1800s kicks up. The **Massacre Rocks Rendezvous** includes a tipi village, traders' market, black-powder shoot, and more. Call (208) 548–2672 for additional information on the park and celebration.

From Massacre Rocks travel 45 miles west on Interstates 86 and 84 to Rupert and then 40 miles south on Highway 77 to Almo and the desert fantasy land of the **Silent City of Rocks,** so christened by pioneers who traveled the California and Mormon trails. Names, smeared in axle grease, can still be seen on some of the granite spires, and gold, stolen from an Overland Stage in 1878, reportedly remains buried amid the rocks. For overnight accommodations in this area of limited facilities, consider calling on the **Old Homestead** B&B at (208) 824–5521.

Circle back up through Oakley, which holds one of Idaho's greatest concentrations of nineteenth-century buildings. Here the **Oakley Pioneer Museum** (208–678–7172; open from 10:00 A.M. to 5:00 P.M. Tuesday through Saturday) informs visitors about the area's past, and July's **Pioneer Days** features Pony Express rides, a rodeo, and a Dutch-oven cook-off.

Burley's **Cassia County Museum,** at East Main Street and Highland Avenue, includes information on and a map of the several pioneer trails that converged in the area; west of town along Highway 30 is the **Milner**

Ruts Interpretive Site, where several miles of wagon ruts are marked. Call the Chamber of Commerce at (208) 678–7230 for more information.

Southwest Idaho

Travel 5 miles south of Hansen on the road to the Magic Mountain Ski Area; then go 1 mile west on 3200 North to the Rock Creek Store. Established in 1865 as a stage station, the place evolved into the first Oregon Trail trading post west of Fort Hall. Also on site is the 1900 Stricker House and an accompanying stone root cellar. Call (208) 423–4000 or 733–3974 for information.

In Twin Falls the Herritt Museum, on the campus of the College of Southern Idaho, and the Twin Falls Historical Museum, 3 miles west of town on Highway 30, offer glimpses of the past. The town's Western Days, held in early June, include gunfights in the street, barbecues, and a chili cook-off. From 6 miles west of Twin Falls on Highway 30/93, follow Highway 93 south to the Hollister port of entry—then another 3 miles, to the fascinating Heritage Museum, with its thousands of Indian artifacts and one of the most amazing mounted-wildlife displays you'll find anywhere. Summer hours are 10:00 A.M. to 4:00 P.M. Tuesday through Sunday; hours vary the rest of the year. Call (208) 655–4444 for information.

Take Interstate 84 west from Bliss to Glenns Ferry and Three Island Crossing State Park, where buffalo and longhorn cattle roam today. During pioneer days the site was considered the most treacherous river ford along the entire length of the Oregon Trail; not to cross, however, meant a longer route with less water and poorer grazing for stock. Approximately half of the emigrant parties chose to ford the river here, and many lost wagons, stock, and even human lives. The park visitor center, open daily from 8:00 A.M. to 5:00 P.M., includes excellent displays of Oregon Trail lore, including compelling passages from emigrants' diaries. The Three Island Crossing Reenactment takes place the second weekend in August in the park. Call (208) 366–2394 for information.

In beautiful Boise head straight for the impressive Capitol building—the only statehouse in the United States heated with geothermal energy—at Capitol Boulevard and Jefferson Street. A highlight, found on the fourth floor: the mural by Montana artist Dana Broussard, commissioned by the state of Idaho, depicting a vivid overview of Idaho's vibrant history.

The **Idaho Historical Museum** presents a good look at Idaho's past, from prehistory through the fur-trapping, gold-mining, and homesteading eras. Highlights include a Wild West saloon, a summary of the westward migration along the Oregon Trail, and trappings of the cowboying trade. The museum, located on Capitol Boulevard in Julia Davis Park, is open from 9:00 A.M. to 5:00 P.M. Monday through Saturday and from 1:00 to 5:00 P.M. Sundays and holidays. Call (208) 334–2120 for information.

Boise is home to more Basques (thought to be the oldest European ethnic group) than any town in the United States. To learn more about them, visit the **Basque Museum and Cultural Center** at Sixth and Grove streets in, fittingly, Boise's oldest home, the Cyrus Jacobs house. Beginning about 1910 the place served as temporary housing for scores of young Basque men who traveled to the American West from their native northern Spain to work as sheepherders. The museum is open between May 1 and September 30 on Tuesday through Friday from 10:00 A.M. to 4:00 P.M. and October through April on Thursday through Saturday from 11:00 A.M. to 3:00 P.M. Call (208) 343–2671 for information. The Basque museum is in the **Old Boise** section of downtown, also home to the **Historic Idanha** (208–342–3611) at 928 Main Street, a hotel that has served grub to nearly a hundred years' worth of visitors to Boise.

The **Old Idaho Penitentiary,** near the east end of Warm Springs Boulevard at 2445 Old Penitentiary Road, was in business for more than one hundred years until it was replaced in 1973. A gaggle of Wild West desperadoes called the place home, as illuminated in the slide show and self-guided tour offered to visitors. The **Idaho Transportation Museum,** housed in the pen's old shirt shop, includes among its varied collection an array of stagecoaches and buggies. The penitentiary is open daily from noon to 5:00 P.M. during summer and from noon to 4:00 P.M. the rest of the year. Call (208) 334–2844 for information.

Festivals abound in greater Boise and southwest Idaho, including the **National Old Time Fiddlers Contest,** held in Weiser the third full week in June (the associated **National Old Time Fiddlers' Hall of Fame,** at 8 East Idaho Street, is open year-round from 9:00 A.M. to 5:00 P.M.); Nampa's **Snake River Stampede/Buckaroo Breakfast,** which dishes out some of Idaho's best family Western entertainment during the third week in July; and the **Old Fort Boise Days,** held in Parma the third week-end in May. Old Fort Boise, a replica of the Hudson's Bay Company post established here in 1834, is open to the public Friday through Sunday from 1:00 to 3:00 P.M. during the summer months. Guided tours can be arranged at other times of the year by calling (208) 722–5138 or 722–5086.

The Old West thrives in five-million-acre Owyhee County, which occupies the arid southwest corner of Idaho. Although it sounds Indian, the name *Owyhee* is actually an early-day twist on the spelling of Hawaii. The county earned the name because of some native Hawaiian trappers who vis-ited in the early 1800s.

Stop first in Murphy, the county seat, at the **Owyhee County Historical Museum** (208–495–2319), where you'll learn about the area's mineral-rich past. The museum is open Wednesday through Friday from 10:00 A.M. to 4:00 P.M. Then travel to **Silver City,** the gem of Idaho's ghost towns. Silver City lies 28 miles southwest of Murphy, most of those miles on a dirt road generally open from late May through mid-October. (Even during that period you should inquire at the museum in Murphy about current road conditions.) Some seventy old buildings remain in Silver City, including the **Schoolhouse Museum,** the **Wells Fargo Depot,** and the offices of the *Owyhee Avalanche,* the first newspaper in the territory.

Where to Eat

Pierre's Playhouse, Victor, (208) 787–2249
Wood River Restaurant & Saloon, Pocatello
Pioneer Saloon, Ketchum, (208) 726–3139
Lazy "A" Ranch, Lava Hot Springs, (208) 776–5035

Where to Stay

Jameson House, Wallace, (208) 752–1252
Idaho Rocky Mountain Ranch, outside Stanley, (208) 774–3544
Twin Peaks Ranch, outside Salmon, (208) 894–2290
Old Homestead Bed & Breakfast, near City of Rocks, (208) 824–5521
Historic Idanha, Boise, (208) 342–3611

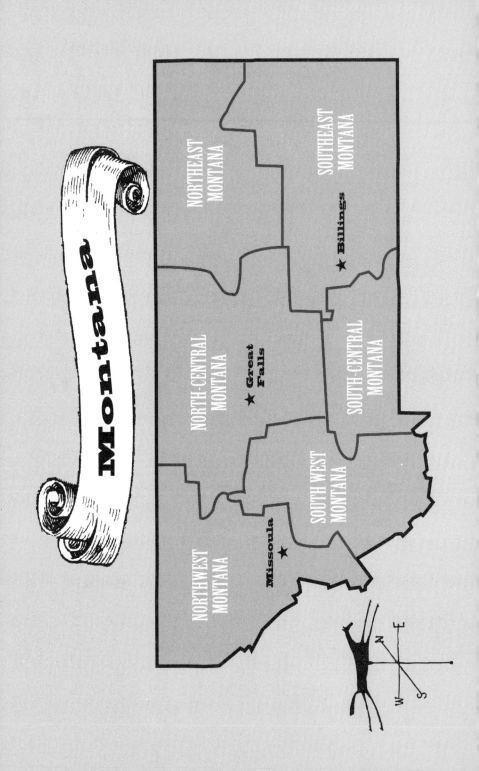

MONTANA

▼▼▼

OST FOLKS don't need to be told that the Old West thrives in Montana as in few other states. If you were to drive across the state, in fact, you'd almost have to have your eyes closed *not* to see cowboys, herding cattle or mending fences, or a pack train headed for higher ground.

Montana is a big state—only Alaska, Texas, and California are larger—and a diverse one. East of the Continental Divide, you'll see the high, arid plains that fit the stereotypical image of Montana; many visitors, however, are surprised by the lushness and heavy timber cover found in many areas on the wetter, west side of the Divide.

The narrative begins by twisting through northwest Montana. From there it makes a counterclockwise loop through the state accurately described by writer Joseph Kinsey Howard, in the title of his 1943 book, as *High, Wide, and Handsome.*

Northwest Montana

Three miles south of the winter-summer resort town of Whitefish, pull into the **Diamond K Chuckwagon** for a cowboy supper of barbecue beef, chuckwagon beans, foil-wrapped baked potatoes, and hot biscuits. After dinner the Diamond K Wranglers shake the walls of the meeting hall, with Old West pickin', fiddlin', and story tellin'. The proprietors guarantee that the whole family will have a good time at the Diamond K, which also boasts an RV park. From mid-June through mid-September, meals are served nightly at 7:00 (try to arrive by 6:15), and the show starts at 8:00 P.M. Call (406) 862–8828 for reservations.

In bustling Kalispell visit the **Conrad Mansion,** the opulent home of one of the town's founding families. After making his fortune in the river trade at Fort Benton, Montana, Charles E. Conrad brought it to northwest Montana, where he built his Norman-style mansion in 1895. Daughter Alicia Conrad Campbell donated the property to the city in 1975 "to be maintained in perpetuity as an historic site," and it remains one of the best-preserved nineteenth-century mansions in Montana. The home, located 6 blocks east of Main Street on Fourth Street East, is open for tours daily from 10:00 A.M. to 4:30 P.M., from May 15 through October 15. Call (406) 755–2166 for information.

Southwest of Kalispell, just out of Marion in the Thompson River valley, the **Hargrave Cattle & Guest Ranch** does its darndest to make cowboys and cowgirls of its guests. The handmade log cabins at the working Charolais cattle ranch date from 1906, and the delicious family-style meals are from an earlier day, as well. The historic 87,000-acre ranch is open year-round. Call (406) 858–2284 for more information.

In Polson, 55 miles south of Kalispell on the shores of colossal Flathead Lake, the **KwaTaqNuk Resort** beckons. Opened in 1992, the resort represents an emphatic statement from the Confederated Salish and Kootenai tribes that they're not going to just sit back and watch others profit from the tourism boom that is exploding in their native land. The large resort, which includes a full-service marina, is staffed primarily by tribal members and features an art gallery that overflows with first-class Western and Native American art and photographs. Call KwaTaqNuk (which means "where the water leaves the lake") at (406) 883–3636 for reservations.

The Confederated Salish & Kootenai also welcome visitors (but not their alcohol) to the **Standing-Arrow Powwow,** held in Elmo in late July, and the **Arlee Powwow and Fourth of July Celebration,** in Arlee. Call the tribal headquarters at (406) 675–2700 for more information.

Several prestatehood structures have been moved to the grounds at the engaging **Four Winds Trading Post,** lending the post an air of authenticity. An impressive array of new and old Native American trappings are on display and/or for sale, including quillwork, tools, tobacco twists, traditional dress, weapons, and medicine pouches. Components of the historically correct collection have played cameo roles in *Dances with Wolves, Son of the Morning Star,* and other movies. Four Winds Trading Post (406–745–4336)

Sweetheart

M any a match was made in the Old West by ranchers and home-steaders who took out advertisements in the eastern and midwest-ern newspapers, "shopping" for a wife. Thousands of young ladies, yearning for better lives, responded to such ads.

Sweetheart magazine is sort of a cross between the old mail-order bride system and the Singles section common in newspapers today. Doling out old-fashioned romance and heartfelt values, spiced with a Western flair, the down-home magazine is published by Charlie "Cowboy Cupid" James (a distant relative of Jesse James) and Cupcake, his wife of more than thirty years. Along with daughter Lise, who serves as office manager, the Jameses compile the monthly publication out of their log home on the Sweetheart Ranch outside St. Ignatius, where they also tend a small herd of black Angus cattle.

According to Cupcake James, since commencing publication in 1988, the magazine has spawned at least 500 lasting relationships. Each issue is brimming with personals, from both men and women, many of them accompanied by photographs. Standing alongside a favorite pony or in one's best Western finery are popular poses.

Each entry is unique, but this composite might be considered repre-sentative:

> *WM, 37, 5'10", 190#, rancher/heavy-equipment contractor with 1,200 irrigated acres in southeast Montana. I'm quiet and my looks are average. I like to ride, dance (even though I've got two left feet), and take a drink now and then. But mostly I'd like to have someone to cuddle in front of the fire with when the Montana wind's a-howlin' and snow's a blowin'. I'm not looking for a goddess, just a companion to take the lonely edge off living on the prairie. If you're a gal who loves wide-open spaces and fiery sunsets, and can handle the solitude and hard work that go with ranch-ing, give me a call.*

Call (406) 745–4209 to request a copy of Sweetheart.

is located 3 miles north of St. Ignatius on Highway 93 and is open daily from 10:00 A.M. to 6:00 P.M.

The beauty of the **St. Ignatius Mission** is bested perhaps, in the immediate vicinity, only by the stunning Mission Mountains, which serve as its backdrop. The church was built in 1891, with bricks fired on the spot, by Native Americans under the supervision of Jesuit missionaries. The walls and ceilings are adorned with the murals of Brother Joseph Carignano, who painted the masterpieces in his time off as mission cook. The house of worship, just off Highway 93 in St. Ignatius, is open daily to visitors from 8:00 A.M. to dusk. Call (406) 745–2768 for information.

As many as fifty million bison roamed the plains in the early 1800s; unbelievably, by 1900 indiscriminate killing had reduced the number of these wild animals to only twenty known individuals. (Fortunately, several private herds had also been maintained.) The **National Bison Range,** 10 miles northwest of Ravalli at Moiese, was created in 1908 to help bolster the beast's dwindling numbers.

Today some 400 to 500 of the shaggy giants roam the range's 19,000 acres. Drive the 19-mile Red Sleep Mountain Drive, keeping an eye out not only for bison but also for elk, black bear, Rocky Mountain goats, bighorn sheep, mule deer, and pronghorns. The visitor center, featuring films, displays, and photographs, is open from 8:00 A.M. to 6:00 P.M. daily from June 1 through Labor Day and, the rest of the year, weekdays from 10:00 A.M. to 6:00 P.M. and weekends from 8:00 A.M. to 4:30 P.M. Call (406) 644–2211 for information. Red Sleep Mountain Drive closes at 9:30 P.M.; travelers must set out no later than 7:00 P.M.

In Missoula pull up to the earthy **Oxford** bar and cafe, a classic Old West saloon that is surviving in the new West. Night and day, the place is jammed with poker players and old-timers who are having a beer or a cup of coffee. If you've the nerve—and a low-enough cholesterol count—order a plate of calf brains and eggs, the house specialty. The "Ox" is located downtown at 337 North Higgins Avenue.

Hunger abated, head to the **Historical Museum at Fort Missoula,** off South Avenue just west of Reserve. Fort Missoula was established in 1877 to provide settlers with protection from Indians and other perceived threats of the frontier. Today an array of displays highlights the fort's compelling past, and several structures have been moved in, including an aged fire-lookout tower. Just gaining momentum is a push for the Northern

Bicycle Touring, 1890s Style

The 25th Infantry, one of four U.S. Army regiments composed of the Buffalo Soldiers (see Kansas, page 344), was stationed at Fort Missoula in the late 1800s. The Missoulian newspaper regularly complimented the black soldiers for their good works and relations within the community. They also earned great respect by managing to keep the peace under martial law, without resorting to violence themselves, in Wallace, Idaho, during the pressure-cooker mine strikes of the 1893 depression.

In 1897 Lt. James Moss, a white officer, and twenty of his soldiers mounted a bicycle expedition that led from Fort Missoula to St. Louis, Missouri. The corps pedaled primitive, 1-speed Spalding bicycles the 1,900 miles—over dirt tracks and muddy roads—in the better-than-respectable time of forty-five days.

The Army never did buy into Moss's idea of using the bicycle for large-scale troop transport. The 25th Infantry, meanwhile, was one of the first regiments mobilized to Cuba in 1898 for the Spanish-American War, where some of the infantrymen fought beside Teddy Roosevelt and his Rough Riders at San Juan Hill. After the war they stayed behind to patrol Havana, again mounted on bicycles.

Rockies Heritage Center, which promoters say ultimately will bring a bevy of diverse historical museums to the grounds of Fort Missoula. The existing museum (406–728–3476) is open summers Monday through Saturday from 10:00 A.M. to 5:00 P.M. and Sunday from noon to 5:00 P.M. It is open on a reduced schedule in winter.

To locate **Garnet Ghost Town,** one of Montana's best preserved, go 27 miles west of Missoula on Highway 200; turn off the highway near the 22-mile marker and proceed for 11 miles on a well-signed gravel road.

Placer mining had been going on in the area since the 1860s, but it wasn't until the mid-1890s, when thousands of miners were unemployed after the repeal of the Sherman Silver Purchase Act (which made silver all but worthless), that things shifted into high gear at Garnet. At its zenith the gold-mining town consisted of a doctor's office, numerous cabins, a union hall that boasted one of the best dance floors in Montana, thirteen taverns, four stores, and more. Remaining structures include the three-story J. K. Wells Hotel, built atop a wooden-post foundation in the winter of 1897. Two newer, 1930s-vintage cabins are available for rent in winter, making Garnet a popular destination for cross-country skiers and snowmobilers. For information call the Bureau of Land Management (BLM) at (406) 329–3914.

Stevensville, south of Missoula up the Bitterroot Valley, is Montana's oldest town and original state capital. The adobe-and-log **Fort Owen**

The Black Robes Come West

T he arrival of the Jesuit missionaries or, as the Indians called them, the "Black Robes," marked the opening of the West to white exploration and settlement. This ultimately was the undoing of many Native American cultural traditions; ironically, however, the missionaries came at the invitation of the Indians.

It was said that even before Lewis and Clark passed through, the prophet Shining Shirt had learned through visions that men in long black robes would one day appear and give the Indians newfound strength.

A delegation of four braves traveled to St. Louis in 1831 in an attempt to persuade priests to come back west with them. The first recruiting trip was unsuccessful, and so were two subsequent ones. At last, however, a group of Indians met in Council Bluffs, Iowa, with Father Pierre-Jean DeSmet and convinced him to return with them. Via Wyoming, DeSmet was led to the Bitterroot Valley, where he supervised construction of St. Mary's Mission.

(406–542–5500) was built in 1850 by Maj. John Owen as a regional trade center. The nearby **St. Mary's Mission** (406–777–5734) was established by Father Pierre-Jean DeSmet in 1841, only thirty-five years after Lewis and Clark had passed through the Bitterroot Valley. Tours run daily from April 15 to December 31 between 10:00 A.M. and 5:00 P.M.

Europeans Guido and Hanny Oberdorfer dreamed for years of owning a spread in the American West, and when they happened across West Fork Meadows, they knew they'd come home. Today their remote **West Fork Meadows Ranch,** where guests sleep in comfy log cabins beneath billowy down comforters, mixes Old World elegance with Old West style and hospitality. The chef changes the menu with the seasons, mixing Montana meats, fish, and vegetables with secret herbs, spices, and sauces to create spectacular feasts. From 3 miles south of Darby, the wilderness oasis is situated deep in the backcountry at the end of miles of dirt forest roads. Call (406) 349–2468 for reservations and an all-important map.

Southwest Montana

From Darby drive south to cross the Continental Divide at Lost Trail Pass; then drop along Highway 43 into the Big Hole River valley, the "valley of 10,000 haystacks," where you'll spot Sunny Slope, or "beaver slide," haystackers, standing about like so many quiet giants.

Big Hole Battlefield National Monument, 14 miles east of the pass, marks the site of one of the most violent clashes of the Indian wars. On the morning of August 9, 1877, Chief Joseph and his band of several hundred Nez Perce were attacked early in the morning by Col. John Gibbon and his soldiers and civilian volunteers. Nearly one hundred Nez Perce died, many of them women and children, as the U.S. forces were repelled; the survivors continued their journey, which ended two months later in the Bear's Paw Mountains of north-central Montana.

Outdoors an interpretive trail leads through the encampment area, a spot still sacred to the Nez Perce. The visitor center, with its thought-provoking displays, is open from 9:00 A.M. to 7:00 P.M. in summer and from 9:00 A.M. to 5:00 P.M. the remainder of the year. Call (406) 689–3155 for more information.

Bannack, Montana's territorial capital, is now a state park and well-preserved ghost town. On July 28, 1862, John White and a group of fellow Coloradans found gold in Grasshopper Creek; the discovery was the first documented strike in the Montana Territory, and it triggered a gold rush: Within a year some 3,000 persons lived in Bannack. Today more than fifty structures remain, many of them in outstanding condition, thanks largely to the area's dry climate, which permits unpainted wood to endure. **Bannack Days,** held the third weekend in July, vividly revives the town's colorful past, with horse-and-buggy rides, buffalo barbecues, and old-time music and crafts. For more information call (406) 834–3413.

The **Beaverhead County Museum** (406–683–5027) is one of

Montana's best small-town repositories of the past. The historic log building in downtown Dillon features collections of Indian artifacts and displays on the area's mining and ranching heritage. A pioneer's log cabin and 1909 Union Pacific depot are also found on the grounds, open year-round from 9:00 A.M. to 9:00 P.M. weekdays and from 1:00 to 4:00 P.M. weekends.

Tiny Dell, 40 miles south of Dillon along Interstate 15, is home to **Yesterday's Calf-A,** one of Montana's most unusual eateries. The restaurant occupies a building that served as a school from 1903 until 1963, and the daily family-style specials are written with chalk on the schoolroom's blackboard. The interior and the yard surrounding the building are brimming with antiques and memorabilia: from an old piano with yellowed sheet music and crosscut saws to spurs, kerosene lanterns, bison skulls, and wagon wheels. A pot of cowboy coffee is on at 7:00 A.M. every day at Calf-A.

To reach Highway 87 turn east onto gravel at the near–ghost town of Monida and progress through a swath of Montana's most beautiful backcountry. You'll skirt the **Red Rock Lakes National Wildlife Refuge,** established in 1935 primarily to help the rare trumpeter swan regain a foothold. After about 60 miles turn north onto Highway 87 and drive through the sprawling, open Madison River valley, where the deer and the antelope truly do play. If nightfall is near as you approach the fishing-and-hunting mecca of Ennis, hole up at the classic **El Western Motel.** From the tidy log-frame cabins to the lampshades and artwork, the hostelry is pure, unadulterated Western. Call (406) 682–4217 for information.

Virginia City, 14 miles west of Ennis, was the richest of Montana's bonanza towns; the area yielded some $30 million in gold during the first three years of mining activity. Ten thousand people lived in Virginia City by 1863, with another 25,000 scattered along the 11 miles of adjacent Alder Gulch.

Virginia City's fate was not typical of that of many boomtowns, thanks to a number of factors, but largely because of a no-holds-barred restoration effort, begun some fifty years ago, by Senator Charles Bovey and his family. Now thousands of visitors experience the Old West along the boardwalk-lined streets of Virginia City, enjoying dancers performing at the **Virginia City Brewery,** a snack at the **Wells Fargo Coffee House,** or a drink in the **Bale of Hay Saloon.** Another favorite is the crowd-pleasing **Virginia City Players,** who perform classic nineteenth-century melodrama at the **Virginia City Opera House** six nights a week during summer. The **Alder Gulch**

Short Line offers rides between Virginia City and nearby **Nevada City,** where old structures from around Montana have been brought in to re-create the original mining town.

Historic-lodging opportunities include the **Nevada City Hotel;** the **Fairweather Inn,** in the heart of Virginia City; and the **Daylight Creek Motel,** tucked behind an Old West facade. A movement currently afoot by the National Trust for Historic Preservation is promoting the idea of turning

The Vigilantes

The population boom at Bannack, which began in 1862, was short-lived: Within two years most of the miners had moved on to golder pastures, such as those found in Alder Gulch camps like Virginia City. The territorial court determined that Bannack and Virginia City, 70 miles apart, needed only one sheriff, and Henry Plummer got himself elected to that post. During his eight-month tenure as sheriff, an office that charged him with protecting the interests of the citizens, Plummer and his gang of "Innocents" worked the road that connected Virginia City and Bannack, killing no fewer than one hundred individuals and relieving countless others of their burdens of gold.

Justice prevailed when the Vigilantes Committee was formed late in 1863: Plummer was hanged a few months later from the gallows he himself had built only a year earlier, and the rest of his gang were either hanged or banished. The graves of Plummer and several of his road agents can be visited at Boot Hill, high above Virginia City, where their tombstones stand hard against the horizon.

Virginia City into a national park; for the latest information and for reservations at the hotels or tickets for the Virginia City Players, call (406) 843–5377.

According to some people, **Robber's Roost,** a few miles northwest of Nevada City, is where Henry Plummer and his Innocents plotted their attacks on prospectors; others say the place wasn't built until several years after Plummer's death. Regardless, the two-story, hand-hewn log building is an uncommon example of frontier architecture. At one time a stage stop and tavern, today the structure houses a used-book and curio shop, providing a good excuse to see the inside of the venerable structure.

Butte, a hard-edged, blue-collar town that is absolutely lovable, is home to the **World Museum of Mining on Hellroarin' Gulch.** The 1899 re-created town, sitting on twelve acres at the site of the old Orphan Girl silver and zinc mine, is a world-class attraction where one can readily while away a day. The cobblestone streets are lined with dozens of buildings that are brimming with relics of the past: an assay office, a Chinese herbal-healing enterprise, a funeral and embalming parlor, and even a sauerkraut factory.

The museum proper, occupying the two stories of the Orphan Girl's old hoist house, includes among its eclectic collection compelling photographs of old Butte. Hell Roarin' Gulch, located at the west end of Granite Street, is open daily from mid-June through Labor Day from 9:00 A.M. to 9:00 P.M. and in spring and fall from 10:00 A.M. to 5:00 P.M. Tuesday through Sunday. Call (406) 723–7211 for more information.

The **Dumas Red Light Antique Mall** (406–723–6128) is housed in a structure built in 1890 specifically as a bordello. The place didn't shut down until the early 1980s, after a violent robbery and under subsequent public pressure. Today the similarly sized and shaped rooms, some with beds still in them, are filled with antiques and curios. The Dumas is located at 45 East Mercury Street, in the Venus Alley section of timeworn uptown Butte. It is open from 10:00 A.M. to 5:00 P.M. daily.

Passing through Anaconda you can't miss glimpsing the inactive **Anaconda Smelter Stack,** where tons of Butte copper were smelted, beginning in the late 1800s. Crest Flint Creek Pass on Highway 1 and continue to Philipsburg, a sort of living ghost town. In the old Courtney Hotel and Overland car dealership, you'll find the intriguing **Ghost Town Hall of Fame,** consisting primarily of high-quality framed photographs that depict many of Montana's ghost towns during their prime. The Hall of Fame is open daily from 10:00 A.M. to 6:00 P.M. in summer and from noon to 5:00 P.M. the rest of the year. Call the Chamber of Commerce at (406) 859–3388 for more information.

In Deer Lodge hold onto your wallet and enter the **Old Montana Prison,** the first territorial prison established in the western United States. In addition to the expected cellular accommodations, found within the prison walls is the **Montana Law Enforcement Museum;** also, the **Old Prison Players** perform for "captive" audiences here during the summer. The prison (406–846–3111) is located at 1106 Main Street.

The **Grant-Kohrs Ranch National Historic Site** resurrects the past at one of the first and most successful cattle spreads carved from the Montana frontier. Johnny Grant, a mountain man from Canada, started raising cattle here in the 1850s. In 1866 he sold out to German immigrant Conrad Kohrs, and the place flourished: At its zenith Kohrs's company ran cows on more than a million acres in four states and parts of Canada. As time progressed, the cowboy's role changed from range rider to that of bale-bucker and fence-mender, an evolution well documented in the visitor center.

Cattle still graze, horses still tug plows, and National Park Service personnel demonstrate both the old and new ways of accomplishing various ranching tasks at the historic site, located at the north end of Deer Lodge and open daily year-round. Numerous buildings are open for touring, including Johnny Grant's 1862 house. The site is open from 8:00 A.M. to 5:00 P.M. daily in summer and 9:00 A.M. to 4:00 P.M. the rest of the year. Call (406) 846–2070 for more information.

Near the top of MacDonald Pass, 15 miles east of Helena, swing into fabulous **Frontier Town,** whose restaurant menu boasts Mulligan stew and Trapper's Chicken. When John R. Quigley, years ago, began building his log-and-rock "town" that straddles the Continental Divide, neighbors in the valley below must've considered him one crazy cowpoke. His buildings, however, did not come crashing down the mountainside when battered by winds and snow, as had been predicted.

Quigley died in 1979, and his widow sold Frontier Town in 1992, but the new owners have retained the magic: The place includes an expansive Western-memento shop, a museum of frontier life, and a one-piece Douglas-fir bar, where adults straddle saddle bar stools and watch as the bartender mixes drinks with spring water that pours from the mountainside. Frontier Town is open daily between April and October from 9:00 A.M. to 10:00 P.M., with the restaurant serving from 5:00 until 10:00 P.M. Call (406) 442–4560 for information.

Gold was discovered in 1864 at **Last Chance Gulch,** now a fun-filled and history-rich pedestrian mall in downtown Helena. **Last Chance Tours** offers open-air coach tours of Helena and its dozens of historic sites, including the **Reeder's Alley** miners' district and the **Original Governor's Mansion.** Tours depart several times daily between May 15 and September 30. Call the Chamber of Commerce at (406) 442–4120 for more information.

The unsurpassed **Montana's Museum,** located at 225 North Roberts Street and immediately across from the state capitol, includes an excellent exhibit on F. Jay Haynes, the official turn-of-the-century photographer for both Yellowstone National Park and the Northern Pacific Railroad. His photographs are displayed, along with railroading and park artifacts from the day.

The Mackay Gallery of Charles M. Russell Art boasts more than sixty Russell oils, pen-and-inks, watercolors, and sculptures, along with several of his comical illustrated personal letters. The gallery showpiece, in the eyes of many, is the stunning *When the Land Belonged to God.* The painting depicts a herd of bison cresting a dry-country rise above a river bottom, with the early-morning sun banking off their backs and steam rising from their nostrils. Montana's Museum is open daily from Memorial Day through Labor Day from 8:00 A.M. to 6:00 P.M. weekdays and 9:00 A.M. to 5:00 P.M. weekends. The rest of the year the hours are 8:00 A.M. to 5:00 P.M. weekdays and 9:00 A.M. to 5:00 P.M. weekends. Call (406) 444–2694 for information.

The history-rich **Sanders Bed and Breakfast** (406–442–3309) occupies the home built in 1875 by Wilbur Sanders, who came to Bannack by wagon train in 1863 and was instrumental in forming the Vigilantes. The seven-room inn, appointed with many of the Sanders family's original furnishings, is found at 328 North Ewing.

The **Wolf Creek Wild Game Feed** offers, literally, a taste of the Old West, with gustatory possibilities that include breaded rattlesnake, bear meat loaf, elk chow mein, mountain lion strips, and beaver tail. A fund-raiser for the local emergency services, the feed is held on St. Patrick's Day in Wolf Creek, 35 miles north of Helena in the scenic Missouri River canyon. Call the Oasis Bar and Cafe at (406) 235–9992 for information.

South Central Montana

In Three Forks, 65 miles south of Helena, one could spend hours exploring the **Headwaters Heritage Museum,** at the corner of Main and Cedar. Just outside town the tranquil **Headwaters State Park** surrounds the point where three rivers merge to become the Missouri. Lewis and Clark, who passed through in 1805, named the "three noble streams" the Gallatin,

John Colter's Run

Wildlife, including beaver, historically was abundant in the Headwaters region. Two of the earliest trappers into the area were John Potts and John Colter, both formerly of the Lewis and Clark expedition. They were dispatched in 1808 from Manuel Lisa's Fort Remon, armed with the mission of persuading Indians to come and trade with Lisa.

Unfortunately for Potts and Colter, by this time the fearsome Blackfeet had assumed control of the Headwaters, and the pair had the bad luck of encountering a party of several hundred Piegan warriors. Potts was killed immediately, but Colter, the story goes, was given the opportunity to retain his life: After convincing the chief that he was a lumbering runner (although known among his peers as fleet of foot), Colter was stripped and released, and he began running—barefoot and bare naked—for his very life.

With Piegans pursuing him over a rough, rocky, and cactus-covered terrain, Colter escaped by hiding in brush along the banks of the Madison. He appeared at Fort Remon eleven days later, tattered, battered, and starved, but his epic adventure further enhanced his reputation as one of the wiliest and toughest of the wild mountain men.

Some 300 people celebrate Colter's trek yearly (the first Saturday after Labor Day) by participating in the 7-mile **John Colter Run.** Harriers ford the Gallatin River and run cross-country, probably over some of the same terrain Colter traversed. Today's runners are permitted to retain their shorts and shoes. Call (406) 587–4415 for information on the run.

Madison, and Jefferson, after the U.S. secretary of state, the secretary of the treasury, and the president, "the author of our enterprize." The park, complete with campground, fabulous fly-fishing, and the ghost-town remains of Gallatin City, can be contacted by calling (406) 994–4042.

Three Forks Saddlery, The Working Cowboy's Store, is located at 221 South Main Street. For more than thirty-five years, the business has outfitted real and wannabe cowboys, with a full line of clothing, hats, and boots; it's also known for its popular Kelly Roper and Montana Packer saddles. The aroma of fresh-tanned leather greets visitors after they open the door, upon which hangs a sign that reads COME IN AND SAY HELLO—YOU'RE ALWAYS WELCOME. Also in Three Forks: **The Sacajawea Inn** (406–285–6515), a historic hotel named for Lewis and Clark's female Shoshone companion. The 30,000-square-foot inn is open year-round.

The **Willow Creek Cafe,** one of Montana's best-kept culinary secrets, is located 7 miles south of Three Forks in the town of Willow Creek. The fresh fruit pies served here, made of locally grown produce, are something to behold. Breakfast and lunch entrees—with names such as the Gold Nugget, the Potosi, and the Boss Tweed—honor the gold and silver mines surrounding the owner's beloved hometown of Pony, Montana. The eatery and adjacent saloon occupy a historic building that was formerly a tavern-barbershop-dancehall complex. In summer it's open from 11:00 A.M. until 9:00 P.M. Monday through Saturday and from 9:00 A.M. to 8:00 P.M. on Sunday. For information on winter hours, call (406) 285–3698.

In burgeoning Bozeman head to the **Museum of the Rockies,** considered one of the top ten museums in the West. Known particularly for its dinosaur collection, the museum also boasts excellent exhibits on Lewis and Clark, the trappers and explorers, and many other subjects. Outside are the 1889 Tinsley Homestead house and outbuildings, transplanted from Willow Creek, which provide a living-history look at the everyday lives of a successful Montana homesteading family. The museum is situated on the campus of Montana State University at 600 West Kagy Boulevard. It is open daily Monday through Saturday from 9:00 A.M. to 5:00 P.M. and on Sunday from 12:30 to 5:00 P.M. Tours of historic Bozeman, in a restored 1936 Yellowstone National Park touring bus, originate at the museum, too. Call (406) 994–DINO (3466) for information.

Overnighting opportunities in Bozeman include the elegant, circa-1883 **Voss Inn,** at 319 South Willson. Each of the six guest rooms has a private bath, and the majestically appointed guest parlor makes afternoon tea an irresistible affair. Call (406) 587–0982 for reservations.

Compelling displays on the mountain men, Native Americans, and U.S. Cavalry are found at the **Museum of the Yellowstone** (406–646–7814) in West Yellowstone. Perhaps the most compelling of all the displays is the Famous Indian Portrait Gallery, with its vintage photographs of the great chiefs of the Nez Perce, Cheyenne, Blackfeet, and other tribes. The museum, located at 124 Yellowstone Avenue, is open daily between May and

October from 8:00 A.M. to 10:00 P.M. The **Burnt Hole Rendezvous,** a gathering of modern-day mountain men and women, includes a traders' row, a black-powder shooting competition, and a frying-pan throw. It takes place in late August outside West Yellowstone; for information call the Chamber of Commerce at (406) 646–7701.

From Mammoth Hot Springs in the northwest corner of Yellowstone National Park, follow the dancing Yellowstone River north into the glorious Paradise Valley. The **Ranch Kitchen,** in Corwin Springs, is owned and operated by the Church Universal and Triumphant, a controversial New Age religious group, which calls the Paradise Valley home. There's no controversy surrounding the quality of the food served here: It's doggone good, home-grown home cookin'. On Fridays and Saturdays between Memorial Day and Labor Day, the evening buffet is followed at 7:00 P.M. by the Old West entertainment of the **Paradise Players.** The Ranch Kitchen is open noon to 2:00 P.M. for lunch and 5:00 to 8:30 P.M. for supper; it is closed Tuesday. For information and reservations call (406) 848–7891.

After detouring at Emigrant to soak in the hot water and Western ambience of **Chico Hot Springs** (406–333–4933), pull into Livingston and up to the **Depot Center,** at 200 West Park Street. Built in 1901–2 for $75,000, the imposing old Northern Pacific station is one of Montana's most impressive structures. The depot began to suffer after the railroad abandoned it in the 1980s, so the Livingston Depot Foundation was formed to raise the funds necessary to restore it to its original grandeur. The foundation was unquestionably successful, and today you'll find on the inside exquisitely displayed Western and Native American art, artifacts, and photographs. Traveling exhibits are commonly brought in, such as the recent "Beautiful, Daring Western Girls: Women of the Wild West" show. (Livingston was an appropriate place for the display, for early residents included the likes of Calamity Jane.) For more information on the Depot Center, call (406) 222–2300.

Saddle up for the **Sixty Three Ranch,** nestled against the precipitous Absaroka Mountains, 12 miles southeast of Livingston. The ranch, which began running cattle in 1863 (hence its name), has been in the hands of the Christensen family since 1929, and in 1982 it became the first Montana dude ranch listed as a National Historic Site. Some of the diversions at hand include photography workshops, horseback riding, bird-watching, and fishing on Mission Creek, which bubbles and gurgles across the ranch for a lengthy 3½ miles. Square dancing and "sweat lodging" are a couple of popular evening activities. A week-long package at the traditional dude ranch includes a private cabin, three meals per day, and the use of a saddle horse and all ranch facilities. Call (406) 222–0570 for reservations.

Nine miles east of Clyde Park, which is 20 miles north of Livingston, the "town" of **DeadRock** sprawls across part of a working ranch nestled below the splendid Crazy Mountains. Guests can hide out in one of the old-West settlement's two lodges or four cabins, far from the worries of the world (as long as they leave behind their computers and cellular phones). Trout fishing in the ranch's forty-acre lake, mountain biking, and horseback riding and packtrips are all popular pursuits in summer, while winter attracts snowmobilers and cross-country skiers. During the fall DeadRock offers outstanding pheasant hunting. Call (406) 686–4428 or (888) 332–3762 for additional information or to make reservations.

Downtown Big Timber features a number of Victorian brick buildings, raised during the town's early days as a cattle railhead. The **Grand Bed and Breakfast** was built as a hotel in 1890, when it served as a center for social gatherings and as a home-away-from-home to those arriving by rail. Recently renovated, the Grand has ten rooms for rent, most with a private bath. For reservations call (406) 932–4459. Big Timber's **C. Sharps Arms,** at 100 Centennial, displays the guns that won the West, as well as accessories manufactured in the 1870s by Sharps and Winchester. It's open to visitors weekdays from 8:00 A.M. to 5:00 P.M. Call (406) 932–4353 for more information.

For an up-close and personal look at some of Montana's most splendid scenery—and at some of its real working cowboys—head for the **Road Kill Cafe,** 16 miles south of Big Timber near tiny McLeod. Bear scat (deep-fried cheese balls) and a beer never tasted so good, and the jukebox kicks out lively country tunes at the Road Kill. The McLeod area also hides a cluster of classic dude ranches, including the **Boulder River Ranch** (406–932–6406) and the **Hawley Mountain Guest Ranch** (406–932–5791).

The streets of tiny Reedpoint serve as the venue for the **Big Montana Sheep Drive,** which, according to some spectators, is matched only by the running of the bulls in Pamplona, Spain. A sheepherder-poetry reading, a sheep-shearing contest, and competitions for the prettiest ewe and smelliest sheepherder are all part of the woolly affair, held the first Sunday in September.

Leave Interstate 90 at Columbus and head south on Highway 78, passing along the mountain-embraced irrigated hayfields that line the Stillwater River. In the spot on the map known as Dean, 8 miles southwest of Fishtail, check out the trio of establishments collectively known as **Montana Hanna's.** The **Trout Hole Restaurant** serves fabulous soups and steaks in surroundings appointed with Western artifacts, and the **Stillwater Saloon** and **Coyote Corner Crafts Shoppe** round out the scene. Call (406) 328–6780 for information.

The **Grizzly Bar,** located in Roscoe, is another establishment whose bounty is well worth the tasting. Its interior is pure Montana, with local cattle brands burnt into the knotty-pine woodwork. Outside, the East Rosebud River gurgles by, and a life-sized grizzly bears down on those entering. Call (406) 328–6789 for dinner reservations.

In the mountain village of Red Lodge, a curious but irresistible mix of Old West and Old World, visit the **Carbon County Historical Museum.** Included is the homesteading cabin of legendary mountain man John Johnston, better known as "Liver Eatin' Johnson," who served a spell as the first marshal of Red Lodge. Also included are exhibits on the rodeoin' Greenough family, whose rich legacy of riders now includes 1993 Professional Rodeo Cowboys Association (PRCA) bareback champ Deb Greenough. The museum, located at the south end of town, is open daily Memorial Day through Labor Day.

To be tempted by some neo-Western furniture and art, swing into **Kibler and Kirch,** at 22 North Broadway. Log-and-iron furniture, cowboy picture frames, willow baskets, and a lot more are ready for the buying. Before leaving the Red Lodge vicinity, detour to the top of Beartooth Pass on the **Beartooth National Scenic Byway.** Indisputably one of North America's most spectacular roads, the byway pokes through some of the wildest Western country surviving. For a detailed tour brochure, call the U.S. Forest Service at (406) 446–2103.

Southeast Montana

Begin touring the Magic City, as Billings is known, by driving up Twenty-seventh Street onto the rimrocks to enjoy the view and find your way along the chuck-holed Black Otter Trail to **Yellowstone Kelly's Grave.** Here a sign reads:

> *A long breach-loading Springfield rifle covered from muzzle to stock with the skin of a huge bullsnake was carried by Major Luther Sage "Yellowstone" Kelly, Shakespeare-quoting Indian fighter and scout. Kelly, a New Yorker born April 19, 1849, and Civil War veteran, guided government expeditions in the 1870s and '80s in the Yellowstone River Valley. . . . He asked to be buried on this point overlooking the area he had scouted. . . . Yellowstone Kelly was the little big man with a big heart.*

The castlelike **Moss Mansion,** with its stone-block construction and distinctive red-tile roof, remains virtually unchanged from the day in 1903 when the Preston B. Moss family moved in. Finely woven Persian rugs and woodwork of polished mahogany, oak, and red birch lend the home a rich vibrancy. For decades the place was shrouded in mystery, as Miss Melville Moss continued living there alone, hermitlike, after the rest of her family had passed away. When she died in 1984 at the age of eighty-eight, Billings residents finally had the opportunity to see what they'd been missing: The mansion's elegance stunned them, and a community-wide determination quickly mounted to save the grand home. No secret today, even Hollywood has discovered the Moss Mansion; several scenes from *Son of the Morning Star* were shot in its interior. Visitors are welcome at the mansion, located at 914 Division Street, Tuesday through Sunday. For information call (406) 256–5100.

"A thousand smiles and a million memories" await at the **Huntley Project Museum of Irrigated Agriculture,** in Homesteader Park, 3 miles east of Huntley. The museum features artifacts used in the early days of farming and irrigation, and details how this arid country was converted into the lush, crop-filled valley seen today. Among the best times to visit is the third weekend in July, when the Huntley Project Lions Club hosts its **Homesteader Days** at Homesteader Park.

Pompeys Pillar National Historic Landmark rises from the prairie 16 miles northeast of Huntley. On April 25, 1806, as he was returning to the East, Captain William Clark carved his name on the face of the butte, where it can still be seen today. Clark wrote that from the summit he could see the Bull Mountains to the northwest and the snow-capped Rockies to the southwest, while huge numbers of buffalo, elk, and wolves moved about on the prairie before him.

Captain Clark named the feature Pompy's Tower, in honor of Baptiste Charbonneau, the young son of Sacajawea, whom Clark had nicknamed

Plenty Coups

Plenty Coups was born near the present location of Billings in 1848, and he died in 1932. At his grave, where two of his wives—Strikes the Iron and Kills Together—also are buried, an American flag flutters atop a tall pole, reminding us that here lies not only a heroic Indian chief but a great American.

When chosen to represent all Indians of the Americas in a ceremony at the Tomb of the Unknown Soldier in 1921, Plenty Coups's brief speech was said to have brought tears to the eyes of more than one tough old cavalryman:

For the Indians of America I call upon the Great Spirit . . . that the dead should not have died in vain, the war might end and peace be purchased by the blood of red men and white.

Plenty Coups was a proud man who had come to terms with the whites, realizing that to keep fighting them would, in the long term, hurt the Crow people more than help them. When deeding his property to the nation in 1928, Plenty Coups mandated that it must become a park for all people to use together. "It is given as a token of my friendship for all people, both red and white," he said, further stipulating that the park was not to be a memorial to him, but to the Crow Nation in its entirety.

"Pompy," or "little chief" in Shoshonean. The name was changed to Pompeys Pillar when Lewis and Clark's journals were published in 1814. The site was recently obtained by the Bureau of Land Management (BLM) and is open to the public daily, Memorial Day through Labor Day, from 8:00 A.M. to 8:00 P.M. For information call (406) 875–2233.

From the Lockwood interchange on Interstate 90 (exit 452), go south for ¹/₂ mile, and turn right onto Old Pryor Road, which quickly leads into a folded land of sandstone cliffs, timbered buttes, and verdant bottomlands, the historic home of nomadic Plains Indians and immense buffalo herds. Turn right after 10 miles, following Old Pryor Road. Then in the Crow Indian village of Pryor, after another 23 miles, find your way to the **Chief Plenty Coups Memorial.**

The park, which celebrates the last great war chief of the Crows, is a tranquil spot: Pryor Creek gurgles below a stand of box elders, and black-capped chickadees—revealed through Plenty Coups's dreams as his own good medicine—flutter about. The museum displays Plenty Coups's personal items and others from the Crow culture. Nearby is the chief's stout, square-hewn log house, raised in 1885 around a chimney of bricks salvaged from Fort Custer. The memorial is open from 8:00 A.M. to 8:00 P.M. daily, May through September, and October through April by appointment. For more information call (406) 252–1289.

Southeast of Pryor dirt and gravel roads lead to the **Pryor Mountain Wild Horse Range,** home to what some say are direct descendants of the mustangs brought to America in the 1500s by the Spanish conquistadors. This is wild country, and the roads can be impassable when wet, so before striking out stock up on water and supplies and call (406) 657–6361 or 666–2412 for up-to-date maps and information.

Along the east side of the deep cleft in the earth known as Bighorn Canyon, the **Yellowtail Visitor Center** is operated by the National Park Service. Here you can learn about the region's rich prehistory and perhaps pick up a tip on where to hike to locate an ancient *pishkun* (buffalo jump) or vision-quest site. You can also arrange for a ranger-led tour to the privately held site of Fort C. E. Smith, established in 1866 to protect Bozeman Trail travelers from Indian attacks. The visitor center is open daily from 9:00 A.M. to 5:00 P.M. Memorial Day through Labor Day and from 10:00 A.M. to 4:30 P.M. during the remainder of the year. Camping is available in the area, where the boating and fishing opportunities are world class. Call (406) 666–3234 for information.

On June 25, 1876, at the site of the **Little Bighorn Battlefield National Monument** (formerly Custer Battlefield), Gen. George Armstrong Custer lost his entire detachment of 210 soldiers when they were boxed in by Sioux and Northern Cheyenne warriors. (The only U.S. Army survivor was a horse named Comanche.) Although the battle was a resounding victory for the Indians, the net result for them was far more negative: Custer's defeat so embittered and unified the nation that the government became more committed than ever to making the frontier safe for whites. The Army jacked up its presence, and within a few short months the Sioux and Cheyenne were compelled to surrender their struggle.

The Custer Battlefield monument was created in 1879, in what was perhaps the only war memorial named for a losing general. Fairness prevailed in December 1991, however, when the name was changed to reflect less bias. The National Park Service has re-created the world-famous battle via displays, signs, and tape recordings that are so realistic that one can almost hear the reports of rifles and screams of soldiers and Indians and smell a tinge of gunpowder on the breeze. Exhibits at the visitor center focus on findings from archaeological excavations undertaken during the 1980s, work that shed radically new light on the battle. Rangers also guide daily bus tours, which offer the best way to come to understand and appreciate the battle, the conditions that led up to it, and the events that followed.

Little Bighorn National Monument is just west of Interstate 90 from a point 2 miles south of Crow Agency. The visitor center is open from 8:00 A.M. to 8:00 P.M. Memorial Day through Labor Day, from 8:00 A.M. to 6:00 P.M. during spring and autumn, and from 8:00 A.M. to 4:30 P.M. during winter. Call (406) 638–2621 for more information.

Crow Fair heats up on the third weekend in August at Crow Agency, the Tipi Capital of the World. The fair boasts a world-class rodeo and performances that include bareback riding by the Crows, considered the best horsemen among the Plains Indians. Crow Fair also includes one of the premier powwows for all of North America's native peoples; members of tribes come from afar for the dance competitions. Crow Fair is held at the tribal campgrounds along the Little Bighorn River. You can't miss it; just look for the city of tipis that flood the bottomlands.

In Hardin visit the **Big Horn County Historical Museum and Visitor Center,** which incorporates eleven buildings on twenty-four acres. Old-time goodies abound, such as early farm machinery and railroading memorabilia, and within view is the site of old Fort Custer. The museum, located just off Interstate 90 at exit 497, is open daily during the summer from 8:00 A.M. to 8:00 P.M. Call (406) 665–1671 for information.

The renowned **Custer's Last Stand Reenactment** takes place several times during Hardin's four-day **Little Big Horn Days,** held in late June. The script, historical notes for which were provided by Crow tribal historian Joe Medicine Crow, reenacts the story of the fateful battle from the Indian perspective. The drama, with a cast of 300 that includes direct descendants of both Indians and whites who took part in the battle, tells the story of Custer's plan to divide his regiment into three parts and how the plan backfired. The drama culminates in a furious, breath-stealing battle. For information call the Hardin Chamber of Commerce at (406) 665–1672.

In Miles City (120 miles northeast of Hardin on Highway 47 and Interstate 94) aim straight for the **Range Riders Museum and Memorial Hall,** dedicated to the great American cowboy and cowgirl. Miles City became the queen of eastern Montana cowtowns after the Northern Pacific Railway arrived in 1881, and herds were driven from afar to the railhead here. (The television miniseries *Lonesome Dove* was based on a cattle drive from Texas to Miles City.)

The Miles City area has produced some of the country's best bronc riders, and the group known as the Range Riders formed in the late 1930s to preserve and promote that heritage. There's much to be seen at their center; Memorial Hall, for instance, displays plaques that honor some 500 pioneer cowboys, and the vaultlike Gun Building features a priceless, 500-piece collection of firearms donated by the Bert Clark family. The museum is found at the west end of Main Street, at the site of Gen. Nelson A. Miles's Cantonment #1, built in 1873 to serve as a temporary quarters for soldiers who were awaiting the construction of nearby Fort Keogh. It's open daily between April 1 and October 31 from 8:00 A.M. to 8:00 P.M. and by appointment the rest of the year. For more information call (406) 232–4483.

The Jaycees' **World Famous Bucking Horse Sale,** held the third weekend in May, is a celebration equaled in renown by few others in Montana. Miles City pulls out all the stops for this one; round-the-clock festivities include a wild-horse drive, street dances, cowboy-poetry readings, barbecues, rodeo, and much, much more. "Buck-outs" are regularly contested, with the wildest, orneriest, and buckingest horses drawing top dollar from rodeo-stock contractors from throughout North America. For information on the always-popular Bucking Horse Sale, call the Miles City Chamber of Commerce at (406) 232–2890 and book your room early!

A trio of Main Street musts before hitting the dusty trail: the **Montana Bar** at 612 Main Street, a true Old West saloon; the **Miles City Saddlery,** Montana's largest Western store, at 808 Main Street; and **Riggs Camera and Gifts,** just across the street, which sells reproductions of works by early photographers, including Evelyn Cameron and Christian Barthelmess, who was called "Shadow Catcher" by the Native Americans he captured on film. His photographs also include shots of early Fort Keough.

For further details on Miles City and information on the remains of **Fort Keogh** and its living-history **Fort Keogh Days,** call the Chamber of Commerce at (406) 232–2890.

Terry's **Prairie County Museum,** occupying the marble-floored 1915 State Bank of Terry building, houses the compelling **World of Evelyn Cameron** photographic display. Cameron, an Englishwoman, came to the Terry area in 1889 with her naturalist husband, Ewen (whose biggest claim to fame was bagging Montana's Boone and Crockett record grizzly bear, in the Missouri Breaks in 1890). Cameron took up photography in 1894, and for the next three decades incessantly lugged around her cumbersome 5 x 7 Graflex camera and associated paraphernalia, photographing the eastern Montana landscape. Excerpts from Lady Cameron's biography, *Photographing Montana (1894–1928): The Life and Works of Evelyn Cameron,* by Donna Lucey, appear alongside the vivid images of cowboys, wolves, farm wives, buggies, and sheepherders. The museum is located at 204 South Logan; for more information call (406) 637–5575.

Northeast Montana

Back in Miles City pull onto lonesome Highway 59 north and into that part of Montana known as The Big Dry or The Big Open. In Jordan, the most isolated county seat in the contiguous United States, check out the fossil-rich **Garfield County Museum,** open daily from 1:00 to 6:00 P.M., June through Labor Day. The **Hell Creek Guest Ranch,** north of Jordan near the Hell Creek Arm of expansive Fort Peck Lake, is a remote badlands spread, homesteaded in 1913 by Elmer Trumbo. Trumbo's son, John, and several of the original buildings remain to greet visitors today. Hell Creek offers ranch-style home cooking and rustic-yet-modern accommodations, with hiking, photography, and fossil digging some of the readily available diversions. In the fall ranch hands guide hunters in pursuit of wild turkey, elk, and trophy mule deer. Hell Creek Guest Ranch is located 21 miles north of Jordan; for reservations and additional information, call (406) 557–2224.

The cattle are milling, dawn's a-breaking over the prairie, and the rich aroma of cowboy coffee is tempting you out of your sleeping bag . . . while the chill in the morning air is tempting you to stay put. The **Foss Cattle Drive,** headquartered in Culbertson, obliges its partakers by permitting them to work as much or as little as they choose, and they can ride on horseback or buckboard, or a combination of both. Meals, created out of the horse-drawn chuckwagon, are sized for a wrangler's appetite. For information call (406) 787–5559.

Sitting Bull surrendered to U.S. troops in July 1881 near the present site of Plentywood, in the extreme northeast corner of the state, and a monument to the great Sioux chief stands sentinel at the **Sheridan County Museum,** located at the entrance to the county fairgrounds. Not long after the Sioux were subdued, outlaws, including Butch Cassidy's infamous Wild Bunch, traveled through the area on the Outlaw Trail, occasionally holing up in the rough breaks of the Big Muddy River valley. You can find out more about the Indians, outlaws, and homesteaders at the museum, open daily May through September.

In Wolf Point, 100 miles southwest of Plentywood on Highways 16 and 2, Native American and white cowboys and cowgirls whoop it up at the **Wild Horse Stampede,** the grandaddy of Montana rodeos, first held in 1915. The wild-horse race, an uncommon addition to more typical rodeo events, features teams of three that compete to be the first to saddle and ride an unbroken horse to the finish line. The three-day festival, held over the second full weekend in July, also includes parades and Indian cultural displays. For more information call (406) 653–2012.

The showpiece of the **Valley County Pioneer Museum** in Glasgow,

50 miles west of Wolf Point on Highway 2, is the **Stan Kalinski Collection.** The collection, for years on display at Stan's Bar on Front Street, includes some 300 mounted animals, including the head of a bison that was butchered for the feast that honored Franklin Roosevelt's visit to Glasgow in the 1930s. Stan's ornate Buffalo Bill Cody bar—bullet hole and all—resides here, too. The museum, open from Memorial Day through Labor Day, is hard to miss; it's the only building on Highway 2 West with an Air Force jet protruding from the front.

"My god man! It would cost a million dollars to build a dam across there!" are the words attributed to Glasgow mayor Leo B. Coleman when informed of the U.S. Corps of Engineers' plan to build a dam across the Missouri River near his town. The **Fort Peck Dam** was built, however, and Coleman was way off—it cost nearly $150 million to build it, along with the lives of six men who were killed in a slide and who remain buried in the dam today.

The huge Depression public-works project became the largest earth-filled dam in the United States, with embankments reaching 4 miles across the Missouri. The lake it impounds claims a mind-boggling 1,520 miles of shoreline. During construction eighteen boomtowns, with a combined population of nearly 40,000, exploded where previously only a few hundred farmers had scratched meager livings. The sight moved Pulitzer Prize winner Ernie Pyle to write:

You have to see the town of Wheeler to believe it . . . it is today the wildest wild-west town in North America. Except for the autos, it is a genuine throwback to the '80s, to Tombstone and Dodge City.

The beautiful Swiss-chalet-style **Fort Peck Theatre,** built in the 1930s for showing movies to the dam workers and their families, today is home to the Fort Peck Summer Theatre. Professional shows, many with an Old West twist, are performed from mid-June through August on Friday, Saturday, and Sunday evenings at 8:00 P.M. For information call (800) 828–2259, extension 185. Tours of Fort Peck Dam and environs are given on the hour from 9:00 A.M. to 5:00 P.M. Call the Corps of Engineers at (406) 526–3431 for more information.

North Central Montana

En route to Lewistown, consider driving the **Missouri Breaks Back Country Byway** to view wild country virtually unchanged since Lewis and Clark passed through. The Missouri River and adjacent breaks comprise a diverse range of habitats; you've a good chance, for instance, of seeing prairie elk in the river bottoms and bighorn sheep atop the ridges and in the timbered coulees.

Note: The 65-mile loop is suitable for passenger cars in dry weather only. The gumbo clay of the Missouri Breaks is notorious for becoming impassable when wet, and people have been stranded for days in the bottoms. Go equipped with plenty of provisions and water, and before striking out call the BLM at (406) 538–7461 to acquire a detailed map and brochure.

Cowboy poetry, a uniquely Western art form, reflects on the life of the range rider, and the emotions it triggers range from joy to heartbreak. To hear it read by those who write it, mosey into Lewistown for the annual **Montana Cowboy Poetry Gathering,** held in mid-August at the Park Inn. Rhymin' wranglers from across Montana and beyond gather to share their poetry and music and to participate in workshops and social activities. Sessions are conducted for cowboy-poetry first-timers and old-timers alike. Call (406) 538–5436 for more information.

Head west on Highway 87, which dips and twists through the heart-stopping, lonesome beauty of the Judith Basin country. Windham's **Sod Buster Museum** (406–423–5358), at the Zimmer Ranch, makes for an interesting stop. In the Utica area several guest ranches beckon: Among these are the **Homestead Ranch** (406–423–5301), and the **Circle Bar Guest Ranch** (406–423–5454).

Turn north onto Highway 80 at Stanford, home to July's **C. M. Russell Stampede Rodeo.** Some 30 miles later you'll skirt the imposing **Square Butte,** used prehistorically as a vision-quest site by Native Americans and now home to a whopping array of critters. The feature appears as a backdrop in several of Charlie Russell's paintings.

Fort Benton, at one time unflatteringly known as "the bloodiest block in the West," has more recently been nicknamed the "Birthplace of Montana." The development of broad-bottom steamboats in the 1850s permitted travel into the treacherous upper reaches of the Missouri River, and by the mid-1860s Fort Benton had become a vital port, controlling trade between the eastern markets and the goldfields of southwest Montana.

Along Fort Benton's riverfront main street, you'll find the **Lewis and Clark State Memorial,** one of master sculptor Bob Scriver's finest works. Cast larger than life, Clark, Lewis, and Sacajawea stand sentinel over the river they traced westward for so many hundreds of miles. Directly in front of the memorial, mired in river mud, lie the sunken remains of the *Baby Rose,* one of the last steamboats to wend its way to Fort Benton.

Also nearby, and much more visible, is the replica of the keelboat *Mandan,* built for the filming of a movie based on A. B. Guthrie's *The Way West.* The **Museum of the Upper Missouri,** open from mid-May through mid-September, focuses on the period between the 1840s and the late 1880s, when the railroad finally pushed through, effectively ending river trade. One highlight is an 1860s trapper's cabin, transported from its original site on the Teton River. The facility is situated at the edge of well-shaded **Old Fort Park,** site of the town's original fur-trading post. Call the Chamber of Commerce at (406) 622–3864 for more information. Farther up the street toward downtown is the BLM's **Lewis & Clark National Historic Trail** headquarters, featuring associated displays.

On October 5, 1877, one of America's epic journeys ended at Snake Creek in the Bear's Paw Mountains at the site known today as the **Bear's Paw Battlefield** (406–357–3130), 16 miles south of Chinook on Highway 240. Chief Joseph of the Nez Perce had seen enough of death and bloodshed, and it was here he was reported to have said:

> *It is cold and we have no blankets. The little children are freezing to death.... Hear me, my chiefs! I am tired. My heart is sick and sad. From where the sun now stands, I will fight no more forever.*

Chinook's **Blaine County Museum** (406–357–2590) runs interpretive tours to the site and also offers an audiovisual presentation on the subject, entitled *40 Miles from Freedom.* The museum, located at 501 Indiana Street,

The Lewis and Clark State Memorial

is open May 1 to September 30, Monday through Saturday from 8:00 A.M. to 5:00 P.M. (closed noon to 1:00 P.M. for lunch) and on Sundays from noon to 5:00 P.M.

The territory north of the Missouri River and east of the Rocky Mountains in Montana is known as the Hi-Line, a term used to describe both the route of the Great Northern Railway and the countryside surrounding it. At the edge of Havre, the Hi-Line's largest community, the 2,000-year-old **Wahkpa Chu'gn Archaeological Site** fascinates those who visit. The site, used throughout prehistory by at least three different cultural groups, includes both a traditional buffalo jump, or *pishkun,* and a pound. Pounds were traps—sometimes appointed with sharpened, upward-pointing sticks—into which the Indians herded individual and small groups of bison.

Tours to the site leave every Tuesday and Thursday evening in the sum-

The End of a Gallant Journey

The Bear's Paw Battlefield is a spot that seems little changed since 1877: Snake Creek still twists across the swath of barren prairie, willow thickets crowding the banks. Its peaceful nature belies a turbulent past.

When Chief Joseph and the Nez Perce surrendered to Col. Nelson A. Miles at the Bear's Paw, it ended their arduous, often brilliant, trek of 1,500 miles. The journey began in Oregon's Wallowa Valley; from there the Indians passed through northern Idaho, meandered through Montana's Bitterroot and Big Hole valleys, progressed into Yellowstone National Park, and reentered Montana. After unsuccessfully garnering sanctuary with their Crow Indian allies, the Indians continued north, intending ultimately to join Sitting Bull in Canada.

But they were caught in the Bear's Paw Mountains, 40 miles short of the border. Although, after several days of fighting, the Indians were still holding off the soldiers, the chiefs couldn't agree on their next move. Ultimately 300 Nez Perce followed Chief Lookingglass to Canada, and Chief Joseph surrendered for the rest.

mer from the **H. Earl Clack Memorial Museum** at the Hill County Fairgrounds. On display at the museum itself are a collection of artifacts from Wahkpa Chu'gn, an exhibit on the Minnesota-Montana homesteading migration, and a history that details the Prohibition-era Bootlegger chain, which ran between Havre and Canada. The museum (406–265–4000) is open May 15 through September 15 from 9:00 A.M. to 9:00 P.M.

Browning, the eastern gateway to Glacier National Park and headquarters for the Blackfeet Nation, is home to the **Museum of the Plains Indian.** The museum showcases the arts, crafts, and cultural artifacts of the Blackfeet and other Plains tribes, including the Crow, Northern Cheyenne, and Sioux. The sales shop, operated by the Indian-owned Northern Plains Indian Crafts Association, offers a broad selection of contemporary Native American products. The museum (406–338–2230) is open daily June through September from 9:00 A.M. to 5:00 P.M. and, the remainder of the year, Monday through Friday from 10:00 A.M. to 4:30 P.M.

North American Indian Days take place in July at the Blackfeet Tribal Fairgrounds, next to the museum. The event, which brings together Indian tribes and white visitors from throughout North America, includes dancing, sporting events, and more. Call (406) 338–7276 or 338–7840 for information. Also in Browning, the **Bob Scriver Studio & Wildlife Museum** (406–338–5425) features the work of Montana's best-known Western sculptor, as well as that of other artists. It's open daily May through September from 8:00 A.M. to 5:00 P.M.

The city of Great Falls, 128 miles southeast of Browning on Highway 89, was named for the Great Falls of the Missouri River, a source of great concern for the Lewis and Clark expedition. Their portage route, now a National Historic Landmark, can be followed by obtaining the self-guiding tour brochure *The Explorers at the Portage.* The city celebrates its annual **Lewis and Clark Festival** in late June, with river tours, visits to expedition sites, buffalo-hump barbecues, running races, and presentations of *Proceeding On,* a drama based on the party's journals. For information on the festival or to obtain the tour brochure, call the Great Falls Visitors Bureau at (406) 761–4434.

The name "Russell" is celebrated in Great Falls and throughout Montana, and the **C. M. Russell Museum Complex** houses the world's largest collection of Russell's works and belongings. The 46,000-square-foot museum includes seven galleries, holding originals by Russell and several other Western artists. The impressive Browning Firearms Collection is also found

A typical "Big Sky" landscape not far from Great Falls

within the museum, and the Museum Store offers Russell reproductions and other artwork and books for sale.

Next door are Russell's log-cabin studio and the house in which Charlie and Nancy Russell lived from 1900 until he died in 1926. In his studio Russell was often known to boil up a pot of bubbling cowboy beans and enjoy the companionship of friends as he painted. The cabin is packed with cowboy tack, Indian goods, buffalo skulls, and other items that Russell studied in order to accurately depict the rapidly disappearing Western frontier.

The museum, located at 400 Thirteenth Street, is open from May 1 through September 30 on Monday through Saturday from 9:00 A.M. to 6:00 P.M. and on Sunday from 1:00 to 5:00 P.M. During the rest of the year, it's open from 10:00 A.M. to 5:00 P.M. Tuesday through Saturday and from 1:00 to 5:00 P.M. on Sunday. In March the museum hosts the annual **C. M. Russell Auction of Original Western Art,** a fund-raiser that attracts

America's Cowboy Artist

Charles Marion Russell was born in 1864 in St. Louis, the Gateway to the West. When, at sixteen, he set out for the Montana plains to become a cowboy, his parents assumed he'd get it out of his system and quickly return home, but young Charlie fell in love with the place and lived out his life there.

After cowboying for a decade in places like the Pigs Eye Basin, in 1892 Russell moved to Great Falls, where he set up his studio and began producing paintings. Most of these depicted the open-range period of Montana's cattle industry, and they earned him the title of "America's Cowboy Artist." Russell made the landscape south and west of Great Falls familiar to people far beyond the borders of Montana.

Charlie Russell became incredibly popular—almost synonymous with wild Montana—and successful far beyond his own expectations because of his uncanny talent for re-creating on canvas the things he'd seen and experienced; his down-to-earth nature; and his wife, Nancy, who possessed the sense for marketing that Russell himself apparently lacked.

Charlie Russell was the kind of celebrity that is all too rare today, a modest one. Just before dying he wrote: "To have talent is no credit to its owner; any man that can make a living doing what he likes is lucky, and I'm that. Any time I cash in now, I win."

Western-art aficionados from throughout the world. For more information call (406) 727–8787.

Before leaving Great Falls check out the **Montana Cowboys Association Museum** (406–761–9299), at 311 Third Street Northwest, where cowboy trappings and Old West memorabilia are copiously displayed.

Where better to end a visit to the paradise of Montana than at the **Heaven on Earth Ranch**? This peaceful getaway, located on the Smith River 55 miles south of Great Falls, offers Old West afternoons filled with fishing, wagon rides, target shooting, photography outings, steak dinners, and, get this, golfing, on perhaps the most remote and underutilized course in North America. Call (406) 452–7365 for information on an unforgettable day trip.

Where to Eat

Diamond K Chuckwagon, Whitefish, (406) 862–8828
Yesterday's Calf-A, Dell, (406) 276–3308
The Oxford, Missoula, (406) 549–0117
Willow Creek Cafe, Willow Creek, (406) 285–3698
Ranch Kitchen, Corwin Springs, (406) 848–7891
Chico Hot Springs, Emigrant, (406) 333–4933
Road Kill Cafe, McLeod, (406) 932–6174
Trout Hole Restaurant, Fishtail, (406) 328–6780
Grizzly Bar, Roscoe, (406) 328–6789

Where to Stay

Hargrave Cattle & Guest Ranch, outside Marion, (406) 858–2284
KwaTaqNuk Resort, Polson, (406) 883–3636
West Fork Meadows Ranch, outside Darby, (406) 349–2468
El Western Motel, Ennis, (406) 682–4217
Nevada City Hotel, Virginia City–Nevada City, (406) 843–5377
Fairweather Inn, Virginia City–Nevada City, (406) 843–5377
Daylight Creek Motel, Virginia City–Nevada City, (406) 843–5377
Sanders Bed & Breakfast, Helena, (406) 442–3309
Sacajawea Inn, Three Forks, (406) 285–6515
Voss Inn, Bozeman, (406) 587–0982
Chico Hot Springs, Emigrant, (406) 333–4933
Sixty Three Ranch, outside Livingston, (406) 222–0570
DeadRock, outside Clyde Park, (406) 686–4428 or (888) 332–3762
Grand Bed & Breakfast, Big Timber, (406) 932–4459
Boulder River Ranch, outside McLeod, (406) 932–6406
Hawley Mountain Guest Ranch, outside McLeod, (406) 932–5791
Hell Creek Guest Ranch, outside Jordan, (406) 557–2224
Homestead Ranch, outside Utica, (406) 423–5301
Circle Bar Guest Ranch, outside Utica, (406) 423–5454

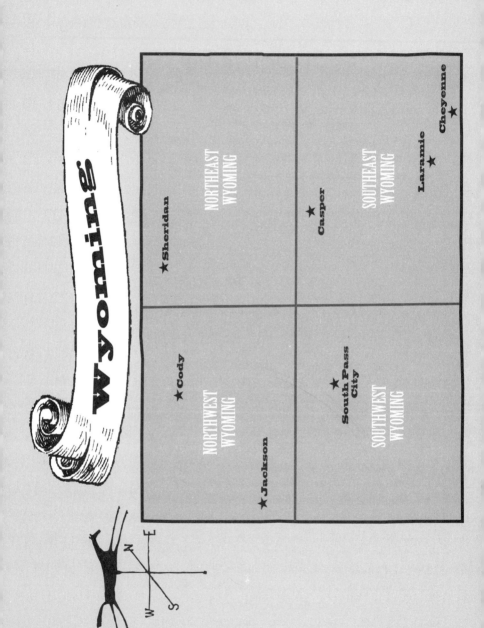

WYOMING

▼▼▼

YOMING is the Cowboy State, pure and simple. Consider the capital city, for instance: Cheyenne Frontier Days is the country's premier rodeo, and the 18-foot *Spirit of Wyoming,* a bronze statue of a cowboy fighting to stay on his rearing stallion, symbolically graces the grounds outside the capitol building.

Wyoming is a state of firsts: the first national park, first national forest, first national monument, and—what may seem paradoxical in a state that's always been full of "men's men"—the first state to grant women the right to vote. But there's also a "last" that Wyoming residents are proud of: Their state ranks fiftieth, dead last, in the number of people living there. Yes, there's plenty of elbow room in Wyoming.

The narrative begins in the northeast, then proceeds to the southeast, southwest, and, finally, the superlative northwest quadrant of the Cowboy State.

Northeast Wyoming

The lively and lovely town of Sheridan, situated at the foot of the Big Horn Mountain's east slope, is well known for its **Trail End Historic Site.** This state-run facility comprises the remarkably lavish 1913 home of former Governor and U.S. Senator John B. Kendrick, who came north in 1872 from his native Texas as a hired hand on a longhorn-cattle drive. Kendrick progressively bought up land and eventually became a cattle baron, riding herd on more than 200,000 acres in Wyoming and adjacent Montana. Located west of downtown at the north end of Kendrick Park, the mansion/museum is open daily from 9:00 A.M. to 6:00 P.M. in summer and from 1:00 to 4:00

P.M. in spring and autumn (closed December 15 through March 15). Call (307) 674–4589 for more information.

When a Wyoming cowboy isn't wearing a cowboy hat or sleeping, chances are he's wearing a King Ropes baseball-style cap. You can get yours at **King's Saddlery,** at 184 North Main, where a dividend for visiting is the excellent Western Museum in the back of the store. It's filled with old saddles, chaps, rifles, Indian artifacts, and more. The saddlery is open Monday through Saturday from 8:00 A.M. to 5:00 P.M. (Now that you're wearing your official hat, you're qualified to enter the **Mint Bar,** immediately across the street, a classic cowboy drinkery with animal-trophy wall hangings and shellacked-burlwood beams.)

Twelve miles southwest of Sheridan, near Big Horn on Highway 335, is another monument to big-time ranching: the **Bradford Brinton Memorial Ranch.** The highlight at the Quarter Circle A Ranch, as Brinton called it, is the twenty-room ranch house, filled to overflowing with relics of the Old West, including Brinton's world-class collection of Western books and art. Works by Charlie Russell, Frederic Remington, John James Audubon, and many others are displayed. The museum (307–672–3173) is open May 15 to Labor Day from 9:30 A.M. to 5:00 P.M., Monday through Saturday.

In Big Horn proper visit the **Big Horn Mercantile** and **Bozeman Trail Inn** tavern, both straight out of the early 1880s and still running. Mid-June's **Cowboy Round-Up** features Western storytelling, ranch-dog competitions, and more. It's the community's biggest to-do—other than when the queen of England comes to town, as she did in 1984, to visit and ride with the family of U.S. Senator Malcolm Wallop, who descends from British gentry. Wallop's Big Horn Equestrian Center, south of town on Bird Farm Road, is replete with America's oldest polo field.

Classic area dude ranches include the world-famous **Eaton's Guest Ranch** (307–655–9285 or 655–9552), an operation that has been running cattle along Wolf Creek since 1904 and is considered the grandaddy of dude ranches; and the **Spear-O-Wigwam Ranch** (307–674–4496 or 672–0002), sitting pretty high in the Big Horns (and where guest Ernest Hemingway reportedly wrapped up *A Farewell to Arms* in 1928).

As Montana-bound gold seekers traipsed through Sioux country north along what became known as the Bozeman Trail, the Powder River basin became central to the Indian wars of the 1860s. No frontier outpost in the

West saw a more violent time of it than **Fort Phil Kearney,** where between 200 and 300 soldiers were garrisoned to watch over the "Bloody Bozeman." The names ring in infamy: the Battle of Tongue River, the Wagon Box Fight, and the Fetterman Fight, all in the mid-1860s; and, several years after the Bozeman Trail had been closed and Fort Fetterman abandoned, then burned by the Sioux, the Dull Knife Battle, fought five months after Custer's demise at the Little Big Horn.

Today at Fort Phil Kearney, a national historic landmark managed by the state parks department and located off Interstate 90 at exit 44 between Sheridan and Buffalo, you'll find signs that mark the locations of the Bozeman Trail and the old post's buildings, as well as a visitor center/museum and the excavated remains of several foundations. The center is open daily from 8:00 A.M. to 6:00 P.M. mid-May through September and Wednesday through Sunday from noon to 4:00 P.M. the rest of the year, except for December through March, when it's closed. **Bozeman Trail Days** commemorate the fort's dark past with living-history reenactments, chuckwagon dining, and more. Call (307) 684-7629 for details and directions to the well-signed battle sites named above and other locations where you can stand in Bozeman Trail ruts.

Buffalo, at the center of sheep country, boasts the outstanding **Jim Gatchell Museum,** with its incomparable collection of more than 10,000 prehistoric Indian artifacts. Also within the two-building complex: a scale version of Fort Phil Kearney, a bonanza of historic photographs, and artifacts from the Fetterman Fight and the Little Big Horn, as well as from the infamous Johnson County War of 1892, which pitted absentee cattlemen who belonged to the Wyoming Stock Growers Association against nearly everyone else: local ranchers, homesteaders, even rustlers. The museum, located at the corner of Fort and Main streets, is open daily from 9:00 A.M. to 8:00 P.M. during the heart of summer, while May 15 through May 31 and September 1 through October 15 it's open from 9:00 A.M. to 5:00 P.M. Monday through Friday. Call (307) 684-9331 for further details.

Some 15 miles south toward Kaycee, you can hole up at the **TA Ranch** (307-684-5702), which is precisely what the "Invaders" (members of the Wyoming Stock Growers Association) did after attacking the KC Ranch during the Johnson County War. Ask to see the bullet holes from those violent times. (The KC Ranch was originally located at the site of present Kaycee's **Hoofprints of the Past Museum.)**

Southeast Wyoming

The oil-rich, misspelled town of Casper (it should be Caspar) is home to the intriguing **Fort Caspar,** a diamond in the rough. The 1930s WPA reconstruction of the original fort includes an Oregon Trail stage station, a sutler's store with Old (and new) West items for sale, and several other structures; during summer tours are led by guides dressed as 1860s cavalrymen. There's also a fine museum and a replica of the original Mormon ferry, built in 1847 to transport emigrants and their wagons across the swollen and dangerous North Platte River. Fort Caspar, located at the west end of Thirteenth Street in suburban Mills, is open in summer Monday through Saturday from 9:00 A.M. to 5:00 P.M. and on Sunday from noon to 5:00 P.M.; the rest of the year it's open Monday through Friday from 9:00 A.M. to 5:00 P.M. and on Sunday from 1:00 to 4:00 P.M. For additional details call (307) 235–8462.

Fort Caspar's **Mountain Man Rendezvous** attracts hordes of folks in early June, as does late July's **Platte Bridge Encampment.** Perennial performers include the acclaimed Casper Troopers Drum and Bugle Corps, known throughout the Rocky Mountain West and beyond.

Douglas, the epicenter of jackalope country, boasts the superlative **Wyoming Pioneer Museum,** located on the Wyoming State Fairgrounds. (Jackalopes, by the way, are those rare and odd creatures with the body of a rabbit and the antlers of a deer.) Old guns, rifles, tack (including a saddle that formerly belonged to Tom Horn), spent ammo from the Battle of the Little Big Horn, and Native American pots and other artifacts are all featured. The museum (307–358–9288) is open Monday through Friday from 8:00 A.M. to 5:00 P.M. and Saturday from 1:00 to 5:00 P.M.

Fort Fetterman State Historic Site, 6 miles northwest of Douglas on Highway 93, commemorates the frontier post established in 1867 and named for Brevet Lt. Col. William J. Fetterman, who died a year earlier at the hands of Red Cloud's Sioux warriors near Fort Phil Kearney, in what became known as the Fetterman Massacre. Fetterman had been a successful Civil War soldier; as Jim Bridger told him, however, "Your men who fought down South are crazy. They don't know anything about fighting Indians." Sure enough, Fetterman lost his entire attachment of eighty men, dispatched from Fort Phil Kearney, which represented the worst U.S. losses in the Indian wars until Custer's Last Stand, ten years later.

Situated along the Bozeman Trail and the last of Wyoming's frontier forts to be built, Fort Fetterman was called "Hell Hole" by the soldiers doing time there, whose only entertainment amid the wind-blown bleakness was found at the sin-central "hog farm" north of the North Platte, the down-and-dirtiest den of debauchery in the territory. A couple of original buildings remain at Fort Fetterman today, one of them housing a museum, open daily during summer from 9:00 A.M. to 5:00 P.M. Call (307) 358–2864 for further information. (Incidentally, Alferd Packer, the infamous Colorado cannibal, was apprehended in the Fort Fetterman vicinity in 1883. See p. 205.)

The proprietors of the **Pellatz Ranch,** perhaps taking their cue from Tom Sawyer, will actually let you pay to help them mend fences, shear sheep, and brand and move cattle. This 8,000-acre spread, located outside Douglas, also offers overnight trail rides and B&B accommodations. It doesn't get any more authentic than this. Call (307) 358–2380 for information and reservations.

The Cheyenne-to-Deadwood Stage Road, leading to the Black Hills goldfields, ran through Lusk, beginning in the late 1870s; later the Texas Cattle Trail skirted to the east, along which hundreds of thousands of longhorns were driven north to open range. Lusk's outstanding **Stagecoach Museum** interprets those trails and times and includes as its centerpiece an Abbott & Downing Coach that ran for years between Cheyenne and Deadwood. The museum, located at 342 South Main, is open daily in July and August and Monday through Friday in May, June, September, and October.

Oregon Trail evidence abounds in the Guernsey area, southwest of Lusk on Highway 18/20 and Highway 270. **Register Cliff,** south of town across the North Platte River, is a rock outcrop that contains a mishmash of graffiti that's a hundred-plus years old: names, dates, destinations, and other information. Closer to town is **Oregon Trail Ruts National Historic Landmark,** where wagon ruts, carved several feet deep in the sandstone, remain as perhaps the most vivid evidence anywhere of the mass migration west in the mid-1800s.

North of Guernsey in Hartville, the **Miners Bar,** reportedly the oldest libation house in the state, boasts a German cherrywood backbar, fabricated in 1864 and moved to here from Fort Laramie in 1881. Hartville's **Boot Hill Days,** held over the Labor Day weekend, includes shoot-outs in the streets and other events contested in the "spirit" of the local cemetery, where numerous men were buried with their boots on. North and east of Hartville is the 10-by-40-mile area known as **Spanish Diggings,** which brims with prehistoric quarry and camping sites, including the important Hell Gap paleo-Indian site.

Lonesome, windswept Fort Laramie, situated at the confluence of the Laramie and North Platte rivers, owns perhaps the most colorful history of any of the Western-frontier outposts. The fort began life in 1834 as Fort William, a fur-trading post established by and named for William Sublette. It quickly grew into the most important outfitting point along the entire network of the Oregon, Mormon, and California trails. In 1849 Fort Laramie became Wyoming's first garrisoned military post, commissioned as a base for both cavalry- and infantrymen. In its role as a military fort, Fort Laramie is perhaps best known as the signing place of the Treaty of 1868, which was among the most blatantly disregarded agreements ever forged between the U.S. government and Native Americans. The wording promised the Sioux the Powder River country "as long as the grass shall grow and the buffalo shall roam," a promise quickly broken after Gen. George Custer's exploratory party discovered Black Hills gold in 1874. (See South Dakota, p. 399.)

Just as hordes of emigrants filtered by in the 1840s and 1850s, thousands make the pilgrimage today to **Fort Laramie National Historic Site.** Operated by the National Park Service, the fort encompasses two dozen original structures, with rangers and docents milling about dressed in garb straight out of the eras through which Fort Laramie served a burgeoning frontier. The **Old Fashioned Fourth of July Celebration** and late August's **Native American Heritage Days** are particularly opportune times to visit. The visitor center at this 800-acre historic site is open daily year-round from 8:00 A.M. to 7:00 P.M. mid-May through mid-September and from 8:00 A.M. to 4:30 P.M. the remainder of the year. For more information call (307) 837–2221.

The name "Cheyenne" resounds through the chronicles of the Old West; here muleskinners and cattlemen rubbed elbows with railroad workers, rustlers, and early legislators and lawmen. It seems that all of Wyoming's residents and half of Colorado's mosey over and up to the capital city for the **Cheyenne Frontier Days,** the most prestigious buck-off in North America. Some 300,000 visitors—from all fifty states and several foreign countries—come every year to watch the country's top rodeoers and to observe or participate in associated events, which include wild-horse racing, chancy chuckwagon races, Indian dancing at the tipi village, square dancing,

Original Oregon Trail wagonwheel ruts

chili cook-offs, parades, running races, and more. If you get carried away amid all the revelry, you can even cleanse your soul at the cowboy worship services, held nightly at the rodeo grounds at 7:00. Closing out its first century—the first was in 1897—Frontier Days roars through southeastern Wyoming for ten days, beginning with the last full week in July. For more information call (307) 778–7222 or (800) 227–6336.

Regardless of whether or not you make it to town during the "Daddy of 'Em All," be sure to saunter over to the **Cheyenne Frontier Days Old West Museum.** On display are Indian artifacts and clothing, horse-drawn vehicles, an old saloon, and other Old West relics, including leftovers from the original Frontier Days bash, which was part rodeo and part Wild West show. The museum, adjacent to the rodeo grounds in Frontier Park, is open in summer Monday through Friday from 9:00 A.M. to 5:00 P.M. and weekends from 10:00 A.M. to 5:00 P.M.; the rest of the year it's open Monday through Friday from 9:00 A.M. to 4:30 P.M. and weekends from 11:00 A.M. to 4:00 P.M. Call (307) 778–7290 for more information.

Also in Cheyenne is the **Wyoming State Museum** (307–777–7022), a heritage-packed attraction with displays on sheep and cattle raisers, Plains Indians, trappers, pioneers, soldiers, and others vital to the state's past. It's located in the Barrett Building, on Central Avenue between Twenty-second and Twenty-fourth, and open Monday through Friday from 8:30 A.M. to 5:00 P.M., Saturday from 10:30 A.M. to 2:30 P.M., and Sunday (summer only) from 1:00 to 5:00 P.M.

The **Cheyenne Gunslingers** battle it out each summer weekday evening at 6:00 and at noon on Saturday at Carey and Lincolnway streets; nearby there's a replica of the gallows used in 1903 to hang convicted murderer Tom Horn. Chuckwagon suppers and horseback rides can be arranged at **Blue Ribbon Horse Center,** a couple of miles west of town at 406 North Fort Road. Before hopping on your horse, you can get outfitted like a true cowhand by ambling over to **Cheyenne Outfitters,** at 210 West Sixteenth, or **The Wrangler,** at 1518 Capitol Avenue. (When it comes to Western wear, if one of these two places don't got it, it probably ain't made.)

Mr. T Dies

Early in April 1994, the legendary bucking bull Mr. T passed away at the John Growney ranch in Red Bluff, California, where he had spent his last four years. Mr. T, who was sixteen, was the most feared and revered rodeo bull in the nation during a 5½-year period when not one cowboy managed to stay aboard him for the eight seconds required to earn a score. Mr. T was named Bucking Bull of the Year once and Bucking Bull of the National Finals Rodeo twice. His perfect string, during which he threw 188 cowboys, ended at the 1989 Cheyenne Frontier Days rodeo, when Marty Staneart of Sanger, California, hung on and rode out the eight seconds, earning a score of 93, the highest-scored bull ride in Frontier Days history.

Guilty or Not Guilty?

Tom Horn was, in a sense, the last of his breed, a go-anywhere-do-anything hired gun and highly skilled stock detective who worked for the Wyoming Stock Growers Association. After being raised during part of his youth by Apache Indians, Horn did a stint as an Indian scout, rode with Teddy Roosevelt's Rough Riders in the Spanish-American War, and served as an investigator for the Pinkerton Agency.

Horn was hanged in Cheyenne on November 20, 1903, after being found guilty of murdering fourteen-year-old Willie Nickell. Debate as to whether or not he truly was guilty began before he died, however, and continues to this day. Many maintain that young Nickell, mistaken for his father, was actually shot and killed by a feuding neighbor on July 18, 1901, and that Horn wasn't the cold-blooded killer he's been made out to be.

At a recent reenactment of his trial in Cheyenne, using evidence that has surfaced since the hanging, Horn was acquitted of the murder. Still, the debate continues.

And don't leave town without stopping at the **Manitou Gallery,** at 1715 Carey Avenue, a leading purveyor of Western and Native American collectibles.

The **Plains Hotel** (307–638–3311), one of the Cowboy State's growing number of refurbished historic hostelries, is situated at 1600 Central Avenue. If you'd rather sleep on the lone prairie, consider the **Adventurers' Country Bed and Breakfast,** located at the poetically named Raven Cry Ranch. The B&B features four rooms with private baths and a three-room suite that sleeps up to four. Three- and seven-day horseback adventures into the Medicine Bow Mountains are also available through the Raven Cry. Call (307) 632–4087 for additional information.

Note: Make your hotel reservations far in advance if you're coming in for Frontier Days (the ten-day period that begins the last full week in July).

Chuckwagon suppers are available at the **Terry Bison Ranch,** south of Cheyenne on Interstate 25 near the Wyoming-Colorado border. Horseback riding and horse-drawn tours of the 2,000-head herd are also offered, and an Old West town, complete with accommodations in a seventeen-room bunkhouse. Call (307) 634–4171 to learn more.

Laramie was named for the river of the same name, along which French-Canadian Jaques LaRamie was killed in 1818 or 1819 by Arapaho Indians (so said Jim Bridger, anyway). Laramie boasts the only four-year college in a state that's alone in having only one, and today the city is a sweet, if windy, mix of country cowboy and 1990s savvy.

If you stop only once in Laramie, do so at the outstanding **Wyoming Territorial Park,** located west of town on the Snowy Range Road. This multicomponent facility does a remarkable job of resurrecting the Old West of southeastern Wyoming; its centerpiece is the restored 1870s Wyoming Territorial Prison, in which roomed the likes of Butch Cassidy. There's also an end-of-the-tracks tent-and-shanty boomtown, where craftspersons ply their trades and folks like Calamity Jane and Jaques LaRamie mill about. Also featured are stagecoach rides, nonstop living-history reenactments, and food and Western entertainment at the Horse Barn Dinner Theatre, which also holds "America's Star," the national collection of the 200-year-old U.S. Marshal Service. The park is open daily from 10:00 A.M. to 5:00 P.M. in summer, with everything but the frontier town remaining open through mid-October. For more information on the museum or its Fourth of July **Mountain Man Rendezvous,** call (307) 745–6161 or (800) 845–2287.

The gracious 1892 Ivinson Mansion, on Ivinson Avenue between Sixth and Seventh streets, houses the **Laramie Plains Museum** (307–742–4448). The mansion is packed with Laramie-area historical items, including immaculate turn-of-the-century furniture, hand carved at the Wyoming Penitentiary in Rawlins. The museum is open in summer Monday through Saturday from 9:00 A.M. to 6:00 P.M. and Sunday from 1:00 to 4:00 P.M., and the rest of the year on a restricted schedule.

The University of Wyoming's new 127,000-square-foot **American Heritage Center** is both a research facility and an exhibition hall, with an associated art gallery. (The gallery's hours are Thursday and Friday from 9:30 A.M. to 4:30 P.M., Saturday from 10:00 A.M. to 5:00 P.M., and Sunday from noon to 4:30 P.M.) The center features an eclectic, world-class collection of Western-America items: one of Tom Mix's saddles and Hopalong Cassidy's six-shooters, for a couple of examples. The Wyoming and the West archives include some 4,500 manuscripts and books, along with more than 70,000 historic photographs and records from hundreds of early ranches. Western art originals are also displayed, including the priceless *Rendezvous Near Green River, Oregon Territory,* an oil painted by Alfred Jacob Miller, based on his own experiences at the mountain-man gathering. The center is open in summer from 7:30 A.M. to 4:30 P.M. on weekdays and from 11:00 A.M. to 5:00 P.M. on Saturday. Weekday hours the rest of the year are from 8:00 A.M. to 5:00 P.M. Call (307) 766–4114 for more information.

The **Two Bars Seven Ranch** is located outside Tie Siding, just north of the Colorado border, 24 miles south of Laramie and a few miles west of Highway 287. The main lodge sleeps twenty-five guests, who can participate in ranch work, dude rodeos, spring and fall cattle drives, trail rides, fishing, and overnight pack trips. Call for information and reservations at (307) 742–6072.

Head west out of Laramie along Highway 130, passing through Centennial before climbing into the superlative Medicine Bow Mountains. In Encampment visit the namesake **Grand Encampment Museum** (307–327–5308), which celebrates, among other things, the late 1830s rendezvous where Indians and French-Canadian trappers converged on the area for their Grand Encampment, to trade and socialize. More than a dozen old buildings (including a two-story outhouse) compose the ghost town/frontier town, and artifacts out of mines in the nearby Sierra Madre Range, old photographs, nineteenth-century cowboy apparel, and more are displayed. It's open Monday through Saturday from 10:00 A.M. to 5:00 P.M. and Sunday from 1:00 to 5:00 P.M. Memorial Day through Labor Day; weekends only in September and October; and by appointment at other times. **Woodchoppers Jamboree,** held in late June, is a wildly popular celebration, drawing folks from throughout the Cowboy State and beyond to watch logging contests, rodeo, and melodramas, and to partake of spill-into-the-street fun.

Between Wolcott Junction and Sinclair, pull off the interstate and into **Fort Steele State Historic Site,** and try to imagine what life would have been like here in the 1870s and 1880s for soldiers charged with protecting the railroad from Indian attack (in a word—*lonely*). The fort, like many settlements in southern Wyoming, exploded onto the scene in 1868, the year the Union Pacific tracks reached across the wild Wyoming landscape.

If you're hungry when you pull into Rawlins, steer straight for **Rose's Lariat,** at the east edge of town at 410 East Cedar Street, for some of the best Mexican food north of Santa Fe. Try to avoid the tiny restaurant between noon and 1:00 P.M. and between 6:00 and 7:00 P.M., however, for available seating is inversely proportionate to the Lariat's sizable reputation.

The grisly **Old Frontier Prison** in Rawlins served as the state penitentiary from 1903, when it was moved from Laramie to Rawlins, until 1982, and the place saw more than its share of the despicable and ornery, as well as the not-so-mean, such as William Carlisle, the "gentleman train robber," a nickname earned because he was known never to take money from female passengers. Fascinating tours are offered daily on the hour and half-hour between 8:30 A.M. and 4:30 P.M., June through Labor Day; spooky flashlight outings are also offered summer nights by reservation. Call (307) 324–4422 for more information on these and on off-season tours.

For accommodations in Rawlins, try out **Ferris Mansion** B&B, an elegant 1903 Victorian, featuring four rooms with private baths, located at 607 West Maple Street. Julia Ferris built the Queen Anne–style home after her husband, George Ferris, was killed on the way home from his copper mine in the mountains south of town. George's death resulted from a runaway team of horses. Call (307) 324–3961 for reservations.

Southwest Wyoming

The massive Oregon Trail feature **Independence Rock State Historic Landmark** is located on the Sweetwater River, 50-odd miles southwest of Casper. Semi-impromptu Fourth of July celebrations erupted here during the years of westward migration, as wagon trains arriving here by that date were well on schedule to reach Oregon. During the middle of the nineteenth century, thousands upon thousands of names were chipped, scratched, painted, and dug into the soft face of the rock by passing emigrants. Many of the old names are still visible today, along with, unfortunately, some newer ones.

Lander, base camp for the acclaimed National Outdoor Leadership School (NOLS), sprawls along the banks of the Popo Agie River. (Say it as it looks if you want people to know you're not from these parts; otherwise, pronounce it *po-PO-zhuh.*) The **Pioneer Museum,** at 630 Lincoln Street, centers around the log cabin that first opened as a museum here in 1915. Exhibits include an outstanding collection of Indian artifacts and other relics, among them the grisly skull of a local farmer who was killed in a nearby Indian raid in 1870, the wagon bolt that was driven through his head still in place. Another room celebrates Lander's annual One-Shot Antelope Hunt. The museum is open in summer Monday through Friday from 9:00 A.M. to 5:00 P.M. and 10:00 A.M. to 3:00 P.M. Saturday; the rest of the year Monday through Friday from 1:00 to 5:00 P.M. and Saturday from 1:00 to 4:00 P.M. Call (307) 332–4137 for more information.

In early June the **Popo Agie Rendezvous** commemorates an 1829 mountain-man bash held in the area, and **Pioneer Days,** the city's really big show, parties on for three days in early July, with Indian dancing and a rodeo that's been happening annually for more than one hundred years. Call the

Nineteenth-century graffiti on Independence Rock

Chamber of Commerce at (307) 332–3892 for more information.

The gold-camp-turned-high-country-getaway of Atlantic City boasts several enterprises that occupy ghostly, timeworn structures. The adobe **Atlantic City Mercantile** (307–332–5143) and the **Miner's Delight Inn** (307–332–0248) are a couple of classics, both offering historic lodgings and regionally renowned grub. "Calamity Jane" Canary spent time here and in nearby Miner's Delight, now a ghost town with a scattering of log structures.

The tiny South Pass City settlement, 5 miles southwest of Atlantic City, mushroomed in 1867, years after the majority of some 350,000 emigrants had already crested the Continental Divide at nearby South Pass and set up farm or shop in Oregon or mine in California. The rash of would-be prospectors might simply have stopped here, if only they'd known: There was gold in these hills. With the success of Henry Reedal's Carissa Lode and the Miner's Delight Lode shortly thereafter, word spread, and, within a year, more than 2,000 people lived at South Pass City, which suddenly found itself the region's largest settlement and a contender for the title of territorial capital. No fewer than thirty gold mines erupted on the surrounding hillsides; things played out quickly, however, and the town was all but deserted by 1875.

Boomlets happened several times over the ensuing decades, so South Pass City never did entirely die out. It almost picked up and moved to California, however, and it's only because a group of concerned Wyomingites outbid Knott's Berry Farm in the mid-1960s that the venerable settlement still resides in the high country of Wyoming instead of the coastal lowlands of the Golden State. The state of Wyoming bought it from the citizens a year later, and today at **South Pass State Historic Site** (307–332–3684) you'll find a couple of dozen restored structures, packed with local artifacts and old-fashioned goods and goodies for sale. The buildings are open daily in summer from 9:00 A.M. to 6:00 P.M., but you can wander through the streets any time of year, assuming you don't encounter a Wind River Range blizzard en route, which also can happen at any time of year. If you're interested in participating in old-fashioned ways over the Fourth of July, there's no better place to be than here. (For information on multiday Oregon Trail wagon outings that originate at South Pass City, call **Trails West** at 800–327–4052.)

The Red Desert town of Rock Springs, which started life as a stage station on the Overland Trail, was also the scene of the infamous Chinese Massacre of 1885, in which some thirty Chinamen were slaughtered, allegedly for taking mine jobs that "should" have gone to whites. Calamity

160

It Should Be Called the "Cowgirl State"

It was from here, the rough-and-tumble, male-dominated boomtown of South Pass City, that in 1869 territorial representative William Bright came and introduced to the inaugural territorial-legislature gathering a bill designed to give women the right to vote and hold political office. It was the first such state or territorial bill that passed in the United States. A couple of months later, Esther Hobart Morris—whose likeness is cast in bronze outside the capitol in Cheyenne—was named South Pass City's justice of the peace, making her the first female judge in the country. She replaced a man who quit in frustration and anger at the passage of the women's-suffrage bill. (Morris, apparently, was simply in the right place at the right time and was not, counter to popular story, a suffrage activist.)

Jane and George LeRoy Parker hung out here in those days. Parker had assumed his pseudosurname of "Cassidy" back home in Utah, but it was here in Rock Springs, where he worked as a butcher, that he took on the nickname "Butch." You can learn more at the **Rock Springs Museum** (307–362–3138), housed in the old castlelike city hall at 201 B Street. It's open Monday through Saturday from 9:00 A.M. to 9:00 P.M. and Sunday from noon to 6:00 P.M.

Rock Springs's big **All Girl Rodeo** is held in early May, and the **Red Desert Round Up,** western Wyoming's largest rodeo, is contested in early August. Call the Chamber of Commerce at (307) 352–6789 for information.

Photographs from the intrepid John Wesley Powell's 1869 river expedition into the Southwest (see Utah, p. 231) are on display at Green River's **Sweetwater County Historical Museum.** The ramshackle fledgling railroad camp was only a year old when Powell and his crew of nine put in the Green River here and headed for the unknown. The museum resides in the county courthouse, at 80 West Flaming Gorge Way; it's open Monday through Friday from 9:00 A.M. to 5:00 P.M. year-round and also Saturdays in summer from 1:00 to 5:00 P.M. Call (307) 872–6435 for more information.

The absorbing **Fort Bridger State Historic Site** marks the spot where the Oregon and Mormon trails parted ways. Several buildings from the

1858–90 military era have been restored and are open for touring: the Bridger-Vasquez Trading Company, for instance, where you can purchase items that range from old-fashioned clothing to a bull-scrotum medicine bag; the first schoolhouse in the state; and the grand 1884 commanding officer's residence. This outstanding museum contains a model of the old fort, a selection of Jim Bridger's own belongings, and scores of other artifacts. The site is open daily April 15 to October 15 and weekends only the rest of the year. Living-history reenactments take place throughout summer, and the spectacular **Fort Bridger Rendezvous** resurrects the fur-trading era during Labor Day weekend. Upward of 500 free trappers, company traders, Indians, and hunters come, as do some 10,000 spectators. A highlight is the performance of *A Ballad of the West,* written by Bobby Bridger, a distant relative of Jim Bridger. Call (307) 782–3842 for more information on the Labor Day weekend event.

In and around false-fronted, cold, and high Pinedale, 100 miles north of Rock Springs, you needn't use your imagination to picture the Wild West, especially if you arrive during the early-summer cattle drive, when hundreds of riders from dozens of ranches push thousands of cows to summer pasture in the Wind River Range high country. The area is yet another of Wyoming's hotbeds of dude ranches and outfitters; here they run trips into the dizzying Bridger Wilderness. This area was a focal point of early Rocky Mountain fur-trade doings, a fact expounded upon at the **Museum of the Mountain Man,** up the hill at 700 East Hettick Street. The museum interprets how, why, where, and when the trappers went about their business of tracking down and processing beaver and trading their plews. There's even a rifle that once belonged to the king, Jim Bridger, on display. The museum (307–367–4101) is open daily from 10:00 A.M. to 6:00 P.M. in summer and on demand the rest of the year.

If you can only go to one mountain-man rendezvous of the many that are highlighted in this book, make it Pinedale's very large and festive **Green River Rendezvous,** which brings thousands to town the second weekend in July. The celebration began in the mid-1930s, a century after the original events took place nearby. Living-history presentations, black-powder shooting, cowboy-poetry readings, Western dancing, rodeoing, frontier-crafts demonstrations—these and more are included, as everyday folks dress in buckskin, chomp on pemmican, and generally transform themselves into mountain men and women. For more information call the Chamber of Commerce at (307) 367–2242.

Of the bounty of bodacious guest ranches that sprawl over the surrounding countryside, the **Darwin Ranch** is perhaps the most picturesque. It's certainly the most remote; the Darwin, in fact, is possibly the most isolated and hard-to-reach dude ranch in the Lower 48. It's found (if you're lucky) north up the Green River Lakes Road, then over miles of bumpy four-wheel-drive paths, via Kinky Creek, in the headwaters of the Gros Ventre River. Many guests find it easier to fly in. Fred Darwin homesteaded here after his friend, Teddy Roosevelt, apparently gave the 160 acres to him by presidential decree. Today's guests carry on traditions that would have pleased T.R.: Fly-fishing, horseback riding, hiking, climbing, and wildlife photography are among the possible pursuits. Because of the remote loca-

Fort Bridger

A lot of history passed through Fort Bridger, which was established in 1843 by the king of the mountain men, Jim Bridger, and his Mexican partner, Louis Vasquez. Crucially located along the Oregon and Mormon trails, the fort evolved into the most important emigrant supply point west of Fort Laramie. Brigham Young and his Mormons, envious of the thriving enterprise, eventually chased Bridger out, built Fort Supply 12 miles to the south, and then took over and expanded on Fort Bridger itself in 1855.

(This was not the first time Bridger had trouble with Mormons. It seems that the first of his several wives was a Latter-day Saint, who divorced him when he wouldn't convert to her religion. Having learned his lesson, the rest of his wives were all Indians. Bridger retired to a farm in Missouri with wife number four, the daughter of Chief Washakie of the Shoshones.)

Not wanting to leave anything for the army, the saints burned both forts during the "Mormon War" of 1858, after which Fort Bridger was rebuilt and converted into a military garrison. In the early 1860s the post served first as a Pony Express station, then as an Overland Stage station, and troops from here helped keep the overland routes open during the subsequent restive times with the Indians. The fort was abandoned by the military in 1890.

tion, a stay at the Darwin Ranch closely resembles the experiences guests enjoyed at northwest Wyoming dude ranches much earlier in this century. During the high season (late July through August) only week-long stays are available; the rest of the summer overnighters are welcome. Call (307) 733–5588 for more information and reservations.

Northwest Wyoming

From Pinedale travel north to the skier's mecca of Jackson, cresting the Hoback Rim and passing through Bondurant, all the while edging through a cross-section of country that defines the best in Western landscape. Touristy Jackson, namesake of mountain man David Jackson, sits at the southwest edge of Jackson Hole. (A "hole," in mountain-man terms, was a large mountain-ringed basin.) This is the renowned Teton country, considered by many the most beautiful region on earth. **Old West Days,** held in Jackson over Memorial Day weekend, is the community's biggest West fest, with Indian dancing, rodeos, a mountain-man rendezvous, and a lot more on hand to keep things kickin'. The **Jackson Rodeo** heats up every Wednesday and Saturday during summer at 8:00 P.M. at the county fairgrounds; for kids it's a hands-on affair: All comers are invited to join in on the hilarious, hooves-hide-and-hair-everywhere calf scramble. For more information visit the imposing **Wyoming State Information Center** (307–733–3316), at 532 North Cache.

Try not to bump into any fellow visitors as you thread your way along the boardwalks that surround Town Square. The **Jackson Hole Museum** (307–733–2414), a block west of the Square at 105 North Glenwood, displays artifacts from the days of the Indians, trappers, and early cattlemen. It is open daily mid-May through mid-October from 9:30 A.M. to 6:00 P.M. Monday through Saturday and 10:00 A.M. to 5:00 P.M. Sunday. Another worthwhile stop is the **Teton County Historical Center** (307–733–9605), found at the corner of Mercill and Glenwood and open Monday through Friday from 8:00 A.M. to 5:00 P.M. in summer. Old books and photographs, along with fur-trade and Native American collections are displayed at the research center. An impressive array of wildlife art—some by masters like Russell, Catlin, Bodmer, and Schwiering—is displayed at the **Wildlife of the American West Art Museum** which moved to its new, 51,000-

square-foot building in September 1994. Situated just north of town, immediately across highway 89/191 from the National Elk Refuge, the stunning facility was designed to resemble a Southwest cliff dwelling and to blend in with its dry, rocky hillside setting.

Half a score of Western- and Indian-art galleries are found in and around Jackson; among the more comprehensive: the **Wilcox Gallery** (307–733–6450), also north of town on Highway 89/191. For quality dude-ranch-style furniture and Western collectibles, hit **Fighting Bear Antiques,** which specializes in the highly regarded furniture of the master, Thomas Molesworth, at 35 East Simpson Street, or **T and A Antiques,** at 155 West Pearl.

Several family-oriented chuckwagon-dinner enterprises operate in the area. A favorite is the **Bar T-5** (307–733–5386), which leads wagon outings upstream from its base along Cache Creek at the southeast edge of town. The Bar T-5 (and several other places around Jackson Hole) also rents horses for trail rides; ride sharp in the saddle, for Cache Creek is a favorite route among the local mountain-biking crowd as well.

Not surprisingly, Jackson Hole is endowed with more than its share of traditional dude ranches. The **Red Rock Ranch** (307–733–6288), located in stunning surroundings south of the Gros Ventre River about 30 miles outside Jackson, is a classic; so is the **Heart Six Ranch** (307–543–2477), 40 miles northeast of town on the Buffalo River.

Once you're tired of sightseeing, go do what you've really been wanting to do: Mount a saddle bar-stool at the **World Famous Cowboy Bar,** on the west side of the Town Square, and order a round of tall, cool ones. You can even take a country-swing dance lesson here on Thursday nights.

John Colter, early on the scene and late of the Lewis and Clark expedition, passed through the Dubois (pronounced DU-boys) area in 1807 en route to Jackson Hole. Originally christened Never Sweat, Dubois is nestled along the east slope of the Rockies near where the Wind River Mountains merge northward into the Absaroka Range. South and east of town red-rock badlands dominate: all in all, one of the prettiest and most frontier-feeling spots in the state, with log construction common throughout the small community. Old-time cow-outfits-turned-dude-ranches and hunting outfitters abound; a couple of possibilities out of the fifteen or twenty in the immediate vicinity (which here, as in much of the spread-out West, can mean anywhere within a fifty-mile radius): the **Lazy L & B**

Ranch (307–455–2839), featuring week-long stays in log-cabin accommodations, square dancing, and good country cooking on a one-hundred-year-old ranch; and the historic 1922 **Brooks Lake Lodge** (307–455–2121), situated in the high country not far from the Continental Divide and boasting a spectacular main lodge with several outlying log cabins. The **Dubois Museum** (307–455–2284), located at 909 West Ramshorn, is open May through September from 10:00 A.M. to 5:00 P.M. Monday through Saturday and from noon to 5:00 P.M. Sunday. Displays center around the local ranching heritage, the mysterious Sheepeater Indians, and the tie hacks, early northern European loggers who came into the region to fell trees and hew timbers for the approaching railroad.

For Western-flair shopping head to **Green River Traders,** at 104 East Ramshorn, or the **Trapline Gallery,** at 120 East Ramshorn; then pop across the street to wet your whistle at the distinctly Wyoming **Rustic Pine Saloon.** A pair of mountain-man rendezvous stir up during summer: the **Little Fawn Rendezvous** in June, for kids only, and the **Whiskey Mountain Buckskinners Rendezvous,** held in mid-August. Call the Chamber of Commerce at (307) 455–2556 for information.

The 2.25-million-acre Wind River Reservation is home to the Northern Shoshone and Eastern Arapaho peoples, traditional enemies who were forced to live together by an insensitive nineteenth-century government and are still coexisting in an oftentimes uneasy truce. (Whites also own about a quarter-million acres within the reserve.) Lower Arapahoe, just southwest of Riverton, is the venue for the **Northern Arapaho Powwow,** in early August, and home to the **St. Stevens Indian Heritage Center** (307–856–4330). Historic photographs and artifacts are displayed, and dolls, moccasins, beadwork, Arapaho artwork, and other items are for sale at the facility, open Monday, Tuesday, Wednesday, and Friday from 9:00 A.M. to noon and 1:00 to 3:00 P.M. Fort Washakie, center for the reservation's administrative and business concerns, hosts the **Eastern Shoshone Powwow and Rodeo,** one component of late June's larger Treaty Day Celebration. The **Shoshone Cultural and Resource Center** (307–332–6120), found within the Bureau of Indian Affairs compound, is open Monday through Friday. The **Sacajawea Cemetery,** the probable burial place of Lewis and Clark's teenage female Shoshone companion (there's some debate as to whether or not the woman buried here truly is Sacajawea), is located west of Fort Washakie. Follow South Fork Road out of town, passing also the grave of

Chief Washakie and sculptor R. V. Greeves's gallery.

The **Hot Springs Museum and Cultural Center,** at 700 Broadway in steaming, hot-water-filled Thermopolis (80 miles northeast of Lander), contains a large collection straight out of the Old West, including the original Hole-in-the-Wall Saloon's backbar. A Native American collection (including a beautiful elk hide, hand-painted by Chief Washakie), vintage photographs, old wagons, and several old cabins and shops are also on hand at the museum, open Monday through Saturday from 8:00 A.M. to 5:00 P.M. Call (307) 864–5183 for more information. Ask also about the **Outlaw Trail Ride,** which leads a maximum of one hundred horseback riders through the Hole-in-the-Wall country to Thermopolis in early or mid-August, roughly following a route once traced by Butch Cassidy. Call (307) 864–2287 for more details.

About 60 miles northeast of Thermopolis, the tiny, picturesque tourist- and cowtown of Tensleep (so named because it was halfway between, or "ten sleeps" from, each of two Sioux Indian destinations) erupts during the **Tensleep Fourth of July** celebration, which includes a rodeo, parade, dance, and street party. From here trace the dusty road that leads north through the hot and dry Big Horn Basin to even tinier Hyattville to glimpse a brown-and-gray badlands swatch of Wyoming, the low-lying portions of which have been turned marvelously green by irrigation waters. Among Hyattville's earliest settlers was Asa Mercer, who came here after shipping two boatloads of potential wives from the East Coast around Cape Horn to Seattle (see Seattle's Frontier Cupid, Washington, p. 81). One of North America's most important archaeological sites, now encompassed by **Medicine Lodge State Park,** is 6 miles northeast of Hyattville on Cold Springs Road and the state park road. For about 10,000 years a progression of Native Americans, from Paleo-Indians to historic Crows, found this area along Medicine Lodge Creek ideal for encampments, with its high sandstone rim that both blocked the north winds and absorbed the warming rays of winter sun. Full-scale excavations began in 1973 with a crew from the University of Wyoming (which included the author of this book). Prehistoric rock art decorates the cliff, which rises sharply above the small visitor center, an ex-cowboy bunkhouse about one hundred years old (new by the surrounding ancient standards). The center is open in summer Monday through Friday from 8:00 A.M. to 8:00 P.M. and weekends from 9:00 A.M. to 8:00 P.M. Pleasant present-day campsites in this uncommonly beautiful canyon are found just west of the archaeological area; call (307) 469–2234 for more information.

Fifty miles northwest of Thermopolis in teeny-weeny Meeteetse (named for an Indian word that means "meeting place"), the **Charles Belden Western Photography Museum** features stunning old photographs, many of them taken early in this century at the famous Pitchfork Ranch. The museum is open from 8:00 A.M. to 8:00 P.M. daily in summer and from 8:00 A.M. to 5:00 P.M. Monday through Friday the rest of the year. The **Outlaw Cafe/Cowboy Bar,** which drips with Western ambience, also has on display early Meeteetse photos.

In a state that thrives on its cowboy culture, Cody, 30 miles north of Meeteetse, just might be the cowboyingest town of all. Here you'll find— and spend a week at, if you're not careful—the superlative **Buffalo Bill Historical Center,** the premier Western museum in the world and arguably the finest museum of any kind west of the Mississippi, and maybe east of it, as well. This sprawling facility encompasses four primary components, all dedicated to the Old West: the **Buffalo Bill Museum,** the **Whitney Gallery of Western Art** (holding more than one hundred originals each of Russells and Remingtons and also select Morans, Catlins, and others), the **Plains Indian Museum,** and the **Cody Firearms Museum,** featuring the world's largest collection of American-made firearms.

The Buffalo Bill Museum houses a staggering collection of Bill Cody's belongings; among the most compelling finds are Lucretia Borgia, his buffalo-slaughtering Springfield rifle, and actual film footage of the Wild West Show. You can even visit Cody's boyhood home, sawn in half in 1933 and transported here by rail from LeClaire, Iowa. *The Scout,* a big, bold bronze statue of the legendary Buffalo Bill—a man who seemed to be everywhere and do a little of everything during western expansion—also stands sentinel on the grounds outside the museum.

The Buffalo Bill Historical Center is open daily from 7:00 A.M. to 10:00 P.M. June through August; from 7:00 A.M. to 8:00 P.M. in May and September; from 8:00 A.M. to 5:00 P.M. in October; Tuesday through Sunday from 10:00 A.M. to 3:00 P.M. in March and November; and Tuesday through Sunday from 8:00 A.M. to 5:00 P.M. in April. It's closed December through February; call (800) 227–8483 or (307) 587–4771 for more information.

Another sure bet in Cody is **Trail Town,** among the most authentic Old West theme towns found anywhere. Among the two dozen buildings moved

Young Bill Cody

By the time he was twenty-one, long before his Wild West Show began, William Cody had done things most men in his day only dreamed of. Born February 26, 1846, near LeClaire in Scott County, Iowa, Cody moved with his family when he was seven to the Salt Creek Valley of Kansas. At eleven, he hired on as an ox-team driver; then, at the ripe old age of fifteen he was named assistant wagonmaster for a Russell, Majors, and Waddell bull train bound for Fort Laramie. When he got there, young Cody fell in for a while with a group of trappers headed for the Chugwater River country.

In 1859 Cody rushed west to look for gold around Pikes Peak, Colorado; then, in 1860, he became one of the youngest employed Pony Express riders, as well as a bit of a legend, by once exhausting twenty horses as he rode 322 miles in twenty-one hours and forty minutes. During the Civil War he served the Union forces as a scout in Missouri and along the Santa Fe Trail. On March 6, 1866, he married Louisa Federici, and together they ran the Golden Rule House hostelry in Salt Creek valley.

In 1867, at twenty-one years of age, Cody was hired by the Goddard brothers to kill buffalo and provide meat for workers on the Kansas Pacific Railroad, during which time he was reported to have killed 4,280 bison in one eight-month period. He acquired the title of "Buffalo Bill" when he outshot another buffalo hunter named Bill—Bill Comstock—in a contest that culminated in 115 dead bison: Cody killed 69 of the animals to Comstock's 46.

in to accompany the 1880s trading post already standing here are Butch Cassidy's Hole-in-the-Wall cabin and the oldest bar from these parts, replete with bullet-hole-ridden door. Several Western notables—most famously, John "Liver Eatin' Johnson" Johnston—are buried on the grounds. Trail Town (307–587–5302) is open daily from 8:00 A.M. to 7:00 P.M. mid-June through mid-September.

Cody has become somewhat of a mecca for pilgrims captivated by Western collectibles. **Prairie Rose,** at 1030 Twelfth Street, hawks authentic Plains Indian pottery, pouches, and other items; some of the store's inventory has appeared in the epics *Dances with Wolves* and *Return to Lonesome Dove*. **Big Horn Gallery,** at 1167 Sheridan Avenue, sells cowboy-style furniture that is symbolic of New West decorating.

Be sure to take in the **Cody Night Rodeo** (307–587–5155), an institution here for more than half a century. The PRCA-sanctioned action whoops it up down at the town's covered grandstand each night at 8:30 P.M. June through August. The huge **Cody Stampede** (307–587–2297) takes place over the Fourth of July, when the town fills with cowboys, mountain men, and tourists.

April's **Cowboy Songs and Range Ballads** brings to town cowboy poets and the sweet sounds of authentic Western music. The **Cowboy Antiques and Collectibles Show,** meanwhile, draws Western-Americana collectors from throughout North America to Cody in late June. Also in June is the **Frontier Festival,** conducted at the Buffalo Bill Historical Center, which features demonstrations of the skills needed by mountain men to make their way in the wilderness, such as hide tanning and rawhide braiding. Call the Chamber of Commerce at (307) 587–2297 for information on these and other frontier-flavored events that fill the calendar in Cody.

A good place to room in Cody is the **Irma Hotel,** built by Bill Cody in 1902 and named for his daughter. The opulent saloon on the premises features a remarkable cherrywood bar presented to Buffalo Bill by Queen Victoria of England. Summer gunfights happen regularly on the porch of the hotel, located at 1192 Sheridan Avenue. Call (307) 587–4221 for information and reservations.

If you prefer out-of-town accommodations, stay at one of the more than two dozen dude ranches and lodges scattered along the Shoshone River's Southfork Valley and the stunning, wilderness-embraced Wapiti Valley, which leads to the wonders of Yellowstone National Park. **Bill Cody's Ranch Resort** (307–587–2097), 25 miles west of Cody, is run by Buffalo Bill's namesake grandson and his wife, Barbara. The historic **Crossed Sabres Ranch** (307–587–3750) is a weekly-stay guest ranch, 9 miles east of the park, that started life in 1898 as a stage stop and today specializes in pack trips. **Pahaska Tepee** (307–527–7701), like the Irma, built by Buffalo Bill to shelter Yellowstone-bound tourists and also to house himself and his friends during hunting trips, is located 2 miles east of the park's east entrance.

Where to Eat

Rose's Lariat, Rawlins, (307) 324–5261
Atlantic City Mercantile, Atlantic City, (307) 332–5143
Outlaw Cafe & Cowboy Bar, Meeteetse, (307) 868–2585

Where to Stay

Eaton's Guest Ranch, outside Sheridan, (307) 655–9285
Spear-O-Wigwam Ranch, outside Sheridan, (307) 674–4496
TA Ranch, outside Kaycee, (307) 684–5702
Pellatz Ranch, outside Douglas, (307) 358–2380
Plains Hotel, Cheyenne, (307) 638–3311
Terry Bison Ranch, outside Cheyenne, (307) 634–4171
Adventurers' Country Bed and Breakfast, outside Cheyenne, (307) 632–4087
Two Bars Seven Ranch, outside Tie Siding, (307) 742–6072
Ferris Mansion Bed & Breakfast, Rawlins, (307) 324–3961
Miner's Delight Inn, Atlantic City, (307) 332–0248
Darwin Ranch, outside Pinedale/Jackson, (307) 733–5588
Red Rock Ranch, outside Jackson, (307) 733–6288
Heart Six Ranch, outside Jackson, (307) 543–2477
Lazy L & B Ranch, outside Dubois, (307) 455–2839
Brooks Lake Lodge, outside Dubois, (307) 455–2121
Irma Hotel, Cody, (307) 587–4221
Bill Cody's Ranch Resort, outside Cody, (307) 587–2097
Crossed Sabres Ranch, outside Cody, (307) 587–3750
Pahaska Tepee, outside Cody, (307) 527–7701

THE
SPANISH FOUR CORNERS

▼▼▼

Colorado
Utah
Arizona
New Mexico

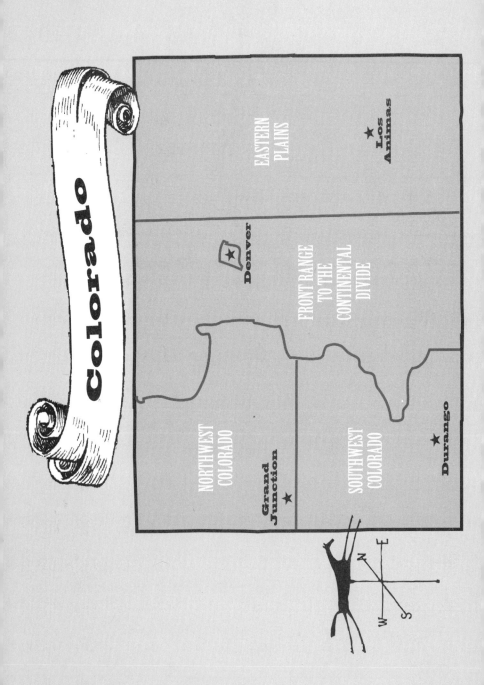

COLORADO

▼▼▼

N ENTIRE volume could readily be devoted to the Old West heritage of Colorado. The southern reaches brim with reminders of prehistoric Anasazi Indians and early Mexican settlers, whereas the eastern plains served as battlegrounds for some of the bloodiest skirmishes of the Plains Indian wars. Central and northern Colorado are steeped in the history of mountain men and cattlemen and in the lore of ore and the wild towns that erupted around high-mountain mineral finds.

Beginning in Julesburg in the northeast, the narrative leads southward across the plains, then swings north, winding back and forth between the Front Range cities and the Continental Divide. Finally it makes another pass, north to south, visiting the abundant vestiges of the Western Slope's colorful past.

The Eastern Plains

Most tourists hurry across "Colorado's Outback" in their rush to reach the mountains, but there's a wealth of history here, much of it tucked away in unassuming small-town museums. Not to investigate this part of the state is to ignore an important chapter in the settling of the West.

Today's Julesburg is actually the fourth rendition of this tenacious and mobile town, an earlier version of which allegedly was judged "The Wickedest City in the West" by Mark Twain. West of town on Highway 138, near Ovid, a monument commemorates Jules Station, Colorado's one-and-only Pony Express depot. It was here, in 1860, that fourteen-year-young William F. Cody signed on as an Express rider. The short-lived mode of communication is revisited at Julesburg's annual **Pony Express Re-Ride** in June. You can call (970) 474–3504 for information on the event.

After the demise of the Pony Express, Cody served as an army scout out of nearby Fort Sedgwick, established in 1864 to protect Overland Trail travelers from raiding Indians. (Years later Cody staged the swan-song performance of his Buffalo Bill's Wild West Show in Julesburg.) Highlights at the **Fort Sedgwick Historical Museum,** located in Julesburg's old railroad depot, include an unusual display of barbed wire and the trappings of Thad Sowder, a Cowboy Hall of Famer who rode with Buffalo Bill. In summer the museum (970–474–2264) is open from 9:00 A.M. to 5:00 P.M. Monday through Saturday, from 11:00 A.M. to 5:00 P.M. on Sunday, and by appointment the rest of the year (call 970–474–3344).

Sterling's **Overland Trail Museum** (970–522–3895) memorializes the route followed by thousands to the promised land of California. The replicated native-stone fort includes pioneer memorabilia, Native American artifacts, and a large collection of branding irons. It's located east of town on Highway 6 and open daily in summer and Tuesday through Saturday the rest of the year.

Museum personnel can direct you to the locations of several stations that formerly existed along the Overland Trail, including **Fort Godfrey,** or Fort Wicked, so named by the Indians because the tenacious defense put up by agent Holden Godfrey and his family resulted in its being one of the only forts between Julesburg and Fort Morgan not destroyed by Plains tribes during their 1864 rampage.

In Strasburg, 40 miles east of Denver, the Kansas Pacific Railroad laid the final stretch of track in 1870 to complete the first interconnected, coast-to-coast rail system, linking New York and San Francisco. The **Comanche Crossing Museum** (970–622–4322), open daily in summer from 2:00 to 5:00 P.M., details that vital accomplishment. The **Deer Trail Historical Museum,** 20 miles southeast of Strasburg on Interstate 70, also contains artifacts from early life on the plains. The museum (970–769–4677) opens by appointment.

The boardwalks and red-brick streets of Burlington's **Old Town** lead to two dozen old—and built-to-look-old—buildings that brim with turn-of-the-century memorabilia. Cancan shows, melodramas, and shoot-outs happen regularly in summer, and seasonal celebrations fill the remainder of the

The Last Battle

The Overland Trail was a breeding ground for conflict between whites and Indians as soon as the first emigrants filed along it in the late 1840s. In the summer of 1869, in a last, crazy gasp at asserting dominance, Chief Tall Bull and several hundred Cheyenne Dog Soldiers repeatedly made bloody attacks on settlers in western Kansas, a rampage that culminated in the abduction of two women from a Swedish settlement.

Maj. Eugene A. Carr, stationed at Fort McPherson in Nebraska, was ordered to end the attacks. Along with 300 men of the 5th U.S. Cavalry, 150 Pawnee scouts, and a young white scout named "Buffalo Bill" Cody, Carr chased the Cheyennes onto the high plains of eastern Colorado. On July 11, 1869, he attacked their camp at Summit Springs; many Cheyenne, including Tall Bull, were killed in the surprise assault, and several hundred of their mules and horses were captured.

The battle at Summit Springs was the final one fought in Colorado between the U.S. Cavalry and the Plains Indians. Today a monument marks the disquietingly peaceful spot, 16 miles south of Sterling. A reenactment of the battle became a regular feature in Buffalo Bill's Wild West Show.

calendar year. Here you can hop aboard the draft-horse-drawn **Old Town Express** for a tour that takes in the ornate **Kit Carson Carousel,** located at the fairgrounds. The forty-six-critter carousel, a National Historic Landmark, was hand-carved in 1905 by the Philadelphia Toboggan Company for the Elitch Gardens amusement park in Denver. Old Town is open from 8:30 A.M. to 7:00 P.M. in summer and from 9:00 A.M. to 6:00 P.M. the rest of the year. Call (800) 288–1334 for information.

Cheyenne Wells, 40 miles south of Burlington on Highway 385, claims the **Cheyenne County Museum.** Housed in the 1892 jail, it still holds the original cellblock and an array of historical items. The museum (719–767–5773) opens afternoons from Memorial Day through September 30. The town of Kit Carson, 25 miles west of Cheyenne Wells, sprouted not far from a trading post established by the famous frontiersman in 1838. The **Kit Carson Museum** (719–962–3350) highlights the town's Indian-fighting and buffalo-hunting days and boasts one of Carson's own six-shooters. It's open daily from 9:00 A.M. to 5:00 P.M. in summer. The town's **Mountain Man Rendezvous** kicks up the dust in Kit Carson in late April, and **Kit Carson Day,** in early September, features rodeo and old-time melodrama performances. Call (719) 962–3248 for information on the celebrations.

When driving south toward Highway 50, consider detouring east to the marked site of the infamous **Sand Creek Massacre,** located on County Road 96, north of Chivington. Early on the morning of November 29, 1864, Col. John Chivington and his 3rd Colorado Cavalry mercilessly marauded the encampment of Chief Black Kettle, who was under the obviously mistaken impression that an armistice stood between the whites and the Cheyenne. Between 100 and 200 Cheyenne were killed, the majority of them women and children. More than any other event, this fanned the flames of bitterness and precipitated the rash of attacks mounted by Plains Indians on whites over the ensuing five years.

Chivington and his "bloody third" regiment were dispatched from Fort Lyon, near present-day Lamar. That post was abandoned in 1867 for **New Fort Lyon,** near Las Animas, where today you'll find the **Kit Carson Museum** (the scout died near here in 1868), housed in an adobe built in

The "Picketwire" River

The stream that flows north into the Arkansas River near Las Animas is called the Purgatoire River on maps but is known locally as the "Picketwire." Apparently the local cowboys and ranchers, not in tune with the tongue-twisting nuances of the French language, found this word easier to say and close enough for their needs.

The early Spaniards called it *El Rio de Las Animas Perdidas en Purgatorio* (The River of Lost Spirits in Purgatory) to honor Spanish explorers who died along the river's banks without having received the last rites of the Roman Catholic Church. Later, French settlers changed the spelling and shortened it to "Purgatoire."

But you can call it the Picketwire, pardner.

the 1940s to hold German prisoners of war. **Boggsville,** undergoing reconstruction 2 miles south of town, is where Carson and his family lived at the time of his death. (The town's founder, Thomas Boggs, moved on to become the territorial governor of New Mexico in 1877.) Also in Las Animas is another **Kit Carson Museum** (719–456–0453), at Ninth Street and Bent Avenue; this one features an eclectic historic collection, open for viewing from 1:00 to 5:00 P.M. daily Memorial Day through Labor Day.

Between Las Animas and La Junta (where Bat Masterson served a five-week stint as sheriff in 1884) is **Bent's Old Fort National Historic Site,** which offers one of the premier living-history experiences in the West. Completed in 1833, the privately owned post, situated on the Mountain Branch of the Santa Fe Trail, became a regionally dominant fur-trading center, with trappers and buyers arriving from Mexico, Wyoming, and points beyond. And founder William Bent, a great friend to the Native Americans, became one of the most influential people in the region in the mid-1800s.

After extensive historical and archaeological research, the adobe fort was reconstructed by the National Park Service in 1975–76 to look much as it did in 1845. Costumed mountain men, Mexicans, Indians, and cavalry troops are now on hand to explain the fort's heyday. The site is open daily in summer from 8:00 A.M. to 5:30 P.M. and in winter from 9:00 A.M. to 4:00 P.M. The sights, smells, and sounds of the beaver and buffalo fur-trading days are revived at the **Old Time Fourth of July** at **Bent's Old Fort.** Another particularly good time to visit is early December, during the reenactment of **Christmas 1846.** Call (719) 384–2596 for information on these and other special events.

The **Koshare Indian Kiva Museum,** situated at 115 West Eighteenth Street in La Junta, is home to the Boy Scouts of America's renowned Koshare Dancers, a traveling group that began in the 1930s. The dancers perform here on Saturday nights during summer and during Christmas week; the associated museum features gorgeous displays of the art and artifacts of Plains and Southwest Indians. It is open daily from 10:00 A.M. to 5:00 P.M. year-round. Call (719) 384–4411 for information.

Southeast of La Junta some 100 miles, along the Oklahoma border in remote Baca County, the **Kirkwell Cattle Company** runs western adventure and overnight chuckwagon tours into the rough cedar-breaks country out of the town of Pritchett. Call them at (719) 523–4422 or 324–9292 to learn more.

Front Range to the Continental Divide

Trinidad, a small city with a south-of-the-border flair (and plenty of opportunities to sample south-of-the-border fare), was a tough, hell-raising Old West town that sprouted around the Santa Fe Trail. It's said that Billy the Kid once strolled through the streets, and Bat Masterson, who apparently spent a lot of time acting as a rent-a-sheriff in these parts, served as town marshal for a year.

A trio of attractions in the **Corazon de Trinidad National Historic District** includes the 1870 Territorial-style adobe **Baca House,** at 300 East Main Street; the nearby **Bloom Mansion;** and the **Santa Fe Trail Museum,** found behind the Baca House. The Pioneer Museum interprets the fascinating history of the area's immense cattle companies and also claims one of Kit Carson's beaded buckskin coats. The three facilities are open from 10:00 A.M. to 4:00 P.M. daily, from May 1 through September 30, with guided tours given every half hour. Call (719) 846–7217 for information.

The **A. R. Mitchell Museum of Western Art** (719–846–4224) is named after the artist whose work is displayed there. The annual **Santa Fe Trail Festival,** held downtown on the second Saturday in June, includes performances by La Junta's Koshare Dancers and Wild West gunfighting troupes. Call (719) 846–9285 for information.

Folks have been digging for coal around Walsenburg since the 1860s. You can learn about the rough life of the pioneer miners at the **Walsenburg Mining Museum,** at Fifth and Main streets. The **Barbed Wire Museum,** in the Old Train Depot on Main Street, is dedicated to the fencing material that helped tame the West, and dozens of twists on the subject are displayed. It's open Memorial Day through Labor Day, Monday through Saturday, from 9:00 A.M. to 4:00 P.M. Call the Chamber of Commerce at (719) 738–1065 for more information.

In the laid-back village of La Veta, nestled at the foot of the stunning Spanish Peaks, the **Fort Francisco Museum** informs visitors about the days in the early 1860s when the fort served as a trading post and as protection for settlers. Historical documents, including Kit Carson's will, are displayed; a blacksmith shop, a saloon, and the 1876 Ritter Schoolhouse round out the complex, open daily from 9:00 A.M. to 5:00 P.M. during summer. The **Spanish Peaks Cowboy Poetry and Arts Gathering,** held in May, celebrates the unique contributions the American cowboy has made to the arts. Call (719) 742–3676 for information.

Competing for your attendance on Memorial Day weekend is the **Rendezvous of the Cultures,** held at the Fort Garland Museum (40 miles west of La Veta on Highway 160). The rendezvous recalls the days when the Indians, U.S. soldiers, and Hispanics first encountered one another in the region. The museum (719–379–3512), housed in an adobe fort raised in 1858, is open daily between April and October, and Thursday through Monday the remainder of the year.

Every day during summer and early fall the **Cumbres & Toltec Scenic Railroad** puffs its way from a depot in tiny Antonito to Chama, New Mexico, some 65 miles south. America's longest and highest narrow-gauge railway still running, the line was laid in 1880 by the Denver & Rio Grande to service the rich mining towns of the San Juan Mountains. It passes through tunnels and over high trestles, slicing through a swath of Colorado's most captivating high country. The trip, which takes a full day, includes a van ride back to Antonito (a fresh load of passengers boards the train in Chama). For information and reservations call Antonito Station at (719) 376–5483.

Salida, boasting one of the state's largest historic downtown districts, today is a mecca for river runners and backpackers. After floating the Arkansas, you can hole up and dry off at the **Jackson Hotel,** an 1878 stagecoach stop in nearby Poncha Springs, where Old West notables like Billy the Kid and Jesse James reportedly slept (that was before the place was appointed with classy touches such as Austrian featherbeds). The hotel also houses a Mexican-food and steak restaurant. Call for reservations at (719) 539–4861.

Winnow your way through the crop of tourist attractions sprouting around the Royal Gorge of the Arkansas River to **Buckskin Joe & Railway.** At the sprawling, re-created 1860s mining camp, visitors enjoy panning for gold, horseback riding, and witnessing gunfights. This Old West town has appeared in numerous movies, including *The Cowboys* and *The Duchess and the Dirtwater Fox.* Its Gold Nugget Restaurant serves buffalo burgers and other hearty Western fare. The long-running **Royal Gorge Scenic Railway** joined forces with Buckskin Joe in 1990; together they are open daily Memorial Day through Labor Day from 9:00 A.M. to 7:30 P.M. Call (719) 275–5149 for information.

Note: If you really enjoy visits to filming locations, before traveling to Colorado call (800) 933–4340 and request a copy of Travel the Movie Trail. *The free brochure leads to more than a dozen sites, mostly in the southwest quadrant of the state, where classic Westerns were filmed.*

Canon City's **Colorado Territorial Prison Museum** graphically preserves the past at the facility, which, during its 120-plus years in business, has housed more than its share of the grisly and despicable. For example, Alferd Packer, the only person convicted of cannibalism in U.S. history, was a guest between 1886 and 1901. The museum, located at First and Macon streets, is open from 8:30 A.M. to 6:00 P.M. daily in summer and in winter from 10:00 A.M. to 5:00 P.M. Friday through Sunday. Call (719) 269–3015 for more details.

The **Historic Rudd Cabin and Stone House** (719–269–9018) are located at 612 Royal Gorge Boulevard. The prominent Rudd family, which settled here in the late 1850s, lived in the log cabin for twenty years and in the large stone house for the next twenty-three. The houses, open daily, are appointed with period furnishings and appliances.

The Bureau of Land Management's **Gold Belt Tour Backcountry Byway** offers an exciting way to travel to and from the high-mountain gold camps nestled on the west slope of Pikes Peak. The byway's component roads are narrow, and the winding and bumpy paths are not suitable for RVs or trailers or for the faint of heart. One of them, the thrilling and aptly named Shelf Road, was literally blasted and chiseled into the rock wall of Fourmile Canyon. Call (719) 269–8500 to request a pamphlet that describes the drive.

The on-again off-again boomtown of Cripple Creek, where donkeys roam free in summer, is on again, thanks to the recent legalization of limited-stake gambling. Before chancing your change in a game of blackjack, however, spend a bit of it on seeing some local history. The **Cripple Creek**

District Museum, at Fifth Street and Bennett Avenue, comprises a trio of buildings that display historic mining gear, ore samples, and much more. A brochure detailing a self-guided walking/driving tour is also available here. The museum is open from 10:00 A.M. to 5:00 P.M. daily Memorial Day through September and on weekends from 10:00 A.M. to 4:00 P.M. the remainder of the year.

At the captivating **Mollie Kathleen Gold Mine** (719–689–2466), 1.5 miles east of town, you'll descend 1,000 feet into the ground to see how early gold miners performed their risky jobs. It's open daily from 9:00 A.M. to 5:00 P.M. May through October.

Next, to appreciate how *some* miners whiled away *some* of their time spent above ground, visit the **Old Homestead Parlour House Museum.** The Homestead was the upper crust of Cripple Creek's abundant bordellos. The parlor and bedrooms are fully appointed in the style of the late 1800s, to the extent of featuring mannequins dressed as the Homestead girls. The museum (719–689–2519) is located on Meyers Avenue.

At the turn of the century, the **Imperial Hotel** (719–689–2922), Cripple Creek's oldest standing structure, was an oasis of gentility in the rowdy town. Completely renovated, it still operates as a Victorian-appointed hotel and casino. Throughout the summer the hotel's Gold Bar Theatre stages regionally renowned, rip-roaring melodramas. It's located at 123 North Third Street.

Jump aboard the **Cripple Creek–Victor Narrow Gauge Railroad** (719–689–2640) for a steam-locomotive tour of the fascinating historic district. Trains depart every 45 minutes from the Midland Terminal at the head of Bennett Street. Both companies operate from May through October.

Victor, the second-largest of the district's dozen boomtowns, hasn't been buffed and boutiqued to the extent of Cripple Creek, and so it presents, perhaps, a more authentic feel for turn-of-the-century Colorado. The inimitable world traveler and reporter Lowell Thomas lived here when young, and at the **Lowell Thomas Museum** you'll find memorabilia from his family and the early days of mining in Victor.

Kids of every age shoot it out—with paintball guns, not real six-shooters—at **Hot Pursuit Park.** The fifty-acre Old West theme park is one of the newer attractions near Victorian Victor. Call (719) 527–0200 for information.

"The World's Greatest Gold Camp"

As busy as Cripple Creek is today, it's still difficult to imagine the town at its zenith, when some 25,000 people lived here, making it Colorado's fourth-largest city. Exclusive boutiques, featuring the latest in European fashions, drew high-society men and women from Denver and beyond.

Cripple Creek claimed a stock exchange and approximately sixty brokers, forty assay offices, sixty lawyers, and thirty men's clubs. It also boasted two opera houses, sixteen churches, eight newspapers (three of them dailies), a business college, and two hospitals with nearly a hundred doctors. Then there was notorious Myers Avenue—several blocks brimming with parlor houses, gambling joints, and taverns—according to moral reformist Carry Nation, a "foul cesspool." Boxing was big, too, and Jack Dempsey, a local mine worker, began his celebrated fighting career in and around Cripple Creek in 1912.

There was fabulous wealth, but it couldn't prevent epidemics of typhoid fever, small pox, and other diseases from striking. Stark evidence of this fact can be witnessed at the hillside Mount Pisgah Cemetery, at the west end of town, where row after row of people—many entire families—who died from the diseases are buried. The gracious landscape was ravaged, too: Mining scars tarnish the mountainsides, and ugly mine-tailing dumps litter the valley floor.

The city of Pueblo began life as the Fort Pueblo trading post, the business enterprise of black mountain man James Pierson Beckwourth. At **El Pueblo Museum**, 905 South Prairie Avenue, you'll find a full-scale replica of the 1842 post. One of many highlights: a cross-section of Old Monarch, an ancient cottonwood felled in 1883 and said to have served as the hanging tree for fourteen desperadoes. The museum is open Tuesday through Saturday in summer and Wednesday through Saturday the rest of the year.

A walk through Pueblo's **Union Avenue Historic District** turns up more than thirty buildings dating from the late 1800s. (A tour map can be obtained at the Chamber of Commerce, at 302 North Santa Fe Avenue.) The

Pueblo County Historical Museum (719–543–6772), located at 217 South Grand in the historic Vail Hotel, features a railroading exhibit and a collection of saddles fashioned by local craftspeople. The 1891 **Rosemount Museum** (719–545–5290), at Fourteenth and Grand streets, is an amazing three-story, thirty-seven-room mansion constructed of pink rhyolite stone blocks. Tours of the home are offered daily in summer and Tuesday through Sunday the rest of the year, except January.

While visiting Pueblo, consider holing up in historic surroundings at the 1906 **Abriendo Inn,** at 300 West Abriendo Avenue. An overnight includes a sumptuous and generous breakfast that is fast becoming legendary in these parts. Call (719) 544–2703 for reservations.

Wealth filtering in from the Cripple Creek district was largely responsible for Colorado Springs's transformation from a resort town into a cosmopolitan city; here the Old West and new West meet today, and both thrive. Begin your tour at the **ProRodeo Hall of Fame and Museum of the American Cowboy,** at 101 Pro Rodeo Drive (north of town off Interstate 25 at exit 147—just watch for the buckin' bronc' sculpture). Among the many highlights are cowboy gear both new and old, live rodeo animals, dozens of captivating photographs, and the Hall of Champions, honoring rodeo's best. Through a sort of virtual-reality photographic arrangement, visitors can also earn a pain-free sense of what it's like to try to stay atop a Brahma bull for eight seconds. The museum is open daily from 9:00 A.M. to 5:00 P.M. Call (719) 593–8840 for more information.

Check out the **Western Museum of Mining and Industry** (719–488–0880), north of town off Interstate 25 near the north gate to the U.S. Air Force Academy. This large and impressive mining museum includes hands-on displays, where visitors learn gold-panning techniques and operate venerable steam-driven mining machinery. It's open throughout the year Monday through Saturday from 9:00 A.M. to 4:00 P.M. and from noon to 4:00 P.M. on Sunday.

Learn about late-nineteenth-century life in the Pikes Peak region at the **White House Ranch Historic Site,** located at the entrance to the magical sandstone world known as Garden of the Gods. The ranch (719–578–6777) is open from 10:00 A.M. to 4:00 P.M. Wednesday through Sunday in summer and on weekends the rest of the year.

Some of the West's tastiest cowboy tunes and barbecue can be sampled at the **Flying W Ranch,** 2 miles north of Garden of the Gods on Thirtieth

Street. The working ranch, situated amid heart-stoppingly beautiful surroundings, also features a reconstructed Old West town, overflowing with
Western memorabilia. Since 1953 hundreds of thousands of wannabe cow-
folks have joined the Flying W for its chuckwagon supper and after-dinner
show that features the Flying W Wranglers, whose sweet melodies and
four-part harmonies are reminiscent of the acclaimed Sons of the Pioneers.

The gates to the South Pasture open daily, mid-May through late
September, at 4:30 P.M., with dinner served at 7:15 P.M. (6:45 P.M. after
Labor Day). In winter, excepting January and February, on Friday and
Saturday from 5:00 to 8:00 P.M., the Flying W runs an indoor steak house.
Call (719) 598–4000 for reservations, a must.

When planning an overnight stay in Colorado Springs, don't overlook
the stunning, world-famous **Broadmoor Hotel** (719–634–7711), one of
the most lavish getaways in Colorado. The thirty-building complex, situated in the Rocky Mountain foothills at 1 Lake Avenue, was built in 1918

The Flying W Wranglers

by Spencer Penrose, who made a fortune from his Cash-on-Delivery Mine in Cripple Creek.

For lodgings less extravagant but no less steeped in history, check into the **Buffalo Lodge,** at 2 El Paso Boulevard, close to the Academy Riding Stables and the Garden of the Gods' trading post. The place is pure West, with shellacked-pine walls decorated with stuffed-animal trophies and Navajo rugs. Call (719) 634–2851 for information.

Just west of Garden of the Gods is Manitou Springs, once a frontier spa and now a resort town that features a curious mix of the tasteful and tasteless. **Miramont Castle,** a forty-six-room mansion that incorporates nine architectural styles, was built in 1895 by an ailing French priest who came for the purported therapeutic values of Manitou Springs's mineral waters. The castle, located at 9 Capital Hill, boasts 2-foot-thick stone walls and a 200-ton sandstone fireplace. It's open for touring daily from 10:00 A.M. to 5:00 P.M.

When hunger strikes, strike out for the **Stagecoach Steak & Ale** (719–685–9400), at 702 Manitou Avenue. Originally an 1880s stage stop, the structure later served as a power plant and then as a summer getaway for Helen Hunt Jackson, author of *Ramona* (see California chapter, page 29). For lodging, have a look at **Frontier's Rest Bed & Breakfast Inn.** This Victorian inn is Old West all the way, from the tile-and-oak fireplace in the parlor to the four antiques-filled guest rooms, each of which has a private bath. The inn's hearty breakfast will prep you for a day of sight-seeing; in fact, you may not need to eat again until the next day. Fontier's Rest, where breakfast and evening desserts are included, is located at 341 Ruxton Avenue, within an easy walk of downtown and the Pikes Peak Cog Railroad. Call (719) 685-0588 for reservations.

For more information on Manitou Springs, call the Chamber of Commerce at (800) 642–2567.

Located about 85 miles west of Manitou Springs on Highway 24, Buena Vista is situated, as its name might indicate, within view of some of the prettiest mountain scenery in the state. The town, famously wild in the 1880s, is better known today as the Whitewater Capital of Colorado. The **Heritage Museum** (719–395–8453), housed in the old county courthouse, offers a thorough look at local history. It's open from 9:00 A.M. to 5:00 P.M. daily throughout the summer.

Devote at least a day to ore- and lore-packed Leadville, and plan to move at a snail's pace at the lofty 10,152-foot altitude. The flagship of Leadville's numerous museums is the impressive **National Mining Hall of Fame and Museum** (719–486–1229), located at 120 West Ninth Street. Tours through the large facility are offered year-round and run hourly at varying times (daily in summer and Monday through Friday in winter).

The grandiose **Tabor Opera House** was built in 1879 by Horace Tabor, Leadville's first postmaster and mayor, and among its most colorful characters; the Great Houdini was among the hundreds of acts who appeared in the ensuing years. Today you can take a self-guided tour of the opera house, accompanied by a taped narrative; it's located at 310 Harrison Avenue and is open from 9:00 A.M. to 5:30 P.M., Sunday through Friday, Memorial Day to September.

Horace divorced his first wife, Augusta, in 1883 for his new love, Elizabeth McCourt "Baby" Doe. Their **Matchless Mine** and **Baby Doe's Cabin** (719–486–0371), situated 2 miles east of town on Seventh Street, are open daily from 9:00 A.M. to 5:00 P.M., Memorial Day through Labor Day.

Another worthwhile stop is the **Healy House and Dexter Cabin,** located a block north of the business district at 912 Harrison Avenue. The Healy House, built as a private residence in 1878, was transformed into a boardinghouse two decades later, when a third story was added. Today's visitor enters a boardinghouse of 1899, where tours are led by "boarders" dressed in the Victorian garb of the day. The adjacent cabin, which was moved to the spot from its original location on West Third Street, looks like just another rough-hewn Colorado log cabin on the outside. On the inside, though, are displayed the opulent belongings of the cabin's builder, James V. Dexter, an early Leadville resident who earned a fortune in mining and other investments. The house and cabin are open daily from Memorial Day through Labor Day and by appointment the rest of the year. Call (719) 486-0487 for additional information.

Leadville resurrects its past each summer with the **Annual Boom Days Celebration,** in early August, which includes the International Pack Burro Race, in which teams of two runners, one human and one mule, ascend 13,186-foot Mosquito Pass. ("Get Your Ass over the Pass," the bumper-sticker reads.)

For more information on Leadville attractions, celebrations, and historic-lodging opportunities, call the Chamber of Commerce at (800) 933–3901.

Horace and Baby Doe Tabor

The Matchless Mine made Horace Tabor a rich man—until the 1893 repeal of the Sherman Act, that is, which changed the dollar standard from silver to gold and rendered silver all but worthless. Horace kept the mine, however, and his last words to wife Baby Doe before dying in 1899 were, "Hang on to the Matchless."

Baby Doe moved to the mine and worked it for more than three decades. The once fabulously wealthy woman died a destitute recluse: She was found at the mine, frozen, in 1935. Her one-room cabin, today a museum, still contains her sparse belongings.

The chamber, located at 809 Harrison, also offers a terrific slide show entitled *The Earth Runs Silver—Early Leadville.*

After getting your car and yourself over Mosquito Pass, drop into 900-square-mile South Park. In Fairplay, which became a full-blown, fired-up mining town not long after gold was discovered in 1859, you'll find the open-air **South Park City Museum.** More than thirty old buildings are situated here, including the old South Park Lager Beer brewery and structures from several other mining camps in the Fairplay Diggings district. The museum (719–836–2387) opens daily at 9:00 A.M. and closes at 4:30 P.M. from mid-May through mid-October.

Near Grant (28 miles northeast of Fairplay on Highway 285), detour north from Highway 285 onto the rough-and-tumble **Guanella Pass Road** and commence the scenic 22-mile drive to the Silver Plume–Georgetown–Empire–Idaho Springs district and its bonanza of mining history. A sampling: Silver Plume's **George Rowe Museum** (303–569–2562), a tribute to nineteenth-century family life, housed in an old schoolhouse; the **Hotel de Paris** museum in Georgetown (303–569–2311), formerly an elegant hostelry run by an eccentric Frenchman; and, in Idaho Springs—where the precipitous walls of Clear Creek Canyon permit precious few rays of sun during the long winters—the **Underhill Museum** (303–567–4709) and **Phoenix Gold Mine** (303–567–0422), a privately owned and operated underground gold mine that offers public tours.

Empire's **Peck House** (303–569–9870), an eleven-room inn opened in 1862, is the oldest operating hotel and restaurant in the state. Some of the hardwood pieces are originals, brought from Chicago via stagecoach by Mrs. James Peck. The twelve-person spa and certain other amenities are substantially newer. The historic **Red Men Hall,** located on Highway 40 in Empire, showcases and sells Native American artwork for the serious collector. Jewelry, Hopi baskets, paintings, kachinas—both antique and by current masters—and more are featured.

The locomotive-drawn **Georgetown Loop Railroad** hauls visitors between Silver Plume and Georgetown, from Memorial Day through early October. The narrow-gauge track dramatically loops over itself to gain elevation at the 300-foot-long Devil's Gate High Bridge, and the 6-mile round-trip includes an optional guided tour of the Lebanon Silver Mine. Call (303) 569–2403 for more information.

Request a tour map at the Idaho Springs Visitor Center; then follow legendary precipitous **Oh My God Road** north toward Central City, through endless evidence of the mining activities once rampant in this part of the world. Central City–Blackhawk, epicenter of "The Richest Square Mile on Earth," has yielded more than half a billion dollars worth of minerals. As at Cripple Creek, some of that money is belatedly returning, for the district recently introduced limited-stakes gambling—and it's booming.

If you can unwrap your white knuckles from the steering wheel and wrangle a parking spot, stroll over to the 1878 **Central City Opera House** (303–582–3200), at 200 Eureka Street. The immaculately restored 750-seat gem is the oldest performing arts center in Colorado, with English-language opera performed June through August. The *Ballad of Baby Doe* was first produced here in 1956 and has since become a signature American opera. Next door is the **Teller House,** with its collection of Victorian furnishings and other artifacts, many of them once owned by Baby Doe Tabor. Built in 1872 as a hotel, this is the location of the bar that sports the famous *Face on the Barroom Floor.* Created on a lark by Herndon Davis in 1936, the painting inspired the opera of the same title, which was commissioned for the Central City Opera House's centennial in 1978.

At the **Central City Gold Mining Museum,** Main and Spring streets, and the **Gilpin County Historical Society,** 228 East High Street, you can learn a lot about the colorful past of the district. Call (303) 582–5251 for more information on Central City and nearby Black Hawk.

Golden, the territorial capital of Colorado from 1862 until 1867, was born in 1859 as Golden City, a vital staging and stocking center for the mountain gold camps. Mineral-rich Colorado clearly owns one of the richest railroading histories of any state, and a mile east of town, at 17155 West Forty-fourth Avenue, the **Colorado Railroad Museum** summarizes the legacy in a replica of an 1800s masonry depot. More than 50,000 pieces are housed inside, and in the basement is a huge HO model railroad, featuring miniatures of important Colorado railroad towns. Some fifty narrow- and standard-gauge locomotives and rail cars fill the grounds outside. The museum is open daily throughout the year; call (303) 279–4591 for further information.

For some spirited fun and solid Western grub, take in the **Lazy H Chuckwagon Supper & Western Show** (303–278–1938) at Heritage Square, located between Interstate 70 and Sixth Avenue on Highway 40. Reservations are a must at the popular barbecue and stage show, which lets loose Wednesday through Saturday evenings and at a Sunday matinee.

Follow the signs on the Lariat Trail (Nineteenth Street), leading to Lookout Mountain and the **Buffalo Bill Memorial Museum,** where that icon of the Wild West is buried. (Incidentally, the night view of Denver from Lookout Mountain is stupendous.) The museum explores Buffalo Bill's life in detail, from his childhood encounters with Indians to his teenage stint with the Pony Express, his scouting and buffalo-hunting days, and his career as a showman. Photographs, publicity posters, and dime novels—more than 700 of which featured Buffalo Bill as the hero—are displayed, and the Women of the Wild West are also celebrated. The museum, maintained by the Denver Parks & Recreation Department, opens at 9:00 A.M. daily. In summer it closes at 5:00 P.M.; in winter, 4:00 P.M. Call (303) 526–0747 for more information.

Before descending into sprawling Denver, arguably the capital of the Wild West, detour south along Highway 470 to Morrison, where you'll find a surprising replica of Bent's Old Fort. **The Fort** restaurant dishes up gourmet food "from the Early West," such as buffalo-hump roast, charbroiled quail, and elk medallions. Those with a bolder taste for adventure can sample Rocky Mountain oysters, buffalo tongue ("the nineteenth century's finest gourmet food"), and armadillo eggs. Drinks include Chimaja Whiskey, "sprinkled with wild mountain parsley and reputed to make a man strong as a bull in love."

Sam Arnold—Yale-educated mountain man, writer, gourmet chef, and world-class marketing man—and a crew of twenty-five from Taos, New Mexico, built the 80,000-adobe-brick structure in the early 1960s. Since then the unique eatery has been written up in numerous national publications and has attracted a long line of customers and celebrities, including Bryant Gumbel and Jane Pauley, when the *Today* show visited in Denver. (Arnold served them Buffalo Eggs, hard-boiled quail eggs wrapped in buffalo sausage.)

Service people, dressed in accurately re-created Sioux Indian and mountain-man garb, will take beaver pelts in lieu of cash. (The current rate of exchange is $20/pelt; no kits accepted.) Smoking isn't permitted in the restaurant, but it is in the tipi outside; in fact, free kinnikinnick is provided. (Kinnikinnick is a low-growing evergreen shrub whose dried leaves were ground up and used by Indians and mountain men as a tobacco replace-

A scene from the 1860s living-history farm at the Littleton Historical Museum

ment.) The Fort (303–697–4771) is located just south of Morrison on Highway 8. A suggestion: Sample the dish called Bowl of the Wife of Kit Carson.

If you overindulged on rattlesnake, hare, or whatever, check into **The Cliff House** lodge and cottages in Morrison. At the sandstone Victorian, built in 1873 by town founder George Morrison, a gourmet breakfast is part of the deal. Call (303) 697–9732 for reservations.

From Morrison follow Highway 470 southeast to the Denver suburb of Littleton. The fourteen-acre **Littleton Historical Museum,** at 6028 South Gallup Street, is a living-history wonderland. Costumed interpreters inhabit and work both an 1860s homestead—complete with pig sty, oxen shelter, and pasture—and a turn-of-the-century farm, with post-and-beam barn, Littleton's first schoolhouse, and a blacksmith shop. The park is open year-round from 8:00 A.M. to 5:00 P.M. on weekdays, from 10:00 A.M. to 5:00 P.M. on Saturdays, and from 1:00 to 5:00 P.M. on Sundays. Call (303) 795–3950 for more information.

Denver pulls out the stops for the two-week, mid-January **National Western Stock Show & Rodeo,** touted as the world's largest livestock exhibition. Thousands of visitors from all fifty states and dozens of foreign countries arrive for the event, which has been running since the early 1900s. One of many highlights: the International Sheep Shearing Contest. Call (303) 297–1166 for ticket information.

Before taking in the stock show, pull into **Miller Stockman,** at 1600 California Street, since 1918 among America's foremost Western-wear stores. Here you can outfit yourself by choosing from one of the most extensive selections of cowpoke apparel on earth.

A fair share of the Old West's cowboys were black. This and other information concerning the important role African Americans played in the settling of the West is revealed at the **Black American West Museum & Heritage Center,** at 3091 California Street. The museum is open Wednesday through Friday from 10:00 A.M. to 2:00 P.M., and from noon to 5:00 P.M. on Saturday and Sunday. Denver's **Annual Bill Pickett Invitational Rodeo,** the second weekend in August, likewise celebrates the black cowboying heritage, while also honoring Bill Pickett, the "father of bulldogging." Call (303) 292–2566 for more information.

Four Mile Historic Park, a fourteen-acre living-history farm at 715

South Forest Street, holds Denver's oldest house. Since 1859 the structure has served variously as a stage stop, saloon, and farmhouse. Several pioneering professions, including blacksmithing and beekeeping, are pursued here, and stagecoach rides are offered. At the Living History Day Camp, kids aged six to eleven can spend a week as "Colorado pioneers." The park is open in summer from 10:00 A.M. to 4:00 P.M., Wednesday through Sunday, and in winter from 11:00 A.M. to 3:00 P.M., Friday through Sunday. Call (303) 399–1859 for information.

The **Colorado History Museum** (303–866–3682), downtown at Thirteenth and Broadway, sums up, in a very large nutshell, the history of Colorado, with detailed dioramas, black-and-white photographs, films, and a lot more. The museum is open Monday through Saturday from 10:00 A.M. to 4:30 P.M. and on Sunday from noon to 4:30 P.M. The nearby Denver Public Library (303–640–6291) contains a comprehensive collection of photographs, newspapers, books, and manuscripts about the settling of the West. The **Western History Collection** is open from 10:00 A.M. to 9:00 P.M. Monday through Wednesday, from 10:00 A.M. to 5:30 P.M. Thursday through Saturday, and from 1:00 to 5:00 P.M. on Sunday.

The **Museum of Western Art,** one of the best of its breed, features classic works by Frederic Remington, C. M. Russell, Georgia O'Keeffe, and others. The museum is at 1727 Tremont Place, in the old Navarre building, formerly an upscale brothel and casino. Call (303) 296–1880 for information.

If you'd like to room in historic elegance, look no farther than the **Brown Palace Hotel.** The Brown Palace has served as home away from home for a wide-ranging collection of folks for more than a hundred years, from cowboy star Monty Montana—who rode his horse, Rex, up the Grand Staircase to a meeting of the Rodeo Cowboys Association—to those lovable Liverpool cowboys, the Beatles (who have a suite named after them). Even if you can't justify spending between $150 and $250 on a bed, swing in for the walking tour of the lavish lodgings. A brochure that describes the highlights is available at the front desk. Call (303) 297–3111 for information and reservations.

Larimer Square, a block full of restored Victorians, is Denver's oldest commercial area. The sixteen buildings here, all built between 1870 and 1890, were saved from the wrecking ball in the 1950s; thanks to a subsequent restoration effort in the 1960s, the 1400 block of Larimer Street now brims with shopping and dining opportunities amid historic surroundings.

There's no sense eating at any of those downstream fast-food joints while in Denver, for eateries celebrating the Western way in food and decor are as thick here as Platte River water. The grandaddy, **The Buckhorn Exchange,** at Tenth and Osage, has been feeding famished wranglers since Indian scout Henry Zietz opened it in 1893. The Buckhorn is famous for its collections of antique firearms, Indian artifacts, Buffalo Bill memorabilia, and big-game trophies. One of the more than 500 trophies is that of a "duffle bird," a legendary winged critter that lives on a diet of hot chili peppers and has to fly backward to cool its tail feathers! The place also owns and displays the first liquor license issued by the state of Colorado.

Fort Vasquez, approximately 30 miles north of Denver on Highway 85 (1 mile south of Platteville), is a 1930s reconstruction of a fort established a century earlier. The adobe-walled original fort was built during the second half of the 1830s, under a partnership formed by Louis Vasquez and Andrew Sublett. After the wane of the beaver- and buffalo-fur trades, Vasques joined with Jim Bridger to build and operate Fort Bridger in southwest Wyoming. Sublett also moved on, eventually succumbing to a grisly-bear attack in California. Their fort, meanwhile, served a variety of functions during the ensuing decades, including that of a shelter for Pikes Peakers during the gold rush of 1859, a refuge for Civil War troops, and a stagecoach stop. Finally, settlers used what was left of the fort in building their own places, and it was largely in ruins by the turn of the century. The museum houses artifacts excavated at the site as well as sizable collections of Plains Indian and fur-trader trappings. Between Memorial Day and Labor Day, it's open Monday through Saturday from 10:00 A.M. to 5:00 P.M., on Sunday from noon to 5:00 P.M., and on a reduced schedule the rest of the year. The annual **Fort Vasquez Fur Trapping Rendezvous** revives the days of the mountain men, with contests, demonstrations, and games. Call (303) 785–2832 for information.

Greeley was the inspiration for *Centennial,* James Michener's classic novel about the settling of Colorado. The town's **Centennial Village** opened in 1976 in honor of the state's one-hundredth birthday. The six-acre complex, located at 1475 A Street, holds some two dozen historic buildings, and its summer History Alive program dramatizes the region's early days. Also of note is the **Meeker Home Museum,** 1324 Ninth Street, a two-story adobe built in 1870 by Nathan C. Meeker, who founded Greeley as the cooperative Union Colony, one of the most fascinating agricultural experiments undertaken in the Old West. (For more information about Meeker, see page 198.) Both museums are open April 15 through October 15 on changing schedules. The **Municipal Archives,** at 919 Seventh Street, is open year-round from 10:00 A.M. to 4:00 P.M., Monday through Saturday. Call (970) 350–9220 for information on the triad of museums.

The **MacGregor Ranch Museum,** near Estes Park, remains substantially unchanged from when Alexander Q. MacGregor homesteaded here in the early 1870s. Antique furnishings and tableware and historic letters and paintings are among the items displayed. The spread, located north of Highway 34 on Devil's Gulch Road, is open Tuesday through Saturday between June 1 and August 31 from 10:00 A.M. to 4:00 P.M. Call (970) 586–3749 for information.

At about the same time that A. Q. MacGregor settled in the Estes Park area, the fourth Earl of Dunraven visited and decided that he'd like to acquire the entire region as a personal hunting preserve. The homesteaders didn't care much for his plans, and MacGregor, an attorney, spearheaded the battle against the wealthy and presumptuous Dunraven. You can learn about the compelling story at the **Estes Park Area Historical Museum,** found at 200 Fourth Street. A Children's Discovery Room and the original Rocky Mountain National Park headquarters building are also on site. The museum is open May through September from 10:00 A.M. to 5:00 P.M. Monday through Saturday and from 1:00 to 5:00 P.M. on Sunday. Call (970) 586–6256 to learn more.

Several traditional ride-and-relax dude ranches, where you're promised a good horse and a good time, are situated in the Estes Park–Allenspark area: for starters, the **Wind River Ranch** (800–523–4212), the **Lazy H Guest Ranch** (800–578–3598), and the **Aspen Lodge Ranch Resort** (800–332–6867).

Northwest Colorado

After threading your way through spectacular Rocky Mountain National Park and over breath-stealing Milner Pass, drop into the relatively wide-open and sparsely settled spaces of northwest Colorado. The nifty little town of Grand Lake, with its decidedly Old West atmosphere, began as a resort when turn-of-the-century Denverites discovered the area's natural beauty. The **Kauffman House Museum,** 407 Pitkin, was built in 1892 as one of the town's first vacation hotels. Tours of the restored hostelry are given from 1:00 to 5:00 P.M. daily, June through Labor Day.

Horseback trail rides are popular in Grand Lake; call the Chamber of Commerce at (970) 627–3402 for a listing of the possibilities. For lodging consider the charmingly rustic 1921 **Grand Lake Lodge** (970–627–3967), situated on a hillside that overlooks the town and lake.

Outside of Granby (15 miles south of Grand Lake on Highway 34) you'll find a couple of the most highly acclaimed dude ranches in the West: the **C Lazy U Guest Ranch** (970–887–3344) and the **Drowsy Water Ranch** (800–845–2292), with a choice of log cabin or lodge accommodations.

Note: For a terrific free brochure detailing the historic sites of Grand County, call (970) 887–2311 and request the Grand County Exploration Guide.

Heading west along the upper Colorado River on Highway 40, you'll pass through a pair of cow towns where you don't need museums to get a feel for the Old West; nevertheless, you might want to swing into the **Grand County Museum** in Hot Sulphur Springs and, in Kremmling, the **Kremmling Museum.**

From Kremmling go south down Highway 9 into Summit County, better known today for its world-class skiing opportunities than its rich mining heritage. Huge piles of dredged-up river cobbles, however, remain as testimony to the area's rabid gold-mining past. A trio of museums in the area will lead to a better understanding of those early times: the **Montezuma Schoolhouse Museum** (970–453–9022) in Montezuma (an isolated village 8 miles east of Keystone; this also includes the **Washington Gold Mine** and **Lomax Placer Gulch**), the **Frisco Historical Park** (970–668–3428) at Second and Main in Frisco, and the **Summit Historical Society's Public Museum** in Breckenridge. At the latter, situated in the 1896 Romanesque Revival home of William Harrison Briggle, you can begin a self-guided walking tour of Breckenridge's historical district.

Head west along Interstate 70 through the new, sanitized resort mass of Vail–Beaver Creek, and at Wolcott turn north onto Highway 131. Interesting stops along the route to Steamboat Springs include the **Oak**

Creek Outdoor Mining Museum in Oak Creek and the 1903 **Royal Egeria Theatre** in Yampa, where weekly melodramas run in summer. The real draw, however, is the tranquil countryside: Cattle graze in broad meadows, flanked by aspen-studded foothills that rise to grand mountains . . . this is the West as it was and as it should remain.

Steamboat Springs has a long history of skiing. In 1913 Norwegian ski champion Carl Howelsen built a ski jump on the hillside above town, and the town still remained a relatively sleepy ranching community until the Steamboat Springs Ski Area was developed in the mid-1960s. Big-hill skiing and big-time cattle ranching are the major industries today, and the two coalesce at the **Tread of Pioneers Museum** (970–879–2214), at Eighth and Oak, where rooms are devoted to both ranching and skiing. The Fourth of July tradition since 1903, features a parade, a footrace, picnics, and the Steamboat Springs PRCA ProRodeo. One of the more popular spectator events at **Winter Carnival** is "horse skijorning," with horses pulling snow skiers through the streets and over jumps. Call (970) 879–0880 for more information.

Craig, 40 miles west of Steamboat Springs, is home to the **Marcia Railway Car,** named after the daughter of Denver railroad tycoon David Moffat. The lavish Pullman, parked at 341 East Victory Way, was built in 1906 for $25,000, an immense sum, even for a house, at the time. It's open for touring in summer Monday through Friday from 8:00 A.M. to 4:30 P.M. and on weekends from 10:00 A.M. to 3:00 P.M.

Craig's **Grand Olde West Days,** held Memorial Day weekend, include a Wild Game & Roadkill Cookoff (*yuck*) and an Old West gunslingers exhibition. Call the Chamber of Commerce at (970) 824–5689 for information on this and details for area driving tours. The **Wyman Elk Ranch and Pioneer Museum,** located approximately 30 miles southeast of Craig, offers guided tours that show off their impressive elk herds and wild western surroundings. Call (970) 824–6431 for information and reservations, which are required.

The site of the **Meeker Massacre** is marked with an interpretive sign 2 miles west of Meeker on Highway 64. The town was named for Indian agent Nathan C. Meeker, founder of Greeley, who was killed here, along with nine of his employees, in a Ute Indian raid in 1879. The incident precipitated the removal of the Utes from Colorado to a reservation in Utah.

In the fall of 1896, three low-down characters out of Brown's Park, the remote hiding grounds of many a notorious outlaw, blew their attempted robbery of the Bank of Meeker. The trio were shot and killed while exiting the bank, and their bodies were laid out on public display for several days thereafter. They're buried at the local Highland Cemetery. The **White River Museum,** occupying an original 1879 cavalry building located at 565 Park Street in Meeker, includes the pistols used in the botched bank robbery. The museum is open from 9:00 A.M. to 5:00 P.M. daily in summer and on weekends the remainder of the year. Call (970) 878–9982 for information.

The names of the restaurants in Rangely (57 miles west of Meeker on Highway 64) address the town's isolation and Western flair: **Last Chance Restaurant** and **Cowboy Corral.** The capital of Colorado's Isolated Empire began life as a Ute trading post in the 1880s. At the **Rangely Museum** you can learn about the outpost's past and can obtain directions for a driving tour of *Cañon Pintado* (Painted Canyon), with its abundant Ute and Fremont Indian rock art. The museum, housed in the town's original schoolhouse at 434 West Main, is open during summer Monday through Saturday from 10:00 A.M. to 5:00 P.M. and on Sunday from 1:00 to 5:00 P.M. Call (970) 675–2612 for information.

Many of the attractions in Grand Junction (90 miles south of Rangely), the Western Slope's major city, concern the *really* old West—when dinosaurs roamed the countryside. Highlights include the rugged, picturesque terrain of nearby **Colorado National Monument** and the **Museum of Western Colorado** (970–242–0971), at Fourth and Ute. The museum's **Cross Orchards Living History Farm,** located at 3073 F Road (also known as Patterson Road), is a working turn-of-the-century farm, complete with costumed guides. From 1896 to 1923 the farm was operated by the Cross family, owners of the Massachusetts-based Red Cross Shoe Company. It was one of the largest apple orchards in the state, with 22,000 trees spread over 243 acres. The farm is open from 10:00 A.M. to 4:00 P.M., Tuesday through Saturday; noon to 4:00 P.M. Sunday between April 1 and November 1; every day from Memorial Day through Labor Day; and on several days the rest of the year, when special activities take place. Call (970) 434–9814 for information.

Head east along Interstate 70 to Glenwood Springs, where the natural hot springs have attracted humans since prehistoric times. The famous dentist-turned-gunslinger John Henry "Doc" Holliday is buried at Linwood Cemetery, on a hillside overlooking town at Bennett and East Thirteenth streets. Henry "Kid Curry" Logan, a notorious member of Butch Cassidy's Hole-in-the-Wall Gang, also rests here. Logan died of a self-inflicted gunshot when cornered in a canyon outside town, after he and two accomplices robbed the bank in Parachute.

The **Frontier Historical Museum,** housed in a 1905 home at 1001 Colorado Avenue, includes the one-time possessions of Horace W. and Baby Doe Tabor, of Leadville fame. The museum is open from 1:00 to 4:00 P.M. Monday through Saturday in summer and Thursday through Saturday in winter. Call (970) 945–4448 for information.

Historic **Hotel Colorado,** a century old and still running, served as the "Little White House of the United States" when President Teddy Roosevelt went bear hunting on the nearby Flat Tops plateau. The Teddy Bear purportedly was born here, when T.R. returned empty-handed one day and several maids stitched together a small bear to console him, using scraps of fabric. A reporter heard about the incident and coined the term "Teddy Bear," and a toymaker picked up on it. The hotel (970–945–6511) is located at 526 Pine.

From Carbondale, 12 miles south of Glenwood Springs, take a side trip to Aspen, originally a mining camp known as Ute City. By 1893, when the town's population had reached 12,000, nearly 20 percent of the silver mined in the United States came from the Aspen area. It was all downhill from there, however, until 1936, when a ski lodge was built and the Roaring Fork Winter Sports Club was formed. From then on, it was *literally* downhill, and today the place is a human zoo of sorts and a mecca for wealthy skiers.

Still the Old West beckons. The Aspen Historical Society maintains the **Wheeler Stallard Museum,** at 620 West Bleeker Street, built in 1888 by entrepreneur Jerome B. Wheeler. The museum is open during summer and the ski season from 1:00 to 4:00 P.M. Tuesday through Friday; guided historical walking tours that take in a selection of the town's many National Historical Register sites run on Tuesday and Thursday. Call (970) 925–3721 for times.

Hotel Jerome, an Aspen tradition since 1889, has been extensively and sumptuously restored to beyond its original grandeur. An overnight stay costs an arm and a leg—say, from $190 to $630—but drop in and have a look even if you're bunking elsewhere. You may run into a movie star or two in the hotel's Victorian-appointed bar. It's located at 330 East Main; call (970) 920–1000 for reservations.

Ashcroft, 13 miles south of Aspen up Castle Creek, and **Independence,** southeast along the Roaring Fork River on Highway 82 near Independence Pass, are ghost towns open for touring during summer. The **T-Lazy-7 Ranch** (970–925–7040) offers horseback rides in summer and snowmobile and horse-drawn sleigh tours in winter, which often include visits to historic mining camps.

Back in Carbondale, continue south along the Crystal River to Redstone, a former company town, now home to artists and summer vacationers. Outside town you'll spot the old "beehive" ovens once used to carbonize coal. **Redstone Castle** (970–963–3408), the forty-two-room home of coal baron John Cleveland Osgood, can be toured by appointment, and the **Redstone Inn** makes for a great overnight. (It's far less expensive than Aspen's Jerome, although it's run by the former owner of that hotel.) No typical turn-of-the-century building, the old English-tavern replica was built to house Osgood's bachelor miners. The original Seth Thomas clock tower has kept locals apprised of the time of day since day one, in 1902. For reservations call (970) 963–2526.

Southwest Colorado

Crest alluring McClure Pass on Highway 133 and cruise through Paonia, small-town home to the influential environmental tabloid *High Country News* ("A Paper for People Who Care about the West"). Just before Delta take a side trip up Highway 65 to Cedaredge, situated on the flank of Grand Mesa. Here you'll find the Surface Creek Valley Historical Society's **Pioneer Town,** open from 9:00 A.M. to 4:00 P.M. Monday through Saturday and 1:00 to 4:00 P.M. Sunday, from Memorial Day through Labor Day and by appointment the remainder of the year. The Old West village (970–856–3280) includes more than twenty buildings, including the Lizard Head Saloon, a jail, and a museum. From there consider continuing up to the mesa top, reputedly the world's largest flat-topped mountain, for an overnight stay in a log cabin at **Grand Mesa Lodge** (970–856–3250).

Fort Uncompahgre, established in 1826 by Antoine Robidoux, is under restoration at the town of Delta's Confluence Park. Accurately attired guides and interpreters greet visitors and invite them to participate in chores and fur-trading activities. The museum, located at the west end of Gunnison River Drive, is open from 10:00 A.M. to 5:00 P.M. Tuesday through Saturday between March and November and abbreviated hours the rest of the year. For information call (970) 874–8349.

Thunder Mountain Lives Tonight recaps Colorado's Old West history in one dramatic, raucous evening. The performance includes Ute Indian ceremonies, the 1893 McCarty Gang shoot-out in Delta, a subterranean mine cave-in, the story of cannibal Alferd Packer, and more. The Western saga explodes at the outdoor Thunder Mountain Amphitheatre in Confluence Park between July 4 and Labor Day, Thursday through Saturday at 8:00 P.M. For ticket information call (970) 874–8616. (Note: Be sure to call ahead. The show was on hold until 1997 but is expected to reappear in subsequent years.)

The **Montrose County Historical Museum** (970–249–2085), housed in Montrose's old railroad depot, features a vast and varied collection of Western Slope pioneering paraphernalia. It's open between May and October on Monday through Saturday from 9:00 A.M. to 5:00 P.M. and on Sunday from 1:00 to 5:00 P.M. The **Ute Indian Museum and Ouray Memorial Park** (970–249–3098), 17253 Chipeta Drive, celebrates the life of Chief Ouray, at the site of his last residence. The museum contains the most extensive Ute collection in the state, with beadwork, feather bonnets, dance skins, and more. It's open from May 15 to September 30 Monday through Saturday from 10:00 A.M. to 5:00 P.M. and from 1:00 to 5:00 P.M. on Sunday (and by appointment the rest of the year). Call (970) 249–3098 for information.

At Ridgway detour south on Highway 550, the incredibly beautiful Million Dollar Highway, to Ouray and Silverton. The old mining towns have hit pay dirt with tourists today, and browsing for new things in old buildings can readily steal away a day. In Ouray, a hotbed for four-wheel-drive tours, you can either rent a Jeep or hire a guide to drive one for you. High and historic places like Yankee Boy Basin and Camp Bird are regular stops on the tours.

Lofty Silverton, 9,300 feet in elevation, is the northern terminus of the **Durango & Silverton Narrow Gauge Railroad** (see Durango, p. 206).

Walk the streets of the Victorian-rich old mining town and you'll feel as if you've stepped back in time a hundred years. A good place to hole up while there is the **Wyman Hotel and Inn** (970–387–5372 or 800–609–7845), located at 1371 Green Street. The refurbished inn's 2-foot-thick walls are made of locally quarried blocks of red sandstone. All rooms have private baths, and a gourmet breakfast is included in the package.

If you're equipped with a four-wheel drive and nerves of steel, you can tackle one of the toughest jeep outings in Colorado, the **Imogene Pass Road** from Ouray to Telluride, via the Tomboy ghost town, or the much more forgiving one-way **Ophir Pass Road,** beginning near Silverton. If not, backtrack to Ridgway and proceed along the smoothly paved Highway 62.

Placerville, 25 miles southwest of Ridgway, is the southern terminus of the **Unaweep/Tabeguache Scenic & Historic Byway.** The 130-mile route winds, entirely on paved roads, through wonderfully wild desert country near the Utah border to the town of Whitewater. A brochure detailing the route's history and geology is available through the BLM (Bureau of Land Management) in Montrose (970–240–5300).

Telluride, at the head of a box canyon so beautiful it should be illegal, breathes skiing, festivals, and mountain fun. The town was named for tellurium, a rare gold-bearing mineral found in the San Juan Range. "To hell you ride" was a play-on-words phrase used by miners to emphasize the bawdiness of late-nineteenth-century Telluride. George Leroy Parker, later known as Butch Cassidy, was a member of the Tom McCarty Gang when it robbed the bank here in 1889.

The community today, like other mining-camps-turned-ski-meccas, such as Breckenridge and Aspen, proffers an odd mix of venerable Victorians and crackerbox condominiums. The ubiquitous about-town travel brochure includes directions for a self-guided historic walking tour. Among the many highlights is the old stone **San Miguel County Historic Museum,** at the north end of Fir Street, at one time a miners' hospital. It's open from 10:00 A.M. to 5:00 P.M. daily, Memorial Day through mid-October. Call (970) 728–3344 for information.

Prostitution was perfectly legal in old Telluride, as it was in most of the mining camps; in fact, the trade was taxed, and the nearly thirty bordellos provided well for the town coffers. Several old brothels and cribs—where "free agents" not associated with a main brothel worked—can be seen in the old Popcorn Alley along Spruce Street, between Colorado and Pacific avenues. In one of these, the Pick 'n Gad, Jack Dempsey served a stint as a bouncer. (Perhaps he discovered his world-class fighting skills there.)

Telluride's **New Sheridan Hotel** is the place for history buffs to stay while in town. Established in 1891, the hotel is anything but new, and its small rooms and narrow hallways are vestiges of days gone by. It is, however, newly refurbished, and in grand style. The New Sheridan is situated at 231 West Colorado Avenue; call (970) 728–4351 for reservations.

For additional information on Telluride and surroundings, call the visitors bureau at (800) 274–3678, or central reservations at (800) 525–3455.

In Cortez a number of businesses deal in high-quality modern Indian art, such as the **Indian Trading Post Museum,** a half mile east of town on Highway 160. The town also is at the center of southwest Colorado's prehistoric-Indian country. The Anasazi (Ancient Ones) occupied the region from about the time of Christ until they disappeared some 1,300 years later.

Get your bearings at the University of Colorado's **Cortez Center** (970–565–1151), 25 North Market Street, where interpretive exhibits detail the Basketmaker and Pueblo periods of the Anasazi. It's open Monday through Saturday from 10:00 A.M. to 10:00 P.M., Memorial Day through Labor Day, and 10:00 A.M. to 5:00 P.M. the rest of the year. Then travel to the BLM's **Anasazi Heritage Center** in Dolores, 10 miles north of Cortez. The excellent museum, adjacent to the Dominguez and Escalante Ruins, contains thousands of artifacts recovered prior to the flooding of nearby McPhee Reservoir. Kids will go wild over the hands-on exhibits, where they can, for instance, grind corn the old-fashioned way, using a *mano* and *metate.* The museum is open from 9:00 A.M. to 5:00 P.M. daily year-round; call (970) 882–4811 for additional information.

Individuals and families become instant archaeologists at the **Crow Canyon Archaeological Center,** just northwest of Cortez. Here you can work the ongoing excavations at Sand Canyon Pueblo and also explore sites farther afield, in remote canyons and atop lofty mesas. You can even try your hand at throwing a spear with an *atlatl.* Reservations are required for the day and multiday programs; for the latter, four-bed hogans are available as on-site housing. Call (970) 565–8975 for information.

On a cold December day in 1888, when Quaker cowboy Richard

Alferd E. Packer

Having heard about the gold strikes in Colorado, harness maker Alferd Packer and twenty others left Provo, Utah, late in 1873. They arrived at the camp of Chief Ouray, near present-day Delta, in January 1874. The weather was bad, and the Ute chief tried to convince the men to sit out the winter, but Packer and five others persisted into the snowbound San Juans.

They were not heard from again until a robust Packer mosied solo into Saguache the following April. He aroused suspicion when he started spending large sums of money—taken from several different wallets!—at a saloon. Packer told authorities that the others had all died feuding and that he had survived the winter only by eating the flesh of a man he'd killed in self-defense.

That summer a party found five decomposing bodies near the present location of Lake City. Four had been killed from blows to the head and the other from a bullet. Strips of flesh had been removed from their chests and thighs.

Packer was arrested and jailed in Saguache on suspicion of murder. He escaped, however, and remained at large until 1883, when he was tried for and convicted of murder in Lake City, and sentenced to hang. That conviction was overturned, however, and Packer was jailed for manslaughter. He was pardoned by Governor Charles Thomas after only five years in the penitentiary in Canon City. He died of natural causes in 1907.

For a century it was not known for certain if Packer did, in fact, kill and eat his companions. James Starrs, a forensic scientist from George Washington University, in 1989 exhumed the bodies. "Packer clearly cannibalized the five gold prospectors," he reported, adding that he'd "had an insatiable hunger."

The Packer massacre site, just south of Lake City, is marked with a stone memorial and five crosses. "Re-trials" are staged in town in July and August by the Western State College drama department. Packer has been memorialized in many ways and places in Colorado. The most tasteless? Probably the Alferd E. Packer Grill, a snack bar at the University of Colorado in Boulder.

Wetherill and his brother-in-law were searching for cattle lost from their Mancos Valley Ranch, they found much more than a few wayward bovines. The Cliff Palace, Spruce Tree House, and Square Tower House ruins they stumbled across are today at the core of **Mesa Verde National Park,** established in 1906 as the first national park dedicated to the works of humans. Walking through the cliff dwellings (accompanied by a ranger-guide only) can be a truly moving and spiritual experience. The park, 10 miles east of Cortez on Highway 160, is open every day of the year; call (970) 529–4461 or 529–4475 for information.

Ute Mountain Tribal Park, situated on the Ute Mountain Reservation just south of Mesa Verde, was set aside by the Ute Indians to preserve and interpret that which their predecessors left behind. The park, a primitive area covering 125,000 acres surrounding the Mancos River, includes hundreds of Anasazi ruins and prehistoric Ute pictographs. Half-day, full-day, and multiday hiking and mountain-bike tours can be arranged at the **Ute Mountain Pottery Plant,** 15 miles south of Cortez on Highway 666. Reservations and guides are required. Call (970) 565–3751, extension 282, for more information.

In Mancos (6 miles east of Mesa Verde on Highway 160) the **Museum of the Mesa Verde Cowboys,** located in the old George Bauer mansion, is dedicated to Richard Wetherill and Charlie Mason. It's open 1:00 to 4:00 P.M. Monday through Saturday. Consider bunking at the nearby **Echo Basin Dude Ranch** near Mancos, where you can pay and stay by the night. The price of a cabin at this pretty spot includes three meals; call (800) 426–1890 for reservations. If you'd rather commit to a week's duding, contact the **Lake Mancos Guest Ranch** at (970) 533–7900 or (800) 325–WHOA!

Durango, 28 miles east of Mancos on Highway 160, is a vibrant, outdoorsy Western town (the late novelist Louis L'Amour owned a mountain cabin here—need more be said?). Before exploring the town, pardner, outfit yourself properly with a new lid at **O'Farrell of Durango,** 598 Main Avenue, where some of the world's best cowboy hats are fashioned.

Next stroll down the block and jump aboard the **Durango & Silverton Narrow Gauge Railroad.** Of all the historic train rides available in this railroading-rich state, the 115-year-old D&SNG is king. The coal burner makes twice-daily, 45-mile runs up the mountain-embraced Animas River valley between May and late October. It's an all-day affair:

three hours to Silverton, two hours layover, and three hours back; a lot of folks split it up by overnighting in historic Silverton. Make reservations for this very popular excursion at least thirty days in advance by calling (970) 247–2733.

The grand **Strater Hotel,** built in 1887, is where those with a bent for historic surroundings should stay while in town. It's among Colorado's finest Victorian lodgings. At the least, swing into the classic Western **Diamond Belle Saloon** for a quick libation. The enterprise is located at 699 Main Avenue. Call (970) 247–4431 or (800) 247–4431 for reservations.

Another good overnight bet in Durango for western-lore lovers: **The Rochester Hotel,** where each room is appointed with memorabilia from or about Western movies filmed in the area. The hotel (970–385–1920 or –4356) is located at 721 East Second Avenue.

The **Bar D Wranglers** serves a plate of cowboy beans and barbecued beef, spiced with live Western music, that's the best this side of the Pecos. Things get cookin' every evening at 7:30 between Memorial Day and Labor Day. The Bar D spread is located about 8 miles from Durango; call (970) 247–5753 for directions and reservations (required).

Durango's **Western Arts, Film, and Cowboy Poetry Gathering,** in late September or early October, includes showings of art and films, along with plenty of authentic cowboys who spin their special brand of poetry. Call the Chamber of Commerce at (970) 247–0312 or (800) 525–8855 or the Resort Association at (800) 463–8726 for more information.

Just west of Pagosa Springs on Highway 160, drop into the **Fred Harmon Art Museum** (970–731–5785). Dedicated to the hometown boy who created the Red Ryder cowfolk cartoon, which ran from 1938 until 1964, the museum features Western movie memorabilia and original comic-strip art. It's open from 10:30 A.M. to 5:00 P.M. Monday through Saturday, and from noon to 4:00 P.M. on Sundays.

Proceed from Pagosa Springs, via Wolf Creek Pass, to South Fork, through a swath of the most gorgeous Western mountain-and-range country you'll ever run across. Continue to Creede, which, during the silver boom of the 1880s, was home to some 10,000 people. ("It's day all day in the daytime, and there is no night in Creede" wrote poet Cy Wyman about those wild times.) Today it's home to far fewer people and a unique dug-out-rock fire station.

After negotiating Spring Creek and Slumgullion passes, drop into Lake City, kick-off point for the 65-mile **Alpine Loop National Back Country Byway.** The outing is popular among both the four-wheel-driving and mountain-biking crowds, who encounter ghost towns and high mountain summits, including 12,800-foot Engineer Pass. The loop is generally snow-free from early June through October, when nearly two-thirds of it is negotiable by passenger car. Call the Lake City Chamber of Commerce at (970) 944–2527 to obtain a detailed tour pamphlet.

From Lake City head northeast to Gunnison, home of the mid-July **Cattlemen's Days** rodeo and revelry. The town's **Pioneer Museum** (970–641–4530) features impressive collections of historic buildings, photographs, Indian artifacts, and railroad memorabilia. The museum, located at the east end of town on Highway 50, is open from 9:00 A.M. to 4:00 P.M. daily from Memorial Day through Labor Day.

Perhaps due to its end-of-the-pavement isolation, Crested Butte (28 miles north of Gunnison on Highway 135) has retained more of its original character than most of Colorado's abundant mining-towns-turned-ski towns. Still, mountain bikes outnumber horses here today, so when in Crested Butte, do as the locals do: Rent a fat-tire, 21-speed steed and pedal the 5 miles to **Gothic** ghost town, wildest of the wild Gunnison County silver camps.

Crested Butte's annual **Mountain Man Rendezvous** celebrates the days of the fur trappers, with modern-day mountain men and women out-fitted in furs and skins. The festival occurs during late July and early August. Call (970) 349–6438 for information.

Where to Eat

Flying W Ranch, Colorado Springs, (719) 598–4000
Stagecoach Steak & Ale, Manitou Springs, (719) 685–9400
Lazy H Chuckwagon Supper & Western Show, Golden, (303) 278–1938
The Fort, Morrison, (303) 697–4771
The Buckhorn Exchange, Denver, (303) 534–9505
Bar D Wranglers, Durango, (970) 247–5753

Where to Stay

Jackson Hotel, Salida, (719) 539–4861
Imperial Hotel, Cripple Creek, (719) 689–2922
Abriendo Inn, Pueblo, (719) 544–2703
Broadmoor Hotel, Colorado Springs, (719) 634–7711
Buffalo Lodge, Colorado Springs, (719) 634–2851
Frontier's Rest Bed & Breakfast Inn, Manitou Springs, (719) 685–0588
Peck House, Empire, (303) 569–9870
The Cliff House, Morrison, (303) 697–9732
Brown Palace Hotel, Denver, (303) 297–3111
Wind River Ranch, Estes Park, (800) 523–4212
Lazy H Guest Ranch, Estes Park, (800) 578–3598
Aspen Lodge Ranch Resort, Estes Park, (800) 332–6867
Grand Lake Lodge, Grand Lake, (970) 627–3967
C Lazy U Guest Ranch, outside Grand Lake, (970) 887–3344
Drowsy Water Ranch, outside Grand Lake, (800) 845–2292
Hotel Colorado, Glenwood Springs, (970) 945–6511
Hotel Jerome, Aspen, (970) 920–1000
Redstone Inn, Redstone, (970) 963–2526
Grand Mesa Lodge, Cedaredge, (970) 856–3250
Echo Basin Dude Ranch, outside Mancos, (800) 426–1890
Lake Mancos Guest Ranch, outside Mancos, (800) 325–9462
Wyman Hotel and Inn, Silverton, (970) 387–5372 or (800) 609–7845
New Sheridan Hotel, Telluride, (970) 728–4351
Strater Hotel, Durango, (970) 247–4431
Rochester Hotel, Durango, (970) 385–1920 or –4356

Utah

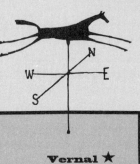

NORTHERN
UTAH

★
Salt Lake
City

Vernal ★

NORTHEAST
UTAH

SOUTHWEST
UTAH

Moab ★

SOUTHEAST
UTAH

★ Escalante

★ St. George

UTAH

▼▼▼

ANY NAMES on the face of Utah—consider Zion, New Harmony, and Moab, for examples—hint at the fact that this once was the promised land for a certain breed of pilgrims. They were the Mormons, members of the Church of Jesus Christ of Latter-day Saints, who in the late 1840s escaped persecution by fleeing their homes in Nauvoo, Illinois. By the thousands they crossed Iowa and entered Nebraska, where they joined in alongside the rushing tide of westward-bound emigrants who were traveling the Oregon Trail.

Today's Mormons, a faithful and proselytizing people, are proud of their ancestors and the hard work they endured under rough conditions to make the arid lands of Utah productive and livable. Most of the towns the "saints" settled are rather plain, in stark contrast with the glorious landscapes that surround them. The southern Utah countryside is, in fact, itself often enough to send a fan of wild Westerns into a frenzy of nostalgia, for scores of shoot-'em-ups have been filmed in Monument Valley, in the Kanab area, and elsewhere in southern Utah.

The narrative begins in the north, courses into the southwestern reaches, then enters southeast Utah, ending finally in the northeast corner of the state.

Northern Utah

In Garden City the **Pickleville Playhouse Summer Theatre** offers Western entertainment and cookouts along the west shore of sparkling Bear Lake. Bear Lake State Park's Rendezvous Beach, on the south end of the lake, is venue for September's **Mountain Man Rendezvous** (801–946–3343), which recalls the days in the 1820s when this area was the setting for the Rocky Mountain Fur Company's annual rendezvous.

Fifteen miles northeast of Logan on Highway 89 in scenic Logan Canyon, then 6 miles south on Temple Fork Road (Forest Road 007), you can visit the grave site of one of the region's most legendary characters. **Old Ephraim,** said to be 10 feet tall and to weigh 1,100 pounds, was among the largest grizzly bears ever taken. Sheepherder Frank Clark, who had tracked the bear for some ten years, finally caught up with him in 1921; Ephraim, sadly, was the last known grizzly to inhabit Utah.

In Logan, whose Center Street has been designated a National Historic District, you'll find the **Daughters of Utah Pioneers Museum** (801–752–2161), at 160 North Main, open between Memorial Day and Labor Day on Tuesday and Thursday from 1:00 to 4:00 P.M., with the addition of 11:00 A.M. to 4:30 P.M. Saturdays during summer. The **Jensen Living Historical Farm** is located 5 miles south of town at 4025 South Highway 89 and is open in summer Tuesday through Saturday from 10:00 A.M. to 4:00 P.M. Actually an outdoor research museum of Utah State University, the place is farmed almost exactly as it would have been by Mormon pioneers in the early 1900s. Special events slated for Saturdays throughout the summer include threshing bees, plowing contests, sheep shearings, and hog butcherings. Call (801) 245–4064 for more information.

The exceedingly popular **Festival of the American West** takes center stage in Logan at Utah State University in late July and early August. The Great West Fair, the heart of the fest, features theme sections that include a Frontier Street, an Indian village, and a mountain-man encampment. Native Americans mix it up with mountain men, Spaniards, pioneers, missionaries, and cowboys in the festival's pageant, *The West: America's Odyssey;* performed nightly at 7:30, the colorful drama features a cast of 200 who relive the saga of the West through dance and music. For information on this one-of-a-kind Festival of the West, call (801) 750–1143.

In Wellsville Canyon, 12 miles southwest of Logan on Highway 91, the outdoor, foot-stomping **Wah-Hoo Revue** is performed by the Wild West Players on Thursday, Friday, and Saturday evenings June through September at the Sherwood Hills Resort. A Western cookout precedes the show. The resort also offers accommodations and indoor dining, along with trail riding on steady horses. Call (801) 245–6055 or 479–4242 to find out more.

The **Brigham City Museum and Gallery** (801–723–6769), with its

The World Championship Dutch Oven Cookoff at the Festival of the American West

large collection of pioneer artifacts, is located at 24 North 300 West in Brigham City (24 miles southwest of Logan) and is open Tuesday through Friday from 11:00 A.M. to 6:00 P.M. The **1870 Methodist Church** at Colorado and South Sixth streets in nearby Corinne, situated along Highway 83 en route to Promontory, is noteworthy because it's believed to be the first non-Mormon church built in the Mormon State. Corinne had twenty-eight saloons at one time and was the most notorious railroad boom town in Utah. Optimistic town founders actually set aside an entire block for a university, which never materialized.

Near Promontory, 35 miles west of Brigham City, the **Golden Spike National Historic Site** marks the spot where, on May 10, 1869, the final spike that linked the first transcontinental railroad was driven. (Actually, the Union Pacific and Central Pacific were more interested in the government land grants that came with developing the railroad than in joining their lines, and they had laid parallel grades for more than 200 miles in Utah before Congress ordered the rails joined at Promontory Summit.) Replicas of a pair of 1869 steam locomotives fire up their engines daily May through October, and the visitor center is open year-round from 8:00 A.M. to 6:00 P.M. Memorial Day through Labor Day and from 8:00 A.M. to 4:30 P.M. the remainder of the year. Every May 10 at the **Last Spike Ceremony,** the event surrounding the driving of the final spike is reenacted—it's a festival celebrating a festival. For information call (801) 471–2209.

In Ogden, which boasts the largest registered National Historic District in the Rocky Mountain region, visit the centerpiece **25th Street.** The complex of museums at **Union Station** (801–629–8444), at Twenty-fifth and Wall, includes the Wattis-Dumke Railroad Museum; upstairs, the Browning Arms Collection honors home-grown Ogden boy John M. Browning. The museums are open year-round Monday through Saturday from 10:00 A.M. to 5:00 P.M., with the addition of 1:00 to 5:00 P.M. on summer Sundays.

Fort Buenaventura State Park (801–621–4808); near the center of town at 2450 A Avenue, is the site of the Great Basin's first permanent white settlement. The park features a replica of the stockade built here by trapper Miles Goodyear around 1840. The park is open daily in summer and on weekends in spring and fall, with a mountain-man rendezvous slated for Easter and Labor Day weekends. Next door to the **Daughters of Utah Pioneers Museum** (801–621–5224), at 2141 Grant Avenue, is Utah's oldest home, a pre-Mormon cottonwood-log cabin built around 1841, also by Goodyear. The cabin and museum are open between May 15 and September 15 Monday through Saturday from 10:00 A.M. to 5:00 P.M.

Up in Huntsville, east of Ogden, you'll find the **Shooting Star Saloon and Cafe,** Utah's longest-running tavern, which was built in 1879. Newer is the **Lagoon Amusement Park,** 17 miles north of downtown Salt Lake City in Farmington, which includes a surprisingly complete and accurate Pioneer Village that the kids will love, if you can drag them from the waterslide and other amusing features also in the park. Stagecoach rides, steamtrain excursions, and a Ute Indian museum are included, and shoot-outs in the street happen daily. The park opens daily Memorial Day through Labor Day and on an abbreviated schedule in April, May, and September. Call (801) 451–8000 for more information.

The **Old Deseret** mid-1800s pioneer village is the centerpiece of Salt Lake City's **Pioneer Trail State Park,** through which runs the final stretch of the Mormon Pioneer National Historic Trail. Costumed docents and craftspersons will bring alive the days of the first Mormon settlers as you tour the adobe houses, public buildings, shops, and renovated Brigham Young Forest Farmhouse. The looming *This Is the Place* monument was erected here in 1947 in commemoration of the one-hundredth anniversary of the arrival of the first Mormon party into the Salt Lake Valley. Another high-light, found in the visitor center, is a huge mural, covering three walls, that depicts the 1,300-mile migration of the Mormons from Nauvoo, Illinois (some 68,000 made the trek). The roles played in Utah by the early Native Americans, Spanish, and mountain men are also explored. The park is located at 2601 Sunnyside Avenue on the east bench of Salt Lake City at the mouth of Emigration Canyon. For information on hours, which change throughout the year, call (801) 584–8391.

The **Fort Douglas Military Museum,** north of Pioneer Trail State Park and run by the U.S. Army Center of Military History, interprets the past at a fort established in 1862 by California-Nevada volunteers. Soldiers were sent to the Utah Territory with the official task of guarding from Indian attack those people who were traveling the Overland Mail route—and with the unofficial task of keeping watch on the Mormons, who were

Pioneer Trail State Park

215

deeply distrusted by many U.S. officials. Commanding officer Col. Patrick Connor and men from Fort Douglas were responsible for the bloody Bear River massacre (see Preston, Idaho, p. 107). Exhibits detail the history of the U.S. military in Utah, the early explorations of the state, and the first Mormon military organizations. A self-guided walking tour of the fort, which takes in the original 1862 cemetery, begins at the museum, open Tuesday through Saturday from 10:00 A.M. to noon and from 1:00 to 4:00 P.M. Call (801) 588–5188 for further details.

Temple Square, in the heart of Salt Lake City, is an immaculately landscaped ten acres that represent the epicenter of the world's Mormon effort. Here, four days after the first pilgrims came into the Salt Lake Valley, Brigham Young stated, "Here we will build a temple to God." The multispired granite temple, begun in 1853, took forty years to complete. Flanking it are two visitor centers and several sculptures symbolic of earlier, tougher times. During the day forty-minute historic tours leave from near the flagpole at the center of the Square (every ten minutes during summer and every fifteen minutes the rest of the year). For additional information go to the city's Visitor Information Center (801–521–2868), located at 180 South West Temple.

The **Museum of Church History and Art** (801–240–3310), at 45 North West Temple Street, features interpretive exhibits, art, historical documents, demonstrations, films, and puppet shows, particularly popular with the kids. Specific highlights include a loaded covered wagon, the very plow that first broke ground in the valley, rare gold Mormon coins from the mid-1800s, a scale model of Salt Lake City in 1870, and a log cabin built in 1847, shortly after the original Mormon party arrived. The museum is open Monday through Friday from 9:00 A.M. to 9:00 P.M. and weekends from 10:00 A.M. to 7:00 P.M.

The **Beehive House,** also on Temple Square, (801–240–2671) was the 1854–77 residence of Brigham Young, who took over the presidency of the Church of the Latter-day Saints after Joseph Smith was assassinated at the Carthage, Illinois, jail in June 1844. Young had a total of twenty-seven wives, so it may seem that such a large house was a necessity; however, only one of them lived with him here at a time. The place is open for touring Monday through Saturday from 9:30 A.M. to 4:30 P.M. (until 6:30 P.M. in summer) and Sunday from 10:00 A.M. to 1:00 P.M.

The **Pioneer Memorial Museum,** operated by the Daughters of Utah Pioneers and located a block north of Temple Square at 300 North Main

Why the Streets Are So Wide in Mormon Country

Salt Lake City was founded on July 24, 1847, by a group of Mormons who had just completed an arduous 1,300-mile journey from Nauvoo, Illinois. The group, led by Brigham Young, consisted of 143 men, 3 women, and 2 children. When the all-powerful Young first viewed the valley, he is reported to have said, "This is the right place."

Immediately the ground was broken by plows, and within just a few days plans were completed for the Great Salt Lake City, named for the nearby inland sea of salt water. Beginning from a point in the center of the city, today identified by the Meridian Marker on Temple Square, blocks were laid out on a grid in ten-acre squares. They were separated by streets that measured 132 feet across—"wide enough for a team of four oxen and a covered wagon to turn around."

This arrangement led to the unusual street addresses common here and in other Mormon-settled towns, which read as if buildings were located on two different streets (for example, 200 North 400 West). The system is actually very efficient and exacting, if somewhat boring.

Street, claims to have the world's largest collection of pioneer artifacts. Paintings, guns, military uniforms, quilts, dolls, books, clothing, furniture, and more are displayed in the main museum. The separate Carriage House, reached via tunnel, features early means of transport: pioneer wagons, surreys, sleighs, bicycles, and handcarts. The museum is open year-round Monday through Saturday from 9:00 A.M. to 5:00 P.M. (also Sunday from 1:00 to 5:00 P.M. June through August). Call (801) 538–1050 for more information.

The **Utah State History Museum** (801–581–4303) is housed in the old Denver and Rio Grande Railroad depot at 300 Rio Grande Street. In the second-level research library, scores of old photographs and books can be perused, while downstairs art and changing exhibits illuminate Utah's compelling past. A top-notch museum bookstore, run by the Utah State Historical Society, is also found on the lower level. The museum is open Monday through Saturday from 9:30 A.M. to 5:30 P.M. and Sunday from noon to 5:00 P.M.

If you're looking for a bite to eat in Salt Lake, look no farther than the

Old Salt City Jail, situated near the University of Utah at 460 South 1000 East. Here you'll dine on prime rib in the old town jailhouse while being serenaded by a singing sheriff! Also of note: **Totem's Club & Cafe,** at 538 South Redwood Road (1700 West), specializing in Mexican and American foods served in a decidedly Western-lodge atmosphere.

The main event at Salt Lake's **Days of '47**—held annually on and around July 24, the date Brigham Young's party exited Emigration Canyon—is the **World Champion Rodeo,** contested at the Delta Center at 301 South West Temple. Related events take place all over town, from old-fashioned pioneer fun and the Annual Dutch Oven Cook-Off at Pioneer Trails State Park to the Western Heritage Art Show at the Utah State Fair Home Arts Building. Parades, concerts, dancing, and a marathon run are also slated; call (801) 325–2000 for a schedule.

Where to stay while in the mecca of Mormonism? One suggestion from scores of possibilities: the **Log Cabin on the Hill** B&B (801–272–2969), located at 2275 East 6200 South, where you'll have a grand view of the Wasatch Mountains and easy access to Salt Lake and the mountain towns beyond.

The **Desert Star Playhouse,** at 4861 South State in suburban Murray, is one of the top family draws in greater Salt Lake. Old-timey melodrama, complete with audience participation, rip-roars through the evenings. Call (801) 266–7600 for information. Also in Murray the **Wagonmaster Steak Company,** the Original Cowboy Steakhouse, at 5485 South Vine, boasts a Dodge City–flavored ambience, with covered wagons, cowboys, and Indians, as well as good food.

In Wanship, northeast of Salt Lake City on Interstate 80, enjoy a wagon ride, Western barbecue, and other Old West fun with the **Blue Sage Hayride and Barbecue Company** (801–268–2020). To the south in the resort village of Park City, the **Park City Stables** offer one- and two-hour trail rides, as well as breakfast and dinner rides that feature great cowboy cooking. Memorial Day through mid-October they'll point you or guide you to trailheads that lead to mountain vistas and broken-down silver mines. The stables (801–645–7256) are located at 1700 Park Avenue.

The **Park City Museum** (801–649–6104), on historic Main Street—a street lined with boutiques, espresso stands, outdoor stores, and specialty shops—incorporates the Utah Territorial Jail, and when you see it, you'll be glad never to have done time there. The museum also includes displays on mining and skiing, this venerable town's two boom industries. It is open year-round on Monday through Saturday from 10:00 A.M. to 7:00 P.M. and on Sunday from noon to 6:00 P.M. The Park City Visitor Information Center shares the building and the same hours, and personnel there will happily provide you with information on the town's historic walking tour.

The **Heber Valley Historic Railroad,** which made its first run in 1899, chugs out of the depot at 450 South 600 West in Heber City, 11 miles southeast of Park City. Regularly scheduled steam-train outings in renovated coaches push through the Heber Valley and Provo Canyon, en route to Vivian Park. For more information call the Heber Valley Railroad Authority at (801) 654–5601.

Butch Cassidy lived in Utah; today the Sundance Kid does, or, anyway, the guy who played him in the movie does. **Sundance Resort** (northeast of Provo on Highways 189 and 92), which Robert Redford began building in the early 1970s, has a neo–Old West feel to it. The stables here rent gentle horses, with guided trail rides that head into the surrounding, dramatic countryside daily between 9:00 A.M. and sundown. For on-site accommodations, contact Sundance Cottages and Mountain Homes at (801) 225–4107.

Between 1858 and 1861 Fairfield (50 miles northwest of Provo on Interstate 15 and Highway 73) boasted a population of 7,000, most of whom were soldiers stationed at Camp Floyd. The soldiers, representing the largest single concentration of troops in the United States during those years, had been sent west to ward off a rumored Mormon rebellion. They were ordered back to Fort Leavenworth, Kansas, in 1861 to serve in the brewing Civil War; as suddenly as they had lost their peace and quiet, the twenty or so families who had settled the fair valley before the Army arrived had it all to themselves again. The main attraction here today is **Stagecoach Inn State Park,** which holds John Carson's two-story adobe-and-wood inn. The restored inn, which contains original furnishings, was built in 1858 to serve as a Pony Express station and an overnight stop for Overland Trail travelers. It's open daily Easter through October 31; call (801) 768–8932 for more information.

Stagecoach Inn State Park is the kickoff point for the **Pony Express Trail National Back Country Byway.** The byway, administered by the Bureau of Land Management (BLM), rolls across 133 miles of uninhabited sagebrush desert and low-slung mountain ranges between here and Ibapah, just short of the Nevada border. (Just off the route northeast of Ibapah, incidentally, is **Gold Hill,** arguably the most impressive ghost town in the state.)

All but 7 miles of the byway are unpaved, but the graded gravel is suitable for passenger cars in all but the worst of weather. Along the way you can expect to see antelope, mule deer, golden eagles, and wild mustangs. You'll find a Visitor Information Site 3 miles west of Faust Junction. For a brochure that details the trail and what to expect while traveling it, contact the BLM in Salt Lake City at (801) 977–4300.

Nephi's **Ute Stampede Rodeo** (801–623–1362), 85 miles south of Salt Lake City, is held the second weekend in July and celebrates the great American cowboy and his boss, the cattleman. Parades, dancing, and victuals are vital components of the fun. While in town, hole up in one of the nine newly remodeled rooms at the **Whitmore Mansion** B&B, a sumptuous accommodation that occupies a 1900 Queen Anne–style Victorian. It's located at 110 South Main; call (801) 623–2047 for reservations.

Southwest Utah

Spring City, 30 miles southeast of Nephi on Highways 132 and 117, is unique in Utah in that every building in town is listed on the National

The Pony Express Oath of Employment

Pony Express riders, whose foremost requirement was that they weigh less than 120 pounds, were issued a Bible meant to help them sustain their brave outlook as they rode solo through a harsh country, sometimes in the company of bandits or hostile Indians.

They also signed an oath, which read as follows:

I hereby swear, before the great and living God, that during my engagement, and while I am an employee of Russell, Majors & Waddell, I will, under no circumstances, use profane language; that I will drink no intoxicating liquors; that I will not quarrel or fight with any other employee of the firm; and that in every respect, I will conduct myself honestly, faithful to my duties, and so direct my acts as to win the confidence of my employers. So help me God.

Register of Historic Places. The past is revived here at the Memorial Day weekend **Heritage Day** (801–283–4321 or 462–2708), with buggy rides, home tours, old-fashioned entertainment, a sheep barbecue, and more. The out-of-the-ordinary **Ephraim Homestead** B&B, at 135 West 100 North in nearby Ephraim, features accommodations in both an 1860s log cabin and an 1880s Victorian country room (over the barn). Call (801) 283–6367 to find out more.

Sixteen miles southwest of Spring City on Highway 89, Manti's **Mormon Miracle Pageant,** Utah's largest outdoor dramatic presentation, recounts tales of Mormon pioneers' toil and romance in the face of remarkable hardship. The spectacle is staged evenings in July, with the imposing hillside Manti Temple, constructed in 1888 of white oolitic limestone, serving as a backdrop and underscoring the saints' resounding success. Call (801) 835–3000 or 835–3823 for schedule and ticket information. A number of historic lodgings grace the picturesque town, including the **Manti House Inn** (801–835–0161), at 401 North Main, which offers rooms in the house where some of the workers who built the Manti Temple stayed more than a century ago.

At 50 West Capitol in Fillmore, 70 miles southwest of Manti, **Territorial Statehouse State Park** contains Utah's oldest government building. Brigham Young directed its construction in anticipation of statehood, but only the south wing was completed, for strife between the Mormons and the U.S. government obstructed anticipated federal funding. Only one full session of the Territorial Legislature, in 1855, was conducted in the building before the seat of government returned to Salt Lake City. Today the state parks department operates the statehouse as a museum, with rooms appointed to resemble typical pioneer rooms. A pair of log cabins and an old schoolhouse also grace the grounds. The park is open daily from 8:00 A.M. to 8:00 P.M. Memorial Day through Labor Day and from 9:00 A.M. to 6:00 P.M. the remainder of the year. For further information call (801) 743–5316.

Imposing **Cove Fort** was built of volcanic basalt in 1867 during the Black Hawk War, to protect stage and freight lines that traversed the Old Spanish Trail. Now restored to its late-1800s condition, the fort is located near the junction of Interstate 70 and Interstate 15 and is open to visitors daily mid-April through mid-October from 9:00 A.M. to dusk.

The **Biggest Little Rodeo in the World** revs up in July in Marysvale, the little town where Zane Grey wrote books, including *Riders of the Purple*

Sage, at his Pines Hotel. Today Marysvale provides access to a number of area ghost towns, such as **Kimberly,** situated high in the gorgeous Tushar Mountains. The unpaved, 16-mile Kimberly Scenic Drive climbs to around 10,000 feet before dropping into Clear Creek Canyon and connecting with Interstate 70 at exit 17. Information is available from the Fishlake National Forest; call (801) 438–2436.

Also along Interstate 70 near exit 17 is the **Fremont Indian State Park & Museum.** The park interpretive center displays a large array of Fremont culture artifacts recovered from the Five Finger Ridge Village, which was discovered during construction of the interstate in 1983. The Fremont culture, prevalent in the area from about A.D. 500 to 1200, is explained via film, exhibits, and a reconstructed pit-house dwelling and granary. Trails lead to Fremont rock art and an outstanding canyon overlook. The museum is open daily in summer from 9:00 A.M. to 6:00 P.M. and the rest of the year from 9:00 A.M. to 5:00 P.M.; for further information call (801) 527–4631.

Rockin' R Ranch near Antimony, 35 miles southeast of Marysvale, is a working cattle ranch first, dude ranch second, which means it's authentic but not necessarily intimate, with its capacity of 300. The 16,000-square-foot main lodge has twenty bedrooms, and there are also cabins and a dormitory for large groups. Riding, roundups, and cow-camp overnights on the Aquarius Plateau are the top diversions, with fishing, boating, and sailboarding on nearby Otter Lake and tubing on the Sevier River also popular. Hayrides and cowboy crooning fill the evening hours. Call (801) 624–3250 for information and reservations.

Just off Interstate 15 at exit 78, Parowan, settled in January 1851, was southern Utah's first town; from here Mormon parties were dispatched to establish settlements elsewhere. Numerous old structures still stand, including the 1858 **Jesse N. Smith Home** (801–477–8190), now a museum open for tours by appointment. Smith and his family lived in this two-story adobe home until 1878, when he was recruited to lead a group of pilgrims to establish the Mormon settlement of Snowflake, Arizona. Across the street is the equally historic **Rock Church** (801–477–3549), completed in 1867, which displays pioneer furniture and other relics and is also open by appointment Memorial Day through Labor Day. For information on the many other historical sites and structures about town, call the Parowan City Office at (801) 477–3331.

Offering rooms and good meals, **Jedediah's Inn & Settler's**

Mormons Gone Bad

The first Mormons in Utah were isolationists. Their lifestyles were unorthodox, and they had endured great persecution in the Midwest; when they moved to Utah, self-sufficiency was a must, with the nearest bastions of civilization hundreds of miles away. Moreover, Brigham Young himself had mandated that the Kingdom should be independent of the "Gentile nations."

From the outset wayward ways among Mormon youngsters were something the oldsters had to contend with. In their unique situation young Mormons inherited both the untamed nature of the frontier into which they were born and their parents' hatred for federal authority. Dancing, fighting, and wild partying among the youth often gave Main Street, or "Whiskey Street," in Salt Lake City a tone more like that of Abilene or Virginia City than of a staid Mormon settlement.

Two young men who carried their "Jack Mormonism" to extremes were Matt Warner, from Levan, and George LeRoy Parker, born and raised near Circleville. When Warner rode to Arizona with his father in 1881 to do work for Brigham Young's son, he wound up robbing a store and hightailing it over the Painted Desert into the canyonlands of southeast Utah. Parker, who got off to a bad start by robbing a clothing store and rustling cattle, later assumed the surname of Cassidy and the first name of Butch and joined the Wild Bunch. (You can visit the cabin where Cassidy was born and raised, 2 miles south of Circleville.)

Restaurant (801–477–3326), at 625 West 200 South in Parowan, also provides horse-drawn wagon rides around the old town, wagon treks into the surrounding mountains, and tours of an operating draft-horse farm and carriage shop. In April the typically quiet town roars to life during the **Iron County Cowboy Days & Poetry Gathering.** In addition to buckaroo-verse recitals, there are horse and mule racing, sheep-shearing demonstrations, and a Western heritage exposition.

Cedar City, 20 miles southwest of Parowan, was settled later in 1851, when a party from Parowan established the Coal Creek settlement to take advantage of the area's rich iron-ore deposits. Historic sites abound in and around town, including **Iron Mission State Park,** which commemorates those pioneer miners, the first to produce iron west of the Mississippi River.

Among the features in the park's large museum is Gronway Parry's extensive collection of pioneer-era vehicles, including a stagecoach riddled with bullet holes allegedly created by Butch Cassidy and his boys. Also on hand are mining and pioneer artifacts and a diorama that details the original foundry operations. The park, located at 595 North Main, is open daily from 9:00 A.M. to 7:00 P.M. in summer and from 9:00 A.M. to 5:00 P.M. the rest of the year. Call (801) 586–9290 for information. (If iron really piques your interest, inquire here for information on the nineteenth-century ruins of **Old Irontown,** situated 20 miles, mostly paved, west of Cedar City.)

When in town for Cedar City's **Paiute Powwow,** held the third week in June, or August's **Jedediah Smith High Mountain Rendezvous** mountain-man festival, swing into **Milt's Stage Stop** in Cedar Canyon, 5 miles east of town, for some of the best steak in Utah.

Easily accessible from Leeds (it's less than 2 miles west of Interstate 15) are the remains of **Silver Reef,** at one time a rip-roaring, but now snoring, silver-mining settlement. With streets paved of river cobbles and its own quarter-horse racetrack, Silver Reef, at its zenith, claimed nearly 2,000 residents, approximately 10 percent of whom were Chinese. The restored Wells Fargo Building, built in 1877 and listed on the National Register of Historic Places, holds the **Wells Fargo Museum and Art Gallery** (801–879–2254), open Monday through Saturday from 9:00 A.M. to 5:00 P.M.

St. George, warm in winter (and boiling in summer), has in recent years grown exceedingly popular as a winter getaway for retired "snowbirds" from the north. It can be argued that Brigham Young himself started the trend, for it was to St. George that he repaired during his last few winters, both to seek relief from rheumatism and to oversee construction of the settlement's mighty temple. The **Brigham Young Winter Home** (801–673–2517), located at 200 North 100 West, is open to visitors year-round from 9:00 A.M. to dark, with free tours that begin at the office on the east side of the house.

Washington (55 miles southwest of St. George) was established in 1857, five years before St. George, as the hub of Utah's "Dixie," to which the church president dispatched families with the mission of growing cotton. The original mill still stands as testimony to Brigham Young's vision of a cotton empire, a dream that never was fully realized. Nearby Santa Clara boasts the 1862 **Jacob Hamblin Home** (801–673–2161), residence of a prolific colonizer who fathered twenty-four children and befriended the local Native Americans. Hamblin's place is located off Santa Clara Drive on Hamblin Drive and is open year-round from 9:00 A.M. to dark. For information on the historic walking tour of St. George and surrounding communities, call the Washington County Travel Council at (801) 634–5747. Included on the tour is **Greene Gate Village,** where six restored pioneer homes, with a total of sixteen antiques-filled rooms, are available for overnighting. Also within the village is the **Bentley Supper House,** with home-cooked country dinners served Thursday, Friday, and Saturday evenings by reservation. The village is located at 76 West Tabernacle; call (801) 628–6999 for lodging reservations or 656–3333 for dinner reservations.

From Rockville (30 miles east of St. George) go 3½ miles south on Bridge Road (200 East) to the well-preserved ghost town of **Grafton.** Settled in 1859, the original town floated downstream three years later, following a forty-day rain storm. If the town looks familiar, that's probably because it was the site of the filming of the famous bicycle scene ("Raindrops Keep Fallin' on My Head . . .") in *Butch Cassidy and the Sundance Kid.*

Springdale, 4 miles northeast of Rockville and settled in 1862, is gateway to spectacular Zion National Park and host to the **Southern Utah Folklife Festival** the second weekend in September. The festival resurrects the days of the pioneers, with crafts demonstrations, food, and old-fashioned music and dancing. The **Bit and Spur Saloon,** at 1212 Zion Park Boulevard, dishes up some of the best Mexican food in Utah, while **O'Tooles' Under the Eaves Guest House** (801–772–3457), at the mouth of Zion Canyon at 980 Zion Park Boulevard, provides comfy accommodations in a sound structure built of locally quarried sandstone blocks.

Forty-three miles southeast of Springdale is Kanab. In this town—nicknamed "Little Hollywood" because so many silver-screen Westerns have been filmed in the vicinity over the past forty years—make your way to the history-rich **Heritage House,** at 100 South Main. It's open in summer from 8:00 A.M. to noon and from 2:00 to 6:00 P.M. **Frontier Movie Town** (801–644–5337), constructed by locals as a monument to the Old West and silver-screen Westerns, is open for touring year-round from 8:00 A.M. to 10:00 P.M. The enterprise also offers cowboy cookouts and Western-entertainment shows.

Note: Kanab offers the easiest access to fascinating Pipe Spring National Monument (see Arizona).

Old Paria ghost town, situated amid a stunning red-rock BLM landscape, is reached by driving 33 miles east of Kanab on Highway 89, then 6 miles north on a dirt road. The town was settled in 1870 by Mormon pioneers who ran cattle and grew nuts and vegetables, while living in sturdy sandstone houses. (Incidentally, some visitors have confused the Hollywood set about a mile from town with the actual ghost town.)

The Mormon people appreciate order—in their lives, their street-naming systems, and the names of their museums. Orderville, site of a Mormon experiment in communal living that began in 1875, has yet another **Daughters of the Utah Pioneers Museum,** this one located on Highway 89 east of town. Hatch, 30 miles north of Orderville, has a similarly named museum.

In the Tropic–Bryce Canyon area, the **B-Bar-D Covered Wagon Company** (801–834–5144) hauls guests around in wagons, serves up hearty chuckwagon meals, and dishes out a foot-stomping Western hoedown. **Canyon Trail Rides** (801–679–8665) will set you up with a horse and saddle for a short trail ride, or they'll lead the more ambitious on the 100-mile, six-day Red Rock Ride, which traverses the remarkable landscape that separates Bryce Canyon and Grand Canyon national parks.

Southeast Utah

Forty miles east of Bryce Canyon, Escalante's **Daughters of Utah Pioneers Museum,** open by appointment, occupies the town's old LDS (Latter-day Saints) Tithing Office. Four miles east of Escalante is the kickoff point for the rough and remarkable **Hole-in-the-Rock Road.** The byway, not to be followed on a lark, leads southeast for some 65 miles to Hole-in-the-Rock, a historic crevice high in a rock wall. Here early in 1880 a party of more than 200 Mormon pioneers dispatched from Parowan, undauntable in their quest to settle the far southeast of Utah, blasted the notch wider so that they could squeeze their wagons through. Then they lowered the wagons over a precipitous pitch to be ferried across the Colorado River. (Lake Powell now lies below Hole-in-the-Rock, but not nearly as far below as did the undammed Colorado.) After an exhausting six-month journey, the party stopped, where they established the town of Bluff.

Boulder's **Anasazi Indian Village State Park** (801–335–7308), 30 miles northeast of Escalante, displays artifacts excavated from the Coombs Site, which was occupied around A.D. 1050 to 1200. A self-guided tour of the ruins starts right outside the visitor center, which is open from 8:00 A.M. to 6:00 P.M. in summer and from 9:00 A.M. to 5:00 P.M. the remainder of the year. If the spectacular high country of Boulder Mountain above town beckons, arrange a trail ride or pack trip in the Hell's Backbone vicinity by calling the **Boulder Mountain Ranch** at (801) 335–7480. The ranch also offers lodging.

Tackle the breathtaking Burr Trail into Capitol Reef National Park, one of the last places in the West explored by whites. Here the National Park Service maintains the old homestead buildings and orchards of **Fruita,** which was settled by Mormons in the late 1870s. Then wend your way to Hanksville and its BLM headquarters (801–542–3461), where you can have a look at the unique and ingenious **Wolverton Mill,** formerly utilized both to crush ore and cut wood.

You can also obtain information at the BLM office on the driving tour of the remote and dramatic **Henry Mountains,** a veritable high-country oasis that rises from the stark desert. The Henrys are home to the last free-roaming, huntable bison herd in North America, numbering around 200 animals. Also ask for directions to the legendary **Robber's Roost Canyon,** at one time an Outlaw Trail hideout along the Dirty Devil River for Butch Cassidy and others of his ilk. This is remote, unforgiving country; if you'd enjoy yourself more in the company of a guide, contact **Outlaw Trails, Inc./Robbers Roost Ranch** in Hanksville, at (801) 542–3421 or 542–3221.

Located in the big empty between Hanksville and Mexican Hat is **Fry Canyon Lodge,** "a country inn disguised as a classic desert outpost." The proprietors claim, accurately no doubt, that their establishment is the most remote desert lodge in Utah. In fact, it's the only business found along the entire 120-mile stretch of the Bicentennial Highway linking Hanksville and Blanding. Fry Canyon was a bustling service center during the mineral-boom days of the 1950s, when it boasted a school, a post office, and numerous abodes housing miners and cowboys. At that time the lodge, which was established in 1955, really was a desert outpost; its original role was that of a mining-supply store. For two years in a row it sold more beer than any establishment in the state—not surprisingly, really, since a captive clientele of some 3,000 thirsty miners was close at hand. Fry Canyon Lodge is situated smack in the heart of the labyrinthine, redrock canyon country, where the hiking and four-wheel-driving opportunities are out of this world. The lodge features six guest rooms, a cafe/bar, and all the comforts of home—despite having to generate its own power and pump its own water. For information and reservations call (801) 259–5334.

Tiny Mexican Hat, immediately across the San Juan River from the vast Navajo Indian Reservation, holds a trio of enterprises that specialize in Native American arts and crafts: **Burch's Trading Post**, the **San Juan Inn & Trading Post**, and **Valle's Trading Post**. All are located along Highway 163. Twenty-two miles southwest in the settlement of Monument Valley, **Goulding's Trading Post** is part museum and part active trading post. This reminder of an earlier day in the hinterland is located in Utah's portion of the Navajo Reservation, 2 miles west of Highway 163. On the grounds is the structure referred to locally as "John Wayne's cabin," which appeared in the Western *She Wore a Yellow Ribbon*. Goulding's also offers lodging and tours of the other-worldly terrain that surrounds the enterprise. Call (801) 727–3231 for information. The nearby **Navajo Tribal Park Headquarters and Visitor Center,** with its displays on Navajo archaeology and art, is open daily 7:00 A.M. to 7:00 P.M. April through October and from 8:00 A.M. to 5:00 P.M. the rest of the year; call (801) 727–3287 for information.

Have a homemade meal or simply enjoy browsing at the **Cow Canyon Trading Post,** 163 Mission Road in historic Bluff (at the junction of Highways 191 and 163), where you can also tour or sleep in the **Pioneer House,** one of San Juan County's first non-Indian structures. For information call (801) 672–2208 or 672–2281.

Several groups of Anasazi Pueblos thrived near present-day Blanding (25 miles north of Bluff) between A.D. 700 and 1200; they are a short hike away from the visitor center at **Edge of the Cedars State Park** (801–678–2238). The visitor center houses an outstanding collection of Anasazi artifacts, as well as exhibits that focus on those groups who came after the Anasazi—Navajos, Utes, and white settlers. The facility, located at 660 West 400 North, is open daily from 9:00 A.M. to 6:00 P.M. May 16 through September 15 and from 9:00 A.M. to 5:00 P.M. the rest of the year.

Huck's Museum and Trading Post, with Indian artifacts on display and a wide selection of Wild West goods for sale, is located on South Highway 191 in Blanding. The **Grayson Country Inn** (801–678–2388 or 800–365–0868), at 118 East 300 South, is a good choice for accommodations while in town, perhaps for the annual **White Mesa Ute Council Bear Dance** in early September.

At the San Juan County Visitor Center (800–574–4386), at 117 South Main in Monticello (25 miles north of Blanding), pick up the brochure that details the incomparable Trail of the Ancients driving tour, which leads the way to Anasazi ruins from **Grand Gulch Primitive Area** on the west to Blanding's Edge of the Cedars and then to **Hovenweep National Monument** on the Utah-Colorado border.

The **MD Ranch Cookhouse** (801–587–3299), located at 380 South Main in Monticello, features "great out West food," live Western music, and a cowboy museum. It's open daily for breakfast from 7:00 to 10:00 A.M. and for dinner from 4:00 to 10:00 P.M. The **Grist Mill Inn** B&B, located at 64 South 300 East, provides comfy accommodations in a converted flour mill. Ten rooms, each with private bath, are available, as are the cozy sitting room with fireplace, hot tub, and third-floor library. Call (801) 587–2597 for information and reservations.

Four-wheel-drive tours and scenic flights through the remarkable and diverse country of the southern Canyonlands can be arranged through the **Needles Outpost.** True to its name, this remote enterprise is located 34 miles west of Highway 191 on Highway 211, at the entrance to the Needles District of Canyonlands National Park. Call (801) 979–4007 for more information.

Pack Creek Ranch, 15 miles southeast of Moab off LaSal Mountain Loop, offers lodging in picturesque, red-roofed cabins, each with a full kitchen. The cabins are available for rent year-round, whereas the restaurant on the premises serves meals March through October only. Hiking, mountain biking, horseback riding (including overnight pack trips), fishing, river running, and four-wheel-drive tours are among the many diversions that can be enjoyed while using the ranch as a base. Call (801) 259–5505 for information and reservations.

Have a meal in Moab in National Historic Register surroundings at the **Grand Old Ranch House** restaurant, a mile north of downtown Moab and open daily for dinner; or head for the **Bar "M" Chuckwagon** (801–259–2276), where cowboys and cowgirls dish up hearty grub and Western songs and tall tales on the banks of Mill Creek at 541 South Mulberry Lane Monday through Saturday from April to October. The community pays homage to its Old West heritage at **Butch Cassidy Days,** slated for early June, when things get even livelier than usual in Moab. Call (801) 259–6226 to learn how to take part.

Fifty miles northwest of Moab, Green River's riveting **John Wesley Powell River History Museum,** overlooking the legendary Green River at 885 East Main, interprets Utah's river history in general and, in particular, the epic Green and Colorado river exploratory floats, undertaken by Powell and his men in 1869 and 1871. Various watercraft used to negotiate the Green—from a round-hulled Indian boat to primitive rafts and modern-day crafts—are among the items displayed. The River Runner's Hall of Fame is also situated within the facility, open in summer daily from 8:00 A.M. to 8:00 P.M. and in winter from 9:00 A.M. to 5:00 P.M. Call (801) 564–3427 for more information.

Wagons creak amid a setting of log cabins and tipis at the **Castle Valley Pageant,** staged 7 miles north of Castle Dale (37 miles northeast of Interstate 70 on Highway 10) at Pioneer Village in late July and early August. The pageant depicts the triumphs and failures of early settlers in the valley: Directed by Latter-day Saints church president Brigham Young, homesteaders head to the desolate Castle Valley, where they proceed to attempt to convert the local Native Americans to Mormonism. A lamb fry is held each day at the Castle Dale city pavilion between 4:00 and 7:30 P.M. in conjunction with the show, which gets underway at 8:30 P.M. For information on the pageant or to arrange for a ride in a covered wagon, call event organizer and wagonmaster Montell Seely at (801) 381–2195.

Northeast Utah

At the Castle Country Travel Council center in Price (800–842–0789), pick up a brochure that leads the way on a self-guided tour of the BLM's **Nine Mile Canyon National Scenic Byway,** where you'll find canyon walls that are the palette for prehistoric petroglyphs and pictographs.

In Helper, 7 miles north of Price, the **Western Mining and Railroad Museum** (801–472–3009) is situated in an old four-story hotel at 296 South Main. Featured are historical photographs and mining memorabilia, including details of the 1900 Scofield mine disaster, which killed 200 men. Here you can also pick up a guidebook that details a driving tour to ten abandoned mine sites in Carbon and Emery counties, including Consumers,

John Wesley Powell

In 1862 Union artillery commander Maj. John Wesley Powell lost his right arm below the elbow to a Confederate rifle ball at the Battle of Shiloh. The stump caused him pain for the rest of his life, but if it slowed him down any it surely didn't show, for Powell went on to live an amazing life as a self-trained naturalist and one of the great explorers of the West.

Not the least of his feats was a trip down the Green and Colorado rivers in 1869. On May 11 of that year, in the rough-and-ready Wyoming Territory settlement of Green River, Powell and a dubious crew of nine—including brother Walter, still reeling from his internment in a Confederate prison, and five drunken trappers—hauled four boats off a Union Pacific railcar and unceremoniously slipped them into the Green.

Our imaginations can only begin to picture what that journey, through wild and unknown waters, must have been like. A thousand miles, a hundred days, and three lives later—close to the end a trio of the trappers jumped ship, climbed the North Rim of the Grand Canyon, and were killed by Shivwits warriors—Powell and his remaining crew popped out of the canyon after negotiating the Separation Canyon rapids and took out near the mouth of the Virgin River.

Years later Powell was asked how he'd managed to make it through the Grand Canyon on his first try. "I was lucky," the explorer quipped.

Hiawatha, and Winter Quarters. The museum is open Monday through Saturday from 9:00 A.M. to 5:00 P.M. May through September and Tuesday through Saturday noon to 5:00 P.M. the rest of the year.

The annual **Northern Ute Indian Powwow** whoops it up at Fort Duchesne (80 miles northeast of Helper on Highway 191) over the Fourth of July, with Indians from throughout the West taking part in the rodeo action and dancing. Vernal, 20 miles northeast, boasts a **Daughters of Utah Pioneers Museum,** at 158 South 500 West, open Monday through Saturday from 1:00 to 7:00 P.M. from May 31 to September 1. The museum includes a large array of pioneerabilia and a replicated Old West settlement. Also in town is the 7,500-square-foot **Western Heritage Museum and Arts Gallery** (801–789–7399), situated in the Western Park complex, with details on both the outlaw and the law-abiding past of the region; it's open from May to September from 9:00 A.M. to 6:00 P.M. Monday through Saturday and 9:00 A.M. to 5:00 P.M. Monday through Friday the rest of the year. The **Outlaw Trail Theatre,** at the Western Park outdoor amphitheater, presents *Rawhide & Lace,* the story of Josie Bassett, the female legend of Brown's Park. The show begins at 8:00 P.M. on summer eves late June through late July. Call (800) 477–5558 for ticket information.

Among the best months to visit Vernal are June and July, during the **Outlaw Trail Festival,** which includes bank robberies and shoot-outs in the streets, an Outlaw Trail Art Show, a competition for poetry that focuses on outlaws and women of the Old West, a Butch Cassidy Outlaw Trail Ride, and a lot more. Call (800) 477–5558 for further information. When in town, try out the **Seven-Eleven Ranch Restaurant,** at 77 East Main, specializing in barbecue and also dishing out great breakfast specials.

From a base in Jensen, **Western Wagon Tours** (801–789–6574) offers carriage rides around venerable Vernal as well as chuckwagon dinners beyond town, while the **All 'Round Ranch** (801–789–7626) teaches horsemanship and cowpunching and offers "cowboy tepee camping."

The very remote **John Jarvie Historical Property,** located in Brown's Park, approximately 50 miles northeast of Vernal, offers a graphic glimpse at turn-of-the-century frontier life. Four original structures, all more than one hundred years old, still stand on this thirty-five-acre site, including a two-room dugout, a corral, and the stone house built by outlaw Jack Bennett, who used masonry skills he picked up in prison. The house now serves as a museum, which, among its displays, ironically includes the pole from which Bennett was hanged by vigilantes. John Jarvie, a well-liked Scot who settled here in 1880 and ran a post office, store, and ferry service, himself died at the hands of outlaws: On July 6, 1909, Jarvie was robbed and murdered, his store ransacked, and his body put in a boat and sent afloat in the Green River. His body was discovered eight days later; his murderers never were. Tours are conducted daily May through October between 10:00 A.M. and 5:00 P.M. For directions and further information, call the BLM in Vernal at (801) 789–1362 and request the *John Jarvie Historic Property* brochure.

Where to Eat

Shooting Star Saloon and Cafe, Huntsville. (801) 745–2002
Old Salt City Jail, Salt Lake City, (801) 355–2422
Totem's Club & Cafe, Salt Lake City, (801) 975–0401
Wagonmaster Steak Company, Murray, (801) 269–1100
Blue Sage Hayride and Barbecue Company, Wanship, (801) 268–2020
Jedediah's Inn & Settlers' Restaurant, Parowan, (801) 477–3326
Milt's Stage Stop, Cedar City, (801) 586–9344
Bentley Supper House, St. George, (801) 628–6999
Bit and Spur Saloon, Springdale, (801) 772–3498
B-Bar-D Covered Wagon Company, Tropic, (801) 834–5144
Cow Canyon Trading Post, Bluff, (801) 672–2208
MD Ranch Cookhouse, Monticello, (801) 587–3299
Grand Old Ranch House, Moab, (801) 259–5753
Bar "M" Chuckwagon, Moab, (801) 259–2276
Seven-Eleven Ranch Restaurant, Vernal, (801) 789–1170

Where to Stay

Log Cabin on the Hill, Salt Lake City, (801) 272–2969
Whitmore Mansion, Nephi, (801) 623–2047
Ephraim Homestead, Spring City, (801) 283–6367
Manti House Inn, Manti, (801) 835–0161
Rockin' R Ranch, Antimony, (801) 624–3250
Jedediah's Inn, Parowan, (801) 477–3326
O'Toole's Under the Eaves Guest House, Springdale, (801) 772–3457
Greene Gate Village, St. George, (801) 628–6999
Boulder Mountain Ranch, Boulder, (801) 335–7480
Fry Canyon Lodge, between Hanksville and Mexican Hat, (801) 259–5334
Pioneer House, Bluff, (801) 672–2208
Grayson Country Inn, Blanding, (801) 678–2388
Grist Mill Inn, Monticello, (801) 587–2597
Pack Creek Ranch, outside Moab, (801) 259–5505

Arizona

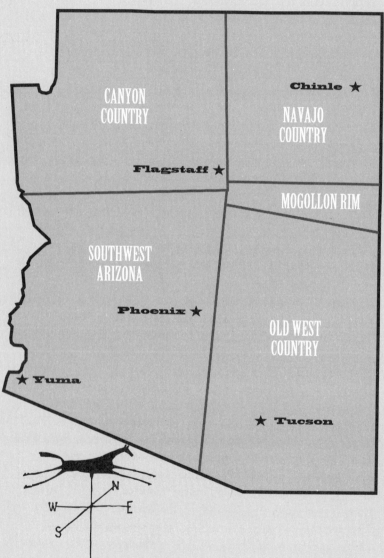

CANYON COUNTRY

Chinle ★

NAVAJO COUNTRY

Flagstaff ★

MOGOLLON RIM

SOUTHWEST ARIZONA

OLD WEST COUNTRY

Phoenix ★

★ Yuma

★ Tucson

N
W — E
S

ARIZONA

▼▼▼

RIZONA and its annals brim with the names of places and people evocative of the Wild West—Tombstone, Geronimo, Wickenburg, Wyatt Earp, and so on. Largely a harsh, hot, arid land, Arizona remained frontier until well into the twentieth century; it was, in fact, the last of the contiguous forty-eight states to gain statehood (it did so in 1912).

Today's visitor sees a relatively new version of the Grand Canyon State, for Arizona's population mushroomed only in recent years, with the perfection of cheap, dependable air conditioning and the successful transport of water to the desert from faraway, impounded rivers.

The narrative begins in the northeast, leads generally southward as it sweeps back and forth across the state, and winds up in Arizona's southeast corner, nicknamed, not accidentally, "Old West Country."

Navajo Country

Northeast Arizona is *Dine' Bi Keyah* (land of the people), the Navajo homeland. An independent nation within America, the Navajo Reservation is big—roughly equal in size to Vermont, New Hampshire, and Massachusetts combined—and a large share of its 200,000 residents lead isolated lives not vastly different from those lived by their nineteenth-century predecessors.

Within the bounds of the nation of the *Dine'* lies the smaller Hopi Indian Reservation, home to a sedentary farming people who differ markedly from the seminomadic Navajos and who have lived in the region several centuries longer. Their mesa-top settlements are the oldest continuously inhabited communities in North America, having been home to the ancestral Hopi since the twelfth century. For information on visiting these traditional and private people, call the Hopi Cultural Center at (520) 734–2401.

Note: Navajo-Hopi country is vast, and services are seldom seen, so careful planning is a must. Although the rest of the state of Arizona does not subscribe to Daylight Savings Time, the Navajo Reservation does. Also, the Native American Tourism Center makes the following request: "Please remember that you are a guest on private land. Show respect for your hosts by obeying tribal laws, and you will be treated with respect." To find out more about the laws and customs applying here, some of which take visitors by surprise, call the NATC at (602) 945–0771.

Canyon de Chelly National Monument is a sacred area considered by many Navajos to be the center of the universe, "where the web of life interconnects all things in creation." Home to Native Americans for at least 2,000 years, De Chelly (pronounced d' SHAY) and its three main tributary canyons—del Muerto (canyon of the dead), Black Rock, and Monument—provide ample evidence that running water is the ultimate sculptor. In all, the park contains more than 100 miles of canyons, whose walls rise from 30 to more than 1,000 feet above the valley floors; the canyons, in turn, hold dozens of prehistoric sites, including several impressive Anasazi (Ancient Ones) cliff dwellings.

The visitor center at Canyon de Chelly is open from 8:00 A.M. until 5:00 P.M. year-round. Jeep, horseback, and hiking trips into the backcountry, led by Navajo guides, can be arranged through several operations in the town of Chinle, 2 miles west. (With the exception of hiking on the 3.5-mile White House Ruin Trail, travel in the canyon is not permitted without a park ranger or an authorized guide.) Camping is available within the park at the peaceful Cottonwood Campground. Call (520) 674–5500 or 674–5501 for more information.

The new **Holiday Inn Canyon de Chelly,** the first resort developed by the Navajo Nation in more than twenty years, offers a deluxe new indoor option to visitors. The lodge restaurant is housed in the historic Garcia's Trading Post, with artifacts from the post's colorful past on display. Call (520) 674–5000 for reservations.

The Long Walk

T imes turned extremely turbulent for the Navajos after the United States took control of their lands from Mexico in 1847. Slave trading was one major problem: By the early 1860s Navajo children were bringing as much as $400 at Santa Fe auction, and it was estimated that as many as 6,000 of them were enslaved.

Gen. James H. Carlton was determined to claim the land of the Navajos and that of the Jicarilla Apaches, both of whom, in his words, "infested this territory." Carlton brought onto the scene Col. Kit Carson who, with a thousand-man army bolstered by Ute Indian war parties, began ravaging Navajo country in the late summer, just before harvest, when food stores were low. They burned fields and homes, killed cattle, and murdered the Indians. Carson finally broke the proud Navajos' spirit in December, when he invaded their sacred Canyon de Chelly.

In what is remembered as the infamous Long Walk, roughly 8,000 Navajos were herded, cold and hungry, to an isolated area in eastern New Mexico known as Bosque Redondo. Along the way soldiers shot those too weak to keep up, and more than a hundred Navajos perished on the journey.

Five years of misery and some 2,000 lives later, President Andrew Johnson ordered Gen. William Tecumseh Sherman to negotiate a treaty at Bosque Redondo. Largely owing to the eloquent pleas of the Navajo spokesman, Barboncito, the Navajos regained a portion of their original homeland, including Canyon de Chelly, the heart of Navajo country.

Millions of acres have been added to that original concession over the ensuing century, and today the Navajo Reservation comprises nearly 26,000 square miles in Arizona, Utah, and New Mexico, making it America's largest Indian reservation.

Erosion of the high, dry tableland known as the Colorado Plateau is responsible for the splendid and unlikely landscapes found in the Four Corners region. Among the more splendid and unlikely: starkly beautiful

Monument Valley, which straddles the Arizona-Utah border just north of Kayenta, a village 85 miles northwest of Chinle.

Giant monoliths of De Chelly sandstone, remnants of a once-continuous 1,000-foot layer of rock, stand sentinel here, spiritlike, over the surrounding arid terrain. The rugged, bizarre scenery has attracted a lot of movie-makers during the past few decades, and dozens of Westerns—including the classics *Stagecoach, The Searchers,* and *How the West Was Won*—have been filmed here.

The 30,000-acre reserve was established in 1958 as the first Navajo tribal park. A scenic drive, mostly within Arizona, begins at the visitor center just across the state line in Utah, 23 miles north of Kayenta. The visitor center is open year-round, excepting New Year's and Christmas days. Camping is available for a $10 fee. For more information call (801) 727–3353.

Numerous outfits offer guided four-wheel-drive and/or horseback tours into Monument Valley—perhaps the best way to enjoy the park, for private travel off the self-guided valley road is taboo. What could be more fun than ambling along on horseback in the shadow of the same spires and pinnacles that John Wayne skirted so many times on the silver screen? For a listing of tour operators, contact the park headquarters or Navajoland Tourism at (520) 871–6436.

Located midway between Canyon de Chelly and the Navajo Nation capital of Window Rock, in the settlement of Ganado, **Hubbell Trading Post National Historic Site** exemplifies the Navajo trading post of the past and present. Here John Lorenzo Hubbell, known as Don Lorenzo to his many Navajo friends, set up shop in the late 1870s. First operating out of a small post purchased from an earlier owner, Hubbell finished building the present post in 1889.

Through the trading of wool, hides, corn, and meat, Navajos earned tokens good for necessities and staples like kerosene, flour, sugar, cloth, and utensils. A trading trip, which typically involved the entire family, often lasted several days. It was an important time for socializing and renewing friend-ships, for Navajo families tended to live remote and isolated lives far from any neighbors (as many still do). Hogans were built on the post's grounds for the benefit of visiting families.

Don Lorenzo's sons continued running the place after he died in 1930; in 1967 his daughter-in-law sold the post and its priceless collection of artifacts to the National Park Service. Today a visit to the oldest continuously run trading post in Navajo country offers a rare glimpse of history in action. During summer weavers are often found working their looms in the visitor center, and among the post's inventory is one of the finest selections of Navajo rugs in the Southwest.

The site is open daily year-round from 8:00 A.M. to 5:00 P.M. For more information call (520) 755–3475.

The five-day **Navajo Nation Fair** kicks up its heels in Window Rock during the week after Labor Day. Billed as the "World's Largest Indian Fair," it is attended by more than 100,000 people each year. Dancers, drummers, and singers representing tribes from throughout the United States and Canada travel to participate in one of the continent's most important powwows.

Other fair highlights include Indian fry-bread competitions, the Native American Music Festival, and the splendidly colorful Navajo Traditional Song and Dance contest, featuring dozens of women dressed in their finest velvet and silk and adorned with turquoise-and-silver jewelry. The showstopping Navajo Nation Fair Rodeo is an All-Indian PRCA (Professional Rodeo Cowboys Association) event and is among the most prestigious of rodeos in Indian country. Throughout the festivities are ample opportunities to shop for Navajo jewelry, handwoven rugs, paintings, and baskets and pottery. For information on the fair and other Navajo celebrations, call the Navajoland Tourism Office in Window Rock at (520) 871–7371.

While in Window Rock, don't miss the **Navajo Tribal Museum,** dedicated to preserving and interpreting the complex culture of the Navajo, and the **St. Michael's Historical Museum,** which details the early influence the Franciscan Friars had on the *Dine'*. The tribal museum (520–871–6673), housed in a new facility in Window Rock, is open Monday through Friday from 8:00 A.M. until 6:00 P.M. (it closes at 5:00 P.M. in winter). St. Michael's Museum (520–871–4171), situated a couple of miles west of town on Highway 264, is open daily May 30 through Labor Day from 9:00 A.M. to 5:00 P.M.

The place to stay in Window Rock is the **Navajo Nation Inn,** "your hogan away from home." The inn's logo, symbolic of the enterprise's importance to the Navajo Nation, is a stylized drawing of the sacred Window Rock sandstone formation set inside the outline of a hogan. The rooms feature a Southwest/Navajo flair, and the restaurant's menu includes a selection of traditional Navajo fare. (As elsewhere on the Navajo and Hopi reservations, alcohol is not served.) For reservations call (800) 662–6189.

Canyon Country

Fourteen miles southwest of Fredonia, in the Arizona Strip country—that part of Arizona lying north of the Colorado River and south of Utah— you'll find **Pipe Spring National Monument,** which memorializes the nineteenth-century cowboy rancher and the indomitable spirit of the Mormon pioneers.

"Pioneers" set up camp at Pipe Spring National Monument.

The first cattleman to ranch the thirsty area was a Mormon convert from Texas, Dr. James M. Whitmore, who arrived in 1863. After spending only a couple of years on the place, Whitmore, along with his hired hand, was killed by Navajo marauders. This incident prompted the Utah Militia to settle at Pipe Spring. Their mission: Keep the Navajo raiders on the south side of the Colorado River.

When peace was forged with the Navajos in 1870, church president Brigham Young picked Pipe Spring as the site for his church's southern Utah "tithing herd," composed of cows donated by Mormon ranching families in lieu of cash. Furor over the polygamous Mormons' lifestyle built to a crescendo in the late 1880s, and, facing confiscation of church-owned property by the federal government, the ranch was sold to a non-Mormon cattleman.

At the center of the monument today is Winsor Castle, a sandstone-and-timber fort built to protect the precious water supply and the missionaries who served at the ranch. The various rooms in the fort—including a kitchen, cheese room, bedroom, and telegraph room—are appointed in period artifacts that reflect the pioneer lifestyle. Numerous outbuildings survive in good repair, too, including the blacksmith shop, harness room, and West Cabin, a bunkhouse used by explorer John Wesley Powell's 1871 survey party. Early tools of the ranching and cowboying trades are displayed throughout and tours are offered on the half hour from 8:00 A.M. to 5:00 P.M.; for more information call the visitor center at (520) 643–7105.

Flagstaff, the four-seasons hub of northern Arizona, with an elevation of 7,000 feet, is home to the Arizona Historical Society's **Pioneer Museum,** located at 2340 North Forth Valley Road (Highway 180). For thirty years the museum has offered visitors glimpses of frontier life, with displays that include old photographs, antique farm machinery, and early medical instruments (many of which will bolster visitors' appreciation of today's less-intrusive medical procedures). The Pioneer Museum (520–774–6272) is open Monday through Saturday from 9:00 A.M. to 5:00 P.M.

Flagstaff began life largely as a supply center for the cattle industry, and ranching is still a way of life for hundreds in the region. Don't miss the **Museum of Northern Arizona,** 3 miles north of downtown on Highway 180. One of the best places to get your bearings when first visiting the Four Corners region, the captivating museum features displays on the geology, history, and prehistory unique to the area. The highly regarded "Native Peoples of the Colorado Plateau" exhibit documents 12,000 years of human occupation in the Four Corners. Revolving displays feature contemporary artwork by the region's Navajo, Hopi, and Zuni Indians, and Native American dances are regularly performed here. The museum is open daily from 9:00 A.M. to 5:00 P.M. Call (520) 774–5211 for more information.

Sedona, 30 miles south of Flagstaff on Highway 89, is widely touted for the scenery of nearby Oak Creek Canyon to the north and the fabulous red-rock formations that surround the town in the other directions. Like the Navajo Reservation's Monument Valley, the natural, rough-hewn beauty of the local countryside caught the eye of Hollywood early on, and dozens of wild Westerns were filmed here.

Sedona has of late been transformed into a trendy hangout for the affluent and for those in search of spiritual/New Age enlightenment. If John Wayne, star of several movies filmed in the area, were to return to the living and visit now, chances are he would regard the former Wild West outpost as the mild West. (A visiting journalist, bemoaning what Sedona has become, dejectedly wrote that "in one block of storefront displays, I counted twenty-two howling coyotes.")

The community's saving grace, however, may be the restrictive envelope of protected federal lands surrounding it: The spectacular red rock responsible for attracting so many people to the area will also limit its future growth.

A four-wheel-drive tour of the red-rock country is a Sedona institution and a must for visitors. Try Pink Jeep Tours or their subsidiary, PJT Ancient Expeditions (800–999–2137).

Sedona's **Western Americana Days,** held on Memorial Day weekend, are a foot-stompin' throwback to the old days. Highlights include an Indian village, a medicine show, and horse-mounted cavalry troops, along with antique cars and airplanes. For information on this and Sedona-area dining and rooming opportunities, both of which are plentiful, call the Chamber of Commerce at (520) 282–7722.

The rich lore of railroading thrives in the town of Williams, 30 miles west of Flagstaff, where turn-of-the-century steam locomotives pull equally old passenger cars to the Grand Canyon along a line laid in 1901. The **Grand Canyon Railway,** originally called the Grand Canyon Line, was conceived

The first passengers arrived at the south rim of the Grand Canyon aboard the scheduled steam train from Williams, Arizona, on September 17, 1901.

as a means of delivering tourists to the Grand Canyon's South Rim that would preclude their enduring the daylong stagecoach ride from Flagstaff.

Over the span of sixty-seven years, this "railroad of cowboys, miners, presidents, and kings" transported millions of tourists—famous, infamous, and regular folks—from Williams to the South Rim. (Better-known passengers ranged from Teddy Roosevelt and John Muir to the likes of Jimmy Durante.) After a twenty-one–year hiatus, an $80 million Arizona tourism-development grant revived the great railroad, and the locomotives are again hissing and chugging over 65 miles of grassy plain, side canyons, and timberland, en route to the Grand Canyon.

The depot is located at the corner of Railroad Avenue and Grand Canyon Boulevard, near the center of Williams. After passengers board refurbished 1920s Harriman coach cars, Engine #18, a 158-ton locomotive built by the American Locomotive Company in 1910, inches out of the station, belching black smoke. Eventually the train reaches a speed of 40 miles per hour.

Children of all ages squeal in delight when Dangerous Dave waltzes through the cars, reciting cowboy poetry or singing Western range ballads. And the finale is classic: A gaggle of banditos, masked and "armed," storm the train on horseback, board, and then proceed to relieve passengers of their gold—all in fun, of course.

The train runs from June through September, departing Williams at 9:30 A.M. and arriving at the South Rim at 11:45 A.M. After a three-and-a-half-hour layover, it heads back to Williams at 3:15 P.M., returning at 5:30 P.M. Schedules vary the remainder of the year. Call (800) THE–TRAIN (843–8724) for more information.

For accommodations in the Williams area, try the **Mountain Side Inn and Resort** (520–635–4431), a two-story farmhouse built on a ponderosa-pine-covered slope at the east end of town. **Miss Kitty's** restaurant, a sure crowd-pleaser, boasts western beef, burgers, and barbecue. Perhaps emulating Matt Dillon more than Miss Kitty, waiters and waitresses sport replicas of Colt .45 "Peacemakers" strapped to their thighs.

Memorial Day weekend, when mountain men run rampant through the streets at the annual **Rendezvous Days,** is an opportune time to visit Williams. Williams was named after the legendary mountain man Bill Williams, and the festival carries on in his spirit. For details call the Chamber of Commerce at (520) 635–4061.

After the copper mines closed in the early 1950s, **Jerome** was well on its way to becoming just another ghost town, but the stubborn old town took on a second life in the late 1960s, when it became a popular artists' colony. The entire hilly town, precariously perched on the side of Cleopatra Hill, has been designated a National Historic Landmark. More than a hundred miles of tunnels, from which a billion dollars in copper was taken, honeycomb the ground below. Saloons, boutiques housed in converted bordellos, galleries, museums, restaurants, bed and breakfasts, and restaurants demand hours of browsing.

Reflecting Jerome's colorful past, the mansion of "Rawhide Jimmy" Douglas sits on a hilltop in **Jerome State Historic Park,** overlooking Douglas's Little Daisy Mine. As you'll see, Jerome is still part ghost town, but you can visit some of the less ghostly and more refurbished residences at the Annual Home Tour in May. For accommodations with a local flair, consider the historic **Jerome Inn** (520–634–5094), located at 309 Main Street, which also serves gourmet meals. When in the area, don't miss venerable **Oldtown** in nearby Cottonwood, with its high sidewalks and false-fronted buildings. For more information contact the Chamber of Commerce at (520) 634–2900.

Southwest Arizona and Phoenix

Thirty-one miles southwest of Jerome on Highway 89 is mile-high **Prescott,** which started taking shape in 1863 after gold was discovered in the nearby highlands. A year later the Arizona Territory was designated, with Prescott the capital. Although Phoenix eventually took over as capital, Prescott continued to thrive and has burgeoned into a major economic and cultural hub.

The **Sharlot Hall Museum,** located in downtown Prescott at 415 West Gurley, preserves the pioneering days in a facility named after a well-known Arizona writer-historian. The complex includes the territorial governor's "mansion" (a log cabin) and the immaculately refurbished 1880s Bashford residence; each July 4 it hosts the frontier-flavored **Territorial Prescott Days.** The museum opens Monday through Saturday at 10:00 A.M. and on Sunday at 1:00 P.M. and closes every day at 5:00 P.M.; call (520) 445–3122 for information.

Other Prescott-area festivities, all focusing on the town's Western heritage, include the annual **Arizona Cowboy Poets Gathering** in August, the Phippen Museum's **Western Art Show** and the **Sheriff's Posse Roping Contest,** both in May, and the **Frontier Days Rodeo & Parade,** held in July. The parade passes through Whiskey Row, a notorious street christened during territorial times for its abundance of watering holes. For more information on Prescott-area attractions, call the Chamber of Commerce at (520) 445–2000 or (800) 266–7534.

The **Double D Ranch Company,** 17 miles north of Prescott on Highway 89, offers horseback adventures and three-day (two-overnight) trips into the surrounding backcountry via covered wagon. The cry of the mule skinner's "Wagons Ho...ooo!" resounds over the high desert, and the spoked wheels of the old wooden covered wagons groan into action, while the scents of leather and mule sweat lift on the breeze, filling guests' senses with the sounds, scents, and sights of an earlier day.

Most guests choose to ride part-time on horseback and at other times in a wagon, quite possibly one of those used in 1940s and 1950s Westerns, such as John Wayne's *Red River.* The rugged terrain traversed includes high mesas, canyons, and timbered mountain slopes. In camp, after a hearty Western meal, wranglers spin tales and sing songs around the roaring fire. During daylight hours greenhorns can practice their target-shooting skills (or lack thereof) with black-powder rifles and bows and arrows. The gathering place for the adventure is at the **O.K. Corral & Museum** on Highway 89, just north of Chino Valley. For information on rates, reservations, and meeting times, call (520) 636–0418.

If you are captivated by cowboying, probably the best reason to head "Out Wickenburg Way," as the town's slogan goes, is the fine **Desert Caballeros Western Museum.** Operated by the Maricopa County Historical Society, the two-story museum is located in the heart of old Wickenburg at the corner of Tegner and Frontier, a street preserved largely in its turn-of-the-century condition.

Welcoming visitors to the museum is the dramatic sculpture *Thanks for the Rain,* which was crafted by Joe Beeler, a cofounder of the Cowboy Artists of America. The museum features a reproduction of a nineteenth-century Wild West town, complete with a general store jam-packed with goods.

A town of 5,000, Wickenburg thrives on its Old West heritage. Annual festivals include the **Gold Rush Days,** held the second weekend of February and soon to celebrate its fiftieth anniversary. A rodeo, "gunfights" in the streets, western dances, mucking-and-drilling competitions, and a melodrama performance entitled *Shoot-out at Hole-in-the-Wall* are all part of the action. Other area celebrations: the festive and popular **Cowboy Christmas Poetry Gathering** in December and the **Septiembre Fiesta,** a tribute to the area's Hispanic settlers. The Fiesta is held at the Desert Caballeros Western Museum and Park during the first week of September. For more information call the Wickenburg Chamber of Commerce at (520) 684–5479.

Those searching for a traditional ranch vacation need look no further than the **Kay El Bar Ranch,** a rustic Hassayampa River getaway listed on the

National Historic Register. Twenty guests, maximum, hole up in the adobe cottages or at the main lodge for a night, a week, or a month. At the ranch, situated 3 miles north of Wickenburg in a secluded Sonoran Desert valley, you can ride horseback through canyons punctuated with giant saguaro cactus, or you can simply relax. The place is open for business from October 15 through May 1 (closing during the scorching summer months). Call (520) 684–7593 for information.

Cowboy Poetry

Cowboy poetry is more popular than ever, and poet gatherings abound, offering great excuses for like-minded cow-folks to get together in the far corners of the West. Wickenburg area resident Carole Jarvis, a regular reciter at the town's Cowboy Christmas Poetry Gathering, sums it up here in "Times, They Are a-Changin' ":

I can't believe how many cowboy poets
Are comin' forth, admittin' that they write
Who'd of thought these tough and rugged cowhands,
Would stand up on a stage, and then recite?!

From Elko it has spread in all directions,
Cowboys everywhere are rhymin' tales.
Memorizin' verses they've composed,
While fixin' fence, or ridin' dusty trails.

We're hearin' now from every Western state.
Why it's hard to find a ranch without a poet,
And if you spend much time around these cowboys,
It won't take long before they show it!

Instead of ropin' calves in their spare time,
These cowboys sit beneath some old dim light
Puttin' down on paper things they've done,
Hunkered over, rhymin' half the night!

Another recommended overnight stop is the **Sombrero Ranch,** a historic bed-and-breakfast establishment sitting high on a fifty-acre grounds a mile from downtown Wickenburg. The desert sunrises and sunsets don't get any better than they do from the ranch's hilltop setting. You can call the Sombrero, situated at 31910 West Bralliar Road, at (520) 684–0222.

First known as Colorado City, then as Arizona City, **Yuma** earned its present name by territorial legislative decree in 1873. The riverside oasis, 175 miles southwest of Wickenburg on Highway 60 and Highway 95, is far from everywhere and generally one of the hottest spots in the United States. Still, the town burgeons.

Beginning in the 1850s and continuing until the "iron horse" arrived in the late 1870s, goods arrived via mule-team freighters at Yuma to be transported to military posts across the Southwest. Many original stone and adobe buildings remain at the **Yuma Crossing Quartermaster Depot,** where costumed interpreters act out the days when the brash settlement served as a major Colorado River crossing and supply hub for a growing region. The facility, operated by the Yuma Crossing Foundation and located at the north end of Second Avenue, is open daily from 10:00 A.M. to 5:00 P.M.; call (520) 329–0471 for information.

Other area attractions include the nearby **Yuma Territorial Prison,** which housed a total of more than 3,000 murderers, larcenists, polygamists, and other undesirables between 1876 and 1909. The prison's infamous reputation notwithstanding, the incarcerated were actually treated reasonably well for the time and place, and so it earned the nickname among the townspeople below as the "Country Club on the Hill." Yuma High School took over the buildings between 1910 and 1914; later, the cells provided free accommodations for rail-riding hobos in the 1920s and for homeless families during the Great Depression. What remains of the prison walls today are encompassed by a state historic park. There's a museum, and ranger-led tours are available between 8:00 A.M. and 5:00 P.M. daily. Call (520) 783–4771 to get more information.

More than two million people live in the capital city of Phoenix and its suburbs. Tucked away in the midst of the city's modern trappings and urban sprawl are numerous Wild West eateries and getaways, so many, in fact, that you'd better plan on at least a week in town if you want to sample them all. For starters try the **Rawhide Steakhouse and Saloon,** found at 23023 North Scottsdale Road. Mesquite-broiled steaks, cowboy beans, and corn on the cob are the standard fare, while the more adventurous can sample fried rattlesnake or Rocky Mountain oysters (don't ask if you don't know). No run-of-the-mill steakhouse, Rawhide offers a rollicking good time for folks of all ages, boasting a Main Street with general store, a working blacksmith shop, several shops and boutiques, and, for the kids, a petting zoo and a western animal display. Shoot-'em-up street entertainers, crooked card dealers, and saucy showgirls all keep the atmosphere rowdy, and desert cookouts, reached via haywagons and complete with dancing and live entertainment, are available for groups. For more information and group reservations (they say they can serve groups sized from 10 to 7,500!), call (602) 502–1880.

If you haven't had enough, also consider trying **Rustler's Rooste,** "the closest thing to cowboy Heaven" (7777 South Pointe Parkway in Phoenix), or **Reata Pass** (27500 North Alma School Parkway in Scottsdale). Both dish up Western-style entertainment and good times, mesquite-broiled steaks, baked beans, and—that's right, pardner—fried rattlesnake.

It seems that for each Old West eatery found in the Phoenix area there's also a Jeep-tour company. The formula, obviously successful: In open-air four-wheel-drive vehicles, "cowboy" guides haul clients over bumpy roads for a day or half-day, taking in prehistoric Indian ruins, isolated desert canyons, and other sights. Along the way guests typically get to enjoy nature walks through the Sonoran Desert and test their quick-draw and six-gun shooting abilities; gold panning is often included, as well. Among the possibilities, most of which are headquartered in the suburb of Scottsdale, are **Wild West Jeep Tours** (602–941–8355); **Desert/Mountain Jeep Tours,** "Scottsdale's Original Jeep Tour" (602–860–1777); and **Pinnacle Adventures** (602–949–8735).

Other attractions worth checking out include the **Buffalo Museum of America,** at 10261 North Scottsdale Road (602–951–1022), a monument to the great beast symbolic of the untamed West. The museum is open Monday through Friday from 9:00 A.M. to 5:00 P.M. **Arizona's Cowboy Camp & Carnival for Dudes,** at 10110 East Jenan Drive in Scottsdale, "turns city slickers into cowboys," after which the former city slickers compete in "authentic Western Olympic games." Sound intriguing? Call them at (602) 860–1777.

The **Pioneer Arizona Living History Museum** keeps the past alive and kicking with a complex of restored buildings—including a bank, an opera house, and a miners' camp—staffed by interpreters in period costumes. Located off Interstate 17 at Pioneer Road, the museum (602–465–0152) is "dedicated to the education and preservation of Arizona's territorial history."

The Mogollon Rim

The town of Payson, 90 miles northeast of Phoenix on Highway 87, claims to be the "Festival Capital of the World," with its several dozen annual celebrations, most of them centered around logging, chili cooking, and cowboying. The year 1995 marks the 111th version of their grandaddy cele-

Shopping for a *City Slickers* Experience

The Hollywood hit *City Slickers* got a lot of folks thinking that maybe they should get in touch with the Old West, as actor Billy Crystal's character and his buddies did.

It's a great idea, and opportunities are abundant in Arizona and elsewhere in the West, but not all Old West outings are created equally. How do you pick from all the options at hand?

Start by determining what most appeals to you and/or your family. Do you dream of bouncing along in a covered wagon, or on the back of a steady horse, in the fashion of a westward-bound Santa Fe Trail traveler? Or would you rather "hire on" to drive cattle over roadless terrain and sleep under a starry sky, emulating the dudes in *City Slickers*?

Maybe what will really tickle your fancy is kicking back at a full-service dude ranch, where you have no responsibility other than enjoying yourself. At these ranches you can usually hike, horseback ride, partake of chuck-wagon meals, and even rope calves and ride bareback in the rodeo arena—but only if you want to.

After deciding what's right for you, call a handful of the appropriate outfits and ask these questions:

1. How long have you been in business? (The longer the better, generally.)

2. Can you provide telephone references in my area?

3. Is the price all-inclusive, or are there add-ons?

Now all that's left is to sign on the dotted line, amble on out, and whoop it up!

bration, the **World's Oldest Continuous Rodeo.** A major event on the PRCA circuit, the big rodeo and accompanying parade, dance, and other festivities take place in mid to late August. For information call the Chamber of Commerce at (520) 474–4515.

Payson, at nearly 5,000 feet in elevation, and the nearby, looming Mogollon Rim—a 1,000-foot-high escarpment that delineates the southern reaches of the Colorado Plateau, which stretches some 200 miles across Arizona—are popular summer getaways for desert dwellers who want to escape the intense heat. Until it was destroyed in the Dude wildfire of 1990, the cabin of celebrated Western writer Zane Grey was nestled against the rim not far from Payson. The **Zane Grey Cabin Site,** however, remains a peaceful spot well worth visiting.

Grey, who hailed from Zanesville, Ohio, graduated from dental school in Pennsylvania, after putting himself through on a baseball scholarship. He built his Arizona cabin in the early 1920s, as a wilderness and hunting retreat. Here, in the shadow of the Mogollon Rim, he wrote *Under the Tonto Rim* and other novels. The caretakers of the former cabin's site, Mel and Beth Counseller maintain a museum in Payson, where they have on display plenty of Zane Grey photographs, books, and other memorabilia. Mel is a cowboy artist, and Beth is a free-lance writer and lecturer, specializing in Grey lore. The cabin site is located about 17 miles east of Payson on Highway 260, then 5 miles north on Forest Road 289. The **Counseller Museum** is situated upstairs at 408 West Main Street and is open Monday through Saturday from 10:00 A.M. to 4:00 P.M. and Sunday from 11:00 A.M. to 2:00 P.M. Call (520) 474–6243 for more information.

In the White Mountains region, a hundred miles east of Payson along the Mogollon Rim, you'll encounter a series of winter-and-summer resort communities. The twin towns of Snowflake and Taylor were settled by Mormon pioneers in the late 1870s, and a walking tour of the towns turns up no fewer than sixteen nineteenth-century pioneer homes, two of them museums listed on the National Register of Historic Places. Pinetop-Lakeside's annual **White Mountain Native American Art Festival,** held in July, brings to town the best in Apache, Hopi, Zuni, and Navajo arts. Individuals and groups—Knifewing Segura, the Chief Jimmy Bruneau School Young Drummers, and the Cuahzihuatl Danza Azteca Dancers, to name a few—perform amid displays of Native American paintings, carvings, flint knapping, jewelry making, weaving, and pottery. Call the Pinetop-Lakeside Chamber of Commerce at (520) 367–4290 for more details.

The mountainous, 1.6-million-acre Fort Apache Indian Reservation, home to the White Mountain Apaches, lies just south of the resort area. At the legendary **Fort Apache** military post, 7 miles south of Whiteriver on Highway 73, you can visit the log cabin resided in by General George Crook during the Apache Wars. At the same location the Fort Apache Cultural Center displays various military and Indian relics and interprets the tribe's unique traditions; the center and its attendant gift shop are open daily from 8:00 A.M. to 5:00 P.M. Also of note is the nearby **1880s Apache Indian Village.** To schedule a tour, call (520) 338–1230.

Old West Country

From the White Mountains region, drive along the beautiful and twisting Highway 191 south as it traces through the Apache-Sitgreaves National Forest. You'll pass through high-elevation towns, such as the appropriately named Alpine, and through pretty Hannagan Meadow, before the road empties into the southern Arizona desert and that portion of the state known as Old West Country.

In Willcox, at the junction of Interstate 10 and Highway 186, the **Museum of the Southwest and Cowboy Hall of Fame,** situated in the Chamber of Commerce Visitor Center, commemorates the history of local Indian cultures and early cattle ranchers. Celebrated at the associated **Rex Allen Arizona Cowboy Museum** is—you guessed it—Rex Allen, the well-known cowboy singer and movie star. For information call the Chamber of Commerce at (520) 384–2272.

From Willcox travel southwest on Highway 186 and pass through Dos Cabezas, an 1885 Wells Fargo station that is almost a ghost town today. Twenty-two miles out, turn onto the graded gravel road leading the 6 miles to remote **Fort Bowie National Historic Site.** Established in 1862, for some twenty-five years the post served as the nerve center for military operations aimed at fighting and subduing the Chiricahua Apaches.

From the parking area in Apache Pass, a 1.5-mile foot trail leads to the adobe remains of historic Fort Bowie. Paralleling an old wagon road, the trail passes the ruins of the Butterfield Stage Station, the fort cemetery, and Apache Spring. A park ranger is usually on duty at the small ranger station–museum, where books, postcards, restrooms, and drinking water are available. There are no other services nearby, and the closest campgrounds and motels are found in Willcox and Bowie. The memorial is open year-round from 8:00 A.M. to 5:00 P.M. daily; call (520) 847–2500 for more information.

Chiricahua National Monument was designated primarily to preserve the spectacular rhyolite spires known as the Wonderland of Rocks. The monument is also home to the **Faraway Ranch,** so named by owner Lillian Riggs because the place was so "Godawful far away from everything." Tours of the ranch compound, a relatively recent addition to the monument, are given daily: weekdays at 10:00 A.M. and 2:00 P.M. and on weekends at 10:00 A.M., 1:00 P.M., and 3:00 P.M. You can visit the house-cum-guest ranch, built by early owner Neil Erickson, and several other structures, including one known as the Dog House. (Ed Riggs, Erickson's son-in-law, built it for himself and his companions because wife Lillian wouldn't permit the men to take liquor in the main house.)

To find Chiricahua National Monument and the Faraway Ranch, continue south for 9 miles on Highway 186 from the turnoff to Fort Bowie National Historic Site, then go 6 miles east. The campground and visitor center (open from 8:00 A.M. to 5:00 P.M. daily) have drinking water and restrooms, but no other services. Call the park at (520) 824–3560 for information.

Drive south from Chiricahua National Monument on Highway 181 and Highway 191 to the town of Douglas, and put up at the historic **Gadsden Hotel.** The hotel opened on Thanksgiving Day in 1907, then burned two years later. Everything was destroyed except the broad marble staircase—the same staircase that the Mexican revolutionary Pancho Villa allegedly once rode up on horseback. The hotel was rebuilt within two years; the formerly splendid structure fell into disrepair in the 1960s and 1970s, but new owners took over in 1988 and have restored it to its former graciousness. Today the 150 rooms in the five-story hotel, listed on the National Register of Historic Places, are available for overnight stays. Call (520) 364–4481 for reservations.

The **John Slaughter Ranch/San Bernardino Land Grant,** 16 miles east of Douglas, is one of the best-preserved nineteenth-century ranches in the Grand Canyon State. Ranch owner "Texas" John Horton Slaughter, sheriff of wild Tombstone during its wildest times, reputedly shot "more than twenty men and numerous Apaches" (the quotation reveals early attitudes concerning Native Americans). The Slaughter Ranch was purchased in 1982 from the Nature Conservancy by the Johnson

Apache Pass and the Chiricahuas

A constant-flowing spring, situated near a low gap that separates the high Chiricahua Mountains and the Dos Cabezas Range, made Apache Pass a natural travel-way for westward-bound emigrants. The main problem, for the whites, was that the pass was in the middle of Chiricahua Apache territory. Taking advantage of horses acquired from the Spanish, the Chiricahuas, led by Cochise, had developed into effective mobile guerrillas, making raids on other tribes and waging warfare to protect their home from outsiders.

When the Civil War broke out, the Confederates had designs on capturing the California gold fields. Their best route was via Apache Pass, and Gen. James H. Carleton led 1,800 volunteers from California to head them off. On July 15, 1862, Carlton's vanguard was ambushed at Apache Pass by several hundred Chiricahuas. Fort Bowie was established on the spot within weeks.

Peace with Cochise finally came when Gen. O. O. Howard offered the Indians a reservation that encompassed their traditional homeland, but after Cochise died in 1874, discontent again mounted. Several bands of Apaches, including the one led by Geronimo, fled to Mexico's Sierra Madre Mountains, and from there they waged occasional attacks in the border region for the next ten years.

Geronimo finally surrendered in 1886 to Gen. Nelson A. Miles, a prolific Indian fighter who also did battle with Crazy Horse, captured Chief Joseph of the Nez Perce in northern Montana, forced the ultimate surrender of Sitting Bull, and helped to quash the Ghost Dance of the Sioux in the early 1890s.

After the Southwest Indian Wars, activity diminished at Fort Bowie; it was abandoned on October 17, 1894. The fearsome Geronimo ended up joining the Dutch Reformed Church in 1903 and, in 1905, marched in Theodore Roosevelt's presidential inaugural parade.

Foundation, based in Sun City, Arizona. Three hundred acres remain of the ranch, which, at its zenith, covered more than 100,000 acres.

The ranch was a small industry, with its own school district and as many as 200 people living and/or working on the grounds. Today turn-of-the-century living is revealed in the spread's numerous structures and their contents. From the house porch visitors can look straight into Mexico. You can visit Wednesday through Sunday, between 10:00 A.M. and 3:00 P.M.; call (520) 558–2474 to find out more.

Bisbee, a mile-high copper-mining town nestled in the Mule Mountains, first boomed in the 1880s and, although large-scale mining stopped being profitable in the mid-1970s, continues booming today. The town has become a center for the arts, and former saloons and other Old West necessities have evolved into galleries, boutiques, and cafes. A dozen or so Victorian homes and old miners' boardinghouses have been converted into B&Bs.

Most of the commercial district dates from around 1910, owing to a 1908 fire that destroyed the heart of Main Street. Surviving the fire were the 1897 Phelps Dodge General Office, now housing the fascinating **Bisbee Mining and Historical Museum** (520–432–7071; open 10:00 A.M. to 4:00 P.M. daily), and the grand 1902 **Copper Queen Hotel** (520–432–2216). A walking tour of town leads through Brewery Gulch, remembered as the "liveliest spot between El Paso and San Francisco," with its nearly fifty taverns. The popular **Queen Mine Underground Tour,** offered seven days a week, leads visitors into an inactive copper mine. For information on these attractions and the annual **Brewery Gulch Days,** held Labor Day weekend, call (520) 432–5421.

Tombstone. The name is practically synonymous with the Wild West. In its early days a brash, high-spirited, and occasionally violent settlement, Tombstone thus far has more than lived up to its reputation as "the town too tough to die." Begin the long, but not tedious, job of getting to know the place at the 1882 **Tombstone Courthouse State Historic Park** (602–457–3311), where the town's turbulent past can be revisited and where a good selection of guidebooks and history books are for sale.

In the 1880s Tombstone was the fastest-growing population center between St. Louis and San Francisco, boasting more than 10,000 people at its peak. In the late 1920s, however, when the silver had played out and Cochise County residents voted to move the county seat to nearby Bisbee,

Tombstone's future looked grim; it appeared as if it might simply wither up, like so many other Western mining camps.

Nevertheless, Walter Cole, editor and owner of the Tombstone *Epitaph* newspaper, wrote optimistically about Tombstone, describing it with the prophetic words "the town too tough to die." Then Hollywood discovered Tombstone in the late 1940s and early 1950s, and the town was transformed into an important tourist attraction. Far-thinking residents were determined that the core of the town should remain in its 1880s condition, and a law was passed to protect the heart of Tombstone from encroachment by modern buildings.

A few years ago a group of art investors, enamored of the history they found alive and kicking in Tombstone, bought and restored several of the more important sites, including **Schieffelin Hall,** the **O.K. Corral,** and the **Crystal Palace,** Tombstone's largest and most popular saloon, even when there were as many as 110 licensed establishments in town. The investors also purchased the *Epitaph* and turned it from a local newspaper into the self-described National Newspaper of Western History (a local edition is still published, as well).

Today you can visit these historic places as well as dozens of others, including **Boothill,** the graveyard used between 1879 and 1884, the **Bird Cage Theatre,** the **Rose Tree Inn Museum** (which houses the "world's largest rose bush" on its patio, covering some 7,000 square feet), and **Big Nose Kate's Saloon,** where the likes of Doc Holliday, Bat Masterson, Johnny Ringo, and the Earp brothers whiled away many an hour. At the **Tombstone Historama** (520–457–3456), near the city park at the west end of Allen Street, an audio-visual presentation on the town, narrated by the late Vincent Price, is run at regular intervals from 9:00 A.M. to 4:00 P.M. daily.

It was at the O.K. Corral where the Earp brothers and Doc Holliday, on an October day in 1881, faced the McLaury and Clanton brothers in the West's most famous gunfight. The **Boothill Gunslingers** kick up the dust at the O.K. Corral at 2:00 P.M. on Saturdays, reenacting that fateful day. On the second, fourth, and fifth Sundays, the **Tombstone Vigilantes** perform either on the streets of town or on the Helldorado Stage. The shoot-'em-uppest time of year is Labor Day weekend, during the **Rendezvous of Gunfighters:** Acts from throughout the Southwest, including the California Gunfighters from Simi Valley and the Oak Creek Gang out of Flagstaff, gather for the bang-fest. All shows are at the O.K. Corral.

Other yearly festivals include **Territorial Days,** held the first weekend in March; **Wyatt Earp Days,** Memorial Day weekend; and the bawdy **Helldorado Days,** which scream through town the third Friday in October.

Overnighting possibilities in Tombstone include the **Buford House B&B** (602–457–3168), featuring five rooms in an 1880s adobe house; the **Tombstone Boarding House** (602–457–3716), which brims with antiques and sports private baths; and **Priscilla's B&B** (602–457–3844), situated in a turn-of-the-century country Victorian home. Another pair of options: the **Silver Nugget B&B** (520–457–9223) and **Victoria's B&B** (520–457–3677).

Tombstone and Bisbee still thrive, but they're exceptions, for littering the landscape of Cochise County are the remains of dozens of towns that might have been. Among these: **Gleeson,** an old turquoise mine, 16 miles east of Tombstone; **Fairbank,** currently under restoration, found northeast of Huachuca City; and **Pearce** mining camp, south of Sunsites off Highway 666, once among the richest gold camps in southern Arizona.

Finally, those who love books as much as touring shouldn't miss the **Territorial Book Trader,** specializing in books on the Southwest, at the corner of Fourth and Allen. For further information on Tombstone and Cochise County, call the Tombstone Office of Tourism at (520) 457–2211; for tours contact **Tombstone Stagelines** (520–457–3234) or **Old Tombstone Tours** (520–457–3018).

Although it wasn't incorporated until 1956, Sierra Vista, 20 miles southwest of Tombstone and the largest city in southeastern Arizona (and the "Hummingbird Capital of the United States"), grew up around old **Fort Huachuca.** Established in 1877 to provide settlers with protection during the Indian Wars, the base is still active today as a U.S. Army center for communications and intelligence training. Fort Huachuca boasts one of the military's finest historical museums, providing an excellent overview of the post.

Among those stationed here during the late 1800s were components of the four regiments known as the Buffalo Soldiers. The 9-foot Buffalo Soldier statue at Fort Huachuca honors the newly freed black men who served their country in the wake of the Civil War. (See Kansas, page 344.)

Buffalo Soldier Days, held in May, celebrates the history of the fort and its black soldiers. The fort's "B" Troop, 4th Regiment, U.S. Cavalry (Memorial), dressed in frontier-era uniforms and riding horseback in for-

Who Was Wyatt Earp, Really?

In his fascinating book *The Earp Brothers of Tombstone,* celebrated Western author Frank Waters (*The Man Who Shot the Deer*) wrote that Wyatt Earp was "an itinerant saloonkeeper, cardsharp, gunman, bigamist, church deacon, policeman, bunco artist, and a supreme confidence man . . . [who] died two years before his fictitious biography [*Wyatt Earp, Frontier Marshal* by Stuart M. Lake] recast him in the role of America's most famous frontier marshal."

Waters's writings were based on the recollections of one "Aunt Allie," the widow of Virgil Earp (Wyatt's brother), whom Waters met when she was a frail octogenarian in the early 1930s. By then the myth of the life that Wyatt Earp lived fifty years earlier was so entrenched in lore that he was widely considered one of the true heroes of the West. Aunt Allie had a different story to tell, however, "in a western vernacular that was all Americana and a yard wide," according to Waters.

Because of threatened lawsuits and, perhaps, public resistance to the dethroning of the king of Tombstone, Waters didn't publish the book right away, although Allie's remembrances were backed by his research. Rather, he donated the manuscript to the Arizona Pioneers' Historical Society in Tucson, as a record for its files.

The society's secretary eventually convinced Waters, twenty-five years later, to publish his manuscript. The society concurred that Aunt Allie's story, not Stuart M. Lake's, was the more factual.

mation, are a popular part of many parades and festivals in the region. Call the Sierra Vista Chamber of Commerce at (520) 458–6940 or (800) 288–3861 for more information.

Twenty miles south of Sierra Vista off Highway 92, the **Coronado National Memorial** is situated in oak woodlands, hugging the Mexican border at the southern end of the Huachuca Mountains. The 5,000-acre memorial commemorates the first major European exploration of the

American Southwest, that of Francisco Vasquez de Coronado, which took place in 1540.

After stopping at the visitor center (open 8:00 A.M. to 5:00 P.M. daily), continue westward up the road to Montezuma Pass. From there hike the half mile to Coronado Peak: Gaze south, far into Mexico and, to the east, into the cottonwood-lined San Pedro River valley, which the Coronado party traced into the future United States eighty years before the Pilgrims landed at Plymouth Rock. For further information call (520) 366–5515.

From Sierra Vista wend your way north, west, and south toward the border town of Nogales.

Note: A shorter, dirt-road route also leads to Nogales from Coronado National Monument. Inquire about road conditions at the visitor center.

North of Nogales, at 30 and 40 miles, respectively, are two historic attractions well worth visiting: **Tumacacori National Monument** (520–398–2341) and **Tubac Presidio State Historic Park** (520–398–2252). Both are open daily from 8:00 A.M. to 5:00 P.M.

Tumacacori holds the remnants of a mission church, now partially restored, built by Franciscans around 1800 and deserted in 1848, for fear of Indian attacks. On display at the monument museum are numerous artifacts, including examples of original wooden statues.

Tubac, the first European settlement in the future Arizona, sprouted as a garrison in 1751, also established to protect settlers. The party that eventually founded the city of San Francisco, California, was dispatched from here in 1776. Today Tubac is a bustling art colony.

Sixty miles north of Nogales and a hundred miles south of Phoenix is Arizona's other metropolis, Tucson. The town began life as a Spanish presidio, and three special areas—**Armory Park, Barrio Historico,** and **El Presidio**—preserve and interpret this special heritage. For information on these and the city's numerous Mexican-flavored festivals, such as the **Fiesta de San Agustin,** contact the Tucson Convention and Visitors Bureau at (520) 624–1817. Also, don't miss the **Arizona State Museum** (520–621–6302) on the campus of Arizona State University.

Old Tucson Studios (520–883–0100), located at 201 South Kinney

Road in Tucson Mountain Park, includes an Old West town that has appeared in countless commercials, Western movies, and television shows. The place also features a fun-filled amusement park, with gunfights, a Kid's Korral, and several restaurants and shops. Just up the road is the world-class and world-famous **Arizona–Sonora Desert Museum,** which details the ecology unique to the Sonoran Desert.

Tucson boasts a bonanza of historic inns hidden among its nooks and crannies; one of many is **El Presidio Inn,** found at 297 North Main Avenue. Occupying an adobe mansion built in the 1800s, the gracious old place has three luxury suites and a guest house and is within walking distance of a selection of Tucson's best restaurants, museums, and shopping opportunities. For information and reservations call (800) 349–6151.

Francisco Vasquez de Coronado

In 1540, accompanied by 336 Spanish soldiers, four priests, several hundred Mexican-Indian allies, and 1,500 stock animals, Coronado set out to look for the fabled Seven Cities of Cibola. Some thirty members of the party eventually made it as far north and east as present-day Salina, Kansas, as they searched for Quivira, where a Plains Indian had told them they would find incredible wealth. (That Indian later admitted that his story about Quivira was nothing but a story, and he was executed by the Spaniards.)

Coronado returned to Mexico in 1542, resuming his duties as governor of the frontier province of New Galicia. He died ten years later at age forty-two, not knowing that he had helped ready the West for its turbulent future: Descendants of the horses left behind by his party forever altered the Native Americans' ways of life. Their religions began to change, too, in response to the teachings of the priests who had traveled with Coronado.

Where to Eat

Miss Kitty's, Williams, (520) 635–9161
Rawhide Steakhouse and Saloon, Phoenix, (602) 502–1880
Rustler's Rooste, Phoenix, (602) 431–6474
Reata Pass, Phoenix, (602) 585–7277

Where to Stay

Holiday Inn Canyon de Chelly, Chinle, (520) 674–5000
Navajo Nation Inn, Window Rock (800) 662–6189
Mountain Side Resort, Williams, (520) 635–4431
Jerome Inn, Jerome, (520) 634–5094
Sombrero Ranch, outside Wickenburg, (520) 684–0222
Kay El Bar Ranch, outside Wickenburg, (520) 684–7593
Gadsen Hotel, Douglas, (520) 364–4481
Copper Queen Hotel, Bisbee, (520) 432–2216
Buford House Bed & Breakfast, Tombstone, (520) 457–3969
Tombstone Boarding House, Tombstone, (520) 457–3716
Priscilla's Bed & Breakfast, Tombstone, (520) 457–3844
Silver Nugget Bed & Breakfast, Tombstone, (520) 457–9223
Victoria's Bed & Breakfast, Tombstone, (520) 457–3677
El Presidio Inn, Tucson, (800) 349–6151

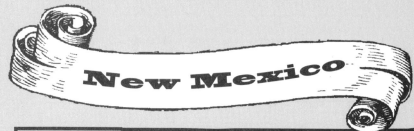

New Mexico

NORTHWEST
NEW MEXICO

NORTH-
CENTRAL
NEW MEXICO

NORTHEAST
NEW MEXICO

★ Gallup

★ Santa Fe

Fort Sumner
★

SOUTHWEST
NEW MEXICO

Lincoln
★

SOUTHEAST
NEW MEXICO

Silver City
★

N
W   E
S

NEW MEXICO

▼▼▼

EW MEXICO became the forty-seventh state in 1912, only a month before Arizona became the last of the Lower 48, yet its capital, Santa Fe, is the oldest capital city in the United States. Here the legacy of the Old West thrives, and a lot of it is exceedingly old.

With its pronounced Mexican and Native American influences, New Mexico often seems like another country; drive the splendid High Road between Taos and Santa Fe, for instance, and you'll be convinced you've been magically transported to Old Mexico. Ties to the past are strong, with present-day Pueblo Indians performing the same ceremonies as those carried out by their nineteenth-century ancestors, and descendants of the early Mexican settlers continuing to celebrate their traditions, as well.

The narrative begins by looping through the northwest quarter of the state. Then, after exploring the very special Santa Fe–Taos area in north-central New Mexico, it circles through the northeast quadrant, leads down into the southeast, and finishes in the southwest, that portion of the state deservedly nicknamed "Old West Country."

Northwest New Mexico

Two dozen Native American reservations are scattered throughout New Mexico; the northwest, however, is generally considered the heart of Indian Country. Before visiting the concentration of living pueblos that surround the village of Bernalillo, travel to the "ghost pueblo" of Kauau at the **Coronado State Monument.** The fifteenth-century ruins, located a mile north of Bernalillo on Highway 44, include a reconstructed ceremonial kiva.

Coronado and his soldiers, on their search for the Seven Cities of Cibola, camped nearby, and among the visitor center's varied collections is a conquistador's armor outfit, complete with headgear. The monument is open daily year-round from 8:00 A.M. to 5:00 P.M. Call (505) 867–5351 for more information.

PUEBLO COUNTRY

BE-PU-WA-VE—WELCOME TO PUEBLO COUNTRY!

*O*f the three native peoples living under sovereign rule in New Mexico today—the Pueblos, the Apaches, and the Navajos—the Pueblo Indians have lived here the longest. Nineteen distinct Pueblo villages are found in the state, and many of their residents lead lives much like those lived by their ancestors in the nineteenth century and earlier (although gambling casinos are springing up at many of the pueblos, detracting some from the ancient look of the villages).

Each pueblo has its unique ceremonies—which typically combine traditional dancing and rituals with a particular Roman Catholic saint's day—and regulations governing visitors. A few general rules of etiquette: Cemeteries and ceremonial kivas are typically off-limits, and alcohol is taboo. When observing dances, don't applaud, move around, or try to talk to participants, for each dance is a prayer that requires your silence and the dancer's concentration. Ask permission before sketching or using your camera or tape recorder within a pueblo (they're often forbidden, especially during ceremonies).

Following is a list of the pueblos, a telephone number to call for additional travel information, and a brief description of each pueblo:

Acoma *(800) 747–0181: Also known as Sky City, Acoma has been occupied since 1150, which makes it one of the longest continuously inhabited settlements in the United States (a competition in which it runs neck-and-neck with the Hopi mesas in Arizona). Early residents scaled the dizzying, 365-foot-high mesa by using a system of ladders and finger-hold trails, but a road leads there today. The San Estevan del Rey Mission, completed in 1640, dominates the skyline. Today most tribal members live in villages below, but Sky City fills during celebrations, when Acoma artists come to sell their acclaimed white-clay pottery. Acoma can be visited only on guided tours, which depart several times daily from the visitor center below.*

264

Cochití *(505) 465–2244: Craftspersons of this pueblo are renowned for their clay Storyteller figures and log-and-rawhide drums, which can be heard resounding at the July 14 Corn Dance.*

Isleta *(505) 869–3111: The largest of the Tiwa-speaking pueblos, Isleta is renowned for the excellent Indian bread made by women of the tribe. The bread is baked in beehive-shaped* horno *ovens and sold in stores as well as out of many homes.*

Jémez *(505) 834–7235: In the 1830s members of the now-extinct Pecos Pueblo merged with the Jémez, and the ceremonials of both tribes are celebrated here today, including the Old Pecos Bull Dance on August 2. The village opens only on feast days, but visitors are always welcome at the Pueblo's Red Rock Scenic Area, where arts and crafts and Indian foods are sold.*

Laguna *(505) 552–6654 or 552–9030: Comprising six villages, Laguna is the largest of the Keresan-speaking pueblos. St. Joseph's Feast Day on September 19 at Old Laguna is their largest celebration, attracting scores of visitors. The shops at Casa Blanca Market Center in New Laguna sell traditional Laguna and Acoma pottery and turquoise-and-silver jewelry.*

Nambé *(505) 455–2036: This pueblo is best known for stunning Nambé Falls, where the annual Nambé Falls Celebration takes place on Independence Day. Traditional dances are performed and Indian food and crafts are sold.*

Picurís *(505) 587–2519 or 587–2957: Settled in the 1200s and abandoned after the Pueblos' 1680 revolt against Spanish rule, Picurís was reestablished in the 1700s. Prior to the uprising it was the largest of the northern pueblos, but today it is among the smallest, with only 250 members. Their Hidden Valley Restaurant serves American and Indian food seven days a week from 11:30 A.M. to 7:00 P.M.*

Pojoaque *(505) 455–3460: A late-nineteenth-century smallpox epidemic nearly eradicated the Pojoaque tribe, but members have made a comeback since reclaiming their pueblo in the 1930s. Now 200-members strong, the tribe owns several businesses, including the Po'suwae geh Restaurant, open daily.*

Sandía *(505) 867–3317: This pueblo was founded around 1300 and visited by Coronado in 1540; today their Bien Mur Indian Market Center opens daily, selling locally made arts and crafts. The St. Anthony Feast Day is celebrated June 13.*

San Felipe *(505) 867–3381: Extremely protective of their traditions, residents welcome visitors only on May 1, their annual feast day, when the Green Corn Dance is performed.*

San Ildefonso *(505) 455–3549: This popular pueblo's polished black pottery, with distinctive black-matte designs, was designed and made famous in the 1920s by Maria and Julian Martinez. Many artists' homes are open for browsing, and the visitor center is open daily from 8:00 A.M. to 4:30 P.M., except on ceremonial days.*

San Juan *(505) 852–4265: Headquarters for the Eight Northern Indian Pueblos Council, San Juan is home of the O'ke Oweenge crafts cooperative, which sells tribal artisans' distinctive redware pottery and many other items (open Monday through Saturday). The annual Artist and Craftsman Show, held in mid-July, boasts nearly a thousand Indian artists, along with traditional dances and foods.*

Santa Ana *(505) 867–3301: The older village of Santa Ana is open to visitors only on January 1 and 6, Easter, June 24 and 29, July 25 and 26 (Feast Day), and December 25–28. The newer village boasts the Ta-Ma-Ya arts and crafts cooperative, with woven belts, paintings, and traditional pottery for sale. It is open on Tuesday, Thursday, and Sunday.*

Santa Clara *(505) 753–7326: Known worldwide for its redware and carved blackware, Kha P'o (Valley of the Wild Roses) offers pottery-making demonstrations and guided tours, which can include a traditional meal in a private home.*

Santo Domingo *(505) 465–2214: Culturally conservative, these people are heralded for their exquisite beadwork and shell jewelry, which can be purchased at roadside ramadas and several private homes and small shops. More than 500 individuals participate in the August 4 Corn Dance, making it among the most colorful and dramatic of Pueblo ceremonials.*

Taos *(505) 758–9593: This is the most famous of the pueblos. The multistory adobe house here is a national historic monument and still home to a few tribal members. (The majority of the tribe lives outside the village walls.) Their San Geronimo Feast Day takes place September 29–30.*

Tesuque *(505) 983–2667: This pueblo is among the most traditional of the pueblos. Tesuque warriors initiated the 1680 Pueblo Revolt, and the Tesuque pueblo celebrates that uprising on August 10. Woven and embroidered Tesuque clothing and other items are sold at the local store.*

Zia *(505) 867–3304: Zia is best known for its ancient sun symbol, which appears on the New Mexico state flag. Adapted from a pottery design, the Zia sun, with its stylized rays, is representative of friendship. Zia's annual Corn Dance is held August 15.*

Zuñi *(505) 782–4481: Claiming a language distinct from the other Pueblos' two language groups, Zuñi is famous for its stonework jewelry, set with pipestone, turquoise, black jet, coral, and opal stones. With nearly 10,000 residents, it is the most populous of the pueblos. The Zuñi Museum Project, open Monday through Friday, features historical photographs and other interpretive exhibits. The Lady of Guadalupe Mission, built in 1629, is decorated with murals that depict Zuñi culture and traditions.*

In Albuquerque start by visiting **Old Town,** 2 miles west of downtown, the site founded in 1706 as San Francisco de Alburquerque (notice the extra *r* that has since disappeared) and named for the Viceroy of New Spain. Gunfights erupt in the streets here in summer, and gift shops, restaurants, galleries, and Native American crafts stores beckon. For the latter try **Gus's Trading Company** at 2026 Central Southwest, which stocks a good selection of pottery, kachinas, jewelry, and drums. **The Albuquerque Museum,** at 2000 Mountain Road Northwest, features extensive art and history exhibits, including the largest collection of Spanish Colonial goods in the United States. The museum (505–242–4600) is open Tuesday through Sunday from 9:00 A.M. to 5:00 P.M.

The **Indian Pueblo Cultural Center,** owned and operated by New Mexico's nineteen Pueblo tribes, features a restaurant that serves traditional fare, along with a gift shop and a pair of museums, including the Pueblo House Children's Museum. Dance and craft demonstrations are presented on weekends and at the annual **American Indian Week** in late April, which also features workshops, lectures, and an art sale. The center (505–843–7270), located near Old Town at 2401 Twelfth Street Northwest, is open daily from 9:00 A.M. to 5:30 P.M.

Another great place to sample traditional New Mexican fare is the **Maria Teresa Restaurant & 1840 Bar,** at 618 Rio Grande Boulevard Northwest. Since 1840, as the name suggests, folks have been gathering at this place, now a registered national historic place. For some of the best chili in the Southwest, head for the **M & J Sanitary Tortilla Factory,** at 403 Second Southwest.

Thoreau, mid-way between Gallup and Grants, is home to the annual **Wild West Days** in July (800–748–2142). Of the several routes that lead to remote **Chaco Canyon National Historical Park,** none is what you'd call convenient. One option: Turn off Interstate 40 near Thoreau and drive north on Highways 371 and 57. The reward at the end of the dusty, bumpy drive is the best-preserved and most impressive Anasazi ruins in New Mexico. The Anasazi, ancestral to today's Pueblo Indians, farmed throughout the Four Corners Region, but it's believed that Chaco Canyon was the heart of their world and that as many as 5,000 of them once lived here.

Begin by stopping at the visitor center; then stroll through Pueblo Bonito, the largest of the dozen or so ruins. The barren but spectacular terrain of the park includes a campground, with water available at the visitor center, but no other visitor services. Chaco Canyon is open daily from 8:00 A.M. to 5:00 P.M.; call (505) 786–7014 for more information and an update on road conditions.

Gallup's long downtown strip, at one time a stretch of legendary Route 66, is packed with pawn shops and trading posts. The capital of Indian Country explodes on weekends, with Indians traveling from afar to trade and socialize. Nearby Red Rock State Park boasts the **Red Rock Museum** and **Outlaw Trading Post** (505–863–1337), with outstanding selections of Native American jewelry, pottery, rugs, and kachinas for sale. The huge **Gallup Inter-Tribal Indian Ceremonial** (505–863–3896) is held in the park in August, with a powwow, arts-and-crafts sale, rodeo, ceremonial dances, parades, half-marathon run, and more.

Long and lonely Highway 666 courses northward through New Mexico's portion of the Navajo Reservation to the settlement of Shiprock, where the colossal **Shiprock Fair** (800–448–1240) explodes in late September. Dancing, rodeoing, powwowing, and art shows are among the festivities.

The **Hogback Trading Company and Wheeler Museum** (505–598–5154), 15 miles east of Shiprock at Waterflow, claims 10,000 square feet filled with one of the most comprehensive selections of Indian art in North America (it specializes in Navajo rugs). Established in 1871 and among the oldest continuously run trading posts in Navajo country, it's currently

The Hogan

The hogan, traditional hexagonal abode of the Navajo, is still a common sight in *Dine' Bi Keyah* (land of the people). The structures blend so well with their surroundings that they appear to be extensions of the earth on which they rest. And, in fact, they are.

There are two general types of hogan. The conical, or forked-stick hogan resembles a mountaintop. The older of the two styles, it's considered the male hogan and today is used primarily for ceremonial purposes. The perpendicular-sided, or walled-log hogan is a rounded log structure with mud or clay chinking and a roof of cribbed logs covered with mud. This hogan is used for cooking and residing in and is the more commonly seen variety.

The interior of the hogan is open, with no center supports to get in the way. An open fire, used both for cooking and warming, vents through a hole in the roof. (Various modern building techniques and features, including chimneys, often are incorporated into newer hogans.) The doorway, which faces the rising sun, is typically the only daylight opening. Electric bulbs or kerosene lamps light the interior, and residents traditionally sleep on piles of sheepskins.

managed by the great-grandson of post founder Joseph Wheeler. The trading company is open Monday through Saturday from 8:00 A.M. to 5:00 P.M.

In Farmington take in the highly regarded *Anasazi: The Ancient Ones,* performed at the Lions' Wilderness Park. The outdoor musical drama relates the story (as well as it is known) of the Anasazi Indians and also of the Navajo and Mormon influences on the Four Corners region. Performances are staged at 8:00 P.M. Wednesday through Saturday, mid-June through Labor Day weekend, with dinner served at the site at 6:30 P.M. For information call the Convention & Visitors Bureau at (800) 448–1240.

Should you for any reason plan to be in Farmington in late March, take in **An Evening of Cowboy Poetry and Tales of the Old West** (800–448–1240) at the Civic Center. Regardless of when you're here, visit the **Farmington Museum,** at 302 North Orchard, to study its overview of Four Corners history.

North-Central New Mexico

Chama, 110 miles east of Farmington, serves as the southern terminus of the **Cumbres & Toltec Scenic Railroad** (see Antonito, Colorado, p. 181). Here the **Gandy Dancer Bed & Breakfast,** whose name celebrates the railroad builders, offers comfy overnight accommodations just a block from the depot; call (505) 756–2191 to make reservations.

Santa Fe historically was a destination of trails. Beginning in the 1500s settlers, soldiers, and priests filtered northward to here from Mexico City along *El Camino Real,* the King's Road; likewise, but beginning some 300 years later, the commerce-driven Santa Fe Trail ran to Santa Fe from Independence, Missouri.

Through it all the Santa Fe Plaza has been a place where a collage of cultures congregated. There is so much to see—and, to taste!—in Santa Fe that it's tough to know where to begin. As good a place as any is the **Palace of the Governors,** the oldest public building in the United States. Built by the Spanish in 1609–10 (fully a decade before the Pilgrims landed at Plymouth Rock), the Palace has served as the headquarters for six ruling governments: the Spanish (1609–80 and 1693–1821), the Pueblo Indians (1680–93), the Mexican Empire (1821–22), the Republic of Mexico (1822–46), the Confederate Army (for less than one month in 1862), and the United States Territory of

Native Americans display their wares at the Palace of the Governors in Santa Fe.

New Mexico (1846–1907). The imposing structure's 385-year history is colorful and fascinating; for instance, it is where Mexican Governor Manuel Armijo nailed to his office wall the ears of invaders out of Texas, where explorer Zebulon Pike was jailed by Mexican patrols, and where territorial governor Lew Wallace wrote his epic novel *Ben Hur*. Today the Palace serves as headquarters for the four-component **Museum of New Mexico,** while simultaneously housing one of those components, the State History Museum, a facility that should not be missed. The Palace of the Governors, situated on the ever-festive Santa Fe Plaza, is open from 10:00 A.M. to 5:00 P.M. daily; call (505) 827–6483 for information. Also mark on your "to-visit" list the hogan-shaped **Wheelwright Museum of the American Indian** (505–982–4636), located at 704 Camino Lejo and open Monday through Saturday from 10:00 A.M. to 5:00 P.M. and Sunday from 1:00 to 5:00 P.M. (in the basement is the fabulous Case Trading Post, which sells rugs, blankets, and other items), and the adjacent **Museum of Indian Arts and Culture** (505–827–6344), open Tuesday through Sunday, from 10:00 A.M. to 5:00 P.M.

Some particularly enticing times to visit Santa Fe: during **Spanish Market** in late July, during the **Mountain Man Rendezvous Trade Fair** in early August (which includes a buffalo roast on the Plaza), or in the midst of the **Santa Fe Indian Market** in late August. All these events, and many more throughout the year, happen in and around the vibrant Plaza and the Palace of the Governors.

Opportunities abound in Santa Fe to overnight in sumptuous old-Southwest adobe-and-wood surroundings, to dine on the best of traditional New Mexican foods, and to shop for the finest in Southwestern art, but nothing comes cheaply in Santa Fe. A couple of lodging suggestions: **La Posada** (505–986–0000), at 330 East Palace Avenue, and **Santa Fe Casitas** (505–982–3332). The latter are available in one- and two-bedroom versions and with kitchens and courtyards. Concerning food, a trip to Santa Fe is incomplete without a night out at the **Pink Adobe,** 406 Old Santa Fe Trail. The restaurant occupies one of the oldest structures in a city filled with venerable buildings. For breakfast, sample the out-of-this-world huevos rancheros at **Pasquals,** a block off the Plaza at the corner of Water and Don Gaspar.

Before leaving town head for **Back at the Ranch,** 235 Don Gaspar, an enterprise that sells vintage Western wear and collectibles. It's an ideal place to pick up a pair of used boots, chaps, or spurs. A couple of other hot spots for purchasing Western relics and clothing: **Arrowsmith's,** at 402 Old Santa Fe Trail, and **Rancho,** 322 McKenzie Street. For more information on the city's many festivals, attractions, accommodations, and restaurants, contact the Convention and Visitors Bureau at (505) 984–6760, or simply start sniffing around. (To help limit the mind-boggling array of possibilities, consider signing on with **Afoot in Santa Fe Tours,** 505–983–3701, for a walking tour or a riding tour in an open-air tram.)

Southwest of Santa Fe along Interstate 25, near La Cienega, the 200-acre **El Rancho de las Golondrinas** exhibits the lifestyles of the early Spanish settlers. The ranch, whose name translates to Ranch of the Swallows, was founded in the early 1700s as a wayside stop along *El Camino Real.* The living-history museum found here today includes several historic buildings, with period-attired residents who tend orchards, vineyards, and goat herds, as well as spin, weave, and cook traditional dishes. The ranch is open to self-guided tours between 10:00 A.M. and 4:00 P.M. Wednesday through Sunday from June to September and to guided tours (by appointment) in April, May, and October. (It's closed November through March.) Call (505) 471–2261 for more information and to learn about special events, including the extremely popular harvest festival in early October.

Near Galisteo, 25 miles south of Santa Fe on Interstate 25 and Highways 285 and 41, guests stay in a gracious hacienda of a vintage similar to that of El Rancho de las Golondrinas. The twelve-room, 250-year-old **Galisteo Inn** (505–466–4000), surrounded by eight country acres, features rooms, well-mannered trail horses, and stellar New Mexican cuisine.

For a stay at a newer accommodation (it's been in operation "only" since the 1920s), head for **Los Piños Ranch.** The spread, 8,500 feet high and steeped in the Western way, is located in the Pecos River headwaters near Terrero, 45 miles east and north of Santa Fe, smack in the heart of the Sangre de Cristo Mountains. A maximum of sixteen guests at a time hole up at the dude ranch, sleeping in rustic log cabins and riding sure-footed horses amid splendiferous surroundings. Los Piños is open Memorial Day through Labor Day; call (505) 757–6213 for more information.

Bypass the main highway and negotiate the circuitous **High Road to Taos,** one of the great American roadways, as it traces through a chain of villages out of Old Mexico: Chimayó, Truchas, Las Trampas, Peñasco, and Talpa. In Chimayó, home to a renowned assembly of traditional weavers (you can buy their goods in local shops), stop at the 1816 **El Santuario de**

Chimayó, open to the public daily from 7:00 A.M. to 4:30 P.M. The adobe chapel is, and has been for decades, the destination for thousands of New Mexicans who make an annual pilgrimage during Holy Week.

After feeding your soul, feed your appetite at **Restarante Rancho de Chimayó,** which serves delectable New Mexican fare with an emphasis on locally grown chiles and other foodstuffs. The century-old adobe, which contains several small rooms for cozy dining, opens daily at noon in summer and Tuesday through Sunday the rest of the year. There's also a B&B associated with the enterprise; call (505) 351–2222 for more information.

After visiting the most obvious attraction in Taos—the incomparable Taos Pueblo—proceed to the **Martinez Hacienda,** perched on the banks of the Rio Pueblo. Located 2 miles southeast of the Taos plaza on Ranchitos Road (Highway 240), the nearly 200-year-old Spanish Colonial fortress at one time protected those within from Apache and Comanche Indian raids, when it served as the northernmost stop on *El Camino Real*. With twenty-one rooms that embrace a pair of courtyards, the grand hacienda offers a living-history lesson on the early Hispanic culture that took root in this part of America. It's open daily from 9:00 A.M. to 5:00 P.M. The **Old Taos Trade Fair** happens at the hacienda in late September; call (505) 758–1000 for information.

The Martinez Hacienda is one of three museums collectively known as the **Kit Carson Historic Museums.** Carson, born in Kentucky in 1809, came to Taos in 1826 after hearing stories of how the settlement was growing into a major center for the fur trade, surrounded as it was by mountains and beaver-abundant streams. In 1843 Carson purchased what is now called the **Kit Carson Home,** as a gift for his new bride. The multiroom adobe, filled with period furnishings, contains displays on Taos's colorful past, including the mountain-man era, in which Carson played a crucial role. The home, just a few hundred yards east of the plaza on Kit Carson Road, is open from 8:00 A.M. to 6:00 P.M. daily in summer and from 9:00 A.M. to 5:00 P.M. the remainder of the year. Call (505) 758–4741 for more information. (In nearby **Kit Carson Park,** the legendary frontiersman, scout, and Indian fighter is buried.)

Another museum that offers a feel for early Taos: the **Governor Bent Home and Museum,** at 117A Bent Street. Artifacts from the frontier, along with family belongings of the first territorial governor, are displayed.

For accommodations, consider **La Posada de Taos,** an adobe hacienda built in the early 1900s by Bert Phillips, a pioneer of the town's now-thriving art community. Six rooms are available at the classic inn, which resides within the historic district; call (505) 758–8164 or (800) 645-4803 for reservations. For information on the many other intimate overnight possibilities in town, call the Taos Bed & Breakfast Association at (800) 876–7857.

Northeast New Mexico

The Santa Fe Trail helped shape early Cimarron, whose very name evokes images of gunslingers and desperadoes. (The name Cimarron, in fact, roughly translates from the Spanish into "untamed.") Guests at the **St. James Hotel,** built in 1873, included Wyatt Earp, Buffalo Bill Cody, Annie Oakley, and Zane Grey. Refurbished in the mid-1980s, the old adobe is appointed entirely in Victorian fashion, with rooms named for some of the famous and infamous who slept in them. Bullet holes can be spotted in the ceiling of **Lambert's,** the on-premises restaurant that formerly housed Lambert's Saloon and Gambling Hall. The hotel is situated in historic Old Town Cimarron; call (505) 376–2664 for reservations.

Five miles south of town is the **Philmont Ranch** (505–376–2281), a 140,000-acre spread donated in 1938 to the Boy Scouts of America by Frank Phillips, founder of the Phillips Petroleum Company. The Philmont Museum interprets the history of the mountain men, cowboys, Indians, and settlers who lived in the region. Approximately 7 miles farther south, at Rayado, is an additional component of the Philmont Ranch—yet another **Kit Carson Museum,** this one a replica of Carson's adobe hacienda.

Fort Union National Monument is located 8 miles north of Watrous on Highway 161 (take Interstate 25, exit 366). The post was established in 1851 to protect from Indian attack both commercial traffic on the Santa Fe Trail and settlers who were piercing the New Mexican wilds. The frontier feel of the place is tangible, thanks to fine displays and audiotapes prepared by the National Park Service and the Santa Fe Trail wagon ruts that are visible on the grounds. The monument (505–425–8025) is open daily from 8:00 A.M. to 5:00 P.M.

Las Vegas, 30 miles southwest of Fort Union, is older, cozier, smaller, and more tame than its famous counterpart in Nevada, although during the railroading boom of the 1880s it was one of New Mexico's leading cities. Here the Rough Riders Memorial Collection at the **City of Las Vegas Museum** includes memorabilia of those hardy troops organized by Teddy Roosevelt for his famous assault on Cuba during the Spanish-American War. Many of T.R.'s men were from New Mexico and brought home with them artifacts from the campaign. The museum, open in summer Monday through Saturday from 9:00 A.M. to 4:00 P.M., is located at 727 Grand Avenue; call (505) 425–8726 for more information. While in Las Vegas, do as trail-weary travelers since 1882 have done, and stay at the **Plaza Hotel** (505–425–3591), one of a bevy of historic buildings that front the comely, tree-lined Old Town Plaza.

Fort Sumner, on the banks of the Pecos River southeast of Las Vegas, holds a number of Wild West attractions, not the least of which are associated with William H. Bonney, a.k.a. Billy the Kid, New Mexico's most enduring (if not endearing) legend, though he lived a mere twenty-one years. The privately owned, multistructure **Billy the Kid Museum** (505–355–2380) features an eclectic collection of Billy's belongings. The museum, located at 1601 East Sumner Avenue, is open daily from 8:30 A.M. to 5:00 P.M. mid-May through mid-September and Monday through Saturday the rest of the year. (It closes in January and February.)

Seven miles southeast of town on Highway 60 and Billy the Kid Road, **Fort Sumner State Monument** (505–355–2573) memorializes the old military fort and surrounding wetlands known as Bosque Redondo. It was to here that Kit Carson herded thousands of Navajos on their Long Walk in the 1860s; it was here that some 8,000 Navajos and Mescalero Apaches were essentially interned for five years. The visitor center at the monument is open from 9:00 A.M. to 6:00 P.M. Thursday through Monday.

The nearby **Old Fort Sumner Museum** (505–355–2942) includes nineteenth-century cowboy, Indian, and military artifacts, along with more Billy the Kid memorabilia, including fascinating old newspaper accounts of his doings. The grave of Billy, who was gunned down at Fort Sumner in 1881 by Sheriff Pat Garrett, is located in the adjacent fort cemetery. (THE BOY BANDIT KING / HE DIED AS HE HAD LIVED, reads the epitaph.) The museum is open daily in summer from 8:00 A.M. to 6:00 P.M. and from 9:00 A.M. to 5:00 P.M. the rest of the year (closed January through March). The

Fort Sumner area's annual, rip-snortin' **Old Fort Days** are held in early June.

Clovis, 60 miles east of Fort Sumner, hosts the **Clovis Cowboy Poetry Gathering** in early May and the **Pioneer Days and PRCA Rodeo** in early June (PRCA stands for Professional Rodeo Cowboys Association). Call the Chamber of Commerce at (505) 763–3435 for more information on this and on the **Caprock Amphitheatre,** found 55 miles north of town. This 1,000-seat outdoor theater, nestled onto the bluffs of the *Llano Estacado* (Caprock), regularly presents the acclaimed musical drama *Billy the Kid* during July and August. **Ben's Barbecue** dishes out a rib-sticking meal prior to the show. Call (505) 461–1694 for tickets and additional information.

Twelve miles southwest of Clovis on Highway 70, the **Blackwater Draw Museum** displays and interprets finds from the nearby Blackwater Draw Site, one of the most important archaeological sites in the New World. Evidence of what became known as Clovis Man, who lived and hunted in North America 11,000 years ago (talk about the *Old* West), was documented here first, in 1932. The museum (505–562–2254) opens Monday through Saturday from 10:00 A.M. to 5:00 P.M. and Sunday from noon to 5:00 P.M. (closed Mondays except in summer).

Southeast New Mexico

Hobbs is the rodeo capital of New Mexico, and its **Lea County Cowboy Hall of Fame and Western Heritage Center** honors Lea County working cowboys, ranchers, and rodeoers. The museum (505–392–1275), situated on the campus of New Mexico Junior College at 5317 Lovington Highway, is open Monday through Friday from 8:00 A.M. to 5:00 P.M., Saturday from 9:00 A.M. to 5:00 P.M., and Sunday from 1:00 to 5:00 P.M. The private **Linam Ranch Museum,** located west of town on Highway 180 and open by appointment only, houses Indian and pioneer artifacts. Call (505) 393–4784 to arrange a visit.

Lofty Cloudcroft is 170 miles west of Hobbs, but it seems a thousand miles north, with the high-country vegetation and low temperatures associated with its 9,200-foot elevation. Visit the **Cloudcroft Historical Museum** (505–682–2733) and the **Sacramento Mountains Historical Society Museum** (505–682–2932); and, if passing through in June, take in the festive **Western Roundup.** While in town stay at **The Lodge,** a

The Lincoln County War of 1878

In a bloody struggle for control of the beef industry and other local business concerns, wealthy English rancher John Henry Tunstall was victim of a hired killing near Ruidoso in February 1878. Lines formed and Lincoln became the battlefield; an April 1 gunfight resulted in the death of Sheriff William Brady, the man reportedly responsible for Tunstall's killing. The Regulators, a group set on avenging Tunstall's death—and which included an eighteen-year-old Billy the Kid, who had worked for Tunstall—barricaded themselves in an adobe compound in Lincoln on July 14.

When Army troops poured in five days later, and the Regulators got a glimpse of the intimidating Gatling gun, most surrendered; several, however, stayed, including Billy, who escaped when the building was set on fire.

Things mellowed when newly appointed Territorial Governor Lew Wallace granted amnesty to all of those who participated in the standoff. Billy, however, was eventually convicted in court at La Mesilla for the murder of Sheriff Brady, in what was widely considered a rigged trial. Sentenced to hang, he was returned to Lincoln to await execution, but he escaped from the courthouse jail on April 28, killing two deputies in the process.

Victorian-appointed inn established in 1899 to serve those arriving at Cloudcroft via railroad. (The original building burned in 1909 and was replaced shortly thereafter.) Call (505) 682–2566 for information and reservations.

The Anne C. Stradling Collection at the **Museum of the Horse** in equine-oriented, Billy-the-Kid-lore-filled Ruidoso contains more than 10,000 horse-related pieces. The museum (505–378–4142), found near the Ruidoso Downs Race Track, is open daily from 9:00 A.M. to 5:00 P.M.

Perhaps more than any town in New Mexico, Lincoln, 35 miles northeast of Ruidoso on Highway 380, keeps the Old West kicking. **Lincoln State Monument** encompasses virtually the entire one-street, restored frontier town and includes the two-story courthouse from which Billy the Kid made his final escape in 1878. (The annual **Old Lincoln Days** in early August includes a reenactment of the famous escape.) The **Lincoln County Museum** includes displays on Billy the Kid, cowboys and Indians, the Lincoln County War, the Buffalo Soldiers, and more. You can pick up a ticket here that's good for admission to the many historical sites in town, all of which are open daily from 8:30 A.M. to 5:00 P.M. May through September (schedules fluctuate the rest of the year). Call (505) 653–4025 for more information.

The reconstructed **Wortley Hotel** offers rooms that look and feel much as those in the original 1870s hotel would have (it burned in the 1930s). The hotel, owned by the Museum of New Mexico, is open year-round, and the restaurant on the premises serves breakfast, lunch, and dinner. Call (505) 653–4500 for more information. Another overnight option: **Casa de Patron** (505–653–4676), on Highway 380 East, a historic adobe whose intimate rooms are filled with antiques.

Southwest New Mexico

Sixteen miles north of Las Cruces and a couple of miles off Interstate 25 at exit 19 are the adobe ruins of **Fort Selden State Monument.** Like most nineteenth-century forts in the West, it was established to protect settlers and travelers from Indian attacks, in this case, Apache. At the visitor center you'll learn of the fort's history and past residents, who included a regiment of the Indian-fighting Buffalo Soldiers. The monument (505–526–8911) is open daily from 8:30 A.M. to 5:00 P.M. year-round.

Get your bearings in Las Cruces at the **Log Cabin Museum** (505–523–0952), at the corner of Main and Lucero. Then travel to the southern end of the city to La Mesilla, the village where the Confederacy established a short-lived southwestern territory capital and where Billy the Kid was convicted of murder and sentenced to hang in 1881. You can learn more at the **Gadsden Museum,** near the plaza on Calle de Parian.

In Deming, 50 miles west of Las Cruces, the **Deming Luna Mimbres Museum** (505–546–2382), at 301 South Silver, is a large red-brick facility that depicts early life in the Southwest, including that of cowboys, miners, and railroaders. It's open Monday through Saturday from 9:00 A.M. to 4:00 P.M. and Sunday from 1:30 to 4:00 P.M.

Columbus, 32 miles south of Deming and just north of the Mexican border and the dusty town of Palomas, Chihuahua, was where Pancho Villa made his bloody 1916 attack on U.S. civilians, an event you can learn more about at the **Columbus Historical Museum** (505–531–2620), located in

Pancho Villa Visits Nuevo Mexico

Pancho Villa, born Doroteo Arango, was considered a Robin Hood by Mexican peasants but a bloodthirsty killer by the American government. He fought against injustice, but often his efforts were misguided. The north-Mexico bandit joined with rebel forces in 1910 to fight for President Madero; then, in 1914–15, he and Zapata helped force President Huerta into exile.

On March 9, 1916, apparently in response to President Wilson's recognition of Venustiano Carranza as the new president of Mexico, Villa and his men attacked the U.S. 13th Cavalry at Camp Furlong, New Mexico. Repelled, they went to the town of Columbus and wreaked general havoc, breaking windows, looting stores, and killing eighteen civilians and wounding another dozen.

A U.S. Army expedition, led by Gen. John J. Pershing, was dispatched the next day. The forces heartily pursued Villa 500 miles deep into Mexico during the next eleven months, killing many of his troops but never cornering their leader.

In some ways more interesting than the egomaniacal, moody Villa was the fact that here we had the changing of the guard—from the old days to the new ways of waging war. It was the first time that motorized vehicles were used by the United States in warfare. Horseback cavalrymen from the Indian wars, including Buffalo Soldiers of the 10th Cavalry, fought side by side with two future heroes of World War I and II: General Pershing and a young protégé officer named George Patton, underscoring how truly short the history of western America is.

Villa, incidentally, was assassinated by the Mexican government on July 20, 1920.

the old Southern Pacific Railroad depot. The **Columbus Raid Commemoration,** held in early March south of town at **Pancho Villa State Park** (505–531–2711), honors those killed in the raid. The park also includes a campground that is landscaped with an incredible array of cactus and other desert plants.

Elegantly Victorian Silver City is yet another New Mexico town where the notorious Billy the Kid made his mark. Sites include the Kid's boyhood cabin, his mother's grave, and the **Star Hotel,** where a young William H. Bonney waited tables. Also in and around Silver City: **Santa Rita del**

Cobre Fort (505–388–2211), a replica of the old Fort Webster trading post, and the **Silver City Museum,** with displays on mining, early women settlers, and the prehistoric Mogollon Indians. (The remains of Mogollon residences can be visited at **Gila Cliff Dwellings National Monument,** deep in the Mogollon Mountains 45 miles north of Silver City.) The museum, itself a historic relic, is an unusual brick Victorian, built in 1881 to serve as home to mining tycoon Harry Ailman. Located at 312 West Broadway, the museum (505–538–5921) is open Tuesday through Friday from 9:00 A.M. to 4:30 P.M. and on weekends from 10:00 A.M. to 4:00 P.M.

Silver City's **Wild West Pro Rodeo** kicks up in early June at the Southwest Horseman's Arena. Other annual festivals include the July 4th **Frontier Days,** the **Cowboy Poetry Gathering** in August, and September's **Mining Days,** which include a chili cook-off, mining competitions, and gunfights in the street. The historic mining settlement of Piños Altos, 7 miles north of Silver City, hides the wild and woolly **Buckhorn Saloon,** serving good food and good drink. Across the street is the log-cabin **Piños Altos Museum** (505–388–1882). For more details on Silver City–area celebrations, accommodations, and attractions, call the Chamber of Commerce at (800) 548–9378.

Photogenic Mogollon, 65 miles northwest of Silver City on Highway 180, then 9 miles east along twisting Highway 159, is 99 percent ghost town, but a few residents still hang on. A 1973 Western starring Henry Fonda, *My Name Is Nobody,* was filmed here and is responsible for the newer facades seen on some of the old buildings in the once-lawless hideout.

Back at Highway 180 go 25 miles north, then 7 miles east on Highway 12 to the San Francisco River town of Reserve. The tiny seat of immense Gila County was founded in the 1860s by Mormon cattlemen. The biggest surprise in town is **Tularosa Dry Goods,** a general store straight out of the nineteenth century, selling late-1800s–style Western wear, including cowboy hats crafted by a local hat maker, and tack, suspenders, enamelware—you name it. It's open Tuesday through Saturday from 10:00 A.M. to 5:00 P.M.

Where to Eat

Maria Teresa Restaurant & 1840 Bar, Albuquerque, (505) 242–3900
Pink Adobe, Santa Fe, (505) 983–7712
Pasquals, Santa Fe, (505) 983–9340
Restarante Rancho de Chimayó, Chimayó, (505) 351–2222
Lamberts, Cimarron, (505) 376–2664
Buckhorn Saloon, Piños Altos, (505) 538–9911

Where to Stay

Gandy Dancer Bed & Breakfast, Chama, (505) 756–2191
La Posada, Santa Fe, (505) 986–0000
Santa Fe Casitas, Santa Fe, (505) 982–3332
Galisteo Inn, Galisteo, (505) 466–4000
Los Piños Ranch, Terrero, (505) 757–6213
La Posada de Taos, Taos, (505) 758–8164 or (800) 645–4803
St. James Hotel, Cimarron, (505) 376–2664
Plaza Hotel, Las Vegas, (505) 425–3591
Wortley Hotel, Lincoln, (505) 653–4500
Casa de Patron, Lincoln, (505) 653–4676

RIVER, MILITARY, AND CATTLE TRAILS

▼▼▼

TEXAS
OKLAHOMA
KANSAS
MISSOURI

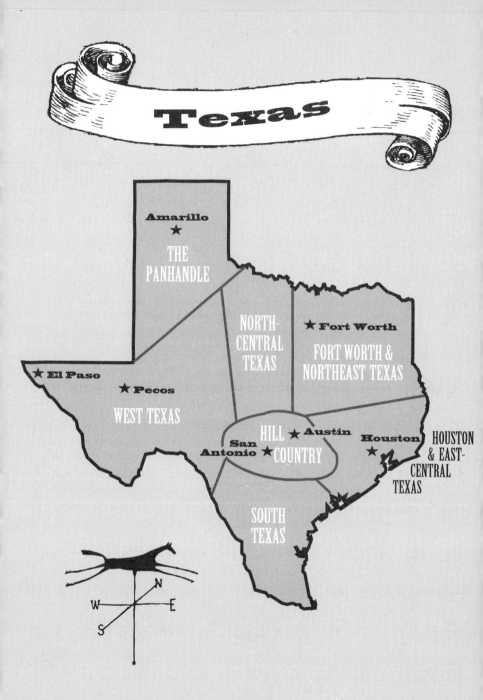

TEXAS

▼▼▼

PEARL BEER, barbecue, boots, bulls, and sweet Western music—that's Texas. It's the Wild West, past and present, where there are more than enough abandoned frontier forts, re-created Old West towns and unabashed cowboyfests to keep anyone happy. The state is big—at 267,000 square miles, almost twice as large as Montana, itself an immense hunk of real estate. True Texans, in fact, regard their state as a "Whole Other Country," as the state travel-bureau slogan goes.

The narrative begins in north-central Texas, adjacent to the Oklahoma border. From there it goes into the northeast and east-central portions of the state and through the picturesque Hill Country. After leading through the rugged western stretches of the Lone Star State, it leads north into the Panhandle, the former haunt of desperadoes like Billy the Kid and west-Texas good guys—like Bob Wills and Buddy Holly.

Note: A comprehensive listing of the numerous guest ranches in Texas is available through the State Division of Travel and Information; call (800) 452–9292.

North-Central Texas

To learn about the region's oil-boom past, visit the **Trails & Tales of Boomtown, USA** in Burkburnett (at the junction of Interstate 44 and Highway 240), a town named for Burk Burnett, former owner of the immense 6666 Ranch, where Teddy Roosevelt hunted wolves in 1905. The comprehensive, two-hour experience includes a video presentation and visits to oil fields, an outdoor oil museum, and a replica of the dugout house lived in by the area's first white settler. Tours run at 10:00 A.M. and 2:00 P.M. on Saturdays from June through October; they begin at the restored Missouri, Kansas & Texas (MKT, or "Katy") Railroad depot on West Third Street. For further information call (817) 569–3304.

Just south of Burkburnett, Wichita Falls, a nondescript Air Force and oil town that typically wouldn't appear on most travelers' itineraries, fires up in late August for the **Texas Ranch Roundup** (817–723–2741). The competition involves a dozen of the most renowned ranches in the state and is designed to determine annually the Best Ranch in Texas. Cowboys battle it out in wild-cow milking, bronc riding, wild-horse racing, branding, and other buckaroo-based events, and dances and other festivities are included for the spectating public. If you'd rather emulate cowboys than watch them, sign on with the **Chaparral Cowboy Country Club,** 4 miles east of the Wichita Falls airport, where horseback trail riding, chuckwagon campouts, and hayrides are offered. Additional activities include black-powder shooting, tomahawk throwing, and, in the evening, storytelling sessions and a Wild West show. Call (817) 723–0297 for reservations and explicit directions.

Fort Belknap, along the Brazos River near Newcastle, between 1851 and 1867 stood guard over area settlers and those persons who traveled through on the Butterfield Overland Mail Route. Six original buildings, along with one replica, remain at the county park, located some 3 miles south of town. The museum and archives are open daily except Wednesday from 9:00 A.M. to 5:00 P.M. The nearby burg of Fort Griffin, meanwhile, grew around a military post that served as a major hide-shipping center in the 1870s and 1880s and was frequented by trappers, buffalo hunters, trail drivers, and soldiers. It's reported that during the outpost's wildest and woolliest twelve-year period, nearly three dozen men perished in gunfights. Today the 500-acre **Fort Griffin State Park** (915–762–3592) encompasses the ghostly remains of several old fort structures, as well as three restored buildings and a quite-alive herd of state-owned Texas longhorns.

The *Fort Griffin Fandangle,* a musical rendition of the old days, is staged in Albany (15 miles south of Fort Griffin) over the last two weekends in June. The unusual blend of ballet and hoedown is performed beneath the stars, with a barbecue supper available on the courthouse square prior to the performance. Call (915) 762–3642 for more information.

Other than some tidy, producing oil fields that surround the town, the **Roaring Ranger Museum** is about the only evidence remaining that the community of Ranger (75 miles southeast of Fort Griffin) was one of the foremost oil-boom towns early in this century. In only a year's time, the population gushed from 1,000 to 30,000, and small landholders became millionaires overnight. Artifacts and photographs from those days are displayed at the museum, housed in the old railroad depot along with the chamber of commerce, at Main and Commerce streets. Pumps, drill rigs, and other items too large to fit inside are displayed on the grounds outside. Hours are Monday through Friday from 10:00 A.M. to 2:00 P.M., Saturday from 9:00 A.M. to 5:00 P.M., and Sunday from 1:00 to 5:00 P.M.

The former enlisted men's barracks does duty today as the museum at **Fort Richardson State Historic Site** (817–567–3506), found at the southwest edge of Jacksboro (80 miles northeast of Ranger). Among the other buildings still standing at the fort—whose commanding officers included Col. Ranald S. MacKenzie, of MacKenzie's Raiders fame—are the impressive stone hospital, the picket-style officers' quarters, and the bakery. Also in Jacksboro is the **Jack County Museum,** which occupies the oldest house in the county, located at 237 West Belknap. The museum houses relics that include artifacts from the early days of ranching. It's open in summer Wednesday through Saturday from 10:00 A.M. to noon and from 1:00 to 5:00 P.M. and Sunday from 2:00 to 5:00 P.M.; the rest of the year it's open Friday and Saturday from 10:00 A.M. to 6:00 P.M. and Sunday from 2:00 to 5:00 P.M.

Fort Worth and Northeast Texas

The accurately renovated **Stonewall Saloon Museum,** at the north end of the Saint Jo town square (at the junction of Highways 82 and 59), displays relics evocative of the days when longhorns were dusting through town up the Chisholm Trail, en route to Abilene, Kansas. The museum is open daily from 10:00 A.M. to 4:00 P.M. year-round except January and February, when it's closed.

Denison, east on Highway 82 and then north on Highway 75, in addition to being the birthplace of Dwight D. Eisenhower, boasts the **Grayson County Frontier Village** (903–463–2487), with more than a dozen renovated, mid- to late-1800s buildings. The village, covering seventeen acres at the southwest edge of town, is open mid-May to October 31 on Wednesday through Saturday from 1:00 to 5:00 P.M. and on Sunday from 1:00 to 6:00 P.M. Also in town: the renovated **Katy Depot,** at 101 East Main, which is listed on the National Register of Historic Places and holds a bonanza of shops and restaurants.

A couple of attractions in Bonham, 28 miles southeast of Denison, that reflect on an earlier day include the **Fannin County Museum,** in the old Texas and Pacific Railroad Depot (903–583–8042) at One Main Street. The museum brims with Indian artifacts, railroading relics, photographs, and historical documents and is open Tuesday through Saturday from 10:00 A.M. to 4:00 P.M. April through August and from noon to 4:00 P.M. the rest of the year. **Fort Inglish Park,** a replica of the stockade and log blockhouse built here in 1837 by Bailey Inglish, is located on West Sam Rayburn Drive. It is open April 1 to September 1 Tuesday through Friday from 10:00 A.M. to 4:00 P.M. and weekends from 1:00 to 5:00 P.M.

Dallas may be the business and cultural capital of Texas, and perhaps it's in Austin where the governor resides, but Fort Worth is undeniably the cowboy and cattle capital of the Lone Star State, and so it's been since the main branch of the famous Chisholm Trail ran through Cowtown, as it came to be called. The Old West thrives in the **Stockyards National Historic District,** approximately 3 miles north of downtown on Main Street. More than forty livestock commissions are headquartered here, and dozens of Western-wear shops (recommended: **Cowboy Trappings of the American West,** at 2739 North Main), eateries, dance halls, saloons, and other enterprises front the traditional boardwalk-lined streets. The huge Mission-style Livestock Exchange Building, at 131 East Exchange Street, contains the **Stockyards Collections & Museum,** with relics relating to the early cattle and meat-packing industries, as well as artifacts collected for the 1986 Texas sesquicentennial celebration. The museum is open Monday through Saturday from 10:00 A.M. to 5:00 P.M. and Sunday from 12:30 to 4:30 P.M. (it is also open on Sunday in June through August from noon to 5:00 P.M.). Call (817) 625–5082 for further details.

Next door the historic **Cowtown Coliseum** hosts the Fort Worth

Championship Rodeo on Saturday evenings at 8:00 P.M. from April through late September, and the **Chisholm Trail Roundup** extravaganza, held annually the second weekend in June. Chuckwagon and armadillo races, cookoffs, shoot-outs, the Texas Old Time Fiddlers Contest, and a lot more are slated in and around the coliseum for three action-packed days. Call (817) 625–7005 for further information. The **Red Steagall Cowboy Gathering and Western Swing Festival** (817–444–5502) is another big Stockyards festival, this one held in late October.

You'll stick out like a sore toe in Cowtown with anything other than cowboy boots on your feet. If you'd prefer to drop a minimum of $400 or $500 on a custom fit, wend your way to **M. L. Leddy's Boots and Saddlery,** at 2455 North Main, or **Ryon's Saddle and Ranch,** at 2601 North Main. If you don't mind a boot made for the masses, go to the **Justin Boot Company** factory outlet, across town at Lipscomb and West Vickery Boulevard, where their more moderately priced boots can be purchased for even less than usual. (Now that your feet are properly outfitted, waddle over and have your picture taken in front of the **Trail Herd Sculpture,** found at the entrance to the Stockyards District.)

Billy Bob's Texas, at 2520 Rodeo Plaza in the Stockyards District, is a honky-tonk of Texas proportions, the world's largest, in fact: It encompasses a 5,000-square-foot rodeo arena, 600 feet of bar rails, and forty-two bar stations, which make a staggering total of 100,000 square feet of floor space. Visit, if for no other reason, simply to see it. The enterprise is open Monday and Tuesday from 10:00 A.M. to 5:00 P.M., Wednesday through Saturday from 10:00 A.M. to 2:00 A.M., and Sunday from noon to 7:00 P.M. Substantially smaller and nearly a hundred years older is the **White Elephant Saloon,** at 106 East Exchange, open Monday through Saturday until 2:00 A.M. and Sunday until midnight. Good Western swing and other traditional country music brings out the dancers nightly. The **Last Great Gunfight of 1887,** which happened the year the White Elephant opened, is reenacted there in early February; call the saloon at (817) 624–1887 for more details.

The place to stay to continue the theme of old Texas and cattle drives is the venerable **Stockyards Hotel** (817–625–6427), at 109 East Exchange Street. The Bonnie and Clyde room is just one of the rooms named for famous and infamous guests the hotel has hosted over the decades. On the lower level **Booger Red's Saloon & Restaurant** features a saddle-stool bar and hearty Cowtown grub.

Cowboy Boots

Cowboy boots—high-topped, tight, narrow-toed and with tall, underslung heels—evolved from frontier-cavalry footwear. Legend says that the early boots in the 1870s and 1880s were so tight that the range rider wearing them wasn't able to walk in them—not to worry, however, for a real cowboy didn't need to walk.

Boot styles, even the way they're worn, differ geographically. A cowhand caught with his pants tucked into his boots in Wyoming or Montana chances being branded a "dude" by his pardners; go to the Cowboy Poetry Gathering in Elko, Nevada, however, and you'll see the majority of the buckaroos' boot tops bared. Cowboys who must run and ride (such as rodeo calf ropers) prefer ropers—those low-heeled boots with rounded toes, built on a shoe last instead of a boot last—which were developed in the 1950s by John Justin, Jr.

Bullhide is the traditional material of choice, whether the boots are custom or factory made. Pigskin is more breathable, but not as water-resistant. Ranchers who spend a lot of time standing around in cow manure prefer waxed calf leather, which stands up well against stomach acid. Ostrich, kangaroo, water buffalo, lizard, llama, shark, and boa constrictor are a few of the more exotic leather possibilities.

The difference between a factory-fit and a custom-fit boot is immeasurable, and no one knows it like a Texan. A leading Montana bootmaker, explaining the difference between Montana and Texas, said, "In Texas, if you see a man wearing a pair of factory-made cowboy boots, you know he's just visiting there."

In 1996 the **National Cowgirl Hall of Fame** pulled up stakes from the small Panhandle town of Hereford and moved to the city. Today you'll find their offices at 111 West Fourth Street, Suite 300, in Fort Worth. The organization exists to honor the women whose lives have advanced the pioneering values and spirit of the great American West. Among the more than 130 current hall-of-famers are well-known individuals—Dale Evans, artist Georgia O'Keeffe, author Mari Sandoz, and singer Rubye "Patsy

Montana" Blevins Rose, to name just a few—as well as a host of rodeo cowgirls whose names are nowhere near as familiar to most Americans. A major museum in the center of the Fort Worth cultural district is under development; meanwhile, the organization invites interested folks to swing by their offices and say howdy. There you'll find an outstanding gift shop and a large research library brimming with related materials available to the public. The offices are open Monday through Friday from 9:00 A.M. to 5:00 P.M. year-round. For an update on the museum's progress or for information on how to become a supporting member of the National Cowgirl Hall of Fame and Western Heritage Center, call (817) 336-4475 or (800) 476-3263.

For a good look at historic Fort Worth, hop aboard the **Tarantula Railroad.** The steam-powered train traces a 7-mile course from its depot at 2318 Eighth Avenue and along the Trinity River and the west side of downtown to the Stockyard Station. The aged engines pull out several times daily on changing schedules; call (817) 763–8394 for information.

The Western-art aficionado can have a heyday in Fort Worth. The two best-known displays are centered in the **Amon G. Carter Museum** and the **Sid Richardson Collection of Western Art,** both of which feature originals by Charlie Russell and Frederic Remington. The Carter Museum, at 3501 Camp Bowie Boulevard in Amon Carter Square, is open Tuesday through Saturday from 10:00 A.M. to 5:00 P.M. and Sunday from 1:00 to 5:30 P.M. It holds the collection bequeathed to the city by Amon Carter, founder of the *Fort Worth Star-Telegram* newspaper. The Richardson Collection, located at 309 Main Street in Sundance Square—named for Harry Longbaugh, the Sundance Kid, who hung out here with Butch Cassidy—is open Tuesday through Friday from 10:00 A.M. to 5:00 P.M., Saturday from 11:00 A.M. to 6:00 P.M., and Sunday from 1:00 to 5:00 P.M.

Also at Amon Carter Square: The **Will Rogers Memorial Center,** featuring a horse-mounted statue of America's beloved cowboy humorist, located on the entrance grounds. The center is a primary venue for the action-packed **Southwestern Exposition Fat Stock Show & Rodeo,** which consumes Fort Worth for two weeks in late January and early February. With roots reaching back a century, the stock show introduced the world to indoor rodeo in 1917, and today it includes the world's longest all-Western parade (no motor vehicles permitted).

Also of note in action- and attraction-packed Fort Worth: the **Cattleman's Museum** (817–332–7064), located at 1301 West Seventh Street and open Monday through Friday from 8:00 A.M. to 4:30 P.M.; and **Fire Station No. 1,** at Second and Commerce streets, tracing "150 Years of Fort Worth," which is open from 9:00 A.M. to 7:00 P.M. The Fort Worth Zoo's outstanding **TEXAS!** exhibit features a replica of a ranch, complete with house, blacksmith shop, livestock corral, and the Yellow Rose Saloon. Livestock and wild critters native to Texas—including pronghorn, javelina, prairie dogs, and bison—thrive at the zoo, located at 2727 Zoological Park Drive, near Texas Christian University. It's open daily from 9:00 A.M. to 5:00 P.M.; call (817) 871–7050 for more information.

In Mansfield, just south of Arlington (which is squeezed between Fort Worth and Dallas), the **Kow Bell Rodeo** kicks up the cowboying action every weekend night, with bull riding on Friday and general events on Saturday and Sunday. Likewise the **Mesquite Championship Rodeo** offers rodeo Friday and Saturday nights April through September at the Mesquite Arena, southeast of Dallas off the LBJ Freeway (Interstate 635) at the Military Parkway exit. There are pony rides for kids and the Bulls-Eye Bar-B-Q Pavilion for all ages. Call (972) 222–BULL (2855) for information.

The sprawling Traders Village flea market and shopping bazaar, at 2602 Mayfield Road in Grand Prairie, just east of Arlington, is the setting for September's **National Championship Pow-Wow.** Dancers from dozens of tribes throughout the Southwest, Rockies, and Dakotas gather to compete for awards in numerous categories. The dancing and arts, crafts, food booths, tipi exhibits, and other associated displays deliver an irresistible vibrancy to the village. Call (972) 647–2331 for more information.

Jefferson, 150 miles east of Dallas, is one of Texas's most history-packed towns. Until the early 1870s the community was the westernmost point to which steamboats, coming out of New Orleans, could navigate the Big Cypress Bayou, which they entered at its mouth on the Red River near Shreveport, Louisiana. In 1873 the Big Cypress suddenly turned unnavigable, however, as its water level fell, due to the blasting and clearing out of a log jam on the Red River. When the water level dropped, so did the town's population, and drastically; Jefferson's long-ago loss is the modern visitor's gain. The mass migration from town left scores of buildings abandoned, and today no fewer than forty old homes have been converted into

Powwow Etiquette

The powwow has been described as the "seed of Indian culture." The gatherings offer Native Americans a chance to renew old friendships and make new ones and, in addition to the dancing and singing, they're also the settings for trading, feasting, and private ceremonies. Participants and organizers alike take great pride in powwows.

Non-Indian spectators are generally welcome at powwows but are expected to learn and practice the appropriate etiquette while attending. Alcohol and drugs are strictly taboo, and spectators should remain watchful, quiet, and respectful at all times. Guests should join in the dancing only at the invitation of the emcee. The dance area is sacred, and out of respect, women should wear shawls when in the area. Spectators generally should not sit on the benches encircling the area or take flash photographs during performances; it is considered polite, in fact, to ask permission before taking any pictures of dancers or singers.

Questions pertaining to what is and is not appropriate should be asked of the emcee and not of performers.

B&Bs—for instance, the grand 1858 **Excelsior House** (903–665–2513), at 211 West Austin. For a listing of the many other possibilities, call (903) 665–2592.

Various sorts of rides available in Jefferson are the best way to learn about and come to appreciate this river port's history. **Bayou Riding Stables** (903–665–7600), also a bed and breakfast, offers guided and narrated horseback tours along the banks of Big Cypress Bayou, whereas the **Jefferson & Cypress Bayou Railroad** (903–665–8400) steam locomotive chugs past historic sites out of a depot on East Austin Street. Narrated trolley rides begin at the corner of Polk and Austin streets, and, finally, the **Turning Basin River Boat Tour** (903–665–2030) penetrates the Big Cypress, with guides who interpret history along the way.

Carthage, 50 miles south of Jefferson on Highway 59, is the hometown of two of Texas's favorite native sons, both country-music legends: Tex Ritter and Jim Reeves. The **Tex Ritter Museum,** located at 300 West

Cynthia Ann Parker

I n 1836 Comanche raiders attacked Fort Parker, killing five members of the Parker family and kidnapping another five. One of those taken was nine-year-old Cynthia Ann, who went on to live with the Comanches for twenty-four years and essentially become one of them. By the time she and her two-year-old daughter, Prairie Flower, were reclaimed by whites in 1860, Cynthia Ann couldn't bear the constraints of the Anglo way of life, so she tried, unsuccessfully, to escape from her biological family on several occasions. Both she and her daughter died about four years after their capture.

Cynthia Ann, who married Chief Nocona, was the mother of the last great Comanche chief, Quanah Parker.

Panola, features memorabilia from the pioneer country-western singer's life. It's open Monday through Friday from 8:00 A.M. to 5:00 P.M. The **Tex Ritter Roundup,** held annually in September or October, celebrates Ritter's life with nonstop music and associated revelry. Call the Chamber of Commerce at (903) 693–6634 for more information.

Texas Highway 21 roughly follows the path of *El Camino Real* (the King's Highway, or the "Old San Antonio Road"), along which a Spanish trading post was established in 1779 in present-day Nacogdoches. The reconstructed **Old Stone Fort** was moved, in celebration of the 1936 Texas Centennial, to the campus of Stephen F. Austin State University, at Griffin and Clark, where it still stands. The fort museum is packed with Indian, Spanish, and pioneer artifacts, along with details on the numerous flags that have flown over it, including those of France, Spain, Mexico, the Republic of Texas, the Confederacy, and, of course, the United States of America. The sound structure is open to visitors Tuesday through Saturday from 9:00 A.M. to 5:00 P.M. and Sunday from 1:00 to 5:00 P.M.

While in Nacogdoches also check out the 1828 **Sterne-Hoya Home,** at 211 South Lanana Street (open Monday through Saturday from 9:00 A.M. to noon and from 2:00 to 5:00 P.M.), and **Millard's Crossing,** a bevy of refurbished nineteenth-century buildings situated at 6020 North Street.

Guided tours at the crossing are offered Monday through Saturday between 9:00 A.M. and 4:00 P.M. and Sunday from 1:00 to 4:00 P.M.

Mission *San Francisco de los Tejas,* the first Spanish mission established in east Texas, is located in the **Mission Tejas State Historic Park,** just southwest of Weches. Established early on, in 1690, for the purpose of warding off a push of French settlers, the mission closed only three years later, then was resurrected in 1716 for a rather uneventful fifteen-year encore. Also within the 118-acre park are a campground, hiking trails, and the log home/stage stop of the pioneering Rice family, built in 1828 to serve those traveling *El Camino Real.* Call (409–687–2394) for more information on the park, which is open daily from 8:00 A.M. to 5:00 P.M.

The reconstructed **Old Fort Parker State Historic Site** graces the grounds of 1,500-acre Fort Parker State Park, 5 miles north of Groesbeck. The fort was established in 1834 by a trio of Parker-brother families to protect their enclave; it was restored in 1936, the year of the Texas Centennial, then again in 1967. Today the zigzag rail fence, stockade, and blockhouse provide a vivid vision from the past. The fort is open daylight hours Wednesday through Sunday.

Other than to dip into Waco's Dr. Pepper Museum, situated in the 1906 bottling plant at 300 South Fifth Street, to test the wild taste of the famous elixir invented in here in the 1880s, the best reason to wander into Waco is to visit the **Texas Ranger Hall of Fame & Museum at Fort Fisher.** The replicated 1837 fort and museum celebrate the unique heritage of the famous free-agent peacekeepers. Initially a private rangering company formed to serve on the west-Texas frontier, the Rangers evolved into a quasi–state military force that battled the Indians and Mexicans essentially on their own terms (that is, with no supervision). In 1935 the Rangers were finally tamed when they were drafted into service as a special investigative force under the auspices of the State Department of Public Safety. The museum includes splendid displays of guns, Indian artifacts, and Western art, along with dramatic dioramas and memorials that commemorate members of the force. It's also the headquarters for the still-active Company F Texas Rangers. The facility, located in a thirty-five-acre park along the Brazos River (take the University Parks Drive exit off Interstate 35), is open daily from 9:00 A.M. to 5:00 P.M.; call (254) 750–8631 for more information.

Houston and East-Central Texas

The **Star of the Republic Museum** interprets the history of the Texas Republic, which ruled the territory from 1836 until 1845, through documents, audiovisual presentations, and exhibits. Located in 154-acre Washington-on-the-Brazos State Park, 25 miles southeast of College Station, the comprehensive museum is open from 10:00 A.M. to 5:00 P.M. daily March through August and Wednesday through Sunday the rest of the year. Part of the original Washington townsite is also within the state park; call (409) 878–2214 for more details.

Huntsville, northeast of Washington on Highway 90 and Highway 30, boasts the **Sam Houston Memorial Museum Complex** (409–295–7824). On display at the complex, situated on fifteen acres that belonged at one time to the important early Texan, are several of his buildings and many of his belongings. It's located at 1836 Sam Houston Boulevard and is open Tuesday through Friday from 9:00 A.M. to 4:30 P.M. and weekends 10:00 A.M. to 6:00 P.M. On San Jacinto weekend in April, the museum hosts the **General Sam Houston Folk Festival,** a lively blend of entertainment and education. Characters straight out of Houston's day greet visitors, and ethnic folk dancers and musicians entertain on six separate stages. Craft and skills demonstrations, dramatic reenactments, and a children's hands-on tent are also featured.

Go east through the Sam Houston National Forest and the Big Thicket to the Livingston-Woodville area and the **Alabama-Coushatta Indian Reservation.** A Living Indian Village, a miniature narrow-gauge railroad excursion, the Inn of the 12 Clans restaurant, and a museum and crafts shop are all part of the visitors complex. It's open in summer Monday through Saturday from 10:00 A.M. to 6:00 P.M. and Sunday from 12:30 to 6:00 P.M.; September through November and March through May it's open weekends (closed December through February). Woodville itself claims the comprehensive **Heritage Village Museum** and living-history center, which includes the Pickett House restaurant, serving delicious family-style meals daily at changing hours throughout the year. The village is open daily from 9:00 A.M. to 6:30 P.M. in summer and from 9:00 A.M. to 5:00 P.M. the rest of the year.

In Beaumont visit the **Spindletop/Gladys City Boomtown** (409–835–0823), evocative of the world's first oil boomtown, which erupted here practically overnight after Anthony F. Lucas's gusher let loose on January 10, 1901. The town that set the stage for the future of east Texas has been re-created; it includes a saloon, livery stable, surveyor's office, and primitive wooden oil derricks. Located on the Lamar University Campus at University Drive and Highway 69 South, it is open Tuesday through Sunday from 1:00 to 5:00 P.M. Also of note is the Beaumont Heritage Society's **French Trading Post & Museum** (409–898–3267), at 2985 French Road, where John Jay French's 1845 home and trading post displays early-day furnishings and utensils. The museum is open Tuesday through Saturday from 10:00 A.M. to 4:00 P.M.

There aren't nearly as many reasons for the Old West devotee to amble into the out-of-control sprawl of Houston (the city's boundaries encompass more than 500 square miles) as there are, say, into Fort Worth or El Paso. A couple of sites, however, shouldn't be missed: the **San Jacinto Battleground State Historic Park,** for instance, where in 1836 Sam Houston's troops turned back Santa Anna's to win for Texas its independence from Mexico. The park, 20 miles east of downtown on Highway 225 and Highway 134 in the northeast portion of Deer Park, includes the impressive San Jacinto Museum of Texas History. Be sure not to miss the half-hour, multimedia history lesson narrated by Charlton Heston and entitled *Texas Forever! The Battle of San Jacinto.* The museum (281–479–2421) is open daily from 9:00 A.M. to 6:00 P.M.

The nineteen-acre **Sam Houston Historical Park,** downtown on Bagby Street, features several restored buildings that recall life in nineteenth-century Houston. The Harris County Heritage Society offers tours Monday through Saturday between 10:00 A.M. and 4:00 P.M. and Sunday between 1:00 and 5:00 P.M. Call (281) 479–2421 for information.

The **Oil Ranch** (281–859–1616), northeast of Houston on Highway 290/6 outside Hockley, offers trail rides, the Fort George Bush maze (!), an "Indian village," and more—even a cow-milking demonstration. It's open Tuesday through Friday from 10:00 A.M. to 4:00 P.M. and Saturday from 10:00 A.M. to 6:00 P.M.

Richmond's **Fort Bend Historical Museum,** regarded as one of the best community historical respositories in the state, features components on the 1820s colonists, the Texas Revolution, early ranching, and the "mother of Texas," local resident Jane Long. The museum, located at 500 Houston Street, is open Tuesday through Friday from 10:00 A.M. to 4:00 P.M. and weekends from 1:00 to 5:00 P.M. The **George Ranch Historical Park** (713–545–9212), situated 8 miles south of town off Highway 762, is a small working ranch (by Texas standards, that is; it's nearly 500 acres) where visitors can chew the fat fireside with cowboys or see how largely forgotten crafts like rope twisting and horseshoe forging are managed. The park opens weekends April through May from 10:00 A.M. to 5:00 P.M. and the same hours Wednesday through Sunday June to December. The park's popular **Ranching Heritage Weekend** is held over Labor Day.

History-rich Columbus, 55 miles west of Houston on Interstate 10, is central to the Cradle of Texas. The region was settled in 1822, the year after the Mexican Revolution, by Stephen F. Austin, who wrangled a land grant from Mexico that opened the way for him to bring 300 American colonists into the Texas territory. "The City of Live Oaks" brims with nineteenth-century homes, many of them converted into B&Bs (call the Columbus Visitor and Convention Bureau at 409–732–5135 for information). On the first and third Thursdays of the month, self-paced walking tours take in a large sampling of the community's venerable businesses, restaurants, inns, and homes, many of which are still private residences. The tours go from 10:00 A.M. to 4:00 P.M.; report to the Chamber of Commerce office in the old opera house for further details.

Hill Country

Austin became capital of the Republic of Texas back in 1839. Perhaps the best reason to visit, however, is not to look back at history but rather to experience the living Wild West on legendary Sixth Street. When it was known as Old Pecan Street, this was Austin's main thoroughfare, until the raising of the present capitol building in 1888, which effected a shift in activity over to Congress Avenue. Sixth Street went downhill after that, way downhill, until a restoration effort was launched in the late 1960s and the 1970s, paralleling the boom of the Austin music scene.

Today most of the city's live-music clubs are concentrated on and around Sixth Street. From nowhere else in the United States—with the possible exceptions of Nashville, New York City, and Los Angeles—is more original music emanating, and it's way more accessible in Austin than in any of those other cities. One suggestion for some hard-hitting country-western or rockabilly is **Headliner's East,** at 406 East Sixth Street. Hit the town on October 31 for **Halloween on Sixth Street** and witness something that you've never seen before: Nearly 100,000 costumed revelers converge for Austin's largest street party.

As in all of Texas, Western wear is big in Austin; the **Cadillac Jack Boot Company,** at 6623 North Lamar, sells revamped handmade boots and other vintage cowpoke clothes; **Texas Traditions,** at 2222 College, fashions some of the most highly acclaimed new custom boots in the United States; and **Lariat Ranch Wear,** at 1610 South Congress, offers real Western clothes at reasonable prices. A sure bet for good Texas grub in restaurant-filled Austin: **The County Line** (which now has restaurants throughout Texas but began in Austin), serving lean barbecue that's too good to be true. It's west of town at 6500 Bee Cave Road (Highway 2244) and is open nightly for dinner.

See a swath of the prettiest country east of the Pecos by hopping aboard the **Hill Country Flyer,** a steam train that runs from Cedar Park (northwest of Austin on Highway 183) to Burnet. The four-hour-plus round-trip, which includes a short layover in Burnet, departs at 10:00 A.M. on Saturday and Sunday; call (512) 477–8468 for information and reservations.

Wimberley, a quaint resort town 40 miles southwest of Austin, is home to **Pioneertown.** This re-created Old West settlement, situated on the 7-A Ranch Resort south of town along the Blanco River, includes a saloon, a general store, an opera house, and a log fort; medicine shows and hiss-and-boo melodramas are regular features during summer. There's also an art gallery that displays Western classics. Pioneertown is open daily in summer from 10:00 A.M. to 10:00 P.M. and weekends the rest of the year from 1:00 to 5:30 P.M.

San Antonio, where Tex meets Mex, is where *Mission San Antonio de Valero* was established in 1718; today it's better known by its subsequent name, **The Alamo.** The old mission became the "Cradle of Texas Liberty" in 1836, when a band of 189 volunteers held off General Santa Anna's huge army of Mexican soldiers for eleven days, from February 24 to March 6. All the Texans died—including Davy Crockett and Jim Bowie—but in doing so they declared independence from Mexico and hurt Santa Anna's army so badly that Sam Houston's men were readily able to finish them off a few weeks later at the Battle of San Jacinto, while crying, "Remember the Alamo!" The extensively renovated Alamo State Historic Site is a modest monument with a huge reputation, tucked humbly amid the skyscrapers on Alamo Plaza between East Houston and East Crockett streets. It is open to visitors Monday through Saturday from 9:00 A.M. to 6:30 P.M. and Sunday from 10:00 A.M. to 6:30 P.M. For more information call (210) 225–1391.

The Alamo was the first of a series of five missions established in San Antonio for the purpose of Christianizing the local Native Americans. The other four, all located along the San Antonio River, compose the **San Antonio Missions National Historic Park.** The Mission Trail, a map for which can be obtained at the Visitor Information Center (800–447–3372 or 210–270–8700) across from the Alamo on Alamo Plaza, leads the way on a 6-mile driving tour that takes in the age-old foursome. Also obtainable at the visitor center is a map for the 2.6-mile **Texas Star Trail** walking tour, which begins and ends at the Alamo and leads to some eighty historic sites.

The **Cowboy Museum and Gallery** (210–229–1257), at 209 Alamo Plaza, is a full-blown 1870s false-fronted town, which includes the Bella Union Saloon, a cavalry fort, and a general store. Displays bring back the days of old San Antone: gunfighters, trail drivers, early ranchers, and others. It's open daily from 10:00 A.M. to 7:00 P.M.

The 200-acre **Fiesta Texas** theme park features four distinct components, all boasting a Texas flair, including *Los Festivales,* which centers on San Antonio's Mexican and Spanish roots, and Crackaxle Canyon, a wild-and-woolly turn-of-the-century west-Texas boomtown. Here the Lonestar Lil theater presents a musical and dance production centered on the oil-boom days; good barbecue can also be had, as can thrills aboard the terrifying Rattler, the world's tallest and fastest wooden rollercoaster. Fiesta Texas, located off Loop 1604 and Interstate 10, is open daily from 10:00 A.M. until after sunset; call (210) 690–8663 for more information.

In this city of festivals, April's ten-day **Fiesta San Antonio** is far and away the most festive. Begun in 1892, Fiesta celebrates Texas's independence from Mexico (won April 21, 1836, at the Battle of San Jacinto) with more than 150 events, including A Night in Old San Antonio, one of the biggest street parties in America. It's held in the quaint, restored La Villita section of town. For more information call the Fiesta San Antonio Commission at (210) 227–5191.

A bevy of historic hostelries line the streets of old San Antonio, including the **Crockett Hotel** (210–225–6500), at Crockett and Bonham. Some two dozen B&Bs are also scattered about the city; for a listing call Bed & Breakfasts of San Antonio at (210) 824–8036. With so many choices it can be tough to pick a restaurant in San Antonio; if you go to only one, make it the **Alamo Cafe** (two locations: 9714 San Pedro and 10060 Interstate 10 West), where Tex-Mex at its best is served. And if you can't find the Western wear you're looking for, you probably haven't looked at **Sheplers,** at Northwest Loop 410 and Ingram Road.

Tiny **Luckenbach,** smack in the middle of the attractive Hill Country, was made famous in the 1970s by "Waylon and Willie and the boys." The town's lone general store is an 1880s structure that also serves as the post office, tavern, and dance hall. Country dances on Saturday night and impromptu Sunday afternoon jam sessions often heat up in the one-horse town, found 60 miles north of San Antonio on Interstate 10 and Highway 1376.

Reach Kerrville and you're getting into real cowboy country. The **Cowboy Artists of America Museum** showcases the works of some of the best contemporary Western artists in the nation, including Joe Beeler and James Boren. Special exhibits and workshops are on the calendar throughout the year, too. Located south of town at 1550 Bandera Highway, the museum (210–896–2553) is open Tuesday through Saturday from 9:00 A.M. to 5:00 P.M. (also on Monday during summer) and Sunday from 1:00 to 5:00 P.M. The rich lore of Texas music is celebrated both at the **Texas Heritage Music Museum** at Inn of the Hills River Resort, 1001 Junction Highway, and at the Texas Heritage Music Foundation's **Jimmie Rodgers Jubilee,** slated for mid-September. Blues, country, and bluegrass resound through the hills in honor of the "father of country music." Call (210) 895–4442 for further information.

The large and historic Y.O. Ranch, 35 miles northwest of Kerrville, is a 50,000-acre exotic-species hunting preserve and guest ranch, which hosts the annual **Y.O. Ranch Longhorn Cattle Drive.** For three days over Memorial Day weekend, experienced hands and greenhorns alike herd longhorns and partake of cookouts and campfire entertainment. To learn more about the historic ranch, established in 1880 by Texas Ranger Capt. Charles Schreiner, ring 'em up at (210) 640–3222.

En route from Kerrville to Bandera, swing into the classic **Camp Verde General Store,** in business since 1857. Nothing remains in the area of the U.S. Army's Camp Verde, headquarters for the compelling but short-lived U.S. Army Camel Corps. Confederates took the camp, fittingly nicknamed "Little Egypt," during the Civil War and either killed or set free all the camels, which had been successfully employed as transport critters on exploratory treks into the Big Bend region.

Bandera, colonized by Mormons in 1854, calls itself the "Cowboy Capital of the World," a claim grounded back in the days when cattle were driven through town on the Western Trail to railhead at Dodge City. Guest ranches, ranging from rustic to refined, surround the town, and the **Frontier Times Museum** houses a staggering array of relics of the Old West and the newer West, as well: photographs, artwork, Indian artifacts, and posters that advertise Buffalo Bill's Wild West Show. Located at 506 Thirteenth Street, the museum is open daily from 10:00 A.M. to noon and from 1:00 to 4:30 P.M. and on Sunday from 1:00 to 4:30 P.M. **Harvey's Old Bank Steakhouse,** at 309 Main, dishes up good Hill Country fare, while the **Cabaret Dance Hall,** at 801 Main, has drawn top country acts to the stage and flashy Texas dippers-and-twirlers to the dance floor for more than half a century.

Among the half-dozen-plus ranches where guests can horse around in the hills that surround Bandera is the area's oldest, the **Dixie Dude Ranch** (830–796–4481), a working ranch since 1901. Other guest ranches include the **Flying L Guest Ranch** (830–460–3001), the **Mayan Dude Ranch** (830–796–3312), the tradition-filled **Twin Elm Guest Ranch** (830–796–3628), and the **Silver Spur Dude Ranch** (830–796–3037), adjacent to the sprawling Hill Country State Natural Area, an area that is tops for riding.

South Texas

The inaugural battle of the Texas Revolution was fought in Gonzales, 70 miles east of San Antonio, hence its nickname "Lexington of Texas." (The

Battle of Lexington similarly was the opening battle of the American Revolution.) Several historic buildings and sites are located in town, including the **1887 Jail,** now housing a museum and headquarters for the Chamber of Commerce and local historical society. It's located on the square at 414 Lawrence Street and is open Monday through Saturday from 8:00 A.M. to 5:00 P.M. and Sunday from 1:00 to 5:00 P.M.

In 1749 Spain built a mission in Goliad for the purpose of converting the local Aranama Indians to Christianity. **Mission Nuestra Señora del Espiritu Santo de Zuniga,** or Mission Espiritu Santo for short, is today the showpiece of sprawling Goliad State Park (512–645–3405), a mile south of town off Highway 183. Nearby **Presidio La Bahia,** built to house Spanish soldiers charged with protecting the mission, grew into a vital frontier fort. (The fort was originally established in 1721 at Matagorda Bay, hence the name *Bahia,* which translates to "bay," and then was moved to here in 1749.) Lovely La Bahia is the best remaining example of the Spanish presidios of Texas; its lavishly restored and still-active chapel is a sight to see. The museum contains artifacts from the Texas Revolution, in which the presidio played a leading role, as well as items from archaeological excavations at the fort. The presidio (512–645–3752), restored in 1967, is a couple of miles south of town on Highway 183, just south of

Maverick

Maverick County, whose seat is out-of-the-way Eagle Pass, was named for early rancher Sam Maverick, one of the signers of the 1836 Texas Declaration of Independence. Maverick had an uncommon method of marking his cattle: He didn't mark them at all. In this way, he rationalized, he could claim any and all unbranded cattle as his. So noteworthy was this unusual strategy that the man's very name, *Maverick,* took on a couple of meanings of its own: (1) an unbranded stock animal and (2) a person who acts independently of or contrary to the norm. It also gave rise to a heckuva good classic television Western, *Maverick,* which starred James Garner (and which was rehashed into a movie, starring Garner and Mel Gibson).

the San Antonio River. It is open daily from 9:00 A.M. to 4:45 P.M.

Also in town is the **General Zaragoza State Historic Site,** birthplace of Ignacio Zaragoza, one of the great military heroes of Mexico. Short on both men and equipment, Zaragoza's Mexican forces in 1862 successfully defended the city of Puebla, Mexico, by repelling an elite force of French soldiers, who not incidentally were en route to Texas to aid the Confederates. The date of the battle was the fifth of May, hence the great Cinco de Mayo celebrations held throughout Mexico and in Goliad and many other towns in Texas and America's Southwest. Numerous other sites of historical significance can be inspected around Goliad; for details stop by the Chamber of Commerce (512–645–3563) at 202 Market Street.

The mostly ghost town of **Helena,** 42 miles northwest of Goliad, was "killed by one gunfight too many," referring to the 1884 shooting death of the son of the area's richest rancher, Col. William Butler. Grieving, peeved, and determined to do in the town that killed his son, Butler convinced the approaching railroad to bypass Helena altogether by offering free land some distance away. A concentration of abandoned buildings that surround the town square, including the **Courthouse Museum,** are open for touring Tuesday through Saturday from 9:00 A.M. to 5:00 P.M.

Fifty miles west of Helena, Pleasanton's **Longhorn Museum** documents the evolution of the great American cowboy, from his Spanish roots in the 1500s to the present. Other displays at the museum, open Tuesday through Saturday from 9:00 A.M. to 5:00 P.M., focus on longhorn-cattle ranching and wild horses.

Just west of Kingsville is the entrance to the dynastic **King Ranch,** established in 1853 and today the biggest spread in the continental United States. Cattle that wear the famous Running W brand graze approximately one million acres of Nueces, Kleberg, Kenedy, and Willacy counties—a ranch larger than Rhode Island. Tours of the ranch are given Monday through Saturday on the hour from 10:00 A.M. to 3:00 P.M. and Sunday from 1:00 to 4:00 P.M. Call (512) 592–8055 for information. The associated **King Ranch Museum** (512–595–1881) is located at 405 North Sixth Street in Kingsville. It's open Monday through Saturday from 10:00 A.M. to 4:00 P.M. and Sunday from 1:00 to 5:00 P.M.

The **Texas Ranger Museum** in Falfurrias (Spanish for "heart's delight," a wildflower common in the region) features photographs, weapons, and

The Seminole-Negro Indian Scouts

Buried at the Seminole Indian Scout Cemetery near Brackettville are several dozen "black Seminoles," the descendants of runaway slaves and Seminole Indians. Along with several groups of Seminoles, the blacks were captured and shipped west to Indian Territory (Oklahoma) in the 1840s; from there they escaped together into northern Mexico and were employed by the Mexican government to fight Apaches and Comanches.

During the next couple of decades, the blacks and Seminoles intermarried, and a distinct ethnic group emerged. The Seminole-Negro Indian Scouts, as they came to be officially known, were drafted into service by the U.S. Army toward the end of the Civil War to help defend the Fort Clark area from Comanches. Between 1871 and 1881 the scouts fought tenaciously in more than two dozen Indian war campaigns, and four of the scouts buried at the cemetery were awarded the Medal of Honor.

The force was dissolved in 1914. A scattering of their descendants still live in the Brackettville area and keep the graveyard maintained.

other artifacts of the early Rangers and settlers in Brooks County. Located on Highway 281 North, it's open Monday through Friday from 9:00 A.M. to 5:00 P.M. and Saturday from 9:00 A.M. to noon. In San Ygnacio, 20 miles north of Zapata (which is 90 miles southwest of Falfurrias), the **La Paz Museum** occupies a 200-year-old Mexican abode, and it features period furniture, photographs of old Zapata, and more. It's found near Benavides Elementary School and is open Monday through Friday from 8:00 A.M. to 3:00 P.M. during the school year (September through May).

Laredo, approximately 90 percent Hispanic, was established in 1755 as the first Spanish settlement in North America not associated with either the military or the Catholic missionaries. Among the sites within the Villa de San Agustín Historical District, site of the original 1755 settlement, is the **Republic of the Rio Grande Building.** Seven flags have flown here, including that of the short-lived Republic of the Rio Grande (1839–41), for which the building served as capitol. It's now a museum, with guns, saddles, and frontier household goods at the core of the collection. The building is

The Cowboy Horse Races at Alamo Village

located on the San Agustín Plaza at 1000 Zaragoza Street and is open Tuesday through Sunday from 10:00 A.M. to 5:00 P.M.

For dining in Laredo try the **Tack Room Restaurant and Bar,** open Monday through Saturday for dinner and found above the Spanish-style **La Posada** hotel (located on the square next to the Republic of the Rio Grande Building); call (210) 722–1701 for information and reservations. Great shopping, eating, and wild times can also be had just across the Rio Grande, in Nuevo Laredo, Tamaulipas. Try, for instance, the **Cadillac Bar,** not far from the international bridge at Ocampo and Belden.

West Texas

Alamo Village in Brackettville is an Old West town set around the replica of the Alamo that was built for the filming of the 1959 John Wayne flick *The Alamo.* The impressive mission, built of bricks manufactured at the site, took approximately 5,000 workers two years to build. The comprehensive Old West town was erected after the movie was filmed but has since appeared in about forty Westerns and countless commercials. (One end of town was patterned after old San Antonio, the other after early Fort Worth.) During summer, music shows and gunfights are staged at the village, which is located on the Shahan HV Angus Ranch, 7 miles north of Brackettville on Highway 674. It is open daily from 9:00 A.M. to 5:00 P.M. On Labor Day Alamo Village hosts the **Cowboy Horse Races,** in which only nonregistered horses and nonprofessional jockeys can take part. The racers, atop Western saddles, thunder through town, competing at various distances up to a quarter of a mile. Call the village at (210) 563–2580 for more information.

Just outside Brackettville is **Fort Clark Springs,** an 1852 frontier fort with the unique distinction of having been transformed into a resort/retirement community. The one-time barracks now serves as a motel, and the Old Guardhouse Museum, open Saturday and Sunday from 1:00 to 4:00 P.M., contains frontier-history exhibits. Also of note: the **Seminole Indian Scout Cemetery,** approximately 4 miles south of town on Highway 3348.

A number of buildings that date from the nineteenth century still stand in Del Rio, "Queen City of the Rio Grande." One of these, the old stone Perry Store trading post, was saved from demolition in the 1960s by the Whitehead ranching family; it has since become the chief component of the **Whitehead Memorial Museum,** dedicated to the legends of the frontier Southwest. A barn, a log cabin, a replica of Judge Roy Bean's Jersey Lilly Saloon, and the graves of Bean and his son are also on the grounds. The museum's Hal Patton Labor Office contains a display on the black Seminoles. The museum (210–774–7568), located at 1308 South Main Street, is open Tuesday through Saturday from 9:00 to 11:30 A.M. and from 1:00 to 4:30 P.M.

Speaking of Judge Roy Bean, the legendary "law west of the Pecos" in the 1880s, be sure to visit Langtry, population thirty. The judge, who presided over court with a six-shooter and a bottle of whiskey, named his tavern/courtroom after his idol, English actress Lillie Langtry, known to the world as "Jersey Lily." Given two choices, Lillie and Lily, Bean still misspelled her name when he dedicated his Jersey Lilly Saloon, which sits out back from the **Judge Roy Bean Visitor Center**/State Travel Information Center.

Lonesome Highway 90 wends westward through the desert to Marathon, then to Alpine, home to Sul Ross State University's **Cowboy Poetry Gathering.** This get-together draws cowboy poets and several thousand spectators to the isolated community in early March. Also noteworthy: the university's **Museum of the Big Bend,** which interprets the region's history through dioramas and artifact displays. It's open Tuesday through Saturday from 9:00 A.M. to 5:00 P.M. and Sunday from 1:00 to 5:00 P.M.

The ordinarily sleepy ghost town of Terlingua, once a mercury-mining boomtown, explodes the first Saturday in November when it hosts the **CASI** (Chili Appreciation Society International) **Chili Championship.** Some 5,000 chili chefs and chiliheads convene for the battle of the "bowls of red"— and the associated nonstop partying—which pits the reigning Texas state champ, as determined at September's Republic of Texas Chilympiad in San Marcos, against contenders from most other states and several foreign countries. (Technically, there's a second, concurrent cookoff contested a ways up the road, and so it's been since the two organizers of the original event had a falling out a few years back.) Terlingua is near the eastern edge of Big Bend National Park, just west of Study (pronounced STOO-dy) Butte. For more information on the chili doings, call (915) 772–2379.

Follow the thrilling River Road, *El Camino del Rio* (Highway 170), from Lajitas to Presidio, where you'll encounter **Fort Leaton State Historic Site** (915–229–3613). The sprawling adobe fortress here was raised in 1848 by frontier trader Ben Leaton, a man who established trade lines with the Apaches and Comanches and was subsequently accused of encouraging Indian raids on Mexican villages. The majority of the more than forty original rooms that surround the plaza have been renovated, and restoration work continues. The attraction is open daily from 8:00 A.M. to

4:00 P.M. (Presidio, essentially a north-of-the-border Mexican village, is reportedly the hottest spot in the very hot state of Texas: in other words, stay away in summer.)

Fort Davis National Historic Site commemorates the frontier post built in 1854 to help guard from Indian attack those individuals who traveled the nearly 600 miles of wilds that separated San Antonio and El Paso. Once the Civil War wound down, the fort became headquarters for the 9th Cavalry of the black, Indian-fighting Buffalo Soldiers. The outstanding restorations and museum are open daily from 8:00 A.M. to 6:00 P.M.; during summer rangers and volunteers, dressed in period attire, give tours, and an 1875 military parade is performed daily at 11:00 A.M. and 4:00 P.M. Call (915) 426–3224 for further information.

The **Prude Guest Ranch,** 6 miles west of Fort Davis off Highway 118 (the road that leads to the McDonald Observatory), was established as a cattle ranch more than one hundred years ago and has been hosting guests since 1911. Wagon cookouts, "star parties," and trail rides in the rugged Davis Mountains are among the activities popular here, where guests stay in batten-and-board cottages or in their own RVs. Call (915) 426–3202 for information and reservations.

El Paso is so far west that it's in the Mountain Time Zone and closer to San Diego than to Houston. From the early 1880s, when the railroads reached town, until well into the twentieth century, El Paso was a Wild West town of impressive proportions, one that truly earned its reputation as "Six-shooter Capital" of the United States. Mexican revolutionaries, Texas Rangers, gunfighters, ladies of the evening, desperadoes, legendary lawmen—Wyatt Earp and Bat Masterson, to name a pair—they all were here. John Wesley Harding, allegedly the fastest gun in the history of the West, is buried at the town's Concordia Cemetery; so is lawman John Selman, who put Harding 6 feet under with a bullet to the head. Both the **El Paso Centennial Museum** (at University Avenue and Wiggins Road on the University of Texas at El Paso campus) and the **El Paso Museum of History** (Interstate 10 at Loop 375/Avenue of the Americas) feature relics and displays that interpret those wild, wild days. They're open Tuesday through Sunday year-round.

Jump aboard the **Trolley on a Mission** for a tour of several El Paso landmarks, including the Ysleta and Socorro missions, both established in the 1680s, making them substantially older than the more celebrated California missions. The 4 1/2-hour outing includes lunch at either the **Old Adobe Horseshoe** or the Tigua Indians' **Ysleta del Sur Pueblo** restaurant. Tours leave from the Civic Center on Tuesday and Thursday mornings at 10:30 A.M.; call (915) 544–0061 for more information. (If you'd rather drive the Mission Trail, pick up a map at the El Paso Tourist Information Center, also on the Civic Center Plaza, or call to request one at 915–534–0653.)

Other sites in and around old El Paso include the 1875 **Magoffin Homestead State Historical Site** (915–533–5147), located at 1120 Magoffin Avenue, open Wednesday through Sunday from 9:00 A.M. to 4:00 P.M.; and the **Fort Bliss Museum,** at Pleasanton Road and Sheridan Drive, open daily from 9:00 A.M. to 4:30 P.M. Fort Bliss, today a city unto itself with more than 20,000 soldiers, began life in 1848. It's where Gen. John J. "Blackjack" Pershing was stationed when dispatched in 1916 onto the trail of Pancho Villa (see Columbus, New Mexico, p. 279). The museum (915–568–5412) includes a group of adobes built to resemble the original frontier post.

It's required to sample south-of-the-border fare while in El Paso; one of many places you can do so is at **La Hacienda,** at 1720 West Paisano, situated in a nineteenth-century building that was formerly a component of Fort Bliss. (The fort has known five different locations around El Paso during its century and a half in existence.) If in town between late June and early September, take in the *Viva El Paso!* outdoor drama, which encapsulates the city's long history, tracing the heritage of the Native Americans, Spanish conquistadors, cavalry, cowboys, and others. The Franklin Mountains serve as backdrop at the McKelligon Canyon Amphitheatre off Alabama Street, where performances are staged Wednesday through Saturday evenings. Call (915) 565–6900 for ticket information and reservations.

Indian Cliffs Ranch, whose Cattleman's Steakhouse boasts the best steaks in the Lone Star State, is situated about 30 miles southeast of town near Fabens. The ranch (915–544–3200) covers more than 20,000 acres of desert country and also offers trail rides and overnight hayrides to a frontier-fort replica.

Most leading Texas bootmakers have factory outlets in El Paso. The **Tony Lama** outlet, for example, is at 7176 Gateway East, and the **Justin** outlet is nearby at 7100 Gateway East. **Morris Saddlery,** at 10949 East Burt, sells saddles and most everything else Western.

The **Coors World Finals Rodeo,** slated for November at the El Paso County Coliseum, closes out the North American Rodeo Commission's year and brings to town riders from several countries. Mexican rodeos, called *charreadas,* are contested on both sides of the international border; you'll find them in El Paso on Sunday afternoons at the Emiliano Zapata Charro Association's arena on Highway 76.

In Pecos, about 200 miles east of El Paso, hitch your pony outside the **West-of-the-Pecos Museum and Park,** which fills an 1896 saloon and two floors of the old Orient Hotel with memorabilia from what was perhaps the most notorious outpost in the Old West. The adjacent grounds contain another replica of Judge Roy Bean's Jersey Lilly Saloon, the old hanging tree, and the grave of Clay Allison, the "Gentleman Gunfighter," whose epitaph reads, "He never killed a man that did not need killing." The museum, located at 120 East First Street, is open Monday through Saturday from 9:00 A.M. to 5:00 P.M. and Sunday from 2:00 to 5:00 P.M.

The **Grey Mule Saloon** at Callaghan and Main streets in Fort Stockton (54 miles southeast of Pecos), another of Texas's numerous communities that grew up around frontier Indian-fighting posts, is a throwback to the past. **Old Fort Stockton** itself, where several original adobe and limestone buildings remain, is on Williams Street between Fourth and Fifth streets. You can learn about the past of the fort and the region in general at the **Annie Riggs Hotel Museum,** located in the old Butterfield stage stop at 301 South Main Street. It's open Monday through Saturday from 10:00 A.M. to 8:00 P.M. and Sunday from 1:30 to 8:00 P.M. Call (915) 336-2167 for more information.

About 110 miles east of Fort Stockton, Ozona's city park holds the **Davy Crockett Monument,** celebrating one of the heroes of the Alamo. The **Crockett County Museum,** at 404 Eleventh Street, contains frontier artifacts that include ones from old Fort Lancaster, now a state historic site located 33 miles west of town on Highway 290. The museum is open Monday through Friday from 10:00 A.M. to 6:00 P.M. Nearby Sonora, on the western slope of the Edwards Plateau, hosts its **Covered Wagon Dinner Theater** mid-June through mid-August. In a small amphitheater near the spectacular Caverns of Sonora, 15 miles southwest of town, costumed storytellers and singers relate the way things used to be in these parts. Call the Chamber of Commerce at (915) 387–2880 for more information.

Roughly 40 miles northeast of Sonora are the well-kept ruins of **Fort McKavett State Historic Site.** All four of the Buffalo Soldier units— two cavalry and two infantry regiments—served here at one time or another. The visitor center, housed in the old post hospital, is open daily from 8:00 A.M. to 5:00 P.M. In the lively and alluring city of San Angelo, **Fort Concho** remains one of the best-preserved frontier forts in the state. This sprawling National Historic Landmark, near downtown at 213 East Avenue D, encompasses two dozen original and reconstructed buildings, including the Robert Wood Johnson Museum of Frontier Medicine. Other buildings hold exhibits that interpret the history of Indian campaigns and old San Angelo. The facility is open Tuesday through Saturday from 10:00 A.M. to 5:00 P.M. and Sunday from 1:00 to 5:00 P.M. The **Fort Concho Living History Program,** reenacted by volunteers, is composed of four historic Fort Concho units, including the 10th Cavalry regiment of black Buffalo Soldiers. Uniforms, gear, tack, and maneuvers are all historically accurate when the units perform at various events throughout the year, including **Sabre, Saddles and Spurs** in April, the festive **Christmas at Old Fort Concho,** and **Frontier Days** in June (one component of the city's large-scale Fiesta del Concho). Call (915) 657–4441, 658–4084, or 653–3162 for further details on the fort and its bounteous activities.

J. L. Mercer, at 224 South Chadbourne in San Angelo, makes some of the most beautiful and sought-after custom boots to be found in Texas. They've been in business since 1923.

Disparagingly nicknamed "hog farms" or "hog ranches" took root outside the boundaries of most frontier army posts, and Fort Concho was no exception. It wasn't until 1946 that Texas Rangers finally closed down **Miss Hattie's Bordello,** a San Angelo attraction (for cowboys and soldiers, especially) for more than half a century. Hattie's was the swankiest of the several "parlor houses" that lined Concho Street; it's reported that there was even a tunnel that led discreetly from here to the bank next door. Now it's a museum, filled with velvet and lace and brass beds, located above Miss Hattie's Antiques. The museum, located at 18 East Concho, is open Tuesday through Saturday from 9:30 A.M. to 4:00 P.M. (Miss Hattie died in San Angelo in 1982, at 104 years of age.)

Swing through Ballinger and have your picture taken with the *Cowboy and His Horse* statue, designed by Pompeo Coppini. This engaging sculpture, located on the courthouse lawn at the intersection of Highway 83 and Highway 67, was commissioned by the family of local cowboy Charles H. Noyes, who was killed in a range accident.

Buffalo Gap Historic Village, located a few miles south of Abilene in the small ranch town of Buffalo Gap, encompasses some twenty frontier structures, including an 1880s bank and a railroad depot. All are furnished in period style, and wagons, firearms, and Indian artifacts are among the objects on display. The attraction is open Monday through Saturday from 10:00 A.M. to 6:00 P.M. and Sunday from noon to 6:00 P.M., mid-March through mid-November and on weekends from 10:00 A.M. to 6:00 P.M. the rest of the year, with guided tours available; call (915) 572–3365 for more information.

Abilene's **Western Heritage Classic** fires up in early May, with working cowboys competing in events that range from wild-cow milking to branding. Ranch-dog trials, cowboy-poetry readings, a longhorn trail drive, and the Championship Campfire Cook-off round out the festivities. For further information call the Convention & Visitors Bureau at (915) 677–7241.

Stamford, 40 miles north of Abilene on Highway 83/277, is known for its **Texas Cowboy Museum,** situated at 113 South Wetherbee Street and open Monday through Friday from 8:00 A.M. to 5:00 P.M., and also for the compelling, hand-carved **Mackenzie Trail Monument.** What Stamford really is known for, however, is the **Texas Cowboy Reunion,** a sight that would have brought tears to John Wayne's eyes. For four days around the Fourth of July, the huge amateur rodeo (no pros permitted) brings some 25,000 visitors to this 4,000-person town. Several hundred cowpokes and horses share the rodeo arena in the main parade, a cacophony of hoofbeats, whinnies, and "whoas." There's even a Little Britches Rodeo for the "cowpokids." Grub is served out of chuckwagons; music, dancing, and other festivities abound. Call the Chamber of Commerce at (915) 773–2411 or Swinson Ranches at (915) 773–3614 for more information.

Sweetwater, 40 miles west of Abilene, hosts the **World's Largest Rattlesnake Roundup** in mid-March. In a "good" year, more than six tons of the wriggling reptiles are weighed in, and upwards of 30,000 spectators—from all fifty states and many foreign countries—show up, out of fascination, fear . . . or something. Some 4,000 pounds of snake meat is deep-fried and feasted upon, while associated activities include a Miss Snake Charmer Queen contest and a 10-kilometer Rattlesnake Run. Call the Chamber of Commerce at (915) 235–5488 for additional information.

Colorado City holds the **Fort Wood** Old West complex, with its saloon, general store, jail, cafe, and Saturday-afternoon gunfights. Midland, another 75 miles up the road, claims the **Museum of the Southwest.** The museum, housed in an immense mansion at 1705 West Missouri Street, is dedicated to the enjoyment and preservation of Southwest culture and art. It's open Tuesday through Saturday from 10:00 A.M. to 5:00 P.M. and Sunday from 2:00 to 5:00 P.M. The Freeda Turner Durham Children's Museum is also situated within the complex; call (915) 683–2882 for more information.

The Panhandle

Boys Ranch was established in the late 1930s by Cal Farley, a Lone Star State businessman and 1920s world welterweight wrestling champ. The successful enterprise, home to some 400 troubled boys, is centered around the Canadian River settlement of Old Tascosa, at one time known as "Cowboy Capital of the Plains." This vital ranch-supply town, which saw more than its share of Wild West figures stroll the wooden boardwalks, was deserted by the 1930s, after the open range was fenced and the railroad bypassed town. There's still a **Boot Hill Cemetery,** maintained by the boys, holding undesirables who died with their boots still on (in gunfights, that is). The **Julian Bivins Museum,** occupying the former Oldham County Courthouse, which also served as the original home for boys, is named for the area rancher who donated the land for Boys Ranch. It features Native American and cowboying items, as well as background on Boys Ranch. It's open daily year-round from 10:00 A.M. to 5:00 P.M. **Cal Farley's Boys Ranch Rodeo** is contested over Labor Day, with bronc riding, chute dogging, and other events for the older boys, and a calf scramble and stick-horse races for the youngsters. Call Boys Ranch at (806) 372–2341 for more information.

In Dalhart, whose city limits span the *Dal*lam-*Hart*ley county line, visit the **Dallam-Hartley Counties Historical Museum,** located at 108 East Fifth Street. Frontier weapons, historic cowboy tack and clothing, furnished rooms, and more are found at the museum, open Tuesday through Saturday and the first Sunday of each month from 2:00 to 5:00 P.M. The **Empty Saddle Monument,** at the north end of the underpass on Highway 87 North, is a favorite Panhandle photography subject, and the **XIT Ranch Rodeo** commemorates what Texans claim was the largest spread under fence in the history of the world. In the 1880s the great XIT Ranch encompassed some three million acres, comparable in size to the state of Connecticut. The northern boundary fence was nearly 200 miles from the southern fence; east to west it spanned about 30 miles. Former XIT hands, their numbers ever-dwindling, are honored at the August bash, and in addition to the world's largest amateur rodeo, the gathering includes parades, Pony Express races, and a huge free barbecue feed—the "world's largest," of course. For information call the Dalhart Chamber of Commerce at (806) 249–5646.

Six miles south of Fritch along the east shore of Lake Meredith, **Alibates National Monument** explores the flint quarries that were worked for more than 10,000 years by prehistoric Native American hunters. (The name derives from former local cowpoke Ali Bates.) The monument, still under development by the National Park Service, can be entered only on ranger-led tours, which leave twice daily, at 10:00 A.M. and 2:00 P.M., Memorial Day through Labor Day and weekends only in spring and fall. Call (806) 857–3151 for more information.

The **Square House Museum** in the town of Panhandle, situated in and around the oldest house in the community, is considered one of the best small-town museums in the state. Guided tours through the grounds interpret the days of the prehistoric Indians, boundless cattle spreads, buffalo hunters, and more. A reconstructed half-dugout on the grounds is appointed in pioneer fashion. The museum, located in Pioneer Park, is open daily.

The **American Quarter Horse Association Heritage Center and Museum** (806–376–5181), in Amarillo off Interstate 40 at the Nelson Street exit, celebrates the rich legacy of the horse that was, is, and probably always will be the favorite of the range-riding cowboy. It opens to visitors daily May through September from 9:00 A.M. to 6:00 P.M. and during abbreviated hours the rest of the year. The management at the **Big Texan Steak Ranch,** an old Route 66 standby, dares diners to down a Texas-sized, seventy-two-ounce slab of beef (how's your cholesterol count?). Watch for the neon cowboy standing sentinel, which might remind you of a west-

Texas Paul Bunyan.

Smell the bacon and eggs frying; listen to 'em sizzle as the sun lifts up over Palo Duro Canyon, and just taste those sourdough biscuits! You won't have to just dream about it if you take in the **Cowboy Morning,** which runs daily at the Figure 3 Ranch, approximately 30 miles south of Amarillo, from April 15 through August 15. Cowboy Evenings are also offered, with Texas-bred steak and all the trimmings, served out of a chuckwagon on the open range. Breakfast is at 8:30 A.M., supper at 6:30 P.M.; call (800) 658–2613 or (806) 944–5562 to sign up. Another Amarillo favorite is the **Old West Show** at the Creekwood Ranch, where guests are hauled in wagons to watch cowboys sing and perform trick roping and other buckaroo feats. The outing, which includes a chuckwagon supper, leaves Thursday through Sunday at 6:00 P.M.; call (800) 658–6673 or (806) 356–9256 for reservations and directions.

The Pioneer Amphitheatre in stunning Palo Duro Canyon State Park, east of the town of Canyon on Highway 217, is venue for the dazzling musical *Texas.* A cast of nearly one hundred—including settlers, Indians, and cowboys—range the huge stage, and riders are spotlighted high above on the 600-foot cliffs that serve as a backdrop, all reliving the history of the Texas Panhandle. The performance, staged nightly except Sunday from early June through late August, draws an average audience of 1,600, and 100,000 in a season. The highly acclaimed show begins at 8:30 P.M., preceded by a barbecue catered by Sutphen's, an Amarillo standby. Call (806) 655–2181 for ticket information and reservations.

Canyon's **Panhandle-Plains Historical Museum** (806–656–2244), on the campus of West Texas State University, is an immense facility containing some two million artifacts that celebrate the region's rich Old West legacy. The Frank Reaugh Collection of Southwestern Art is but one highlight; the extensive collections of guns and brands are a couple of others. The museum is open Monday through Saturday from 9:00 A.M. to 5:00 P.M. and Sunday from 1:00 to 6:00 P.M.

The **Llano Estacado Museum** in Plainview (60 miles south of Canyon), while substantially more modest than Canyon's repository, is a good one all the same, with artifacts from the nearby Plainview Man archaeological site, frontier firearms, and more. The Llano Estacado Museum, named for the Spanish term (meaning "staked plain") for the surrounding

A scene from the musical Texas, *held at Palo Duro Canyon State Park.*

plains, is located on the campus of Wayland Baptist University at 1900 West Eighth Street. It's open on weekdays from 9:00 A.M. to 5:00 P.M. and on weekends (March through November only) from 1:00 to 5:00 P.M. Also in town: the **MacKenzie Statue,** honoring the famous trailblazer and Indian fighter Col. Ranald S. MacKenzie.

The living-history **National Ranching Heritage Center** in Lubbock vividly interprets the story of Panhandle ranching. Some three dozen buildings, spread over a fourteen-acre site well hidden by hills from the city, include a 1909 Victorian home and an 1886 house relocated from the XIT Ranch. The museum, located at Fourth Street and Indiana Avenue, is open daily Monday through Saturday from 10:00 A.M. to 5:00 P.M. and Sunday from 1:00 to 5:00 P.M., when guides in period costume host visitors. The **National Cowboy Symposium and Celebration** is a popular and wildly entertaining regional event held here in early September, and

Candlelight Christmas at the Ranch, held the first Thursday and Friday in December, combines the spirits of the season and of early ranch life. The center, one of a trio of facilities encompassed by the Museum of Texas Tech University, is located at the northeast corner of campus. Call (806) 742–2498 for more information.

Lubbock has produced more than its share of world-class musicians, most of them possessing a country flair—Waylon Jennings and Roy Orbison, to name a couple. Buddy Holly is the most famous native son of all; be sure to have a look at his statue, located at the corner of Eighth Street and Avenue Q, and, if you want, at his grave, situated in the Lubbock Cemetery. For some good dancing and sweet Western swing—one of the brands of music that influenced a young Holly—head for the **Westernaire Club,** at 4801 Avenue Q.

Speaking of Western swing, what better place to wind up a Lone Star tour than in tiny Turkey, home to the King of Western Swing, Bob Wills? The music of Wills and his Texas Playboys exemplifies, practically defines, what it means to be Texan. The **Bob Wills Museum,** at Sixth and Lyle streets, includes boots, fiddles, photographs, recordings, and other Wills memorabilia. It's open Monday through Friday from 8:00 to 10:00 A.M. and from 1:00 to 5:00 P.M. **Bob Wills Day** is celebrated the last Saturday in April, with plenty of live music, dancing, and Texas-style barbecue. Call (806) 423–1253 for information on the event, which brings upward of 10,000 visitors to town, increasing its population by approximately twenty-fold.

Where to Eat

Booger Red's Saloon & Restaurant, Fort Worth, (817) 625–6427
The County Line, Austin, (512) 327–1742
Alamo Cafe, San Antonio, (210) 495–2233
Harvey's Old Bank Steakhouse, Bandera, (830) 796–8486
Tack Room Restaurant and Bar, Laredo, (210) 722–1701
La Hacienda, El Paso, (915) 533–3190
Indian Cliffs Ranch, Fabens, (915) 544–3200
Big Texan Steak Ranch, Amarillo, (806) 372–6000

Where to Stay

Stockyards Hotel, Fort Worth, (817) 625–6427
Excelsior House, Jefferson, (903) 665–2513
Crockett Hotel, San Antonio, (210) 225–6500
Dixie Dude Ranch, outside Bandera, (210) 796–4481
Flying L Guest Ranch, outside Bandera, (210) 460–3001
Mayan Dude Ranch, outside Bandera, (210) 796–3312
Twin Elm Guest Ranch, outside Bandera (210) 796–3628
Silver Spur Dude Ranch, outside Bandera, (210) 796–3037
La Posada, Laredo, (210) 722–1701
Prude Guest Ranch, outside Fort Davis, (915) 426–3202

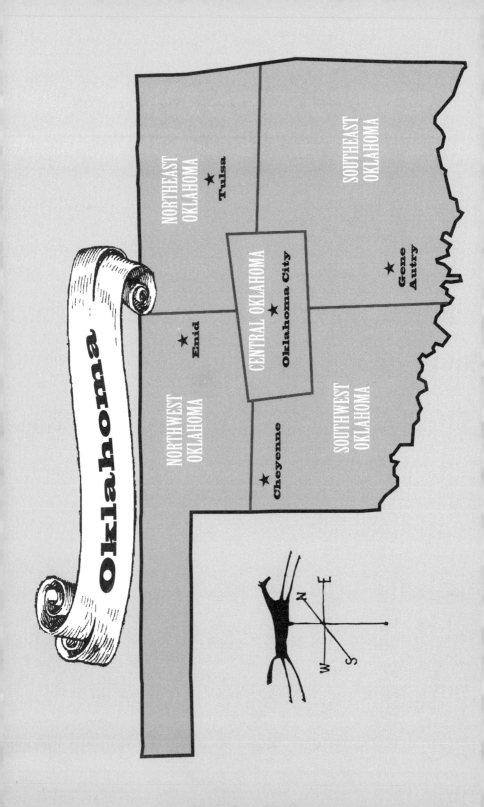

Oklahoma

NORTHEAST OKLAHOMA

★ Tulsa

SOUTHEAST OKLAHOMA

CENTRAL OKLAHOMA

★ Oklahoma City

★ Gene Autry

★ Enid

NORTHWEST OKLAHOMA

★ Cheyenne

SOUTHWEST OKLAHOMA

N
E
W
S

OKLAHOMA

▼▼▼

HAT can you say about a state that claims Will Rogers, Tom Mix, and Gene Autry as native sons? The state even has a *town* named Gene Autry, for heaven's sake.

Oklahoma was considered largely a wasteland in the nineteenth century, when it was officially designated as Indian Territory, the place to which Native Americans were relocated when they got in the way of the white man's Manifest Destiny. Today nearly 250,000 Native Americans reside in Oklahoma—more than in any other state—and Oklahoma City claims the National Cowboy Hall of Fame: This, then, truly is cowboy-and-Indian country.

The narrative begins in the northeast part of the state, then proceeds through southeast, central, southwest and, finally, northwest Oklahoma.

Northeast Oklahoma

Begin in Miami, where the **Dobson Museum,** at 110 A Street Southwest, features a substantial collection of Indian art and venerable tools and mining paraphernalia. It's open Sunday, Wednesday, and Friday from 1:00 to 4:00 P.M. Then go 13 miles south on Highway 69 and 9 miles southeast on Highway 59, where the fascinating **Har-Ber Village** (918–786–6446) includes more than one hundred log cabins that display Indian and pioneer artifacts. It's open daily March through November from 9:00 A.M. to 5:00 P.M.

Just north of Bartlesville, Dewey's **Tom Mix Museum** (918–534–1555), at 721 Delaware, features a collection of clothing, saddles, and other items that belonged to this pioneer cowboy celebrity from Oklahoma. The museum is open Tuesday through Saturday from 9:00 A.M. to 4:30 P.M. and on Sunday from 1:00 to 4:30 P.M., during which time the on-site theater runs Mix's silent movies. Also have a peek inside the **Dewey Hotel** (918–534–0215), at 801 North Delaware, a grand, restored 1899 hostelry. It's open between May and October Tuesday through Saturday from 10:00 A.M. to 5:00 P.M. and Sunday from 1:00 to 5:00 P.M.; call for information. **Prairie Song, Indian Territory** is a replica of an 1800s pioneer village; it's situated on the longest-running ranch in the state still in the hands of the same family. The place, located on the prairie 5 miles east of Dewey, opens by appointment; call (918–534–2662) to arrange a visit.

In Bartlesville you can visit the 1908 **Frank Phillips Home,** former residence of the founder of the Phillips Petroleum Company, at 1107 South Cherokee Street. An even more alluring Phillips-related attraction is the **Woolaroc Museum,** 12 miles southwest of town on Highway 123. (En route you'll go by the **Prairie National Wild Horse Refuge,** where wild mustangs run free.) Frank Phillips's Woolaroc Lodge, evocative of the oil-boom wealth of the 1920s in Oklahoma, is a gracious log structure appointed from the ceiling down in the style of the Old West—from wagon-wheel chandeliers, scores of big-game trophies, and paintings of Buffalo Bill and other characters to Navajo rugs that cover the tables and floors. Woolaroc also houses an extensive display of Indian collectibles and Western art, along with a fine exhibit of Colt firearms and dozens of other early artifacts, more than 55,000 pieces in all. Phillips entertained friends and acquaintances here who included the likes of Will Rogers, Herbert Hoover, and Harry S. Truman.

The surrounding 3,600 acres of wildlife sanctuary are roamed by more than 1,000 bison, elk, and longhorns, the latter descendants of the hardy stock brought into Mexico and Texas by the Spaniards in the 1500s and driven through Oklahoma a century ago along the Chisholm Trail and other stock highways. Woolaroc's Y-Indian Guide Center, affiliated with the national YMCA, exhibits the culture and crafts of some of America's first inhabitants. By taking in the 5-mile North Road Tour, which traverses a pretty stretch of the prairie ranch, you'll also encounter a re-created 1840s Trader's Camp at Bison Lake. Woolaroc—big, wild, and woolly—is open daily from 10:00 A.M. to 5:00 P.M. in summer and Tuesday through Sunday from 10:00 A.M. to 5:00 P.M. the rest of the year. Call (918) 336–0307 for more information.

The **Osage Tribal Museum,** at 600 North Grandview Avenue in

Pawhuska—a town that brims with National Historic Register buildings—features a sizable display of items from that tribe's culture. Among the highlights is a gallery that exhibits early photographs of the Osages. It's open Monday through Friday from 10:00 A.M. to 4:30 P.M.; call (918) 287–2495 for more information. The nearby **Osage County Historical Museum** (918–287–9924), at 700 North Lynn Avenue, features Indian and Old West artifacts, along with a monument to the nation's first Boy Scout troop, organized in 1909; the museum is open Monday through Saturday from 9:00 A.M. to 5:00 P.M. and Sunday from noon to 5:00 P.M. The Nature Conservancy's **Tallgrass Prairie Preserve** begins outside town on Tallgrass Drive and sprawls across 36,000 acres between here and the Kansas border. The preserve comprises the nation's largest intact native grassland of the sort that blanketed the region prior to the introduction of the plow. Like the Ghost Dance prophesy come true (see Wovoka, in Nevada, p. 45), bison are returning to the area in great numbers, and the herd is expected to grow to nearly 2,000 over the next few years. For information on the 50-mile scenic drive, along which numerous endangered species of plants can be inspected, call (918) 287–4803 or 287–1208.

Ponca City's famous **Pioneer Woman Statue,** a 17-foot bronze of mother and child, honors the women who pushed west with their families, enduring tough and uncertain conditions in an unsettled land. The adjacent museum houses displays of early furniture, clothing, implements, and appliances. The complex, located at Highway 77 and Lake Road, is open Tuesday through Friday from 9:00 A.M. to 5:00 P.M., Saturday from 10:00 A.M. to 4:00 P.M. and Sunday from 1:00 to 4:00 P.M.; call (405) 765–6108 for information. The **Ponca City Cultural Center & Indian Museum** (405–767–0427), situated at 1000 East Grand, houses Native American artifacts and relics from the famous Miller Brothers' 101 Ranch. It's open Monday through Saturday from 10:00 A.M. to 5:00 P.M. and Sunday from 1:00 to 5:00 P.M. (The facility also serves as a new tourism center.)

In Foster-Harris's 1955 book *The Look of the Old West,* he asserted that "the famous old 101 Ranch of Oklahoma has about as good a claim as any to having started the now nationwide spectacle sport" of rodeo. The **101 Ranch Rodeo,** a Professional Rodeo Cowboys Association (PRCA)–sanctioned event scheduled for August at the 101 Ranch Rodeo Arena, celebrates that heritage. Call (405) 767–8888 for information.

Twenty-five miles northwest of Stillwater on Highways 51 and 86,

Perry's **Cherokee Strip Museum** displays artifacts from the tumultuous Cherokee Strip Land Run of 1893. Located at 2617 West Fir Avenue, it's open Tuesday through Friday from 9:00 A.M. to 5:00 P.M. and weekends from 2:00 to 5:00 P.M.; call (405) 336–2405 for information. For a snack or a meal before leaving town, check out the **Shady Lady Steak House & Tea Room,** at 502 Fifth Street.

The Cherokee Strip Land Run

In 1889 Indian Territory was opened to white settlement, with acreages distributed through auction, lottery, and a series of five land runs held between 1889 and 1895. The largest and most spectacular of the land runs—in Oklahoma and U.S. history, both in terms of participants and the amount of land up for grabs—took place when the Cherokee Strip, a 226-mile-wide by 58-mile-deep tract of land, was open to settlers.

They came by foot, horseback, train, bicycle, and buggy—from every state in the Union and even from abroad. Most owned little but a dream: to carve out a homestead somewhere within the seven million acres of the Cherokee Strip. On September 16, 1893, more than 100,000 would-be settlers raced out at the sound of a pistol shot, vying for only 42,000 plots of free land.

The countryside changed literally overnight, and towns began springing up where previously there was only unbroken prairie—the largest of them today is Enid—as a result of what might be considered the largest competitive event in the history of the world.

In Stillwater, home to Oklahoma State University, put up at the **Thomasville Bed & Breakfast,** at 4115 North Denver Street. The mansion, built in 1890, is at the center of historic Thomasville, a collection of more than two dozen historical buildings. Four guest rooms grace the sixteen-room mansion, and a library, formal parlor, and morning room are available for visitors' enjoyment. Call (405) 372–1203 for reservations. Stillwater is also the home of Western Publications, publishers of periodicals that keep the Wild West kicking, including *Old West* and *Hunter's Frontier Times.* You can call them at (800) 749–3369.

A half-mile west of Pawnee on Highway 64, the **Pawnee Bill Museum**

& **Ranch** includes the 1908 home of William Gordon Lillie, army scout-turned-showman and proprietor of Pawnee Bill's Wild West Show. Displays from the show as well as Bill's personal effects are exhibited; outside, there's a drive-through buffalo refuge. The park is open Tuesday through Saturday from 10:00 A.M. to 5:00 P.M. and on Sunday from 1:00 to 4:00 P.M. (closed Tuesdays November through April). The annual **Pawnee Bill Wild West Show and Festival** takes place Saturday nights from late June through early August, with some one hundred cowboys and Indians performing Custer's Last Stand, a stagecoach robbery, trick riding and roping, and more. Call (918) 762–2513 or 762–2108 for information.

In Sand Springs, on the western edge of the greater Tulsa area, tie up at the famous **Mock Brothers Saddlery,** where world-class saddles and leather goods are crafted and Western clothes and boots are sold. It's open Monday through Saturday from 9:00 A.M. to 6:00 P.M. Then head to **Discoveryland!,** setting for boisterous performances of the Rodgers and Hammerstein

The Wild West Shows of Oklahoma

Buffalo Bill's turn-of-the-century Wild West Show was the most famous of its genre, but several similar productions toured the country and the world simultaneously, including shows from three spreads in Oklahoma: the Mulhall Ranch, the Pawnee Bill Ranch, and the Miller Brothers' 101 Ranch.

Zack Mulhall, who ran an 80,000-acre ranch outside Guthrie, built a Wild West show that starred his daughter, Lucille, billed as the "world's first cowgirl." She became a favorite of Teddy Roosevelt, as the show toured between 1900 and 1915.

Gordon William Lillie, better known as Pawnee Bill, joined Buffalo Bill's Wild West Show in the late 1800s; then in 1888 he struck out on his own. The biggest crowd pleaser in Pawnee Bill's show was his wife, May, a proper Philadelphia lady who learned to ride sidesaddle and shoot with the best of 'em.

The extremely popular Wild West show out of the Miller Brothers' 101 Ranch near Ponca City toured throughout the world from 1908 until the Great Depression hit America, with Col. George Washington Miller and his three sons riding herd. The Millers are often credited with creating the modern sport of rodeo.

classic *Oklahoma.* A Western musical revue, Indian dancing, and optional preperformance barbecue are also on tap at the get-together, which runs Monday through Saturday evenings from early June to late August. Call (918) 245–6552 for tickets and further information.

The renowned **Frankoma Pottery** works, at 2400 Frankoma Road in Sapulpa, includes among its native-clay products irresistible dinnerware that bears designs based on Native American and classic Western themes. The factory outlet and gift shop, open from 8:30 A.M. to 6:00 P.M. Monday through Saturday and Sunday from 12:30 to 5:00 P.M., is located a mile north of town on historic Route 66.

The **Allen Ranch,** at 19600 South Memorial in Bixby, is a day ranch that offers Western fun for the entire family: trail rides, cowboy shows, barbecues, cattle drives, hayrides, participatory rodeo, and more. It's open year-round, with the popular Chuckwagon Supper & Cowboy Music Show and other events taking place periodically; for more information and schedules, call (918) 366–3010. Similarly, the **Perryman Wrangler Ranch** (918–299–2997), at 11524 South Elm-wood Avenue in nearby Jenks (self-proclaimed Antique Capital of Oklahoma), is a 280-acre spread that provides barbecue cookouts, hayrides, Western entertainment, shoot-outs, storytelling, and Indian dancing.

In Tulsa proper don't bypass the **Gilcrease Museum,** boasting one of the world's finest collections of art by both famous and lesser-known Western and Native American artists. Artifacts and rare books and other documents are also on hand, interpreting the development of America from pre-Columbian times through the nineteenth century. The facility, once home to Cherokee Indian Thomas Gilcrease, is located at 1400 Gilcrease Museum Road and is open Monday through Saturday from 9:00 A.M. to 5:00 P.M. and Sunday from 1:00 to 5:00 P.M. The Rendezvous Restaurant is located on site, also; call (918) 596–2700 to learn more.

The **Tulsa Powwow,** with more than fifty tribes participating, is slated for early August at Mohawk Park. Dancing, arts and crafts, seminars, and sporting events are all part of the festivities. Call the Tulsa Chamber of Commerce at (918) 585–1201 for information.

Three miles northeast of Oologah (25 miles north of Tulsa on Highway 169), go to the **Dog Iron Ranch,** where you can visit the birthplace of the inimitable Will Rogers—cowboy entertainer, philosopher, radio commentator, actor, and Oklahoma's favorite native son. The attraction (918–275–4201) is open daily from 8:00 A.M. to 5:00 P.M. Then head down

Highway 88 to Claremore and visit the other end of Rogers's life at the **Will Rogers Memorial** and grave site, situated on West Will Rogers Boulevard. Rogers's saddle collection, Ziegfeld Follies costumes, photographs, trophies, and manuscripts are displayed at the memorial, open daily from 8:00 A.M. to 5:00 P.M. There's also a 178-seat theater that runs Rogers's films throughout the day. For more information call (918) 341–0719.

Among the displays at the **J. M. Davis Gun Museum** (918–341–5707), at 333 North Lynn Riggs Boulevard, are some 20,000 firearms, including examples of those responsible for winning/stealing the West. It's open Monday through Saturday from 8:30 A.M. to 5:00 P.M. and Sunday from 1:00 to 5:00 P.M. **Will Rogers Days** kicks up in Claremore in November; a Pony Express ride, Wild West show, and more are included. Call the Chamber of Commerce at (918–341–2818) for information.

The **Western Hills Guest Ranch** in Sequoyah State Park, east of Wagoner on Highway 51, offers guests a week-long, kicks-filled "cowboy camp." At the horseshoe-shaped resort ranch, situated on Fort Gibson Lake (named for the nearby historic frontier post), history, conservation, and Western heritage are the primary themes. Possibilities include trail rides, stagecoach and covered-wagon rides, chuckwagon cookouts, and golf and tennis (okay, not *everything* about the place is Old West). Guests eat at the Calico Crossing restaurant and wet their whistles at Black Jack's Saloon. Call (918) 772–2545 to find out more.

Owing to its prime location along the Illinois River, Tahlequah (25 miles east of Wagoner on Highway 51) is the canoeing capital of Oklahoma; not incidentally, it's also capital of the Cherokee Nation. The **Cherokee Heritage Center and National Museum,** 3 miles south of town on Willis Road, features multimedia, stationary, and living-history exhibits that interpret the history of the Cherokee tribe. In summer Tsa-La-Gi, a re-created seventeenth-century settlement, is staffed by Cherokees who act out a village life similar to that of their ancestors. The *Trail of Tears* outdoor drama revisits the tragic trek taken by some 16,000 Cherokees from the East Coast to Indian Territory, in response to the Removal Act of 1830. The drama is presented summer evenings at 8:00 P.M. Tuesday through Saturday. The heritage center is open during summer Monday through Saturday from 10:00 A.M. to 5:00 P.M. and Sunday from 1:00 to 5:00 P.M.; the rest of the year it is open Monday through Friday from 10:00 A.M. to 5:00 P.M. and Sunday from 1:00 to 5:00 P.M. Call (918) 456–6007 for more information.

Why So Many Native Americans Live in Oklahoma

The land now called Oklahoma was set aside in the 1820s by the U.S. government for the "Five Civilized Tribes"—the Choctaw, Chickasaw, Cherokee, Creek, and Seminole—who were forced to move from their traditional homelands between 1820 and 1842.

The removal of the Choctaw, the first tribe relocated to Oklahoma, was a relatively peaceful event. As the relocations progressed, however, they became bloodier and bloodier, and the Cherokees' forced march from their home in the Southeast, through the wilderness of Missouri and Arkansas, came to be called the Trail of Tears because so many died along the way.

In 1890 the five nations were grouped into one entity in the eastern half of future Oklahoma, dubbed "Indian Territory." The western portions were set aside for Plains tribes that were being moved to the area in the wake of the Indian wars—the Nez Perce, Cheyennes, Kaws, Pawnees, and others. This region was called Oklahoma Territory. (*Oklahoma* translates from the Choctaw into "Red People.") Eventually, through little choice of their own, sixty-seven tribes made Oklahoma their home.

In 1905 the Five Civilized Tribes mounted a short-lived campaign to convert Indian Territory into a fully recognized state of the Union, to be named Sequoyah. The government rejected the idea, opting instead for a single state that combined the Indian and Oklahoma territories; this Oklahoma became the forty-sixth state in 1907. Today a quarter of a million Indians live there, with thirty-six tribes maintaining councils in the state.

Southwest of Tahlequah off Highway 62, the **Fort Gibson Military Park** (918–478–2669), Oklahoma's first army base, includes a replica of the 1824 outpost and displays on the 7th Cavalry. Numerous living-history presentations are offered throughout the year at the park, located a mile north of the town of Fort Gibson and open Monday through Saturday from 9:00 A.M. to 5:00 P.M. and Sunday from 1:00 to 5:00 P.M. The national cemetery, a mile east of town, includes the graves of soldiers from every American war campaign.

Nearby Muskogee claims the **Ataloa Lodge** (918–683–4581), featuring one of the nation's largest private collections of Native American arts, crafts, and pottery. It's located on the Bacone College Campus, at 99 Bacone Boulevard and Shawnee Bypass, and is open Monday through Friday from 10:00 A.M. to 4:00 P.M. Also in town is the **Five Civilized Tribes Museum** (918–683–1701), overlooking Honor Heights Park on Honor Heights Drive. Housed in the 1875 Union Indian Agency building, the museum includes a trading post that brims with baskets, beadwork, artwork, prehistoric artifacts, and more. It's open Monday through Saturday from 10:00 A.M. to 5:00 P.M. and Sunday from 1:00 to 5:00 P.M.

Perhaps because the community of Jenks claimed the state's antiques-capital title first, similarly antiques-filled Muskogee bills itself as the Bed & Breakfast Capital of Oklahoma. One of several B&B possibilities: the **Graham-Carroll House**, "legend of Muskogee's Silk Stocking Avenue," where a three-course gourmet breakfast comes with the deal. The establishment is located at 501 North Sixteenth Street; call (918) 683–0100 for reservations.

Southeast Oklahoma

The **Sequoyah Homesite** (918–775–2413), holding the former residence of Sequoyah, the Cherokee responsible for developing that tribe's alphabet, is located 11 miles northeast of Sallisaw on Highway 101 (Salisaw is 50 miles southeast of Muskogee on Highway 64). It was built in 1829, making it one of the oldest structures in the state, and nowadays is open Monday through Friday from 9:00 A.M. to 5:00 P.M. and weekends from 2:00 to 5:00 P.M. Between Sallisaw and Keota you can visit the **Overstreet-Kerr Living History Farm**. A potato house, smoke house, rock barn, and chicken house grace the grounds that surround the 1895 three-story Victorian. It's open Tuesday through Saturday from 10:00 A.M. to 4:00 P.M., with tours available. Call (918) 966–3396 for directions.

North of tiny Tuskahoma on Highway 271 is the **Choctaw National Historical Museum** (918–569–4465), with artifacts, paintings, and photographs that illuminate the Choctaws' unique culture and history. The museum, housed in a structure built in 1884 to serve as capital of the Choctaw Nation, is open Monday through Friday from 8:00 A.M. to 4:30 P.M.

Six miles east of Broken Bow is the **Gardner Mansion** (405–584–6588), home in the 1880s to Jefferson Gardner, chief of the Choctaws. The artifact-filled facility is open daily for touring. Six miles southwest of nearby Haworth, you'll find the 1867 **Henry Harris Home** (405–245–1129), former residence of another prominent Choctaw leader and open to visitors by appointment. Finally, just outside tiny Swink (23 miles west of Idabel on Highway 70), visit the **Choctaw Chief's House,** a hand-hewn log cabin built in 1832 for Chief Thomas LeFlore. It's open to visitors Tuesday through Friday from 9:00 A.M. to 5:00 P.M. and weekends from 2:00 to 5:00 P.M.

In Hugo the **Hugo Heritage Railroad & Frisco Museum** proffers the longest scenic railway ride in Oklahoma, beginning at the town depot on Saturday and Sunday at 2:00 P.M. You can dine at the restored 1914 depot in the **Harvey House Restaurant,** evocative of those oases of civilization that once graced the frontier along the Santa Fe Railway line. The depot is on the 300 block of West Jackson; call (405) 326–6630 for more information.

Sixteen miles north of Durant on Highway 78 and Highway 199, the **Fort Washita Historic Site** includes a museum that highlights the history of the fort, along with restored troops barracks and the commanding officer's cabin. The fort was built in 1842 to provide protection for the "civilized" Chickasaw and Choctaw Indians from the wrath of warring Plains tribes. It's open Monday through Saturday from 9:00 A.M. to 5:00 P.M. and Sunday from 1:00 to 5:00 P.M. Each April the Friends of Fort Washita sponsor the **Fur Trade Era Rendezvous,** with authentically detailed 1840s equipment, costumes, and weaponry abounding. Call (405) 924–6502 for more information.

The Western-flair rooms at Kingston's **Sun Ray Ranch,** situated just a few miles from immense Lake Texoma, feature antiques that date from the days of the Indian Territory. Guests choose from one of three rooms; many also choose to help out as ranch hands. Call (405) 564–3602 for reservations.

Pass through Gene Autry, if for no other reason than simply to say you've been to Gene Autry, Oklahoma. While there, swing into the **Gene Autry Oklahoma Museum** (405–294–3047), with memorabilia from the tune-filled life of the Singing Cowboy. Its regular hours are Saturday from 10:00 A.M. to 4:00 P.M. and Sunday from 1:00 to 4:00 P.M., but it will open at other times if you call ahead. The nationally distributed newsletter *Rope Burns* comes out of this little town, with updates on Western-heritage happenings like cowboy-poetry gatherings and Western-collectibles shows. Call (405) 389–5350 to request a sample copy.

Central Oklahoma

In Oklahoma City, world famous for its Old West ways, make the obligatory stop at the immense Stockyards City for a meal at the **Cattleman's Cafe,** at 1309 South Agnew. Numerous Western-wear stores and saddle shops are nearby, where you can get properly dressed before moseying over to the **National Cowboy Hall of Fame & Western Heritage Center.**

Sponsored by seventeen western states, the facility maintains the largest collection of Western lore in the world and is, in itself, more than an adequate reason to travel to Oklahoma. Included among the finds are works of art by the western masters: Russell, Remington, Moran, and the rest. Three distinct halls of fame are located within the complex: the **Rodeo Hall of Fame;** the **Western Performers Hall of Fame,** celebrating the likes of Gene Autry, John Wayne, Walter Brennan, and the entire cast of *Gunsmoke;* and the **Hall of Great Westerners,** whose 200 elite members represent the West's most admired men and women, whether they be ranchers, cowboys, writers, poets, or explorers. On the grounds outside are the graves of and/or memorials to several champion rodeo critters, including Tornado, the world-famous bucking bull, and the horse known as Steamboat, "Symbol of the Spirit of Wyoming."

Displays with a Native American bent include the heralded 18-foot-high *End of the Trail* statue and John Wayne's own kachina doll collection. Each May chuckwagons from working cattle ranches gather at the National Cowboy Hall of Fame for the **Cowboy Chuckwagon Gathering & Reenactment.** Life as it was on an 1800s cattle drive is resumed. The world-class, world-famous complex is located at 1700 Northeast Sixty-third Street and is open daily from 8:30 A.M. to 6:00 P.M. in summer and from 9:00 A.M. to 5:00 P.M. in winter. Call (405) 478–2250 for more information.

Another trio of sure bets in town includes the resplendent **State**

Museum of the Oklahoma Historical Society (405–521–2491), at 2100 Lincoln Boulevard, open Monday through Saturday from 8:00 A.M. to 5:00 P.M.; the **Harn Homestead & 1889er Museum** (405–235–4058), a ten-acre farm that re-creates the 1889 land run, located at 313 Northeast Sixteenth Street and open Tuesday through Saturday from 10:00 A.M. to 4:00 P.M.; and **Frontier City** (405–478–2412), a Western theme/amusement park that stages Western shows complete with gunfights. The park, located at 11601 Northeast Expressway, is open daily in summer and weekends in spring and fall.

Each January Oklahoma City pulls out the stops for the **International Finals Rodeo,** when the world's top rodeoers compete at the Myriad Convention Center for nearly a quarter of a million dollars. Call (405) 236–5000 for ticket information. While in the area, consider overnighting at **The Grandison,** one of Oklahoma City's oldest and grandest homes. The 1896 house features five guest rooms, including an immense third-floor suite, each with private bath. It's located minutes from downtown at 1841 Northwest Fifteenth Street; call (405) 521–0011 to make reservations.

A bronc buster at the International Finals Rodeo

In El Reno, at the western edge of suburban Oklahoma City, check out **Fort Reno,** today an agricultural station but between 1875 and 1908 an important cavalry post. Items from the horse-soldier days are displayed at the center, which is open daily from 8:00 A.M. to 4:30 P.M. Each June the fort hosts its **Indian Territory Days,** with Indians, trappers, cowboys, soldiers, and pioneers commingling. The fort is located off Interstate 40 at exit 119; call (405) 262–3987 for information. Also nearby and of note: **The Wilds Restaurant & Recreation Area,** where hayrides, cookouts, and horseback riding are offered, buffalo graze, and Western entertainment in the form of the Prairie String Band is enjoyed in the log-cabin restaurant. The Wilds, located on Britton Road between Highway 4 and Highway 81, is open daily in summer; call (405) 262–7275 for more information.

The **Chisholm Trail Festival,** slated for June at the Kirkpatrick Homestead in Yukon (Garth Brooks's hometown) just west of Oklahoma City on Highway 66, commemorates the years 1867 through 1889, during which millions of longhorns were driven from Texas through this area en route to the railhead in Kansas. A frontier trading camp, a cowboy church service, and reenactments of famous Old West events are all part of the family-oriented fun; call (405) 354–3567 for information. Be sure also to have a look at the *Chisholm Trail Mural* downtown, also honoring the trail that hosted hundreds of herds of longhorns.

In Chandler, off Interstate 44 northeast of Oklahoma City, visit the **Museum of Pioneer History** (405–258–2425), at 717 Manvel Avenue. It's open Monday through Thursday from 8:00 A.M. to 4:30 P.M. and Friday from 9:00 A.M. to 3:00 P.M. Then head to the **Read Ranch,** west of town on Highway 66, a 240-acre spread with a determined Western atmosphere that dishes up barn dances, horse-drawn hayrides, trail rides, campouts, Indian dancing, gunfights, chuckwagon suppers, and libations at their new Flying Spur Saloon. Call (405) 258–2999 to learn more.

Guthrie's 1,400-acre Victorian downtown core comprises one of the largest contiguous urban areas listed on the National Register of Historic Places. Old Guthrie served as both the territorial capital and the original state capital. The **Oklahoma Territorial Museum** (405–282–1889), located at 402 East Oklahoma, includes extensive information on the huge land run that took place in this area in 1899, whereas the **State Capital Publishing Museum** (405–282–4123), at Second and Harrison streets, is a four-story Victorian that features a print shop and exhibits on the first newspaper published in the territory. Both museums are open Tuesday through Friday from 9:00 A.M. to 5:00 P.M., Saturday from 10:00 A.M. to 4:00 P.M., and Sunday from 1:00 to 4:00 P.M.

A scattering of taverns and eateries occupy venerable structures in Guthrie's historic district, including the **Blue Belle Saloon & Restaurant,** at 224 West Harrison Street, where Tom Mix served drinks. Victorians-turned-B&Bs in Guthrie include the twenty-three-room **Harrison House** (405–282–1000), at 124 West Harrison; the 8,000-square-foot **Stone Lion Inn** (405–282–0012), at 1016 West Warner; and the somewhat cozier **Caretaker's Cottage Guest House** (405–282–0012), at 1009 West Warner.

Guthrie's **International Tom Mix Festival** (405–282–1947) is held each September, and the city's world-famous **Lazy E Arena** hosts some of America's premier rodeos, stock shows, and country concerts. A couple of the more colorful events: the **Oklahoma Cattlemen's Range Round-Up,** held in May, with working cowboys from throughout the state competing in events designed to replicate true ranch tasks, and the September **Women's National Finals Rodeo,** with the nation's top fifteen cowgirls vying for world championship titles. To find out what's happening and for ticket information, call (405) 282–3004.

The **Chisholm Trail Museum,** at 605 Zellers Avenue in Kingfisher, 30 miles west of Guthrie, displays history from the vital cattle highway named for Cherokee trader Jesse Chisholm. Two log cabins, an old bank and schoolhouse, Indian artifacts, and the 1892 Governor A. J. Seay Mansion are featured. The museum is open in summer Tuesday through Saturday from 9:00 A.M. to 5:00 P.M. and Sunday from 1:00 to 5:00 P.M. (it's closed Tuesdays in winter). Call (405) 375–5176 for more information.

At Roman Nose State Park, located 8 miles north of Watonga, you can rent a cottage or a tipi for the night at Roman Nose Resort, and you can enjoy Native American favorites at the resort's Redbird Restaurant. Call (405) 623–7281 for information.

Southwest Oklahoma

Anadarko bills itself as the Indian Capital of the Nation, and the wealth of museums and attractions bears out this claim. The **Delaware Tribal Museum** (405–247–2448), 2 miles north of town on Highway 281, is open

Monday through Friday from 8:00 A.M. to 5:00 P.M. The **National Hall of Fame for American Indians** (405–247–5555), at the east end of town on Highway 62, displays bronze busts in an outdoor exhibition area open Monday through Saturday from 9:00 A.M. to 5:00 P.M. and Sunday from 1:00 to 5:00 P.M. The nearby **Southern Plains Indian Museum and Crafts Center** (405–247–6221) operates during the same hours. **Indian City U.S.A.,** 2 miles south of town on Highway 8, is an expansive outdoor museum that offers tours of seven Indian villages, each focusing on the lives, religious traditions, and cultures of a different tribe. The indoor portion of the facility exhibits artifacts and historic photographs. Indian City is open daily from 9:00 A.M. to 6:00 P.M. in summer and from 9:00 A.M. to 5:00 P.M. the rest of the year. Call (405) 247–5661 for information.

Also in Anadarko: the **Philomathic Museum,** housed in the old train depot at 311 East Main Street. Displays include railroading artifacts, early military equipment, and a pioneer physician's office and general store. It's open Tuesday through Sunday from 1:00 to 5:00 P.M.; call (405) 247–3240 for information.

Anadarko's **American Indian Exposition** brings more than 500 cere-monial-dancing competitors to town in early August. The National War Dance Championship and Outstanding Indian of the Year competitions also are conducted during the exposition. Call the Chamber of Commerce at (405) 247–6651 for further information.

Meers, population four, is a ghostly reminder of the town that boomed early in this century during a gold rush in the surrounding Wichita Mountains. The blink-and-miss-it settlement is known throughout Oklahoma for the **Meers Store,** a unique enterprise listed on the National Register of Historic Places. Meersburgers, made of pure Texas longhorn beef, rib-eye steak, barbecue, and homemade pies are among the specialties served in the store's restaurant. The Meers Store is open Monday through Friday from 8:00 A.M. to 9:00 P.M. and weekends from 7:00 A.M. to 9:00 P.M.

Lawton, 40 miles south of Anadarko, bustles around a number of sites evocative of a slower time, including the **Fort Sill Museum,** located at 437 Quanah Road. Several buildings remain of the original 1869 fort, including the guardhouse that at one time held Apache leader Geronimo prisoner and others that display exhibits on the frontier army. The Buffalo Soldiers of the 10th Cavalry constructed many of the stone buildings at Fort Sill, where the grounds hold the graves of Geronimo and other Indian leaders. The museum is open daily from 8:30 A.M. to 4:30 P.M.; call (405) 442–5123 for information.

The impressive **Museum of the Great Plains** (405–581–3460), at 601 Ferris Avenue in Elmer Thomas Park in Lawton, details the history and prehistory of the Great Plains up through the early 1900s. A re-created 1840s fortified trading post, with living-history interpretations, is a highlight at the museum, open daily year-round, from 8:00 A.M. to 5:00 P.M. Monday and Tuesday and 8:00 A.M. to 6:00 P.M. Wednesday through Sunday. The annual **Spring Encampment at the Red River Trading Post** living-history celebration, held in early May, sees brightly bedecked dragoons, Plains Indians, and frontier women, mixing with fur traders and merchants. (There's a similar Fall Encampment gathering in November.)

A site worth visiting in Duncan, 30 miles southeast of Lawton, through which the 1852 Military Trail ran: the **Stephens County Historical Museum,** with its Boomer Room, focusing on the lives of the first whites to settle in Oklahoma. Indian and Chisholm Trail artifacts, old photographs, and horse-drawn carriages are also displayed at the facility, open Thursday through Sunday from 1:00 to 5:00 P.M. It's located in Fuqua Park at Highway 81 and Beech Street; call (405) 252–0717 to find out more. Duncan's **Festival of the Cowboy** (405–252–4160), slated for April, celebrates the cowboy way with a rodeo, barbecue, and other Old West festivities.

The **Museum of the Western Prairie** (405–482–1044), at 1100 North Hightower in Altus, 60 miles west of Lawton, interprets the colorful history of southwest Oklahoma. It is open Tuesday through Friday from 9:00 A.M. to 5:00 P.M. and weekends from 2:00 to 5:00 P.M. Nearby Magnum was the historic capital of what was known as the "unassigned territory," as well as the center of an early land dispute with Texas. You can learn about it at the **Old Greer County Museum & Hall of Fame** (405–782–2851), with displays and artifacts representative of life in those early days. The facility, located at 222 West Jefferson, is open Tuesday through Friday from 9:00 A.M. to 5:00 P.M.

Cheyenne, 80 miles north of Altus, boasts the **Black Kettle Museum** (405–497–3929), named for the Cheyenne chief whose people fought against George Armstrong Custer's near here in 1868, at the Battle of Washita—after Custer made a surprise attack on the village. The battlefield, listed on the National Register of Historic Places, is a couple of miles west of town off Highway 47 on Highway 47A and is marked with a memorial. The museum includes artifacts from both the Indians and the 7th Cavalry, as well as early pioneer relics. Located at the junction of Highway 283 and Highway 47, it's open Tuesday through Saturday from 9:00 A.M. to 5:00 P.M. and Sunday from 1:00 to 5:00 P.M.

Northwest Oklahoma

The **Plains Indians & Pioneer Museum** (405–256–6136) is located in Woodward (70 miles north of Cheyenne), home also to stunning Boiling Springs State Park. The museum, featuring a trader's shop, an early-day bank, prehistoric artifacts, and an art gallery, is found at 2009 Williams Avenue and is open Tuesday through Saturday from 10:00 A.M. to 5:00 P.M. and Sunday 1:00 to 4:00 P.M. Fourteen miles northwest of town, along the North Canadian River, is **Historic Fort Supply,** open on appointment by calling (405) 766–3767. The **Fort Supply Military Days,** sponsored in June by the Oklahoma Historical Society, features primitive-skills craftspersons, a cavalry encampment, a buffalo hunters' camp, and regular showings of the video *Custer at the Washita.* Those individuals with horses in tow can participate in the associated **Fort Supply Cavalry Ride.**

Outside of tiny Ames, 80 miles east of Woodward, the **Island Guest Ranch** offers hayrides, horseback riding, cookouts, Western entertainment, and rental cabins. This 2,300-acre spread, situated near the legendary Cimarron River, serves home-grown beef and produce and also features a re-created ghost town, complete with tavern and general store. Call (405) 753–4574 or (800) 928–4574 for reservations and directions.

A couple of attractions in Enid (85 miles east of Woodward)—which, with a population of 43,300, is about 43,000 people larger than Ames—include the **Museum of the Cherokee Strip** (405–237–1907) and the **Railroad Museum of Oklahoma** (405–233–3051). The former, located at 507 South Fourth Street, details the land rush and settlement of the Cherokee Outlet and also features a barn with early farming equipment. It's open Tuesday through Friday from noon to 5:00 P.M. and Saturday from 9:00 A.M. to 1:00 P.M. The railroad museum, situated at 702 North Washington Street, features various artifacts from throughout the West, including telegraph equipment. It's open Tuesday through Friday from 1:00 to 4:00 P.M. and Saturday from 9:00 A.M. to 1:00 P.M.

Alva, 70 miles northwest of Enid, boasts yet another **Cherokee Strip Museum.** This one, located at 901 Fourteenth Street, features nearly forty theme rooms, including a kitchen, living room, chapel, gun room, and one-room schoolhouse, all decorated with artifacts from the late 1800s. The museum is open between May and August Tuesday through Sunday from 2:00 to 5:00 P.M. and weekends only between September and April from 2:00 to 5:00 P.M. Call (405) 327–2030 for more information.

Go west on Highway 64 and take the short detour south to Freedom for a glimpse of the **Cimarron Cowboy Monument,** a 15-foot-high granite memorial to the rough-and-ready cow people who settled the Cherokee Strip. Most of the downtown buildings are fronted with rough cedar, lending Freedom the distinct look of a dusty old cowtown. The **Rodeo & Old Cowhand Reunion** is conducted in August. Call (405) 621–3276 to learn how to join in on the fun.

Keep heading west until you reach the town of Gate, where you'll find the **Gateway to the Panhandle Museum.** Old guns, newspapers, and other artifacts bring to life the early days here in "No Man's Land." The museum (405–934–2004) is open Monday through Saturday from 1:00 to 6:00 P.M. and at other times by appointment.

Beaver, 30 miles west and south, boasts the **Jones & Plummer Trail Museum** (405–625–4439), named for the cattle trail that traced through the panhandle. Situated at the Beaver County Fairgrounds, the museum displays old clothing, saddles, photographs, and other items evocative of earlier times. It's open Wednesday through Friday from 1:00 to 5:30 P.M., Saturday from 1:00 to 5:00 P.M., and Sunday from 2:30 to 5:00 P.M. The **Cimarron Territory Celebration & World Champion Cow Chip Throw** happens here in late April; call the Chamber of Commerce at (405) 625–4726 for details.

Where to Eat

Shady Lady Steak House & Tea Room, Perry, (405) 336–5003
Allen Ranch, Bixby, (918) 366–3010
Perryman Wrangler Ranch, Jenks, (918) 299–2997

Calico Crossing, Sequoyah State Park (east of Wagoner), (918) 772–2545

Cattleman's Cafe, Oklahoma City, (405) 236–0416

Harvey House Restaurant, Hugo, (405) 326–6630

The Wilds Restaurant, El Reno, (405) 262–7275

Read Ranch, Chandler, (405) 258–2999

Blue Belle Saloon & Restaurant, Guthrie, (405) 260–2355

Redbird Restaurant, Roman Nose State Park (north of Watonga), (405) 623–7281

Meers Store, Meers, (405) 429–8051

Where to Stay

Thomasville Bed & Breakfast, Stillwater, (405) 372–1203

Graham-Carroll House, Muskogee, (918) 683–0100

Sun Ray Ranch, Kingston, (405) 564–3602

The Grandison, Oklahoma City, (405) 521–0011

Harrison House, Guthrie, (405) 282–1000

Stone Lion Inn, Guthrie, (405) 282–0012

Caretaker's Cottage Guest House, Guthrie, (405) 282–0012

Island Guest Ranch, outside Ames, (800) 928–4574

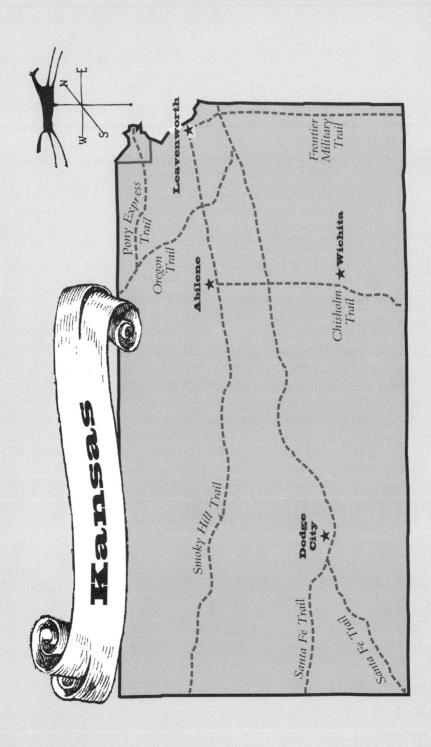

KANSAS

▼▼▼

ANY OF the names on the face of Kansas—Dodge City, Abilene, and Wichita, for instance—evoke images of cowboys, frontier soldiers, desperadoes, and straight-shooting lawmen.

The narrative roughly follows the six historic trails vital to the settling of Kansas in the 1800s: the **Frontier Military Trail**, leading north from Baxter Springs to Fort Leavenworth; the **Pony Express Trail,** which cuts a swath through the extreme northeast corner of the state; the **Oregon Trail,** the first 170 miles of which run through northeast Kansas (the stretch was known as the Independence Road); the **Santa Fe Trail,** leading west across the state to the Colorado border; the **Smoky Hill Trail,** also traversing the state east to west; and the legendary **Chisholm Trail,** over which thousands of cattle were driven to railhead at Abilene.

The Frontier Military Trail

The **Frontier Military Scenic Byway,** comprising Highway 69 and several linking roads, traces the old military road built through Indian Territory between 1838 and 1845. Fifty miles west of the byway from Baxter Springs (the "first cowtown in Kansas" and home to the **Big Brutus Museum,** 316–827–6177) is Coffeyville, which has built a thriving tourism industry around the infamous Dalton Gang. The boys grew up in the area, then died here, on October 5, 1892, when they attempted to rob two banks at once, including the **Old Condon Bank,** now a National Historic Landmark located on the Dalton Defenders Plaza. In nearby **Death Alley** bullet holes from that fateful day can still be seen in the walls of surrounding buildings, and at the old **City Jail,** you can see where the dead bodies of the Daltons were laid out for public view.

Four of the five members of the Dalton Gang who died that day are buried at Elmwood Cemetery, as are two of the four men killed defending the town from the outlaws. The **Dalton Museum,** at 113 East Eighth Street, is dedicated to the defenders and contains Western mementos, including artifacts from the Dalton Raid. The museum is open daily from 9:00 A.M. to 7:00 P.M. **Dalton Defenders Days,** held at the plaza on the Saturday closest to October 5, includes a reenactment of the raid, a saloon show, and a mountain-man rendezvous. Call the Visitors Bureau at (316) 251–1194 for more information on the Dalton festival and museum.

Fort Scott National Historic Site, 60 miles north of Baxter Springs in the center of the town of Fort Scott, features a dozen historic structures built between 1842 and 1845, along with nine reconstructed buildings. Special living-history activities stir to life throughout the year, including the annual **Good Ol' Days** celebration in June, considered one of the premier festivals in Kansas. Fort Scott (316–223–0310), located on Old Fort Boulevard, is open daily from 8:00 A.M. to 5:00 P.M.

Farther up the military road, the town of Trading Post was established as, obviously, a trading post, conceived to enhance trade between the French and the Osage Indians. The **Trading Post Museum Complex** (913–352–6441) encompasses a restored 1857 cabin, an old schoolhouse, and a scattering of antique farm machinery. It's open March 15 through November 30, Tuesday through Saturday from 9:00 A.M. to 5:00 P.M. and Sunday from 11:00 A.M. to 5:00 P.M.

In Leavenworth, just north of Kansas City, visit the **Leavenworth County Museum,** housed in the 1867 Carroll mansion at 1128 Fifth Avenue. Elaborate, handcrafted woodwork and dozens of donated antiques afford an air of aged distinction. A re-created general store occupies one room and a barbershop another. The museum is open Monday through Saturday from 10:30 A.M. to 4:30 P.M. and Sunday from 1:00 to 4:30 P.M. (closed between Christmas and the third week of February). Call (913) 682–7759 for information.

The unique **Harvey Girls Luncheons** are served to groups of fifteen and larger at the Riverfront Convention Center, which occupies the town's historic train depot. The gatherings are particularly popular among senior-citizen tour groups. The original Harvey House Girls, organized by

Fort Scott

ort Scott was built in 1842 as a link in the chain of U.S. Army outposts established to keep peace in the Permanent Indian Frontier, that country west of the line that delineated the western extent of white settlement (which turned out to be anything but permanent). The garrisons, built at intervals along the line reaching from Louisiana to Minnesota, housed infantrymen, along with the more colorfully bedecked and heavily armed Dragoons. These unique corpsmen—each of whom carried a heavy "old wristbreaker" saber, a .52 caliber Hall carbine and a .54 caliber percussion pistol—were trained to fight both on foot and on horseback.

The fort, built in ancestral Osage Indian country, was designed to keep the peace among the nomadic Indians, white settlers, and eastern tribes whom the government had banished to the Permanent Indian Frontier. Peace reigned in the area, however, with military intervention seldom necessary, so the primary function of the soldiers evolved into guarding overland-trail travelers and patrolling the Indian country farther west.

By 1853 Fort Scott had outlived its reasons for being; troops were transferred to Fort Leavenworth, and the post buildings were sold at auction.

Leavenworth's Fred Harvey, worked as waitresses in the Harvey House restaurants, situated in depots along the Santa Fe Railroad line. Today's "girls," in costume, along with an engineer and conductor, greet and serve guests; after the scrumptious luncheon a presentation on the history of Harvey and his girls is offered. Call (913) 651–2132 at least two weeks in advance to make reservations.

Buffalo Bill Cody, born in nearby Iowa, moved to Leavenworth with his family when he was nine. He worked downtown for the Russell, Majors, and Waddell Freight Company before signing on as a rider for the Pony Express, the company's branch enterprise in St. Joseph, Missouri. The annual **Buffalo Bill Days** celebration, held the third week in September, commemorates Cody, Leavenworth's role in opening the West, and the pioneers who passed through on the westward-leading trails. Call the Leavenworth Visitors Bureau at (913) 682–4113 for more information.

Just north of Leavenworth is historic **Fort Leavenworth,** established in

1827 and still in service as the oldest continuously run Army post west of the Mississippi. Among the sights is the 1828 Rookery, the oldest house in Kansas and home to military notables such as George Custer and Dwight D. Eisenhower during their stints at Fort Leavenworth.

In the 1830s and 1840s, branches of both the Oregon and Santa Fe trails crossed Fort Leavenworth's property. The **Frontier Army Museum,** on the base on Reynolds Avenue, is organized around the theme of the Army's role in westward expansion. Highlights include displays of uniforms from the Indian wars and Mexican War periods, an extensive collection of horse-

The Buffalo Soldiers

The 10th Cavalry, organized at Fort Leavenworth in 1866, was one of the U.S. Army's four black Indian-fighting regiments. Whether by design or accident, the Army had created a painfully ironic circumstance: It was using one oppressed people to conquer another. The black soldiers were highly regarded by their Native American adversaries, however, who called them the "Buffalo Soldiers" because of their fuzzy hair and tenacious fighting skills.

The Buffalo Soldiers were sent to the Southwest in 1870, where for ten years they patrolled a region of 100,000 square miles. Even here, far away from the Deep South, they were often scorned by the citizens they were sent to protect. In Texas, for instance, off-duty soldiers came to expect trouble from saloon keepers, cowboys, and townspeople. Even so, the Buffalo Soldiers were extremely dedicated, averaging a desertion rate one-third that of the typical white regiment.

When the Indian wars heated up on the Great Plains, some of the Buffalo Soldiers were transferred to North Dakota and Montana, in spite of a warning from the quartermaster-general that they couldn't tolerate the cold winters. (They did just fine.)

Between 1865 and 1899 eighteen Buffalo Soldiers received the Medal of Honor for service above and beyond the call of duty. Gen. Colin Powell, who served as a one-star general at Fort Leavenworth in the early 1980s, helped provide momentum for the creation of the *Buffalo Soldier Monument* to honor the heroic men. It was dedicated in 1992 on the fort's grounds.

drawn vehicles (including a sleigh owned by George Custer), and the Frontier Fort story hour, particularly popular among kids. It is presented by appointment by the museum's volunteer Musettes. The Frontier Army Museum also serves as headquarters for the **Company B, 1st US Dragoons** living-history unit. Call (913) 684–3191 for a schedule of their performances and other information. The museum is open year-round, Monday through Friday from 9:00 A.M. to 4:00 P.M., Saturday from 10:00 A.M. to 4:00 P.M., and Sunday from noon to 4:00 P.M.

The Pony Express Trail

Pony Express riders dusted through the northeast corner of Kansas for a brief eighteen months, beginning in April 1860. At Seneca, where riders made relay stops to change horses, the **Nemaha County Historical Museum** (913–336–6366) includes displays on the short-lived mail-delivery system. The museum, at Sixth and Nemaha streets, is open Monday through Friday from 1:00 to 4:00 P.M.

At Marysville, 30 miles west of Seneca, the **Bronze Pony Express Horse Rider** statue at the Hall Brothers Pony Express Park on Highway 36 West seems alive, as if horse and rider are tearing across the prairie. The **Pony Express Barn and Museum** (913–562–3825), at 106 South Eighth Street, is the only remaining Express "home station" in its original location. Hours are from 10:00 A.M. to 5:00 P.M. Monday through Saturday and Sunday from noon to 5:00 P.M., May 1 through October 30.

The **Hollenberg Pony Express Station,** 16 miles northwest of Marysville near Hanover, is managed as a museum by the Kansas Historical Society. Built in 1857 by German immigrant Gerat H. Hollenberg, it served initially as his ranch home and as a tavern, country store, and Overland Express stage station. Known then as Cottonwood Station, the place evolved into the most westerly Pony Express station in Kansas. The museum, 2 miles northeast of Hanover, is open year-round Wednesday through Saturday from 10:00 A.M. to 5:00 P.M. and Sunday from 1:00 to 5:00 P.M. Call (913) 337–2635 for information.

Near Republic, 60 miles west of Hanover, the **Pawnee Indian Village Museum** is constructed around the floor of an earth lodge that was used as a residence during the early nineteenth century. The Republican Pawnee village here consisted of some thirty or forty lodges, with an estimated population of 1,000 individuals. Artifacts from the excavations are on display, and twenty-two lodge sites are defined within a six-acre enclosure. The site, located southwest of town, is open Tuesday through Saturday from 10:00 A.M. to 5:00 P.M. and Sunday from 1:00 to 5:00 P.M. Call (913) 361–2255 for more information.

The Pony Express

In 1859 the railroad and telegraph went no farther west than St. Joseph, Missouri. From there horse-drawn stagecoaches and oxen- or mule-drawn wagons took on the mail and freight.

In 1860 the Leavenworth freighting firm of Russell, Majors, and Waddell initiated the Pony Express. Their riders cut across northeast Kansas up to the Platte River in Nebraska, through Fort Kearney and Scotts Bluff, then onto Fort Laramie, South Pass, Fort Bridger, and Salt Lake City. From there they skirted the southern edge of the Great Salt Lake and rode across Nevada and over the Sierra Nevada to Sacramento.

At relay stations, located every 10 to 15 miles, riders changed horses in two minutes or less, with a fresh rider taking over at every third station. The maiden run, which included a freight of forty-nine letters and several telegrams and newspapers, galloped out of St. Joseph at 7:15 P.M. on April 3, 1860. The cargo reached San Francisco, via boat from Sacramento, eleven days and a few hours later.

Although the Pony Express was much faster than any previous means of communicating across the vast expanses of the West, the costs of running it were far greater than the revenues. By October 1861 the Express died; the completion of the telegraph had hammered the final nail into its coffin.

The Oregon Trail

Fort Riley, northeast of Junction City, was established in 1852 as a staging area for horse soldiers who patrolled the overland trails. The expansive **U.S. Cavalry Museum,** located in the 1855 post hospital, celebrates the long and

Kansas

captivating history of the American Horse Soldier, who served from 1775 until 1950 and included the Dragoons, Mounted Riflemen, and Cavalrymen. Weapons, uniforms, and original works by Frederic Remington are exhibited at the museum, open Monday through Saturday from 9:00 A.M. to 4:30 P.M. and Sunday from noon to 4:30 P.M. Call (913) 239–2737 to request a copy of the brochure *U.S. Cavalry Museum Walking Tour.*

The **First Territorial Capitol** State Historic Site (913–784–5535), also found at the still-active military reservation, is open Thursday through Saturday from 10:00 A.M. to 5:00 P.M. and Sunday from 1:00 to 5:00 P.M. The **Custer House,** built of native limestone in 1854, holds displays that depict the life of the frontier soldier during the Indian wars. It's open Monday through Saturday from 9:00 A.M. to 4:30 P.M. and Sunday from noon to 4:30 P.M.

In Manhattan visit the **Wolf-Butterfield Museum** (913–776–7344), at Juliette and Fremont streets. The stone structure served as an overnight station for the Butterfield Overland Dispatch Stage Line in the mid-1860s. It's open Thursday through Saturday from 1:00 to 5:00 P.M. and Sunday from 2:00 to 5:00 P.M.

In the capital city of Topeka, head for the **State Capitol,** where historic murals by native son John Steuart Curry offer dramatic overviews of pioneer Kansas. Then head to the **Kansas Museum of History,** on Sixth Street off Interstate 70 at exit 356. The state's premier repository of things old tells the story of Kansas from prehistoric times through the present. Displays include a Southern Cheyenne buffalo-hide tipi, an 1866 log cabin, an 1880 Santa Fe Railroad locomotive, a sod house, and, for the kids, a hands-on Discovery Room. Workshops and living-history demonstrations are regular features at the museum, open Monday through Saturday from 9:00 A.M. to 4:30 P.M. and Sunday from 12:30 to 4:30 P.M. Call (913) 272–8681 for information.

Some of those individuals who traveled the northern branch of the Oregon Trail crossed the Kansas River, via toll ferry, at the location of today's **Historic Ward-Meade Park.** In 1854 Anthony and Mary Jane Ward purchased 240 acres here from a Pottawatomie Indian (for $100!), and their place became a gathering spot for newly arriving homesteaders. Today their lives are acted out by costumed guides at **Prairie Crossings,** a turn-of-the-century Kansas village, with its Pauline Depot and Caboose, one-room Victor Schoolhouse (replete with "school marm"), and

Mulvane General Store. At the old Ward Cabin, visitors enjoy hearth-cooked prairie meals, topped off with molasses cookies, and at the Lingo Livery Stable, first-class Western grub is accompanied by live bluegrass music. An Oregon Trail display graces the stable's first floor. Historic Ward-Meade Park is located at 124 Fillmore Street, and the office is open from 8:00 A.M. to 5:00 P.M. daily, with tours offered at 11:00 A.M. and 2:00 P.M. Call (913) 368–3888 for further details.

Special Oregon Trail tours can be arranged by reservation at the park, or do-it-yourselfers can call the Topeka Visitors Bureau at (913) 234–1030 and request a copy of *Following the Oregon Trail in Shawnee County, Kansas.* Those wanting to dig deeper should call or visit the **Kansas Center for Historical Research** (913–296–3251), at 120 West Tenth Street.

Midway between Topeka and Lawrence, at Big Springs, the living-history **Sereneta Farms** conjures images of the old Oregon Trail. Staffers don pioneer clothes and tractors pull visitors in covered prairie schooners across open grasslands, where Oregon Trail wagon ruts can be seen. A lip-smacking prairie meal is served along the way, with mealside entertainment that can include a Native American storyteller, pioneer dancers, or live cowboy crooners. The ninety-minute Adventure Tour is offered Wednesday through Saturday at 10:00 A.M. and 5:00 P.M.; the site is open to visitors from 10:00 A.M. to 5:00 P.M. Wednesday through Saturday and 1:00 to 5:00 P.M. Sunday. For more information call (913) 887–6660.

Organized or self-guided tours to Oregon Trail sites in and around Lawrence can be arranged by contacting the Visitors Bureau at (913) 865–4497. Tours include a visit to **Blue Mound,** an important campsite that is considered the first natural landmark for Oregon Trail travelers. Request the brochure entitled *The Oregon Trail through Lawrence, Kansas.*

Local playwright and actress Kay Kuhlmann performs the captivating *Daughters of Courage: Stories from the Oregon Trail.* Her one-woman play, derived from diaries of women who traveled the trail, is performed exclusively for groups by reservation, often during luncheons and dinners. Call the Visitors Bureau for details.

Old West Lawrence, found on Louisiana Street between Sixth and Eighth streets, boasts the town's best turn-of-the-century architecture, and the nearby **Watkins Community Museum,** at 1047 Massachusetts Avenue, includes Oregon Trail exhibits. The museum is open Tuesday through Saturday from 10:00 A.M. to 4:00 P.M. and Sunday from 1:30 to 4:00 P.M.

The **Shawnee Methodist Mission** (913–262–0867), although not along the Oregon Trail proper, was visited by hundreds of emigrants and for many was the last sign of white civilization they encountered before Oregon. Three of the original brick buildings still stand at the twelve-acre state park, located in Shawnee (suburban Kansas City) at 3403 West Fifty-third Street and open Tuesday through Saturday from 10:00 A.M. to 5:00 P.M. and Sunday from 1:00 to 5:00 P.M. Also visit **Old Shawnee Town** (913–268–8772), three blocks west of Nieman on Fifty-seventh Street. Both it and the mission are open Tuesday through Saturday from 10:00 A.M. to 5:00 P.M. and on Sunday afternoons.

The **Bill Pickett Invitational Black Rodeo** (913–472–8900) roars into Kansas City at the end of September. A salute to the Buffalo Soldiers and black cowboys, the rodeo is named after America's most famous black cowboy. After retiring from the 101 Ranch Wild West Show, where he rode with Tom Mix and Will Rogers, Pickett ambled on out to Hollywood and starred in several movies.

The Sante Fe Trail

Travel along the Santa Fe Trail, which spanned the rugged 800 miles between Independence, Missouri, and Santa Fe, began in 1822 and continued until 1880, when the railroad reached Santa Fe. The trail carried millions of dollars worth of goods to Santa Fe, the capital of a Mexican province with abundant natural resources but virtually no manufacturing. The heaviest use occurred in 1860, when a government survey noted 3,000 wagons, 7,000 people, and 60,000 mules along the route. More than half of the trail was within Kansas.

In Lenexa, in southern suburban Kansas City, visit the 1864 **Legler Barn Museum,** a beautiful limestone-and-timber structure that houses an array of nineteenth-century goodies. Guests at the place included scores of Santa Fe Trail travelers and an individual named Jesse James. Adjacent to the museum, the recently restored **Lenexa Depot** houses railroading and other early transportation memorabilia. The venerable pair of buildings, located on the 14900 block of West Eighty-seventh Street, are open Tuesday through Saturday from 10:00 A.M. to 4:00 P.M. and Sunday from 1:00 to 4:00 P.M. Call (913) 492–0038 for information. Restored **Old Town Lenexa**

(913–888–6570), on Santa Fe Trail Drive, includes a general store, restaurants, and antiques shops.

The **Mahaffie Farmstead & Stagecoach Stop** is located at 1100 Old Kansas City Road in Olathe. The Santa Fe and Oregon trails converged here, and the 1865 landmark was important to those people who traveled both trails. Three structures here are listed on the Historic Register: J. B. Mahaffie's stone house, an ice house, and a wooden-peg barn. It's open in summer, Wednesday through Sunday from 1:00 to 5:00 P.M. and, the rest of the year, Monday through Friday from 1:00 to 5:00 P.M. Call (913) 782–6972 for information.

At the **Prairie Center** catch a fleeting glimpse of wind-whipped tallgrass prairie not unlike that which covered thousands of acres of Kansas when the emigrants filed through. The park, at 26235 West 135th Street, includes a campground, displays interpreting the natural history of the tall-grass prairie, and miles of recreational trails. Call (913) 856–7669 for information.

Immediately southwest of Olathe, at a point near Gardner, the Santa Fe and Oregon trails parted company: ROAD TO OREGON, read a solitary sign on the right-hand fork. The Oregon Trail headed northwest through present Lawrence, the Santa Fe southwest through Baldwin City. Santa Fe Trail artifacts are displayed there, at the **Old Castle Museum Complex's** Palmyra Post Office and Bloods Grocery, businesses that served hundreds of Santa Fe Trail travelers between 1857 and 1862. The complex (913–594–6451) is on the campus of Baker University.

Council Grove, brimming with history, was established in a timbered Flint Hills valley in the mid-1800s. Seth Hays, a government-licensed trader with adventure in his genes—he was a grandson of Daniel Boone and cousin of Kit Carson—arrived on the scene in 1847 to do business with several thousand Kaw (or Kansa) Indians who had been recently relocated here by the government.

The **Kaw Methodist Mission,** now housing a museum run by the state historical society, was built in 1851 as a boarding school for Kaw Indian boys, a purpose it served for only three years. The museum, on Mission Street, is open Tuesday through Saturday from 10:00 A.M. to 5:00 P.M. and Sunday from 1:00 to 5:00 P.M. Call (316) 767–5410 for information. The **Last Chance Store,** built in 1857, for a short time was the last chance for Santa Fe–bound freighters to obtain supplies. It's located at Main and Chautauqua streets.

350

Don't miss dining at the **Hays House,** built in 1857 by town founder Seth Hays. It's considered both the oldest continuously run restaurant west of the Mississippi and one of the finest eateries in Kansas. Photographs and artifacts are displayed in the building, which, through time, also has served as a post office, tavern, church, and publishing house for the town's first newspaper. Old West fare is served from 6:00 A.M. until 9:00 P.M. Sunday through Thursday and until 9:30 P.M. on Friday and 10:00 P.M. on Saturday. (All closing times are a half-hour earlier November through March.)

To continue basking in Council Grove's abundant nineteenth-century atmosphere, hole up at **The Cottage House,** which started life in 1867 as a cottage and blacksmith shop. Then in 1871 a two-story brick house swallowed the cottage, and a 5,000-square-foot Queen Anne addition in the early 1880s marked the final major alteration. Recently renovated, the place offers twenty-six rooms of various shapes and decors, with antiques and lace curtains found throughout. The Cottage House (316–767–6828) is located at 25 North Neosho.

Special events fill the calendar year at Council Grove, including the week-long **Santa Fe Trail Ride** in June and the **Voices of the Wind People** historical pageant in late September. For a complete listing of events and a guide map to the numerous historical sites, call the Visitors Bureau at (316) 767–5882.

In Lyons, 115 miles west on Highway 56, the **Coronado–Quivira Museum** (316–257–3941) commemorates the 1541 Coronado Expedition, which found its way as far north and east as this part of Kansas. The museum, also featuring Santa Fe Trail relics and murals by noted regional artist Stan Herd, is open Monday through Saturday from 9:00 A.M. to 5:00 P.M. and Sunday from 1:00 to 5:00 P.M.

Thirty miles west of Lyons on Highway 56, Great Bend's **Barton County Historical Village and Museum** (316–793–5125), on South Main Street, includes an 1871 rock house and Santa Fe Trail and Native American artifacts. It's open April through November, Tuesday through Sunday from 1:00 to 5:00 P.M. Thirteen miles southwest of Great Bend is **Pawnee Rock State Monument,** a primary Santa Fe Trail landmark. The rock was substantially higher—estimates range from between 40 and 70 feet—until pioneer settlers chipped away at it for building materials.

In nearby Larned (23 miles southwest of Great Bend on Highway 56) the **Santa Fe Trail Days,** with its bustle of living-history action, takes place over Memorial Day weekend; call the Chamber of Commerce at (316) 285–6916 for details. Two miles west of Larned on Highway 156, the **Santa Fe Trail Center** (316–285–2054) is dedicated exclusively to studying and illuminating the complex history of the Santa Fe Trail. It's open from 9:00 A.M. to 5:00 P.M. seven days a week. Four miles farther west is **Fort Larned National Historic Site,** guardian of the Santa Fe Trail, established in 1859. Soldiers stationed at the post served to protect those people who moved goods and mail and, later, settlers and railroad-building crews. Nine buildings of timber and sandstone—built in 1868 to replace the original, crumbling adobes—remain, restored to near-original condition. An old barracks houses the visitor center, with its extensive museum collections and sales outlet that features books and "pioneer" toys for the kids.

On summer weekends from 9:30 A.M. to 4:30 P.M., costumed rangers and volunteers interpret topics such as early military weapons and the everyday lives of the Buffalo Soldiers and others stationed at the windy, isolated, and gritty fort. Fort Larned is open daily from 8:00 A.M. to 6:00 P.M.; call (316) 285–6911 for more information.

Fort Dodge (316–227–2121), situated along the Santa Fe Trail 5 miles east of Dodge City, was established in 1865. Since 1890 it has served as the Kansas Soldiers' Home, and today it also includes a history museum/library, open Monday through Saturday from 10:00 A.M. to 4:00 P.M. and on Sundays from 1:00 to 4:00 P.M.

Dodge City, the haunt of legends like Wyatt Earp and Bat Masterson, has been called variously through time the "Queen of the Cowtowns," the "Wickedest Little City in the West," and the "Beautiful Bibulous Babylon of the Frontier." When the railroad reached Dodge in 1872, its future as a trade and transport center was sealed, and nearly a million buffalo hides were shipped east during the next two years. By 1875 the bison were largely eradicated, but Texas longhorn cattle took their place—some five million of them were driven by cowboys up the Western Trail from Texas to Dodge City over the course of the ensuing decade.

By 1886 the cattle drives had ended, but the legend of Dodge City was indelibly etched on the record of Western lore. **Boot Hill Museum,** at the site of the old Boot Hill cemetery in downtown Dodge at Front and Fifth streets, includes a reconstructed **1876 Dodge City.** At the **Long Branch Saloon,** visitors explore the Life of a Cowboy exhibit; during the daytime in summer, they take in **Prof. P. Q. Montgomery's Medicine Show** and,

Buffalo City

With good cause Dodge City was originally known as Buffalo City. Santa Fe Trail caravans passing through the area were sometimes stalled by herds of bison that numbered in the tens of thousands, and it was reported that the endless mass of shaggy beasts, when fording the Arkansas River, sounded like a continuous waterfall.

Buffalo hats, coats, and blankets were already immensely fashionable when, in 1871, an East Coast tanner perfected a method for turning bison hides into high-grade leather. Now boots and machinery belting could be made of the animal's skin. Buffalo hunting by the whites exploded, and hundreds of professional and amateur gunmen poured into western Kansas. An average hunter-skinner team could readily kill and process several dozen bison per day; one hunter, Tom Nixon, bragged that he had bagged 120 in a span of forty minutes at a single stand—and a total of 2,173 in less than five weeks.

Mountains of buffalo tongues, steaks, and hides lined the new Santa Fe Railroad tracks in newly named Dodge City. Buffalo money made the town rich, crazy rich; before the end of the 1870s, however, wanton greed had taken its toll: The magnificent Monarch of the Plains had been virtually eliminated from his former domain, and his bones lay bleaching in the sun, scattered about the hot, dry prairie.

if brave enough, sample his amazing cure-all, Prickly Ash Bitters. There are also the **Dodge City & Panhandle Stage Line** stagecoach rides and gunfight reenactments at 9:00 A.M., noon, and 3:00 P.M. In the evenings Boot Hill boasts Western chuckwagon dinners from 5:30 to 7:30 P.M. and the **Long Branch Saloon Variety Show,** featuring Miss Kitty and her Can Can Girls (reservations required).

Boot Hill Museum (316–227–8188) is open from 8:00 A.M. to 8:00 P.M. daily in summer and, the rest of the year, from 9:00 A.M. to 5:00 P.M. Monday through Saturday and from 1:00 to 5:00 P.M. on Sunday. The parking area is just off Wyatt Earp Boulevard between First and Second streets. Located nearby, within the Kansas Teachers' Hall of Fame at 603 Fifth Street, is the **Gunfighters Wax Museum** (316–225–7311), with its lifelike figures of good guys and bad alike. It's open April through November 8:30

Front Street of Old Dodge City at the Boot Hill Museum

A.M. to 6:00 P.M. Monday through Saturday and 1:00 to 5:00 P.M. Sunday.

The **DCF&B Railroad** (Dodge City, Ford & Bucklin) offers a 16-mile round-trip excursion through "the land of cowboys, Indians, and outlaws," with meals served on board in the dining car. The train pulls out of Dodge at 10:00 A.M. daily from Watersports Campground (follow Second Avenue south across the river and turn east onto Sycamore Street). Special dinner trips run on Friday and Saturday nights at 7:00; call (316) 225-3232 for reservations, which are required.

The brochure *Dodge City, Santa Fe Trail, Fort Dodge Walking/Driving Tour* is available at the Visitor Information Center (316-225-8186) in the Boot Hill parking lot. The tour leads to numerous sites in and outside of Dodge, including a prominent set of Santa Fe Trail tracks west of town and the spot where Coronado is believed to have crossed the Arkansas River on his 1541 expedition.

Dodge City Days, held every August, celebrates the town's past and present, with events that range from turtle races and barbecue cook-offs to street dances, cowboy-poetry readings, and PRCA (Professional Rodeo Cowboys Association) rodeo action. Call (316) 227-3119 for information.

West of Dodge, near the present site of Ingalls, the Santa Fe Trail split into the Dry Route and the more northerly Mountain Branch. The 1892 Santa Fe Railway depot in Ingalls today houses the **Santa Fe Trail**

Museum of Gray County (316–335–5220), open between May and October on Monday through Saturday from 9:00 to 11:00 A.M. and 1:00 to 4:00 P.M. and on Sunday from 2:00 to 5:00 P.M.

In Garden City, along the Mountain Branch of the Santa Fe Trail, the **Finney County Historical Museum** (316–272–3664) at Finnup Park includes a display on the trail's route through the county. The museum is open in summer Monday through Saturday from 10:00 A.M. to 5:00 P.M. and Sunday from 1:00 to 5:00 P.M.; in winter it's open daily from 2:00 to 5:00 P.M. Also of note is the **Finney County Wildlife Area,** south of Garden City on Highway 83, where prairie animals, including a herd of several dozen bison, roam free. It's open year-round, Monday through Friday from 8:00 A.M. to 5:00 P.M.

The Smoky Hill Trail

The Smoky Hill Trail, which served as the shortest route to the Colorado gold fields for many would-be prospectors, runs north of and roughly parallel to the Santa Fe Trail. From Garden City wend your way up to the trail at Wallace, via Scott City. Twelve miles north of Scott City is **El Cuartalejo State Park,** site of the Pueblo Indians' northeasternmost settlement (it was occupied by Taos Indians between 1650 and 1720) and also the first white settlement in Kansas. Call the Chamber of Commerce at (316) 872–3525 for more information.

In Wallace the **Fort Wallace Museum** commemorates "the fightin'est fort in the West." Established as Camp Pond Creek, about a mile south of present-day Wallace, the fort was later moved to a site farther east along the Smoky River. The old post cemetery, fenced off within the Wallace Township cemetery, is all that remains of the fort. The museum (913–891–3564), which includes the original Pond Creek Stage Station and an old Union Pacific depot, is open from early May through September, Monday through Saturday from 9:00 A.M. to 5:00 P.M. and Sunday from 1:00 to 5:00 P.M.

East of Wallace near Russell Springs, the **Butterfield Stage Museum** (913–751–4242) occupies the 1887 Logan County Courthouse. The museum houses a historical research center and displays on the area's past; it's open Memorial Day through Labor Day, Tuesday through Saturday from 9:00 A.M. to noon and Sunday from 1:00 to 5:00 P.M.

From Quinter, en route to Hays, a detour 20 miles north on Highway

24 leads to Studley and the nearby **Cottonwood Ranch.** The site, run by the state historical society, is a full-scale, 1880s living-history farm based on the sheep ranch established here in 1885 by English immigrant John Fenton Pratt. The ranch is open Wednesday through Sunday from 10:00 A.M. to 5:00 P.M.; call (913) 627–5866 for further details.

Hays, founded when the Union Pacific Railway arrived in 1867, rapidly burgeoned into a gathering place for buffalo hunters, Indian scouts, and soldiers. At **Historic Fort Hays,** built to provide travelers with protection from the Indians, you'll find an old hexagonal stone blockhouse, stone guardhouse, and frame-construction officers' quarters. The history of the fort and of the town of Hays, once an unruly place where James B. "Wild Bill" Hickok served a stint as sheriff, is interpreted in the visitor center. Also on the grounds is the **Monarch of the Plains,** an immense sculpture of a bison, the animal once so abundant on the Kansas plains. **Pioneer Days,** held at the fort in September, features mock attacks and demonstrations of pioneer skills, including horseshoeing, rope making, and post-rock cutting. The park is open Tuesday through Saturday from 9:00 A.M. to 5:00 P.M. and Sunday and Monday from 1:00 to 5:00 P.M. Call (913) 625–6812 for information.

The **Ellis County Historical Museum** (913–628–2624), at 100 West Seventh Street, features more than 25,000 artifacts relating to life in a young Ellis County. It is open Monday through Friday from 9:00 A.M. to noon and from 1:00 to 4:00 P.M. and on weekends from 1:00 to 5:00 P.M. The old **Boot Hill Cemetery**—the first cemetery so-named in Kansas, Hays residents are quick to point out—is found at Eighteenth and Fort streets.

A couple of comprehensive tour guides are available for the asking by calling the Convention and Visitors Bureau at (913) 628–8202: *Hays— Where History Walks the Streets* and *Hays and Northwest Kansas,* which leads the way on four historic driving tours in the region. One of these leads to LaCrosse, 30 miles south of Hays, and its unique **Barbed Wire Museum.** The museum, situated in the Chamber of Commerce offices at 120 West First Street, displays more than 500 varieties of the "Devil's Wire," which was so important to the settling of the West, as well as related items such as fencing tools. The museum (913–222–9900) is open Monday through Saturday from 10:00 A.M. to 4:30 P.M. and Sunday from 1:00 to 4:30 P.M.

Brookville, 6 miles south of Interstate 70 at exit 238, is home to the historic **Brookville Hotel.** Originally known as the Cowtown Cafe, it was built in the 1870s, when the town served as a cattle-shipping railhead. Famous since 1915 for its home-style Brookville Chicken Dinners, the place discontinued its hotel service in 1972 and shortly thereafter added its Homestead Dining Room. Jam-packed with antiques and old artifacts, the eatery is open Tuesday through Friday from 5:00 to 8:30 P.M., Saturday from 4:00 to 8:30 P.M., and Sunday from 11:00 A.M. to 7:30 P.M. Reservations are recommended; call (913) 225–6666.

The Chisholm Trail

When the railroad first reached Abilene and entrepreneur Joseph G. McCoy chose it as the site for his new stockyards, the town claimed only 300 people. It quickly mushroomed to 3,000 and boasted the largest stockyards west of Kansas City, several hotels and mercantiles, and dozens of saloons. More than three million head of cattle came to railhead here between 1867 and 1872, and the hundreds of cowboys who drove them along the dusty Chisholm Trail finally got to let go and whoop it up here—earning Abilene its reputation as one of the wildest of the 1800s Wild West towns.

The **Dickinson County Historical Museum** (913–263–2681), at 412 South Campbell, highlights the period of western expansion, including the cowtown era, and the slightly later time when Dwight D. Eisenhower grew to manhood in Abilene. The museum is open April through October on Monday through Friday from 11:00 A.M. to 8:00 P.M., Saturday from 10:00 A.M. to 8:00 P.M., and Sunday from 1:00 to 5:00 P.M.

An elaborate trio of Abilene's abundant Victorians are open for touring: the **Lebold-Vahsholtz Mansion,** at West First and Vine streets; the **Seelye Mansion,** at 1105 North Buckeye Street; and the **Kirby House** (913–263–7336), at 205 Northeast Third Street. Every day of the week lunch (11:00 A.M. to 2:00 P.M.) and dinner (5:00 to 9:00 P.M.) are served at the 1885 Kirby House, one of Abilene's most popular restaurants.

Begin your visit to Wichita at **Shepler's** (6501 West Kellogg; 316–946–3600; open 10:00 A.M. to 9:00 P.M. Monday through Saturday and noon to 6:00 P.M. Sunday), "the world's largest Western store," where you can get properly outfitted before rambling on down to the **Old Cowtown**

Museum, at 1871 Sim Park Drive. One of the premier places in the country to get a picture of life during the days of westward expansion, Old Cowtown brings back Wichita and Sedgwick County of the late 1800s, with more than forty original, restored, and replicated buildings spread over seventeen sprawling acres along the Arkansas River. Included at the major site is the **Empire House Restaurant** where, Thursday through Sunday evenings, a bodacious buffet dinner precedes old-fashioned, family-flavored melodrama performances. The Empire House is also open for lunch from 11:00 A.M. until 2:00 P.M. Monday through Saturday. Call (316) 263–0222 for information about the old Cowtown Museum or reservations at the Empire House.

Also visit the fully stocked general store, the saddle and harness shop, and the Munger House, the first log house and hotel in Wichita. Lectures, events—such as the **Old Sedgwick County Fair**—and living-history demonstrations occur throughout the year at Old Cowtown. It's open daily March through October on Monday through Saturday from 10:00 A.M. to 5:00 P.M., on Sunday from noon to 5:00 P.M., and on weekends the remainder of the year. For more information call (316) 264–0671.

Two additional museums are found along the Arkansas, near Old Cowtown. Located in the arrowhead-shaped Mid-America All-Indian Center, the **Indian Center Museum** features permanent collections that demonstrate the diversity of Native American culture and traditions, with displays on Plains, Southwest and Northwest Coast Indians, and Eskimos. The gift shop sells arts and crafts designed and created by Indians throughout North America. On the grounds, at the confluence of the Big and Little Arkansas, the *Keeper of the Plains* stands sentinel. The 44-foot, five-ton sculpture is the work of the late Kiowa-Comanche artist Blackbear Bosin. The museum (316–262–5221) is open Tuesday through Saturday from 10:00 A.M. to 5:00 P.M. and Sunday from 1:00 to 5:00 P.M. Nearby the **Wichita Art Museum** (316–268–4921) includes among its collection original works by Western artists Frederic Remington and Charles M. Russell. It's open Tuesday through Saturday from 10:00 A.M. to 5:00 P.M. and Sunday from noon to 5:00 P.M.

The **North American Prairie Exhibit,** situated within the immensely popular Sedgwick County Zoo, is home to critters of the frontier West. Grizzly bears, pronghorn, bison, Mexican wolves, eagles, prairie reptiles, and more can be seen on a walk through the prairie preserve, much of it along an elevated boardwalk. The loud and lively prairie-dog town, *Prairie Queen* boat ride, and Prairie Landing Restaurant (specializing in barbecue) are some of the highlights of a visit to this world-class exhibit. The zoo (316–942–2213) is located at 5555 Zoo Boulevard.

For more information on Wichita, contact the Convention & Visitors Bureau at (316) 265–2800.

The three-day **Flint Hills Overland Wagon Train Trips** depart from the cattle town of Cassoday, 40 miles northeast of Wichita. The trip offers perhaps the best way to learn to appreciate the Kansas prairie as experienced by the pioneers. On this paradox-filled tour, you'll travel by both bus and covered wagon, you'll sleep under a roof and under the stars, and you'll stray way off the beaten track but also visit sites in bustling Wichita. Old-time musical entertainment and hearty, campfire-cooked grub add final touches to this unforgettable outing. The cost is $205.00 per person. Call (316) 321–6300 to make arrangements.

More than 150,000 prospective homesteaders participated in America's largest land rush when the Cherokee Outlet territory was open. In Arkansas City, 30 miles west of Caldwell, the **Cherokee Strip Land Rush Museum** features memorabilia of the strip country. It is open year-round from 10:00 A.M. to 4:00 P.M. Tuesday through Saturday and 1:00 to 4:00 P.M. on Sunday. Call (316) 442–6750 for information.

Where to Eat

Prairie Crossings, Topeka, (913) 368–3888
Hays House, Council Grove, (316) 767–5911
Brookville Hotel, Brookville, (913) 225–6666
Kirby House, Abilene, (913) 263–7336
Empire House Restaurant, Wichita, (316) 263–0222
Flint Hills Overland Wagon Train Trips, Cassoday, (316) 321–6300

Where to Stay

Cottage House, Council Grove, (316) 767–6828

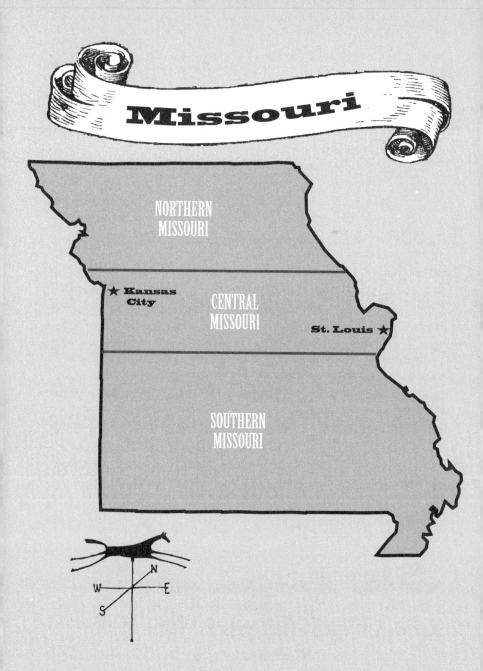

Missouri

NORTHERN MISSOURI

★ Kansas City

CENTRAL MISSOURI

St. Louis ★

SOUTHERN MISSOURI

N
W E
S

MISSOURI

▼▼▼

ISSOURI isn't in the West, so what's it doing here? Well, the Lewis and Clark expedition set out from here, as did those individuals who traveled the Oregon, California, Santa Fe, and Pony Express trails. It's estimated that by 1848, still early in the western migration, some 12,000 people had settled in Oregon, and one in four of them was born in Missouri. Frontiersmen Daniel Boone, Jim Bridger, and John C. Frémont all lived parts of their lives here, and the Rev. Pierre-Jean DeSmet, one of the first Jesuit missionaries to go west to spread the gospel among the Plains Indians, was from Missouri. So was "America's Cowboy Artist," Charlie Russell. Enough said?

The narrative begins with a meandering pass through southern Missouri; then, beginning at St. Louis, it heads west through central Missouri along the Missouri River, where most of the state's history directly related to western expansion is found. Finally, it winds up by making a quick swing through northern Missouri.

Southern Missouri

The **Laura Ingalls Wilder Historic Home** is located in Mansfield, 50 miles east of Springfield. Wilder and her husband, Almanzo, and their daughter, the future novelist Rose Wilder Lane, moved here to the Rocky Ridge Farm in 1894. It's where Laura penned the nine *Little House* books, which describe her family's experiences while farming in the Dakotas during the late nineteenth century. The home, located just east of Mansfield on Highway A, is open from 9:00 A.M. to 5:00 P.M. Monday through Saturday and 12:30 to 5:30 P.M. Sunday from April though November; call (417) 924–3626 for information.

Branson, 70 miles southwest of Mansfield, is a spot everyone should visit once. Don't go there if you want to get away from it all, however, for it's so bustling that it seems everyone *is* visiting, and all at once. Branson has recently become a magnet for musical entertainers, from the Osmond Brothers and Japanese violinist Shoji Tabuchi to Mr. Las Vegas himself, Wayne Newton.

There's a lot of hillbilly music available in Branson, and some fine country sounds, too—theater owners in the area include Roy Clark and Mel Tillis, to drop only a couple of names. The pickins' are slimmer for true Western music, however; one of your best regular bets is Boxcar Willie and the Texas Trainmen, who play the **Boxcar Willie Theatre** (417–334–8696) on West Highway 76.

Long before Nashville and Las Vegas merged in Branson, **Silver Dollar City** brought thousands of visitors to the area. The re-created 1890s setting features a Pioneer Village, complete with grist mill, candy factory, and blacksmith shop. The Frisco–Silver Dollar Line steam train, old-fashioned food, and "lost" crafts demonstrations are other highlights. There's even a Thunderation roller coaster that passes through an underground mine (well, okay, maybe everything isn't realistic Old West, but it's all fun!). Live music regularly resounds at Silver Dollar City, open daily late May through late October and weekends in April, early May, November, and December. Call (417) 336–7100 for information.

Travel to **Prairie State Park** (417–843–6711), some 30 miles north of Joplin, a 3,000-acre remnant of the tall-grass prairie that formerly blanketed much of the Midwest. Native grasses and animals, including bison and prairie chickens, thrive. Next, from the town of Nevada (northeast of Prairie State Park), turn east and go 8 miles on Highway 54, then north on Highway C for 11 miles. Two miles east on a gravel road is the **Osage Village State Historic Site**; between 1700 and 1777, when the earliest Europeans came into the area, it was the site of a large Osage Indian village.

To the north and west of the Indian village is the town of Butler, where the **Bates County Museum of Pioneer History** occupies the former Bates County Jail. Featured are sixteen rooms, spread over three floors and brimming with regional memorabilia—hand tools, musical instruments, furniture, glassware, dolls, photographs—you can just about name it and you'll see it. Beyond the old jail are a turn-of-the-century log cabin, housing some of Daniel Boone's belongings and exhibits of pioneer clothing, an early-day print shop, a harness shop, and a sorghum mill. The museum is located a block southeast of downtown, at 100 East Fort Scott. It's open May through September on Sunday, Monday, Thursday, and Friday from 1:00 to 5:00 P.M. and on Saturday from 10:00 A.M. to 5:00 P.M. Call (816) 679–4777 for information.

Head east to Warsaw, perched on the eastern edge of expansive Harry S. Truman Reservoir. Here the **J & S Old West Museum** (816–438–2631), at 1038 East Main, displays antique riding saddles, Indian artifacts, cavalry gear, cowboying tack, and more. The **Kumberland Gap Pioneer Settlement** living-history village is north of town on Highways 65, T, and TT. A grist mill, restored log cabins, blacksmith shop, and general store are some of what you'll find at the settlement, open May through October.

Central Missouri

St. Louis's **Gateway Arch**—America's tallest monument, which was designed by architect Eero Saarinen—is the epicenter of the ninety-seven-acre **Jefferson National Expansion Memorial.** First take the obligatory and remarkable ride in a five-person capsule up one of the legs of the arch to the viewing room, 630 feet above the St. Louis riverfront, and gaze out upon the spot where the West symbolically began.

Situated beneath the arch, the **Museum of Westward Expansion** offers a fascinating look back to the days of Lewis and Clark and the mountain men, soldiers, and pioneers who traveled from St. Louis into the great western frontier. Exhibits that focus on Native Americans, cowboys, frontier transportation, and the guns that won the West are on view, too. The grand **Old Courthouse,** also within the park, includes numerous displays that trace the development of the United States and regularly offers showings of the educational film *Time of the West.* The associated Arch Museum Shop stocks a large selection of books and Western mementos.

The Jefferson National Expansion Memorial is open daily year-round from 8:00 A.M. to 10:00 P.M. between Memorial Day and Labor Day and from 9:00 A.M. to 6:00 P.M. the remainder of the year. Call (314) 982–1410 or 425–4465 for more information.

Other area must-sees include the **Missouri Historical Society's History Museum** (314–746–4559), housed in the Jefferson Memorial

Building in Forest Park, just west of downtown and north off Interstate 64. The comprehensive state repository, open year-round, includes exhibits on

Gateway to the West

S te. Genevieve, 50 miles south of St. Louis, survived as the sole settlement in the upper Louisiana Territory for some thirty years, until Pierre Laclède established his fur-trading post in 1764 at the confluence of the mighty Missouri and Mississippi rivers.

At this time the Louisiana Territory was ruled by Spain: Although originally claimed for France by LaSalle in 1682, the Spanish assumed rule for forty years beginning in 1762. The territory was secretly ceded back to the powerful French, however, in 1802, but Napoleon Bonaparte considered it a troublesome frontier and quickly unloaded it to the United States for $15 million in 1803.

One country's junk is another's gold; the Louisiana Purchase doubled the land mass of the United States, and President Thomas Jefferson wasted no time in having the region inspected. The Missouri River offered the most obvious route leading west, and so St. Louis became the Gateway to the West when Jefferson dispatched his Corps of Discovery—led by William Clark and Meriwether Lewis—from there in 1804.

the western frontier and the role St. Louis played in opening it. Hours are 9:30 A.M. to 5:00 P.M. Tuesday through Saturday.

The **Taille de Noyer Home** (314–524–1100), at the northern edge of the St. Louis metro area in Florissant, began life as a log-cabin fur-trading post in 1790, and ultimately grew into the seventeen-room mansion of millionaire John Mullanphy. Located at 1896 South Florissant Road, it is open year-round. **The John B. Myers House and Barn** (314–837–7661), at 180 West Dunn Road, is an 1870s complex, now housing quilt, weaving, antiques and craft shops, and a deli. The **Museum of Western Jesuit Missions** (314–837–3525 or 361–5122), situated at 700 Howdershell Road, illuminates the history of the Black Robes, some of the earliest white men to travel west and associate with the Plains and mountain Indians.

St. Charles, northwest of and across the Missouri River from St. Louis, features a historic downtown with a wealth of restaurants and antiques and gift shops. The **Lewis and Clark Center** (314–947–3199), at 701 Riverside Drive in the town that served as Missouri's first capital, includes exhibits on the intrepid duo and their equally adventuresome party members, as well as an extensive collection of Native American artifacts. A recent addition focuses on St. Charles's unique role in outfitting the Lewis and Clark expedition and includes an "1804 store," filled with the sorts of items the Corps of Discovery would have stocked up on before leaving town.

The **Lewis and Clark Rendezvous** (314–946–7776) kicks off annually in May in St. Charles, with a reenactment of the party's departure presented at Frontier Park; the Buckskinners Ball and black-powder shoot are two of the many other events involved. Those fond of exploring nature and history while hiking, jogging, or cycling should check out the **KATY Trail,** which follows the old Missouri-Kansas-Texas (MKT) Railroad right of way. Work is ongoing on the trail, considered a state treasure that ultimately will span 200 miles of central Missouri, beginning in St. Charles.

Historic inns and B&Bs have proliferated in the greater St. Louis area: for one, the **Boone's Lick Trail Inn,** at 1000 Main Street in St. Charles's historic district, where guests sleep on nineteenth-century beds beneath old quilts and surrounded by antiques. The inn (314–947–7000) features five rooms and one suite, all with private baths. For a listing of many more possibilities, call the River Country Bed & Breakfast Association at (314) 771–1993.

No name typifies the American frontiersman more than that of Daniel Boone, the "fighting Quaker." Near Defiance, west of St. Louis on the north side of the Missouri, you can visit the **Daniel Boone Home,** where the trailblazer, Indian fighter, scout, trapper, surveyor, judge, and West Virginia state legislator died in 1820 at age eighty-six. Boone came to the area in 1799 to serve as governor of the then-Spanish-held Missouri territory. Here in the pastoral Femme Osage Valley, he built his final home. It's surely no mountain-man shack; rather it's a limestone mansion, with walls 2½ feet thick, filled today with memorabilia from the Boone family. Nearing completion is the associated **Boonesfield Village,** a full-blown living-history settlement complete with log homes and an at-work blacksmith, cabinet maker, tinsmith, and muzzle-loading rifle smith. The attraction, located on Highway F outside Defiance (signs guide the way), is open for touring daily between March 15 and November 15 from 9:00 A.M. to 5:00 P.M. Call (314) 987–2221 for information.

Head for Jefferson City—en route passing through a string of historic river towns, including Marthasville and the German settlement of Hermann—where you can visit the **Jefferson Landing State Historic Site.** Situated between the State Capitol and the historic Governor's Mansion, the mid-1800s river-trade complex comprises three buildings, including a visitors center that is open daily year-round. Call (573) 751–2854 for information.

In Columbia, 30 miles north of Jefferson City, hit the **State Historical Society of Missouri** library, found on the ground floor of the east wing of the University of Missouri–Columbia's Ellis Library building, at the corner of Hitt and Rollins. Among the bonanzas here for those visitors who want to delve into a particular subject is the Newspaper Library, housing the largest state collection of newspapers in the nation. Newspapers, now mostly on microfilm, date from 1808 to the present. Historic journals, photographs, scrapbooks, and letters are on file, too. The facility is open from 8:00 A.M. to 4:30 P.M. Monday through Friday and from 9:00 A.M. to 4:30 P.M. on Saturday. The society also sells numerous publications that relate to westward expansion. Call (573) 751–2854 for information.

Go west along Highway 40 and pass through quaint Rocheport, once an active riverboat town and now an antiquing mecca. The town is home to numerous historic buildings, including the unique **School House Bed and Breakfast** (573–698–2022), at Third and Clark streets. The **Friends of Rocheport Museum** (573–698–3701), at First and Moniteau streets, displays an extensive collection of historical photographs and other memorabilia.

When passing through Boonville, 12 miles west of Rocheport, visit the **Old Cooper County Jail & Hanging Barn** located at 614 East Morgan. It's open Memorial Day through Labor Day. **Arrow Rock State Historic Site,** where the Santa Fe Trail crossed the wide Missouri, is found 11 miles northwest of Boonville on Highway 41. This National Historic Landmark features a walking tour that leads to a dozen historic buildings, many of them retaining their early-day appearance. Included are the 1830s home of the famous artist George Caleb Bingham, a courthouse dating from the 1820s, and the 1873 jail. The **Old Tavern,** built in 1834 and added onto in subsequent years, has been renovated into a very popular restaurant, which serves traditional country-style meals. Call (816) 837–3200 or 837–3330 for reservations and business hours, which change with the seasons. The village opens daily Memorial Day through Labor Day, with tours given at 11:00 A.M. and at 1:30 and 3:00 P.M. It's open only on weekends during spring and fall.

The adjacent portion of Arrow Rock that is not encompassed by the state park also boasts several historic eateries and accommodations. Call (816) 837–3231 for a listing and for information on the numerous annual events, including the very popular **Arrow Rock Crafts Fair,** held in early October.

When in town also take in the fascinating **John P. Sites, Jr., Pioneer Gunshop,** located between High and Main streets. Sites, born in Virginia in 1821, set up shop as a gunsmith in Arrow Rock in 1844. His timing coincided with the great westward migration; consequently, the shop became a major hub of weapons' outfitting and repair, and his firearms have been found in every state west of the Mississippi. Three of his now-priceless rifles are owned by the Friends of Arrow Rock group and are on display at the museum.

Fabulous **Fort Osage** is found in Sibley, 3 miles north of Buckner on Highway BB. The fort, operational from 1808 until 1827, served as one of the first military outposts and trading houses in the Louisiana Territory. It was built under the direction of William Clark, not long back from his Corps of Discovery's expedition, for the purpose of enhancing trade and political relations with the Osage Indians. Living-history interpreters are on hand to offer insight into early military and civilian life at Fort Osage, which has been accurately reconstructed by using evidence uncovered in archaeological excavations. Special events held each year include the popular "An Expedition of Discovery."

Now step forward a few years in Missouri history at **Missouri Town 1855.** This pre–Civil War farming community, located in Blue Springs, sprawls over some thirty rolling acres on the east side of Lake Jacomo in Fleming Park, off the west end of Cowherd Road. The living-history museum comprises nearly forty buildings of 1820–1860 vintage, with period-attired interpreters who raise crops and tend livestock typical of the day. You'll also find a blacksmith, a housewife, merchants, and others going about their daily tasks. An opportune time to visit is during the bountiful **Fall Festival of Arts, Crafts & Music,** held in early October. Fort Osage and Missouri Town 1855 are both open between April 15 and November 14 Wednesday through Sunday from 9:00 A.M. to 5:00 P.M., and between November 21 and April 14, weekends only, from 9:00 A.M. to 5:00 P.M. Call (816) 795–8200, extension 260, for more information. In Independence, northwest of Blue Springs, follow the straightest path to the **National Frontier Trails Center,** at 318 West Pacific. The facility serves as an archives and interpretive center for the three premier westward-leading overland trails—the Santa Fe, Oregon, and California—all of which originated in or near Independence. Films and displays on the Lewis and Clark expedition and the fur-trapping mountain men, along with emigrants' artifacts, diary passages, and letters, help to produce vivid images of the days of westward expansion. The center is situated near a spring, where hundreds stocked up on water before striking out for the greener pastures of Oregon or the golder fields of California. It's open daily year-round; call (816) 325–7575 for information.

Learn about the Latter Day Saints' aborted plans to put down roots in Missouri—and their subsequent travels north to Illinois, then west to Utah—

Statue of a pioneer woman and child at the National Frontier Trails Center

at the museum at the **Mormon Visitors Center,** located at 937 West Walnut Street. In 1831 founder Joseph Smith designated the Independence area as the site for his new church's city of Zion, a city built on a foundation of righteous living and selfless cooperation. Zealots from New York and Ohio moved in; their controversial lifestyle, however, clashed with that of the traditional Southerners who had settled in the area before them. Persecution followed.

Through artifacts and artwork the center offers insight into what brought the Mormons to Missouri and what made them leave. Displays include a fully appointed frontier cabin. The center is open daily from 9:00 A.M. to 9:00 P.M., with free tours given throughout the day. Call (816) 836–3466 for information.

The Rage to Go West

From the January 22, 1841, Independence *Chronicle:*

The rage for emigration westward seems to be as great as ever—quite an enthusiasm is exhibited in every little knot of citizens we meet upon the street. . . . The young and old alike are anxious for frontier life; all seem to be on tiptoe for adventure. Some of them are even disposing of their farms, some of household furniture, and others of their merchandize [sic], preparatory to their departure for this fabled "land of promise."

Members of the James and Younger gangs were among the more infamous guests accommodated over the years at the **1859 Marshal's Home & Jail Museum.** The structures, accurately restored and featuring top-notch historical displays, are located at 217 North Main and are open year-round, except January, Monday through Saturday from 10:00 A.M. to 5:00 P.M. and Sunday from 1:00 to 4:00 P.M. Call (816) 252–1892 for information.

A glimpse at the opulent side of life in the late 1800s can be had at the remarkably lavish (some might say garish) thirty-room **Vaile Mansion.** Built in 1881 by U.S. mail contractor Harvey Vaile, the place includes a four-story tower and features ceiling murals and ornate furnishings throughout. Located at 1500 North Liberty, it's open for tours April through October and during the Christmas season. Call (573) 836–7111 for more information.

For a good map that shows directions to all these Independence sites and more—including several relating to Harry S. Truman, born in Lamar, Missouri, in 1884, when the West was still wild—call the Tourism

Department at (573) 325–7111 and request the brochure *Where the Trails Start and the Buck Stops.*

In Kansas City proper visit the **Alexander Majors Historic House and Park,** south of downtown at 8201 State Line Road. Majors, a partner in the powerful Russell, Majors, and Waddell freighting company—which owned, among other things, the Pony Express—was largely responsible for the growth of Kansas City and the opening of the West. His restored 1856 antebellum home, featuring the original white pine woodwork, is listed on the National Register of Historic Places. A collection of Conestoga freight wagons and buggies are also found at the site, open between April 1 and December 20 on Saturday and Sunday from 1:00 to 4:00 P.M. Call (816) 333–5556 for information.

An astounding array of booty recovered from a mid-1800s shipwreck is displayed under glass at the **Treasures of the Steamboat *Arabia*** museum. The "Great White *Arabia*" was carrying 130 people and 200 tons of supplies and headed for the frontier when she went down on September 5, 1856, at a location just north of Kansas City. The well-preserved cargo was unearthed at the site, left dry when the Missouri changed its course. The 1988 excavations revealed clothing, whiskey, rifles, beaver hats, appliances—nearly everything manufactured in the 1850s and used by pioneer settlers and miners on the Western frontier. Not everything is under glass; there are also a working, 28-foot paddle wheel and several hands-on exhibits at the museum, located at 400 Grand in the Historic River Market Area. It's open Monday through Saturday from 10:00 A.M. to 6:00 P.M. and Sunday from noon to 5:00 P.M. Call (816) 471–4030 for information.

The 200-acre **Benjamin Ranch,** off Interstate 435 at the East Eighty-seventh Street exit, offers trail rides, sleigh rides in winter, and barn parties that feature country cooking and good old down-home entertainment. It's also venue for the **K.C. Jaycee Pro Rodeo,** held during the Fourth of July week. Call (816) 761–5055 for information.

In Liberty, northeast of Kansas City, the **Jesse James Bank Museum** is the site of the first successful peacetime, daylight bank robbery in America. The culprits were never apprehended, but the notorious James and Younger gangs were assumed guilty. The bank office and vault, downtown at Water and Franklin streets, appear much as they did on the day of the robbery in 1866. The museum is open Monday through Saturday from 9:00 A.M. to 4:00 P.M.; call (816) 781–4458 for information.

One of the most famous men incarcerated at the **Historic Liberty Jail** (816–781–3188) was none other than Mormon Church founder Joseph Smith, who did time during the winter of 1838–1839. Exhibits and an audiovisual presentation relate the story of Smith's imprisonment, which precipitated the movement of thousands of Mormons first to Nauvoo, Illinois, and ultimately to Utah. The facility, located at 216 North Main Street, is open daily from 9:00 A.M. to 9:00 P.M., with tours provided by the proprietors, the Church of Jesus Christ of Latter Day Saints.

The **Jesse James Farm & Museum** near Kearney, north of Liberty, includes the restored family home where Frank and Jesse James grew up. The museum boasts the world's largest collection of James family memorabilia, as well as a gift shop that sells James-related goods. The home, 2 miles east of town on Highway 92 and then 2 miles north on Jesse James Road, is open daily May through September from 9:00 A.M. to 4:00 P.M. and, the rest of the year, from 9:00 A.M. to 4:00 P.M. weekdays and from noon to 4:00 P.M. on Saturday and Sunday. Call (816) 628–6065 for information. Just across the road is the **Claybrook Home,** the restored antebellum home of Jesse James's daughter, also open to visitors.

En route to St. Joseph, follow Highways 92 and 273 to historic Weston. Founded in 1837, the river town quickly evolved into an important Oregon Trail supply and departure point. Floods in the late 1800s, however, changed the course of the Missouri, leaving Weston literally and figuratively high and dry. Nevertheless it bustles again today, with tourists who come to view the dozens of pre–Civil War buildings and to visit sites such as the **Weston Historical Museum** (816–386–2977) and the **McCormick Distilling Company,** founded in 1856 and one of America's oldest. For information on historic lodgings, antiques shops, farmstead tours, and the village's many specialty shops, call the Visitors Bureau at (816) 640–2909.

Northern Missouri

St. Joseph surely added its chapter to the book of Western history: The life of Jesse James ended here, whereas that of the Pony Express began here. The **Jesse James Home** is where the bank robber, living under the assumed name of Mr. Howard, was shot and killed in 1882. Bob Ford, at that time a recently recruited member of the James Gang—and who had been living with James and his wife while they planned a bank robbery in nearby Platte City—killed James for the reward money offered by the governor.

The James Home sits on the grounds of the **Patte House Museum,** built in 1858 as a 140-room luxury hotel. The Russell, Majors, and Waddell freight firm established their Pony Express office here on April 3, 1860. Later the building served again as a hotel and also as a women's college and shirt factory. Highlights at the museum are the 1854 Buffalo Saloon (now serving soft drinks), the restored Pony Express headquarters, and the 1877 train depot from Union Star, Missouri, along with a Hannibal and St. Joseph wood-burning steam locomotive. The museum, situated at Twelfth and Penn streets, is open between Memorial Day and Labor Day on Monday through Saturday from 10:00 A.M. to 5:00 P.M. and Sunday from 1:00 to 5:00 P.M. In spring and autumn it's open weekends only from 1:00 to 5:00 P.M. Call the Pony Express Historical Association at (816) 232–8206 for more information.

The **St. Joseph Museum** and its satellite **Pony Express Stables Museum** further illuminate the most fascinating communications experiment undertaken on the American frontier. The main museum, occupying the forty-three-room 1879 Gothic sandstone Wyeth-Tootle mansion, houses impressive historic, prehistoric, and natural-history displays. The Pony Express Stables Museum includes photographs of all the known Pony Express station sites, exhibits that depict the hazards regularly encountered by the daring riders, and displays that highlight the completion of the telegraph, which sounded the death knell for the Pony Express.

A saddle maker and other craftspersons are on hand to demonstrate old trades. The St. Joseph Museum is located at Eleventh and Charles streets; the Pony Express Museum at 914 Penn Street. Both are open between April and September, Monday through Saturday from 9:00 A.M. to 5:00 P.M., and Sunday from 1:00 to 5:00 P.M. The remainder of the year the main museum is open afternoons Tuesday through Sunday, the Pony Express Museum by appointment. Call (816) 232–8471 for more information.

Among the historic B&B lodging possibilities in St. Joseph: the **Harding House** (816–232–7020), a turn-of-the-century home with unusual antique touches that include a pump organ.

Where to Stay

Boone's Lick Trail Inn, St. Charles, (314) 947–7000
School House Bed & Breakfast, Rocheport, (573) 698–2022
Old Tavern, outside Boonville, (816) 837–3200 or 3330
Harding House, St. Joseph, (816) 232–7020

1860 Pony Express Ad

WANTED: Young Skinny Wiry Fellows, not over eighteen. Must be expert riders willing to risk death daily. Orphans preferred. Wages $25 per week. Apply Central Overland Express.

The Pony Express Memorial Statue in downtown St. Joseph captures one of these "Young Skinny Wiry Fellows" in a larger-than-life bronze sculpture of horse and rider flying across the open prairie.

ROUGHRIDER COUNTRY

▼▼▼

NEBRASKA
SOUTH DAKOTA
NORTH DAKOTA

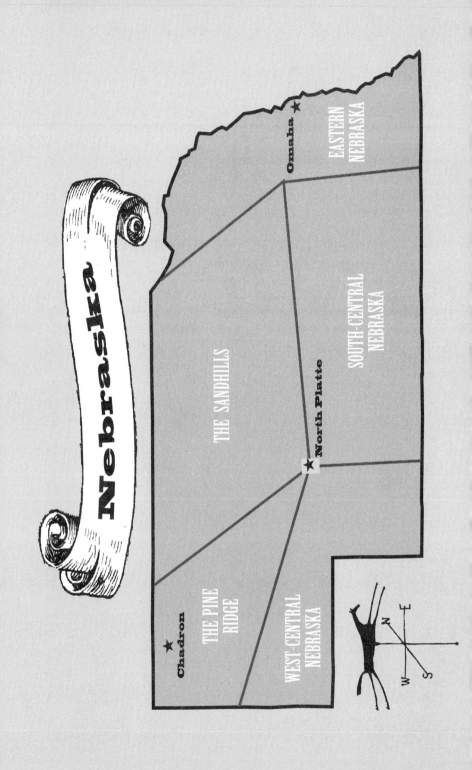

Nebraska

Chadron ★

THE PINE
RIDGE

WEST-CENTRAL
NEBRASKA

THE SANDHILLS

North Platte ★

SOUTH-CENTRAL
NEBRASKA

Omaha ★

EASTERN
NEBRASKA

N
E
W
S

NEBRASKA

▼▼▼

ISTORIC Nebraska: images of hardscrabble homesteaders, residing in houses of sod and barely scratching an existence on the treeless prairie. The state also played a vital role in the Indian wars and in the migration westward along the Oregon Trail. The Lewis and Clark expedition traced the eastern boundary of Nebraska as they followed the Missouri River, and the migrating Mormons, when they evacuated Nauvoo, Illinois, and headed for Zion, crossed Nebraska, too—joining in near Fort Kearney alongside Oregon Trail emigrants (but on the other side of the Platte River from them).

The narrative begins in eastern Nebraska and from there meanders westward across the south-central and west-central portions of the state, then heads north into the rugged Pine Ridge, winding up in the picturesque Sandhills region.

Eastern Nebraska

Six miles southeast of Fairbury, in the southeast corner of the state, is the **Rock Creek Station State Historical Park.** The Oregon Trail road-station-turned-Pony-Express "swing station," where riders quickly changed mounts, is where James Butler "Wild Bill" Hickok began his bloody career as a gunfighter. While working as a stable hand here in 1861, Hickok gunned down, apparently without just cause, the station's owner, Dave McCanles, with a .56 caliber percussion rifle that was owned by the deceased. The 350-acre grounds, with visible Oregon Trail wagon ruts, are open year-round from 8:00 A.M. to 8:00 P.M.; the visitor center is open daily 9:00 A.M. to 5:00 P.M. Memorial Day through Labor Day and on weekends in May, September, and October. Ox-drawn carriage rides are one of many attractions at the station; call (402) 729–5777 for more information.

Homestead National Monument, 4 miles west of Beatrice on Highway 4, encompasses one of Nebraska's first documented homesteads. In a rush to return to his regiment, Daniel Freeman, a Union scout from Iowa, persuaded the land agent in Brownville, Nebraska, to sign him up immediately after the strike of midnight January 1, 1863, when the Homestead Act kicked in. In so doing Freeman became one of the first takers of President Abraham Lincoln's offer of free land.

The monument includes Freeman's original T-shaped homestead, an 1867 log cabin representative of those built by homesteaders in eastern Nebraska, and interpretive trails that wind through more than one hundred acres of restored tall-grass prairie. The visitor center features displays on nearly every aspect of pioneer life; the nearby Freeman school, operational from 1872 until 1967, remains a persuasive reminder of the important role played by schools in frontier America. The park is open daily year-round from 8:30 A.M. to 5:00 P.M. **Homestead Days,** held during a four-day period in late June, revive the ways and the days of nineteenth-century sodbusters, with spinning, apple-butter boiling, and candle-making demonstrations and singing and dancing. Call (402) 223–3514 for more information.

Within Omaha, Nebraska's largest city, there's a bonanza of lore that relates to America's period of westward expansion. Begin by visiting the **Mormon Pioneer Cemetery and Visitors' Center,** at 3215 State Street. En route to the promised land of Utah, 3,000 Mormon immigrants hunkered down here during the winter of 1846–47, one of Nebraska's toughest ever. Some 600 pioneers perished in the brutal weather and remain buried here today. The visitor center is open daily from 9:00 A.M. to 9:00 P.M., with guided tours of the cemetery given by Latter-Day Saint church members. Call (402) 453–9372 for more information.

The **General Crook House,** operated by the Historical Society of Douglas County, once stood sentinel over surrounding Fort Omaha. Originally known as Quarters One, the lavishly restored Victorian was renamed in honor of its most famous resident, Gen. George Crook, Civil War hero, Indian fighter, and one of the nineteenth-century military's most outspoken advocates of Native Americans' rights. The house and immaculate gardens, situated at Thirtieth and Fort on the campus of Metro Community College, are open Tuesday through Friday from 10:00 A.M. to 4:00 P.M. and Sunday from 1:00 to 4:00 P.M. Call (402) 455–9990 for information.

The Homestead Act

Foreseeing the saturation by homesteaders of the far West and the East, expansionist politicians shepherded the Kansas-Nebraska Act of 1854 through Congress, effectively opening the central plains to white farmers. Southern politicians opposed a land giveaway, knowing that free land would benefit working-class whites, who would ultimately vote down slavery as new states were designated. Once the southern states seceded from the Union, however, President Lincoln signed into law the Homestead Act of 1862. The Act declared that any citizen, current or intended, could lay claim to a quarter of a square mile (160 acres) of surveyed government land. After five years, if a dwelling was built and crops were planted, the land became the claimant's, free and clear.

The liberal terms of the Homestead Act, while accomplishing the goal of settling the frontier, proved to work against many of the takers. A quarter-section was plenty of land in the East, but it was often inadequate to support a family in the dry, low-yielding reaches west of the 100th meridian.

Add to the already trying circumstances the hailstorms, prairie fires, blizzards, locust plagues, heavy debt, expensive rail transport, wind, and loneliness, and it's easy to see why a large share of homesteaders called it quits. Others managed to hang on, however, and many of today's high-plains spreads are farmed by descendants of Nebraska's original homesteaders.

The **Union Pacific Historical Museum,** located at 1416 Dodge Street, documents the vital role played by that railroad in expanding the western limits of U.S. settlement. Displays include the funeral car of President Abraham Lincoln, who had close ties to the Union Pacific, and reminders from the May 10, 1869, driving of the Golden Spike in Promontory, Utah, including the original telegram sent by Gen. Grenville M. Dodge announcing the completion of the transcontinental railroad. Also on exhibit: original posters advertising railroad lands for sale, rare guns, and the scalp of a railroad worker who survived an Indian attack! The museum is open from 10:00 A.M. to 5:00 P.M. Tuesday through Saturday and 1:00 to 5:00 P.M. Sunday; call (402) 444–5072 for information.

A couple of other museums well worth visiting: the **Western Heritage Museum** (402–444–5071), in the old Union Station at 801 South Tenth

Street, open from 10:00 A.M. to 5:00 P.M. Tuesday through Saturday and from 1:00 to 5:00 P.M. Sunday; and the **Great Plains Black Museum** (402–345–2212), open from 10:00 A.M. to 2:30 P.M. Monday through Friday. In addition to its more timely displays, the latter's exhibits focus on the Buffalo Soldiers and black cowboys, railroaders, and early settlers.

Fort Atkinson State Historical Park commemorates the first U.S. fort built west of the Missouri River, a post that played a crucial role in the earliest opening of the frontier to the fur-trading mountain men. Here visitors view outstanding films and exhibits that relate to Lewis and Clark—including a replica of Lewis's unusual air gun—and the fur trade, as well as a large-scale replica of the fort during its early-1820s heyday. The fort is being restored, based on this model.

The grounds at fascinating Fort Atkinson, a National Historic Landmark, are open daily year-round, and the visitor center is open Memorial Day through Labor Day and weekends in September and October from 9:00 A.M. to 5:00 P.M.; living-history demonstrations are staged periodically throughout the summer. The fort is located a mile east of Fort Calhoun (9 miles north of Omaha) on Highway 75. Call (402) 468–5611 for more information.

Just across the Iowa border from Blair, Nebraska, the amazing booty of the sunken stern-wheeler *Bertrand,* which went down on April 1, 1865, is displayed and carefully preserved in climate-controlled glass chambers at **DeSoto National Wildlife Refuge** (712–642–2772). (The boat was actually excavated on the Nebraska side of the border, hence its inclusion here.) The visitor center is open from 9:00 A.M. to 4:30 P.M. daily throughout the year, with the *Bertrand* excavation site open from 6:00 A.M. to 10:00 P.M. daily April 15 through September 30. (Much of the refuge is off-limits during the waterfowl migrating seasons.)

In the capital city of Lincoln, visit the **State Museum of History,** located at Fifteenth and P streets. The stories of the people of the plains—Indians, explorers, fur-traders, homesteaders, and town builders—are told through immaculately prepared displays, distributed among three floors. The museum is open from 9:00 A.M. to 5:00 P.M. Monday through Friday and from 1:30 to 5:00 P.M. Saturday and Sunday. Call (402) 471–4754 for more information. Nearby, at the Love Library at Twelfth and R streets, the **Great Plains Art Collection** (402–472–6220) includes nearly 200 bronzes by Frederic Remington and Charles M. Russell, as well as hundreds of paint-

The Bertrand

Steamboats plying the 2,000 miles of Missouri River separating St. Louis and Fort Benton, Montana, served as the lifeline that allowed frontier gold-mining towns such as Bannack and Virginia City, Montana, to thrive. The Missouri's shifting sands and channels and submerged snags made navigation notoriously treacherous, and during the nineteenth and early twentieth centuries, more than 400 steamers went down.

The *Bertrand*, a mountain packet sternwheeler built in Wheeling, West Virginia, in 1864, was specifically designed for negotiating shallow, narrow western rivers; still, the Big Muddy got the best of her. Having lit out from St. Louis on March 16, 1865, she sank on April 1 just north of Omaha, carrying $250,000 worth of merchandise thought to be destined for the Montana gold fields. She was discovered a century later, in 1968, buried in an abandoned Missouri River channel on the DeSoto National Wildlife Refuge.

By the fall of 1969, excavations were completed. Only nine of the anticipated 500 flasks of mercury were found, and the gold and whiskey rumored to be aboard apparently were not. What was found in the remarkable time capsule were more than 200,000 artifacts, providing a vivid glimpse of pioneer life, some of it hinting at a more glamorous lifestyle than we typically imagine: There were the basic picks and shovels for mining, hammers and saws for building new towns, canned food, clothes, and plows. There were *4,000* pairs of men's, women's, and children's shoes. But also on board were silk goods, champagne, French wines, beer from Amsterdam, canned oysters, and silverware and china.

ings and other works of art, along with approximately 4,000 volumes that focus on Great Plains and Western American history—making up one of the great collections of Western documents. It's open Monday through Friday from 9:30 A.M. to 5:00 P.M., Saturday from 10:00 A.M. to 5:00 P.M., and Sunday from 1:30 to 5:00 P.M.

South-Central Nebraska

Grand Island's expansive **Stuhr Museum of the Prairie Pioneer** features several collections of buildings, including the Pioneer Settlement, with its eight structures that emulate one of the "road ranches" that once served westward-bound Oregon Trail travelers. Also on site are a Pawnee earth lodge; buildings from the legendary 10,000-acre Taylor Ranch in Hall County, Nebraska; and Railroad Town, with some sixty century-year-old structures, including the birthplace cottage of Henry Fonda, one of America's favorite silver-screen cowboys. Core attractions at this very large facility, located at the junction of Highways 34 and 281, are open daily year-round from 9:00 A.M. to 5:00 P.M. (Sundays between October 16 and April 30 it's open only from 1:00 to 5:00 P.M.). Call (308) 385–5316 for more information.

From Grand Island head 70 miles northwest on Highways 2 and 11 to Burwell. Southeast of Burwell (home to **Nebraska's Big Rodeo,** slated annually for late July), near Elyria, is **Fort Hartsuff State Historical Park,** a restored 1870 infantry post. The fort, established to help quell confrontations between settlers and the Teton Sioux and other Indians, has withstood 120 years' worth of the elements remarkably well, thanks largely to the fact that its buildings were constructed of concrete. Ample supplies of gravel, but very little timber, were available locally; in fact, troops traveled nearly 100 miles to the northwest to find a 100-foot pine suitable to serve as the post's flagpole.

Living-history demonstrations take place on weekends at the fort, with guides dressed in period uniforms. The grounds are open from 8:00 A.M. to 8:00 P.M. year-round, and the visitor facilities are open daily Memorial Day through Labor Day and on weekends in May, September, and October. Call (308) 346–4715 for more information.

In Red Cloud, 65 miles south of Grand Island on Highway 34/281, the **Willa Cather Historical Center** celebrates the Pulitzer Prize–winning novelist who wrote so vividly about the lives and times of the pioneers. Cather's childhood home, located at 338 North Webster, is open between May and September, Monday through Saturday from 8:00 A.M. to noon and from 1:00 to 5:00 P.M., and on Sunday from 1:00 to 5:00 P.M. The hours are the same during the remainder of the year, except that it's closed on Mondays. Call (402) 746–3285 for more information.

Once you go to **Pioneer Village,** you'll find it no surprise that it is Nebraska's number-one tourist attraction. Spread over twenty acres in Minden,

Harold Warp's outstanding collection includes more than 50,000 pieces of early Americana, distributed among some three dozen buildings, including the Elm Creek Fort from Webster County, where it was built within a stockade in 1869 to protect several families during the Indian wars. Other finds include a Pony Express station out of Bridgeport, Nebraska; an extensive array of wagons, buggies, and carts; a general store, stocked with thousands of old-fashioned items; pioneer farming equipment; and Buffalo Bill's saddle, which Cody used in his Wild West Show and Warp acquired in 1955 (interim owners included Tex Rickard and Rudolph Valentino). For the kids there's a working 1879 steam-powered merry-go-round, still just a nickel per ride.

The above listing merely scratches the surface of what you'll find at the largest "museum of progress" in America, with its beautiful displays that trace America's growth since 1830. The privately owned nonprofit enterprise, with a staff of more than one hundred, is located 12 miles south of Interstate 80 from exit 279. It's open daily year-round from 8:00 A.M. till sundown. Call (308) 832–1181 for more information.

Fort Kearney State Historical Park, 3 miles south of Kearney on Highway 44, then 4 miles east on Highway L50A, celebrates one of the first forts built to protect Oregon Trail travelers. Fort Kearney also served as a Pony Express home station, as a telegraph office, and as an outfitting depot during the earlier Indian campaigns. Mandated by the government for establishment in 1847 "where the road to California encounters the Platte River," Fort Kearney saw some 30,000 emigrants—bound for the gold fields of California and for Oregon and Utah—pass through in one frenetic eighteen-month period, beginning late in 1848. The park, featuring a re-created stockade and several other structures, is open year-round from 8:00 A.M. to 8:00 P.M., with the interpretive facilities open daily only from Memorial Day through Labor Day from 9:00 A.M. to 5:00 P.M. Call (308) 234–9513 for more details. Also in Kearney: **Platte Valley Saddle Shop, Inc.,** which has been creating custom riding saddles since 1942. The business is located at 1908 Central Avenue.

About 100 miles southwest of Kearney on Highway 44 and Highway 6/34, McCook's **Museum of the High Plains** features an eclectic array of memorabilia that highlight the town's origin as a railroad stop. On site are an old-time drugstore; the John Helm cabin, one of the first structures built in Red Willow County; and a display that focuses on the Battle of Beecher Island, which occurred during the Indian wars in nearby eastern Colorado. The museum, located at 421 Norris Avenue, is open year-round from 1:00

Building a House of Nebraska Marble

Unlike the eastern reaches of Nebraska, the central and western portions of the state had little timber cover. Settlers made do with burning buffalo chips for fuel and, for homes, building hillside dugouts or houses of sod, a sight that moved Mark Twain to note, in *Roughing It*, "It was the first time we had ever seen a man's front yard on top of his house."

The short buffalo grass that covered the prairie owned a tough tangle of roots, which held sod together even after it was cut and removed from the ground. Using a specialized plow, sod strips were sliced a foot wide and about 4 inches deep, then cut width-wise into 3-foot sections. Slabs, grass-side down, were laid in double courses and stabilized with four corner posts. A ridgepole was hung from forked upright posts, then branches were laid down to form rafters, upon which more sod, grass-side up, was laid.

A homesteader could typically scrape enough sod from half an acre to build a respectable 16-by-20-foot house. Even after lumber became readily available, many sod-busters chose to continue living in their homes of "Nebraska Marble." The soddies were inexpensive and quick to build; they did an admirable job of keeping out the heat, cold, and wind; and they were fire- and tornado-proof—all covetable qualities for the time and place.

to 5:00 P.M. Tuesday through Saturday and from 1:30 to 5:00 P.M. Sunday.

In Stockville, 50 miles northeast of McCook on Highways 83 and 18, the unusual **Dancing Leaf Earth Lodge** offers "an experience in primitive Native American life." The rolling prairies in this part of Nebraska in prehistoric times were home to the Native Americans known as the Upper Republicans. The proprietors of Dancing Leaf spent 400 hours building their large earth lodge to accurately resemble those once lived in by members of the farming culture. Options at the getaway include overnighting in the earth lodge, dining on buffalo stew and blue-cornmeal muffins, "sweat lodging," bull boat rides, learning primitive living skills (including stone- and bone-tool fabrication), and several somewhat more esoteric endeavors such as "spiritual bonding." (A caveat: True Native American spirituality is not something that can be purchased, or put on and taken off like a shirt.) Call (308) 367–4233 for more information and to make an appointment.

An original 1860 **Pony Express Station** sits in Gothenburg's Ehmen

Park, just north of Interstate 80. Horse-drawn carriage rides through the historic town originate at the station throughout summer daily between 9:00 A.M. and 5:00 P.M. Nearby, just south of the interstate, the popular **Sod House Museum** boasts a re-created farmstead with a barn museum, windmills, and a sod house similar to those resided in by many Nebraska homesteaders. Both attractions are open to visitors daily from 8:00 A.M. to 9:00 P.M. May 1 through October 1. Call (308) 537–2680 for more information.

North Platte's **Buffalo Bill State Historical Park** celebrates the singular man who, among his many feats, was nearly elected to the Nebraska Legislature at twenty-six years of age. In 1878 Cody set up residence in North Platte, having joined in a cattle-growing partnership there the previous year. The Old Glory Blowout he organized for the town's Fourth of July celebration in 1882 is regarded as having set the stage for the popular sport of rodeo in America; in a sense, it also served as the trial run for Buffalo Bill's Wild West Show, which commenced performances the following year.

Cody's ranch, known as Scout's Rest, was built near North Platte during the zenith of his career as a showman, and it was here that he came to relax and recuperate between stints of the show. The sixteen-acre park (the ranch originally encompassed 4,000 acres) includes Cody's original eighteen-room house, a barn, and outbuildings, with displays that interpret the life and times of one of the Old West's most famous and colorful characters.

The ranch grounds, located on Buffalo Bill Avenue, are open daily year-round from 8:00 A.M. to 8:00 P.M.; the house and barn are open daily Memorial Day through Labor Day from 10:00 A.M. to 8:00 P.M. Between April 1 and Memorial Day and between Labor Day and October 31, they're open Monday through Friday from 9:00 A.M. to 5:00 P.M. and closed weekends. Reservations for the park's popular buffalo barbecues—held on Wednesday, Thursday, and Friday nights in July and August, and featuring a cowboy singalong for "dessert"—can be secured by calling (308) 535–8035.

The **Fort Cody Trading Post** and Old West Museum (308–532–8081) in North Platte feature one of the West's largest and most unusual gift shops, specializing in leather goods, jewelry, and Western gifts of nearly every bent. The 20,000-piece Buffalo Bill's Wild West Show in miniature, hand-carved and animated, is a top attraction at the post, found at the junction of Interstate 80 and Highway 83 and open year-round.

North Platte's **NEBRASKAland Days** festival, held in late June, includes the Buffalo Bill PRCA (Professional Rodeo Cowboys Association) Rodeo, barbecues, and cowboy-poetry readings; a Frontier Revue, High

Noon Shoot-Out, Wild West Dance, and hog-calling competition are also on tap. For details call (308) 532–7948.

West-Central Nebraska

In Paxton, 40 miles west of North Platte, don't miss **Ole's Big Game Lounge and Grill,** "Nebraska's Most Famous Waterin' Hole." This unique eatery and tavern is open year-round Monday through Saturday from 8:00 A.M. to 1:00 A.M. and Sunday from 10:00 A.M. to 10:00 P.M. The 1880s bar and backbar here are straight out of the Old West, from the legendary Frontier Bar in Cheyenne, Wyoming. On display, hanging from knotty-pine walls, are two-hundred-plus mounted animal trophies, making up one of the largest private collections of its kind in the country, that of Rosser O. Herstedt ("Ole" to his friends). Ole made hunting sojourns to every corner of the world over the span of many years to bag his collection.

Ogallala, 50 miles west of North Platte on Interstate 80, is situated along the Union Pacific Railway and was the end of the line for the Texas Trail cattle drives that ran between 1875 and 1885; it also was the gateway to the newly opened ranges to the north and west. **Front Street** is a re-creation of early Ogallala, and its **Cowboy Capital Museum** tells the story of the town's wilder days, when it attracted gunmen, showgirls, and gamblers of every ilk. A shoot-out precedes performances of the **Crystal Palace Revue,** a high-octane musical staged nightly, Memorial Day through Labor Day, in the spirit of the old saloon shows. The museum and other facilities are open daily from 11:00 A.M. to 10:00 P.M. May through September and from 9:00 A.M. to 6:00 P.M. October through April. Call (308) 284–6000 for show times and other information.

The **Mansion on the Hill,** a lavish 1887 brick Victorian, houses a museum filled with reminders of the days when cattle was king and Ogalalla queen of the cowtowns, and nicknamed "Gomorrah of the Plains." The mansion, situated at the corner of Highway 61 and North Spruce Street, is open to visitors from 1:00 to 5:00 P.M. Tuesday through Sunday, Memorial Day through Labor Day. **Boot Hill Cemetery,** where cowboys were buried with their boots on, is located 3 blocks west of the Mansion on the Hill. For more information on these and other Ogallala sites, call the Chamber of Commerce at (308) 284–4066.

The site known today as **Ash Hollow State Historical Park** served as a prehistoric Indian camp for thousands of years before the first white traders passed through in 1812. (The party, led by Robert Stuart, unknowingly blazed the Oregon Trail and made way for thousands to follow in their tracks.) Because of the shelter, water, wood, and wild foods it afforded, the veritable oasis appealed to Indians and white travelers alike; eventually, Ash Hollow became a vital layover for Oregon Trail emigrants, and as many as four trading posts sprang up there during the 1840s and 1850s. Today the Nebraska Game and Parks Commission maintains a visitor center that's open daily Memorial Day through Labor Day and weekends in May, September, and October. The grounds, located 3 miles south of Lewellen on Highway 26, are open year-round from 8:00 A.M. to 6:00 P.M. Call (308) 778–5651 for information.

The settlement of Sidney emerged in 1867 when the Union Pacific Railroad's tracks reached this far west. Here the Sidney Barracks, a subpost of Fort Sedgwick, Colorado, was established, primarily to protect railroad workers from Sioux, Cheyenne, and Arapaho raids (the Indians' opposition mounted the farther west the railroad pushed) and to provide "escort services" to emigrants who followed the Oregon Trail. In 1870 the Barracks evolved into the independent Fort Sidney; today the **Fort Sidney Museum and Post Commander's Home** relates the fort's intriguing history, which included roles in the Black Hills gold rush of the late 1870s and in the Indian unrest that occurred during the proliferation of the Sioux Ghost Dance in 1890–91.

The commander's home, at 1108 Sixth Avenue, was purchased by the county historical society in 1962 and renovated to late-nineteenth-century style; the museum, housed in the former Officers' Quarters, is found a block north. The facilities are open May 15 through September 15 daily from 9:00 to 11:00 A.M. and from 1:00 to 3:00 P.M.; in winter from 1:00 to 4:00 P.M. daily, or by appointment. For information call (308) 254–2150.

The Oregon, Mormon, Pony Express, and Sidney-Deadwood trails all passed by the present site of Bridgeport, a fact celebrated at the town's **Pioneer Trails Museum.** Located at the south end of Main Street on Highway 385, the museum (308–262–0108) is open Memorial Day through Labor Day from 10:00 A.M. to 6:00 P.M. Monday through Saturday and 1:00 to 6:00 P.M. Sunday. Four miles south of town on Highway 88 you can visit Courthouse and Jail rocks, two important landmarks used by emigrants in tracking their progression westward. The grounds are open year-round during daylight hours; call (402) 471–4754 for more information.

Chimney Rock National Historic Site is located 23 miles east of

Scottsbluff, at a point 3.5 miles south of Bayard. From far to the east, upward of 30 miles, travelers could see this strange formation looming and signaling the end of the plains and the beginning of the tough Rocky Mountain passage. The Nebraska State Historical Society maintains a trailer with exhibits here, open daily between Memorial Day and Labor Day from 9:00 A.M. to 6:00 P.M.; additional information on Chimney Rock is displayed at the Scotts Bluff National Monument visitor center (see p. 389). The site and hiking trails are open year-round during daylight hours. Call (308) 586–2581 for more information.

The **Oregon Trail Wagon Train** (308–586–1850), headquartered 2 miles south of Bayard, offers 1990s travelers a chance to slow down and experience the Oregon Trail via covered wagon, on tours that last from one to six days. Specified outings come complete with "Indian raids," square dances beneath the stars, black-powder shooting, and cookouts that feature scrump-

It's clear why the Indians called Scotts Bluff Me-a-pa-te, *or "hill that is hard to go around."*

tious pioneer grub like hoecakes, spoonbread, vinegar pudding, cowboy coffee, and homemade ice cream. The enterprise also offers canoe rentals, log-cabin overnights, and tours of its 1910 living-history organic farm.

Scotts Bluff National Monument, 3 miles west of Gering on Highway 92, protects 3,000 acres of prairie grasslands and landforms, including the monolith called Scotts Bluff. Known by its Indian name *Me-a-pa-te* (hill that is hard to go around) until 1828, when fur-company clerk, frontiersman, and Indian fighter Hiram Scott died nearby, the bluff marked the route followed to the mountains by traders and trappers. Their caravan trail evolved into the Oregon Trail, which gold seekers, emigrants, freight carriers, military expeditions, stagecoaches, and Pony Express riders followed west. Among displays at the monument's Oregon Trail Museum are paintings by pioneer artist and photographer William Henry Jackson; outside, a trail leads to a section of still-visible roadbed carved by passing wagons. The monument is open daily from 8:00 A.M. to 7:30 P.M. in summer and from 8:00 A.M. to 5:00 P.M. the rest of the year; call (308) 436–4340 for more information.

The Pine Ridge

From Chimney Rock National Historic Site, travel northeast 50 miles on Highways 92 and 385 to the town of Alliance. Cavalry gear and Native American artifacts are displayed in Alliance's **Knight Museum of High Plains Heritage** (308–762–2384), situated in the city park at 908 Yellowstone Avenue. The primary focus of the museum is the conflict that erupted with the mixing of two distinct cultures, the aggressive white newcomers and the native Indians. The facility is open May 1 through October 31 Monday through Saturday from 10:00 A.M. to 6:00 P.M. and Sunday from 1:00 to 5:00 P.M.

The Wild West still kicks at historic **Fort Robinson State Park,** just outside Crawford, where nearly 22,000 acres of wild country also offer endless recreational possibilities. The fort played a major role in the Indian wars of the late 1800s; in fact, the great Oglala Sioux warrior Crazy Horse was killed here in 1877, stabbed with a bayonet while allegedly resisting arrest. Later, in the early 1890s, the black Buffalo Soldiers of the fort's 9th Cavalry patrolled the Pine Ridge Reservation during the restive times that followed the Wounded Knee uprising. Throughout summer, living-history demonstrations, Western entertainment, trail rides, buffalo-stew cookouts, and jeep and stagecoach rides are popular daytime diversions, while nightly dramatic performances beckon visitors into the Post Playhouse.

You can sleep in a cabin or a lodge room where the blue-coated cavalrymen of the Indian wars formerly bunked, and you can dine in the main-lodge restaurant on buffalo specialties. Fort Robinson is open between Memorial Day and Labor Day Monday through Saturday from 8:00 A.M. to 5:00 P.M. and Sunday from 9:00 A.M. to 5:00 P.M.; hours vary during the off-season. Call (308) 665–2900 for further details.

The top-notch **Museum of the Fur Trade,** 3 miles east of Chadron on Highway 20, is devoted to the story of the American fur trade and the mountain man's role in opening the West to settlement. Included are a reconstructed log-cabin trading post and warehouse, built in 1833 by the American Fur Company, and comprehensive gun and fur collections. The museum, which for three decades has published *Museum of the Fur Trade Quarterly,* is open daily June 1 through Labor Day from 8:00 A.M. to 5:00 P.M. and by appointment the rest of the year. Call (308) 432–3843 for more information.

The **Olde Main Street Inn** (308–432–3380), at 115 Main, is a B&B that is currently being renovated to its gracious 1890s style. Originally known as the Hotel Chadron, the structure has served numerous functions, including that of military headquarters for Gen. Nelson A. Miles during the Wounded Knee uprising. Ten units are presently available in the hotel, buffalo burgers and Indian tacos are served in the adjacent restaurant, and the hotel's 77 Longbranch Saloon features Western entertainment on weekends.

On the second floor of the Administration Building on the campus of Chadron State College, you'll find a room dedicated to Mari Sandoz, author of numerous books about the West (the poignant *Cheyenne Autumn* is probably her best known). Personal effects, photographs, and early manuscripts of one of Nebraska's most powerful literary figures are displayed during regular working hours; to arrange a visit at other times, call (308) 432–6246.

For a map of numerous historic sites in the surrounding area, call the Convention & Visitors Bureau at (308) 432–4401 and request a copy of the brochure entitled *Nebraska Pine Ridge Area.*

In Gordon the **Tri-State Oldtime Cowboys Memorial Museum** occupies a log building that brims with saddles, hats, tools, and boots, as well as a chuck wagon emblazoned with more than 200 local cattle brands. The museum, located in Winship Park (1 block west of Main Street between Third and Fourth streets), is open daily June 1 through mid-September from

1:00 to 5:00 P.M. and by appointment the rest of the year. Call the local historical society at (308) 282–0887 for more information.

Similar to the room dedicated to Mari Sandoz at Chadron State College, Gordon's **Mari Sandoz Room** celebrates Nebraska's famous chronicler of the West; Sandoz's manuscripts and memorabilia are displayed, and her books are on sale. The facility, located at 117 North Main, is open year-round Monday through Friday from 9:00 A.M. to 5:00 P.M. and Saturday from 9:00 A.M. to noon. Here you can also pick up tour maps for several area outings, including the Old Jules Country tour (named for Sandoz's father), which penetrates the picturesque Sandhills. For details on guide-accompanied Sandoz Country Tours, offered on Wednesdays during June, call (308) 282–9972.

The Sandhills

The **Arthur Bowring Sandhills Ranch State Historical Park,** near Merriman (77 miles east of Chadron on Highway 20), preserves the Bar 99 Ranch, where cattle baron Arthur Bowring homesteaded in 1894. The park, a living-history tribute to Bowring and others of his breed, features an interpretive center with photographs and artifacts that document the history of the Sandhills as well as that of Arthur and Eve Bowring and cattle ranching in general. The Eve Bowring Visitor Center is open daily from 9:00 A.M. to 5:00 P.M. Memorial Day through Labor Day, and the park grounds are open year-round. Call (308) 684–3428 to arrange a special tour or to request information on the late-June **Sod House Sunday** celebration, which includes a mountain-man encampment, a cattle-calling contest, and a cow-chip throw.

The remote **Verde Valley Guest Ranch,** 55 miles south of Merriman on Highway 61, then 3 miles west, is an ideal place for a restful Western getaway. Horseback riding, stargazing, hiking, nature photography, and fishing are among the activities suggested by the ranch proprietors, whom you can reach by calling (308) 458–2220.

Where to Stay

Olde Main Street Inn, Chadron, (308) 432–3380
Verde Valley Guest Ranch, outside Merriman, (308) 458–2220

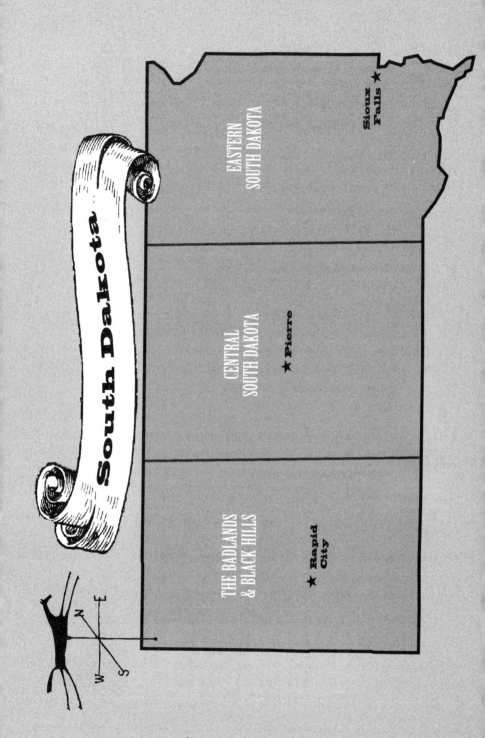

South Dakota

EASTERN SOUTH DAKOTA

Sioux Falls ★

CENTRAL SOUTH DAKOTA

★ Pierre

THE BADLANDS & BLACK HILLS

★ Rapid City

SOUTH DAKOTA

▼▼▼

T O LOOK AT a state road map of South Dakota is enlightening. East of the Missouri River, which cuts off roughly the eastern one-third of the state, the dense tangle of highways and back roads typically run straight at the main points of the compass, creating the right angles of farm country. West of the river, conversely, roads are fewer and farther between, and they snake around, their routes ruled by the terrain: ranch and range territory.

The narrative begins in the east, proceeds along the Missouri River through central South Dakota, then finishes up in the Black Hills, those picturesque and manageable mountains well known for their concentration of Old West lore attractions. Be forewarned, however, and careful where you stop: The Black Hills also hold perhaps the most notorious and tackiest concentration of tourist traps west of the Mississippi.

Eastern South Dakota

Sisseton, nestled into the northeast corner of the state, is home to the **Tekakwitha Fine Arts Center,** featuring arts and crafts of the Indians of the Sisseton and Wahpeton Lake Traverse Sioux Reservations. The ten galleries within are open daily from 9:00 A.M. to 5:00 P.M. Memorial Day through Labor Day; the rest of the year Tuesday through Friday from 9:00 A.M. to 5:00 P.M. and weekends from 12:30 to 4:00 P.M. The facility is found a quarter-mile south of Highway 10, at 401 South Eighth Avenue West. During the Fourth of July weekend, the center hosts the **Coteau Heritage Festival**; call (605) 698–7058 to learn more about it.

The **Canyon Ranch** (605–738–2480), northwest of Sisseton near Veblen, amid the glacially formed Coteau des Prairies (French for Hills of the Prairies), offers guided trail rides and backcountry camping in a 10,000-acre swath of South Dakota that includes picturesque Sica Hollow State Park to the south.

Fort Sisseton State Park, roughly 30 miles west of Sisseton, holds the remnants of one of the best-preserved frontier forts in the Dakotas. More than a dozen structures remain from the post, built in 1864 in response to the Minnesota Uprising of 1862 to protect Dakota Territory settlers from Sioux raiders. It also served as an important layover for emigrant wagon trains and freight wagons headed for the Black Hills goldfields. The fort was abandoned in 1889 after twenty-five years of service; then, in the 1930s, fourteen of its stone and brick buildings were restored by the WPA (Works Progress Administration). The present is the past at the **Fort Sisseton Historical Festival,** slated for the first weekend in June, with a fur-traders' rendezvous, peopled by buckskinners and muzzle loaders who come in from several surrounding states. Also on tap are Dakota Dan's Medicine Show, cavalry parades, art and crafts demonstrations, melodramas, a pioneer costume ball, old-time fiddle music, a Native American encampment, and children's games. The visitor center is open daily from 11:00 A.M. to 7:00 P.M. Memorial Day through Labor Day, and the grounds are open year-round. Call (605) 448–5701 for further information.

In Webster, 23 miles south of Fort Sisseton State Park, swing into the **Dakotah Factory Outlet** on East Highway 12. The enterprise is nationally renowned for its pillows, bed coverings, and other bedroom fashions designed with a Western flair, depicting things like bucking broncos and Native American prints. The sales outlet is open Monday through Friday from 9:00 A.M. to 5:00 P.M. and Saturday from 10:00 A.M. to 3:00 P.M.

Masked bandits storm the train and gunfire rings out aboard the *Whetstone Valley Express* during Milbank's **Trainfest** celebration, held the second week in August. Orange-and-blue Dakota Rail engines, which typically haul cars that brim with barley rather than people, pull passenger cars to nearby Corona and back. For more information call the Chamber of Commerce at (605) 432–6656.

In Brookings the **South Dakota Art Museum** collection includes early Karl Bodmer sketches, Lakota artifacts (such as the feather headdress of Fools Crow), and renderings of nineteenth-century homestead life by painter

Harvey Dunn. The museum (605–688–5423), located at the corner of Medary and Harvey Dunn on the Campus of South Dakota State University, is open weekdays from 8:00 A.M. to 5:00 P.M., Saturday from 10:00 A.M. to 5:00 P.M., and Sunday from 1:00 to 5:00 P.M.

Take a tour of **DeSmet** (35 miles west of Brookings on Highway 14), the "Little Town on the Prairie" made world-famous by author Laura Ingalls Wilder and named for Father Pierre Jean DeSmet, the intrepid Jesuit missionary who tramped the West, spreading the gospel among the Plains Indians. Tours, which run between 9:00 A.M. and 5:00 P.M. daily Memorial Day through September 15, begin at the Ingalls's first residence in town, originally a railroad surveyors' barracks. Also on the itinerary are the **Ingalls House and Museum,** a place built by Laura's father in 1887, and more than a dozen additional sites that appeared in Laura's stories. An excellent time to visit is the last weekend in June or the first two weekends in July, during the annual **Laura Ingalls Wilder Pageant** dramatic presentation, featuring scenes from Wilder's books, including *The Long Winter* and *These Happy Golden Years.* For more information call the Laura Ingalls Wilder Memorial Society at (605) 854–3383.

In Madison, 45 miles southeast of DeSmet on Highways 25 and 34, the **Smith-Zimmerman State Museum** (605–256–5308), located on Eighth Street on the Dakota State University Campus, includes among its large collection a replicated homesteader's shanty and an antique covered wagon. It's open year-round Thursday through Sunday from 1:00 to 4:30 P.M. Just west of town **Prairie Village** (605–256–3644) offers a graphic glance at nineteenth-century life on the South Dakota range, with more than fifty restored buildings filled with antiques and artifacts. The village is venue for the annual **Steam Threshing Jamboree,** which is held the last full weekend in August and includes rug weaving, quilting, spinning, and horse-powered grain grinding. Nearby at Lake Herman State Park is the 1871 oak-log cabin of homesteader Herman Luce. Call the Chamber of Commerce at (605) 256–2454 for more information.

In Sioux Falls, South Dakota's largest city, visit the **Old Courthouse Museum,** downtown at 200 West Sixth Street. The facility displays artifacts and memorabilia representative of the Plains Indians and the region's earliest white settlers. Also housing relics of the past is the **Pettigrew House,** the century-old home of South Dakota's first senator, located at 131 North Duluth Avenue. More information on these two Siouxland Heritage

Museums, both open Tuesday through Saturday from 9:00 A.M. to 5:00 P.M. and Sunday from 1:00 to 5:00 P.M., can be obtained by calling (605) 335–4210. If you're interested in delving into a particular subject relating to the history of the West, head to the **Center for Western Studies** (605–336–4007), on the campus of Augustana College.

The Prairie Star offers for sale a large selection of Native American arts and artifact reproductions, including star quilts, beadwork, pipestone carvings, drums, buffalo skulls, braided horsehair items, and the sterling-silver jewelry of Lakota silversmith Reed Haskell. The enterprise (605–338–9300) is located at 229 South Phillips Avenue in Sioux Falls. Meanwhile the **Jim Savage Western Art Gallery and Historical Center** (605–332–7551), at 3301 East Twenty-sixth Street, sells Old West antiques, collectibles, and wearable art and also displays the wooden sculptures of the late Jim Savage.

Swing into Vermillion's **W. H. Over State Museum** (605–677–5228), on the campus of the University of South Dakota, which displays pioneer relics and photographs, firearms, and an impressive collection of prereservation Lakota Sioux artifacts. It's open Monday through Friday from 8:00 A.M. to 5:00 P.M. and weekends from 1:00 to 5:00 P.M. Also in town and open to visitors is the 1881 **Austin Whittemore House** (605–624–8266), now housing the Clay County Historical Society Museum. The grand Italian Villa–style Victorian is located at 15 Austin Avenue and is open in summer from 1:00 to 4:00 P.M. Friday through Sunday.

In history-rich Yankton, 25 miles west of Vermillion and territorial capital from 1862 until 1883, visit the **Dakota Territorial Capitol Replica,** located in Riverside Park. (For information on tours call 605–665–4501.) The **Dakota Territorial Museum** (605–665–3898 or 665–3636), found in Westside Park, houses valuable relics that remain from the territorial days. On the third weekend in August, the community revisits its past at the **Yankton Riverboat Days** celebration, which includes a rodeo among its numerous events. Call (800) 888–1460 for complete details.

The stunning **Mulberry Inn** B&B, at 512 Mulberry Street in Yankton, was built in 1873 and today is listed on the National Register of Historic Places. The inn features six guest rooms, two parlors with marble fireplaces, and an expansive porch, perfect for lounging. Call for reservations at (605) 665–7116. Finally, while in Yankton visit the **Mother Earth Gallery** (701–665–5113), dedicated to selling Lakota art and to promoting more complete understanding of the cultural traditions of the western Sioux. The enterprise, found 2 miles west of town on Highway 52, is open Tuesday through Saturday from 10:00 A.M. to 7:00 P.M. and Sunday from 1:00 to 5:00 P.M.

Ninety miles northwest of Yankton, Mitchell's unique and world-famous **Corn Palace** was constructed in 1892 as a symbol of the fertility of South Dakota's soil and to draw new settlers to the region. The palace, enlarged in 1905 and then again in 1921, features murals and other artwork, inside and out, composed entirely of thousands of bushels of corn and other grains and grasses. The exterior is redecorated each year to reflect a new theme. The Corn Palace is located at 604 North Main and is open daily in summer from 8:00 A.M. to 10:00 P.M. and during abbreviated hours the rest of the year; call the Chamber of Commerce at (605) 996–7311 for further information.

Also of note in Mitchell: the very large and artifact-filled **Friends of the Middle Border Museum** (605–996–2122), situated at 1311 South Duff and open daily in summer, and the **Mitchell Prehistoric Indian Village** (605–996–5473), located on Indian Village Road on the shore of Lake Mitchell and open daily May 1 through October 31. Tour guides describe life as archaeologists believe it was in this tenth-century village, where as many as 1,000 hunter-farmers lived. A walk-through earth lodge, a complete bison skeleton, and audiovisual presentations are featured.

Swing into Huron (65 miles northwest of Mitchell) to visit the expansive **Dakotaland Museum** (605–352–4626), located on the State Fair Grounds, which depicts earlier times in central South Dakota. It's open Memorial Day through Labor Day on weekdays from 8:30 to 11:30 A.M., 1:00 to 4:00 P.M., and 6:30 to 8:30 P.M. and on weekends from 1:00 to 4:00 P.M. and 6:30 to 8:30 P.M.

Aberdeen, 90 miles north of Huron, holds a pair of intriguing sites. The **Dacotah Prairie Museum** (605–622–7117), at 21 South Main, boasts a collection of early settlers' paraphernalia. It's open Monday through Friday from 9:00 A.M. to 5:00 P.M. and weekends from 1:00 to 4:00 P.M. The other, **Centennial Village,** a concentration of fourteen nineteenth-century buildings located at the Brown County Fairgrounds, is open Sunday only, from 1:00 to 4:00 P.M. Each August during the county fair, costumed good guys and evil characters populate the village saloon and other structures, occasionally shooting it out on the streets. Call the Aberdeen Convention & Visitors Bureau at (605) 225–2414 for more information.

Central South Dakota

The great Sioux chief Sitting Bull, who defeated General Custer at the Little Bighorn, is buried on the Standing Rock Indian Reservation, on a bluff just across the river from Mobridge. The seven-ton granite bust that marks the gravesite was carved by Korczak Ziolkowski, the late sculptor best known for initiating the Crazy Horse Mountain sculpture in the Black Hills. Also in town, adorning the walls of the Scherr-Howe Arena, is a set of ten 16-by-20-foot murals that depict Sioux history and traditions. The stunning pieces are the work of Native American and native South Dakotan Oscar Howe. The **Sitting Bull Stampede Rodeo,** held over the Fourth of July weekend, is Mobridge's biggest and wildest event; call (605) 845–2387 to learn more about it.

In Pierre, South Dakota's delightfully compact capital city, visit the impeccable **South Dakota Cultural Heritage Center,** a beautifully designed structure that appears to grow from the prairie it celebrates. The center, located at 900 Governors Drive, is open Monday through Friday from 9:00 A.M. to 4:30 P.M. and weekends from 1:00 to 4:30 P.M. Call (605) 773–3458 for more information.

In 1743 the La Verendrye brothers, thought to have been the first whites in the South Dakota territory, buried a lead plate at a point near present-day Pierre, claiming the region for France. The **Verendrye Monument,** west of Pierre across the river, marks the spot, and the **Verendrye Museum** (605–223–3191), in downtown Fort Pierre, relates the story of the La Verendryes and that of Fort Pierre Chouteau, the outpost established in 1832 by Pierre Chouteau, Jr., and South Dakota's first permanent white settlement. The museum is open daily from 9:00 A.M. to 5:00 P.M. in summer.

A fun getaway in the Pierre area: **Cow Creek Lodge,** located 16 miles north of the capital city along Highway 1804 on the banks of Lake Oahe. The lodge offers log-cabin accommodations with kitchenettes and a waterfront restaurant that specializes in steaks and barbecue; it's open seven days a week.

In Chamberlain don't bypass the **Akta Lakota Museum** (605–734–3455), located on the campus of St. Joseph's Indian School. The museum explores the art, spirituality, cultural traditions, and history of the western

Sioux people. Included among its displays are paintings, artifacts, and an exhibit that details the vital role that bison played in the everyday lives of Plains Indians. The museum gift shop sells prints, books, quilts, jewelry, and other items. The facility is open from May to September, Monday through Saturday from 8:00 A.M. to 6:00 P.M. and Sunday from 1:00 to 5:00 P.M.; the rest of the year it is open from 8:00 A.M. to 6:00 P.M., Monday through Saturday.

The delightful **Rafter L Bar Ranch** B&B is located along the banks of the White River, 14 miles south of Interstate 90 from a point near Vivian. This unpretentious hideaway offers three rooms with a shared bath, horseback riding, and good home cooking. Call (605) 895–2202 for more information or to make reservations.

The Badlands and Black Hills

This region hosted the last of the great Western-frontier gold rushes, with things erupting after Gen. George Custer's exploratory party found color in the Black Hills in 1874. Custer's outing also once and for all alienated the Sioux people—to whom the Black Hills were vitally sacred—and set the stage for his own undoing at the Little Bighorn.

Rapid City's **Hotel Alex Johnson,** built in 1928, commemorates the great Sioux Nation, with a multitude of artworks and artifacts displayed on every floor. Regional specialties, including buffalo steaks and native game and trout, are served on the premises in the Landmark Restaurant. For information on rooms at this National Historic Landmark, located at 523 Sixth Street, call (800) 888–2539. Or, if you'd prefer to slip out of town, consider the **Madison Ranch** (605–342–6997), a 1920s rodeo and guest ranch situated 5 miles west of Rapid City on Nemo Road. The lodge, featuring five antiques-appointed rooms and a private collection of Western memorabilia and artifacts, is surrounded by 1,000 forested acres located in Box Elder Creek Canyon. Or, if you prefer, mosey out to the **Flying B Ranch** (605–342–5324), where peaceful overnights are possible on a 3,500-acre cattle spread in the foothills of the Black Hills. The ranch is located 3 miles north of Rapid City (take exit 58 off Interstate 90).

Six miles south of Rapid City along Highway 16, next to Reptile

Filming *Dances with Wolves*

Whether you loved it or hated it, Kevin Costner's film *Dances with Wolves* was a huge success (it won seven Academy Awards), and the 1989 frontier epic almost single-handedly revived interest in the Old West and the Wild Western film genre.

The movie was filmed amid the sprawling prairie-scapes of South Dakota and predominantly featured South Dakota's Native Americans as extras. Doris Leader Charge, a Lakota language instructor at the Sinte Gleska College on the Rosebud Reservation, served as dialogue coach and technical adviser and was also cast as the Sioux matriarch Pretty Shield.

Filming locales included Roy Houck's Triple U Ranch, northwest of Pierre along Highway 1806, where the largest private herd of bison in the world, numbering more than 3,000, also served as extras. The Indian winter camp was filmed in the Black Hills National Forest's Little Spearfish Canyon, whereas the summer camp scenes took place along the Belle Fourche ("Bell Foosh") River. Several tour operators—including Dakota Vistas, Inc., out of Sturgis—offer interpretive tours and up-close-and-personal looks at a number of the filming sites, including the recently relocated replica of Fort Hays, Kansas.

At the Atka Lakota Museum in Chamberlain and at South Dakota's Original 1880 Town near Murdo, props used in the movie are exhibited, and at Costner's Midnight Star Casino in Deadwood, costumes worn by Costner and costar Mary McDonnell are displayed.

Gardens (and not to be confused with the Flying B), the **Flying T Chuckwagon Cowboy Supper & Show** brings to life the cowboying way. After the dinner bell gongs at 7:30, Western grub is dished out on tin plates in the chuckwagon barn; afterward, the Flying T Wranglers sing and joke about life on the prairie. The fun runs Memorial Day through mid-September; call (605) 342–1905 for reservations, a must.

Keystone's **Big Thunder Gold Mine** tour begins with a film that illustrates how Black Hills gold was retrieved in the nineteenth century, then takes visitors underground to inspect the old mine and dig for their own gold ore. The enterprise is open daily from 8:00 A.M. to 8:00 P.M. April 15 through October 15; call (605) 666–4847 for further information. Be sure also to stop into the **Historic Ruby House Restaurant,** on Main Street in Keystone, to sample buffalo steak in authentic 1890s surroundings. The Ruby's Red Garter Saloon shakes things up in the evenings with a Western musical revue.

The **Triple R Ranch** (605–666–4605), located on Highway 16A outside Keystone (8 miles from Mount Rushmore), is one of South Dakota's most traditional dude ranches. Western hospitality at its finest is provided to guests, who reside in rustic cabins. Week-long getaways include hiking and horseback riding through the nearby Black Elk Wilderness and Norbeck Wildlife Preserve. There's also the **Bunkhouse Bed & Breakfast,** found outside Hermosa on an isolated Spring Creek cattle spread, far from the madding Mount Rushmore crowds. Comfortable accommodations, highlighted with Western decor, are accompanied by a ranch breakfast sized for a wrangler. Call (605) 342–5462 for information and reservations.

Custer State Park—at 73,000 acres the nation's second-largest state park—features four mountain resorts, including the gracious **State Game Lodge & Resort** (605–255–4541), nicknamed the "Summer White House" after hosting presidents Coolidge and Eisenhower, and the Western-flaired **Blue Bell Lodge & Resort** (605–255–4531), offering trail rides, hayrides, chuckwagon cookouts, and rustic log-cabin accommodations. Also within the park are several campgrounds, a visitor center, numerous historic sites, and a herd of bison that comprises some 1,500 animals. Bighorn sheep, mountain goats, and elk also call the park home, as do feral burros (perpetually on the lookout for a free snack) and a host of smaller critters, including the ever-barking prairie dog. Horseback riding, jeep safaris, rock climbing, and swimming are but a few of the possibilities in this wondrous outdoor playground, located 5 miles east of Custer and open year-round. Call (605) 255–4515 for maps, information, and camping reservations.

Although the in-progress **Crazy Horse Memorial** carving north of Custer has been caked in controversy for many years in this conservative town, most locals today are proud of it. The late Korczak Ziolkowski labored over the project for many years, and his legacy continues: Visitors can watch history in the making, as the sculptor's family and workers continue drilling and blasting away at the mountain of granite to reveal the horse-mounted likeness of Crazy Horse hidden within. When finished, the grandeur of the

Herds of buffalo roam the prairies and meadows of Custer State Park.

great Lakota chief's memorial will rival, perhaps exceed, that of nearby Mount Rushmore. (Crazy Horse's head alone will be nine stories high; the presidents' faces on Mount Rushmore are "only" six stories tall.) The large visitor center includes a one-thirty-fourth scale model of what the memorial will one day look like and also houses the **Indian Museum of North America,** with its huge collection of Native American artifacts. It's open daily in summer from 7:00 A.M. to 7:00 P.M and in winter from 8:00 A.M. to 5:00 P.M. Call (605) 673–4681 for more information.

Grab a bite at the sprawling **Chief Restaurant** (605–673–4402), on Highway 16 West, where you'll be surrounded by Native American displays and entertained with continuous Western-theme slide shows. The **Custer Mansion** B&B (605–673–3333), at 35 Centennial Drive, offers sumptuous Western hospitality and scrumptious home-cooked breakfasts in an 1891 Victorian Gothic. For something a bit more rugged, call on **Dakota Badland Outfitters** at (605) 673–5363. This longtime Custer-based ranching outfit offers four distinct Old West getaways, including wagon rides and pack trips into the Black Hills and the Badlands. If you'd rather view the backcountry from inside a four-wheel-drive van or astride a bicycle than from atop a horse, call **Golden Circle Tours** at (605) 673–4349, with offices located at 40 North Fifth in Custer.

The outdoor **Paha Sapa** pageant, staged in Custer in July, revisits events from the Black Hills' past, including the discovery of gold east of town at French Creek, the founding of Custer, and the hanging of Fly-Speck Billy.

Fourteen miles west of Hot Springs, the 14,000-acre **Black Hills Wild Horse Sanctuary** is the first privately owned reserve in the United States established expressly to protect wild mustangs. Hundreds of these horses, rounded up by the Bureau of Land Management (BLM) and given away in the agency's Adopt-A-Horse program, run free at their new home on the range. Here, where dark pine forests back sprawling Cheyenne River grasslands, visitors can camp in tipis and partake of chuckwagon dinners and tours, offered daily Memorial Day through September. Call (605) 745–5955 for additional information.

The **Black Hills Central Railroad** 1880 steam locomotive pulses four times daily out of the Hill City depot, 14 miles north of Custer on Highway 385, where you'll also find the High Liner Restaurant and Historic Depot Gift Shop. The two-hour trip, traversing hills and meadows, ends at Keystone (where passengers can also board). Call (605) 574–2222 for schedules and reservations. Hill City's **High Country Ranch** B&B (605–574–9003) proffers cabins decorated in Western style; an overnight includes a half-hour trail ride on a gentle horse and traditional Western grub for the first meal of the day. The ranch rests 4 miles west of town. The **Rafter J Bar Ranch** (605–574–2527), 3 miles south of town, also offers trail riding, as well as camping in private, timbered sites.

The town erupts evenings in summer, Tuesdays through Saturdays, when outlaw Sam Bass sprints out of the Hill City Bank and into the streets, carrying an unauthorized withdrawal of loot. Here he faces the sheriff in a shoot-out, as townspeople and saloon girls race for cover. Don't miss it, and don't miss the **Ishnala Wecha Lakota Art Gallery,** with its contemporary Sioux arts and crafts. For more information on these and other Hill City attractions, events, and accommodations, call the Chamber of Commerce at (800) 888–1798.

Located about 18 miles north of Hill City on Highway 385, the **Circle B Ranch** dishes up Western food and fun seven nights a week, from the Saturday preceding Memorial Day through the Saturday before Labor Day. After a hearty supper of tender South Dakota beef, potatoes, baked beans, and campfire biscuits, the Circle B Cowboys croon about the romantic days of the Old West; horse-drawn wagon rides and trail rides on horseback are also possibilities. The gates open at 5:00 P.M., with supper served at 7:30. For reservations, which are required, call (605) 348–7358.

At the north end of the Black Hills in Lead (rhymes with *seed,* not *said*), just up the street from the Homestake Mine, the largest current gold-mining operation in the United States, the **Black Hills Mining Museum** shows and tells how it was done in the old days with the old ways. Displays explain how and why this rugged country was explored and settled, and they also feature historic mining paraphernalia. Visitors can pan for gold and tour a replica of an underground mine at the museum, open daily from 9:00 A.M. to 5:00 P.M. mid-May through September; call (605) 584–1605 for further information.

In downtown Deadwood, all of which is a National Historic Landmark, get your bearings at the **Deadwood Interpretive Center.** Across the street, at 54 Sherman Street, is the **Adams Memorial Museum,** housing relics that relate to Wild Bill Hickok, Calamity Jane Canary, Potato Creek Johnny, and many other of the notables and notorious who spent time here. Nicknamed "Deadwood's Attic" because of the array of long-forgotten items it hides, the museum even includes the biggest nugget ever retrieved from the Black Hills. The museum (605–578–1714) is open May to September Monday through Saturday from 9:00 A.M. to 6:00 P.M. and Sunday from 9:00 A.M. to 5:00 P.M. (closed Mondays October through April).

The **Ghosts of Deadwood Gulch,** a wax museum that encompasses the likenesses of famous Indian chiefs, Jesuit missionaries, miners, and sol-diers, is located in the Old Towne Hall at 12 Lee Street. It is open May 6 through September 30 from 8:00 A.M. to 6:00 P.M. Old Towne Hall also houses the theater where the tumultuous **Trial of Jack McCall** is staged. The re-created trial of the man charged with murdering Wild Bill Hickok in Saloon No. 10 on August 2, 1876, is performed nightly, except Sundays, from late May through late August. The courtroom drama unfolds at 8:00 P.M., but only after a gunfight outside along Main Street culminates in the capture of the evil McCall. Tickets can be reserved or purchased at the wax museum or by calling (605) 578–3583 or, in the off season, 578–2510.

Take in the streets of Deadwood while learning of their bawdy past by jumping aboard one of the many buses that buzz around town. Typically on the itinerary of the hour-long tours are the old Badlands red-light district, Chinatown, and the hillside **Mount Moriah Cemetery,** the resting place for famous Deadwoodians like Preacher Smith, Wild Bill Hickok, and Calamity Jane, whose deathbed plea was to be buried next to Wild Bill, the only man she'd ever truly loved.

Old West eateries and drinkeries proliferate on the streets of

Deadwood Lives

Deadwood exploded onto the frontier in 1876 during the frenzy of the Black Hills gold rush, and things have seldom quieted since. Wild Bill Hickok, who had a reputation for prowess with a six-shooter earned during his gun-fighting and marshalling days in Kansas, left behind his wife in Wyoming and showed up in Deadwood in 1876. Along with thousands of others, Hickok was looking for Black Hills gold . . . but he found his at the town's gaming tables rather than in its mines.

Wild Bill was shot in the back of the head by Jack McCall while playing poker at the No. 10 Saloon. McCall was captured, tried, and aquitted, based on his claim that Hickok had murdered his brother a few months earlier. But Deadwood's paper, the *Black Hills Pioneer,* maintained that "a drunken and irresponsible jury had freed a cowardly killer" and, in fact, McCall was arrested shortly thereafter in Nebraska, when caught bragging about pulling a big one over on the Deadwood jury. He was retried and found guilty in Yankton, and hung on March 1, 1877.

Illegal gambling flourished well into the twentieth century, until a crackdown in 1947, and brothels operated—sometimes discreetly, sometimes not—until the early 1980s. With the legalization of limited-stakes gambling in 1989, it seems that things won't quiet down in Deadwood for some time to come: More than 100 gambling halls now run in the gaming district.

Deadwood's Old Style Saloon No. 10

Deadwood. Among them: **Back at the Ranch,** boasting an open-pit mesquite grill at 681 Main Street, and the **Dakota Territory Saloon,** at 625 Main Street. **Old Style Saloon No. 10,** 657 Main Street, claims to be "the only museum in the world with a bar," offering drinks and gambling in the Main Street saloon where Wild Bill Hickok met his maker. The walls and rafters hold Wild West artifacts, photographs, and even Hickok's wedding license.

Twentieth-century comforts meld with nineteenth-century furnishings at the grand **Bullock Hotel** (605–578–1745 or 800–336–1876), a Deadwood mainstay since it was built in 1895 by the town's first sheriff, Seth Bullock. The stone-block hostelry, located at 633 Main, features twenty-eight luxurious guest rooms; below, gambling goes on twenty-four hours a day in the hotel's gaming hall, and Bully's Restaurant is also on the premises. For more information on area attractions and accommodations, call the Deadwood/Lead Area Chamber of Commerce at (605) 578–1876.

The **Old Fort Meade Cavalry Museum,** a couple of miles east of Sturgis on Highway 34/79, recalls the days of the 7th Cavalry, which was stationed here during the 1880s, after its heavy losses at the Battle of the Little Bighorn. The fort itself was operational until 1945, when it was converted into a VA hospital, and more than a dozen buildings still stand. The fort museum, containing artifacts and displays that illuminate the post's sixty-five years in service, is open daily from 9:00 A.M. to 5:00 P.M. May 1

Fort Meade

Fort Meade was built by the 1st and 11th infantry divisions during the winter of 1878–79, for the purpose of housing troops charged with standing sentinel over settlers and gold seekers who were penetrating the sacred land of the Sioux. Fort Meade was the scene of the court-martialing of Marcus Reno, the major dismissed from the service in disgrace for purported cowardice at the Battle of the Little Bighorn, where he had served as a commander in Custer's 7th Cavalry. Posthumously, Reno was officially absolved of the charges, but the court-martialing ruined his reputation and the rest of his life.

Comanche, the buckskin horse that was the sole U.S. Army survivor of Custer's detachment at the Little Bighorn, retired at Fort Meade with military honors. Comanche was transferred to Fort Riley, Kansas, along with the rest of the 7th Cavalry, in 1888.

A final historic tidbit: Beginning in 1892 Fort Meade was the first army post at which *The Star-Spangled Banner* was regularly played at retreat ceremonies. The practice spread from here to other posts around the United States and led to the 1916 executive order that named it the national anthem.

through September 30 (8:00 A.M. to 7:00 P.M. Memorial Day through Labor Day). Cavalry reenactments are presented occasionally during summer, and the Old Post Cemetery makes for a poignant visit, regardless of the season. Call (605) 347–5240 or 347–2818 to learn more about the fort, which is open from 9:00 A.M. to 7:00 P.M. daily, and call the BLM at (605) 892–2526 for a brochure that details the **Fort Meade Back Country Byway.**

In the peaceful community of Spearfish, visit the splendid **High Plains Heritage Center,** featuring interpretive exhibits as well as artwork that depicts the Old West. A chuckwagon supper and unique "buffalo show" are offered on Monday and Wednesday evenings in summer. The museum, located at 825 Heritage Drive, is open daily from 9:00 A.M. to 8:00 P.M. in summer and 9:00 A.M. to 5:00 P.M. the rest of the year; call (605) 642–9378 for further information.

Where to Eat

Flying T Chuckwagon Cowboy Supper & Show, Rapid City, (605) 342–1905
Ruby House Restaurant, Keystone, (605) 666–4404
Chief Restaurant, Custer, (605) 673–4402
Circle B Ranch, north of Hill City, (605) 348–7358
Back at the Ranch, Deadwood, (605) 578–1300
Dakota Territory Saloon, Deadwood, (605) 578–3566
Old Style Saloon No. 10, Deadwood, (605) 578–3346

Where to Stay

Mulberry Inn, Yankton, (605) 665–7116
Rafter L Bar Ranch Bed & Breakfast, outside Vivian, (605) 895–2202
Hotel Alex Johnson, Rapid City, (800) 888–2539
Madison Ranch, outside Rapid City, (605) 342–6997
Flying B Ranch, outside Rapid City, (605) 342–5324
Triple R Ranch, Keystone, (605) 666–4605

Bunkhouse Bed & Breakfast, Hermosa, (605) 342–5462
State Game Lodge & Resort, Custer State Park, (605) 255–4541
Blue Bell Lodge & Resort, Custer State Park, (605) 255–4531
Custer Mansion Bed & Breakfast, Custer, (605) 673–3333
High Country Ranch Bed & Breakfast, Hill City, (605) 574–9003
Bullock Hotel, Deadwood, (605) 578–1745

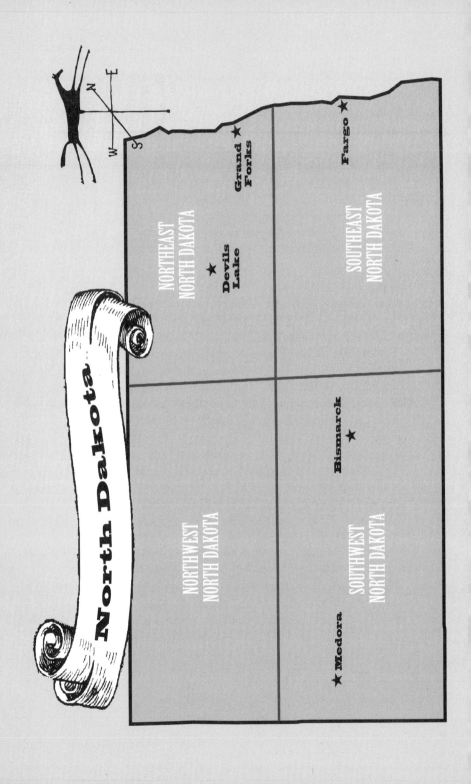

North Dakota

NORTHWEST
NORTH DAKOTA

NORTHEAST
NORTH DAKOTA

★ Devils
Lake

★ Grand
Forks

SOUTHWEST
NORTH DAKOTA

SOUTHEAST
NORTH DAKOTA

★ Medora

Bismarck
★

Fargo ★

NORTH DAKOTA

▼▼▼

MUCH HAS BEEN written about the Oregon Trail, the Santa Fe Trail, and other early emigrant and commerce highways. The first, however, and perhaps the greatest frontier trail of all was the Missouri River, a large share of which cuts through North Dakota, a state that brims with the legacy of Native Americans, trappers, Indian fighters, frontier cowboys, and homesteaders.

The narrative begins in the northeast part of the Peace Garden State, then continues into the southeast and the southwest, ending in the rugged reaches of northwest North Dakota.

Northeast North Dakota

Begin near the south shore of the fishing haven of Devils Lake, where the **Fort Totten State Historic Site** preserves one of the best remaining examples of an Indian-wars–era military fort. Built as an Army outpost in 1867, Fort Totten served longer than most of its peers: The brick buildings evolved into an Indian health-care facility and then a reservation school before finally closing shop in 1959. Sixteen buildings built between 1868 and 1871 remain, with superb exhibits that reflect on the post's past, along with a museum store/interpretive center. The picturesque grounds are open year-round, and the center is open to visitors daily from 8:00 A.M. to 5:00 P.M. between May 16 and September 15. Call (701) 766–4441 for more information.

In Rugby, proclaimed by the U.S. Geological Survey as the Geographical Center of North America, visit the **Geographical Center Pioneer Village & Museum.** Open May 1 through October 1 from 8:00 A.M. to 7:00 P.M. daily, the facility maintains a vast array of artifacts, housed in a correspondingly large collection of historic buildings. Awaiting discovery: antique guns, Indian and Eskimo artifacts, a Great Northern Railroad depot, a Norwegian immigrant's home, a well-stocked general store, a saloon where you can wet your whistle with a frothy root beer, and a lot more. The complex is located on Highway 2 East; call the Chamber of Commerce at (701) 776–5846 for more information.

Walhalla is home to North Dakota's largest concentration of moose as well as one of the state's best ski areas (bet you didn't think North Dakota had *any* moose *or* ski areas). It's also where you'll find **Walhalla State Historic Site** and the transported-in, then rebuilt, 1851 trading post of Norman Kittson. About 1.5 miles northeast of town is the restored **Gingras Trading Post State Historic Site.** Between 1843 and 1873 the log-hewn oak house and store—now the oldest remaining structures built by whites in North Dakota—served the burgeoning Metis (meh-TEE) community of the upper Red River valley. The post, offering replica fur-trade merchandise for sale, is open daily from 10:00 A.M. to 5:00 P.M. May 15 through September 15. Call (701) 549–2775 for more information.

Like hundreds of other people in Iceland in the late 1870s, the Eggert and Rannveig Gunnlaugsson family were forced by harsh conditions to emigrate from their homeland to North America. In 1880 they settled 5 miles west of present Cavalier, where today you can visit **Icelandic State Park** and the Gunlogson Homestead (the spelling of their name changed through time). The homestead includes their farmhouse and barn and a one-room school, while nearby is the new Pioneer Heritage Center, open daily, which details the settlement of the region by Icelandic immigrants and nearly two dozen other ethnic groups that arrived between 1870 and 1920. Twenty-two flags, representing all of these people, fly at the center. The **Pioneer Heritage Days** in June celebrates this rich mix of settlers with arts and crafts, lectures, ethnic foods, crafts displays, and tours. Call (701) 265–4561 for more information.

Pembina, in the extreme northeast corner of North Dakota, became the first European settlement in the region in 1797 when it was chosen as the site for the Northwest Company's Fort Panbian. The **Pembina State Historical Museum** celebrates that early heritage, with displays on the prehistoric Chippewas and Ojibwas, Metis buffalo hunters, frontier soldiers, and early means of transportation—namely steamboats, which plied the Red River beginning in 1859, and the St. Paul-to-Winnipeg stage line, which ran through Pembina in the 1860s. The museum, situated in temporary quarters at the corner of Stutsman and Sixth streets, is open daily Memorial Day through Labor Day from 1:00 to 5:00 P.M. and by appointment (701–825–6209) the rest of the year.

Pass through Grafton and swing into the **Walsh County Heritage Village** (701–352–3280); then proceed to Grand Forks, where the *Dakota Queen,* a 150-passenger side-wheeler riverboat, makes regular lunch and dinner cruises on the Red River during summer, pending repairs to damage caused by the 1997 floods. Call (701) 775–5656 for information.

Southeast North Dakota

Fargo, North Dakota's largest city, is where you'll find **Bonanzaville, USA.** This restored pioneer village includes a wealth of artifacts distributed in more than forty buildings and spread about fifteen acres; they include log and sod houses, antique farm machinery, and a museum filled with Native American artifacts. **Pioneer Days** erupt here in late August, with parades, demonstrations of pioneer skills and crafts, a threshing bee, dancing, and concerts. Bonanzaville, located along West Highway 10 in West Fargo, is open daily year-round, except during the weeks of Thanksgiving, Christmas, and New Year's Day. The village buildings are open for touring every day June through October and Monday through Friday the rest of the year. Call (701) 282–2822 for more information.

North of Wahpeton, in Abercrombie, visit **Fort Abercrombie State Historic Site.** This military post on the Red River was authorized by Congress in March 1857 as one component in a series of similar posts that linked St. Paul with the Montana gold fields. The fort's most dramatic times were during the Minnesota War of 1862, when it was besieged by Sioux Indians over a period of nearly six weeks. The site, at the east edge of town, includes one original building, as well as a reconstructed palisade wall and blockhouses. The interpretive museum is open May 16 through September 15 from 8:00 A.M. to 5:00 P.M. daily. Call (701) 553–8513 for further information.

Ten miles west of Wahpeton on Highway 13, the **Bagg Bonanza Farm** is among the last of a breed of colossal wheat farms that burgeoned with the arrival of the railroad to the Great Plains. In 1873, the year after the

Northern Pacific entered North Dakota, the railroad's primary financier, Jay Cooke, went bankrupt. The Northern Pacific, in order to raise the funds necessary to continue building its line westward, permitted stockholders—who then were holding deflated shares—to buy large tracts of its land at very low prices. Attorney J. F. Downing, from Erie, Pennsylvania, was one stockholder who took the railroad up on its offer; by the time his nephew, F. A. Bagg, joined his enterprise in 1886, Downing owned nearly 10,000 acres of North Dakota prairieland.

When his uncle died in 1913, Bagg took his quarter-interest inheritance, buildings and all, and began his own bonanza farm a mile up the road. Some thirty buildings remain, including Bagg's house, which was originally built as a bunkhouse on his uncle's farm in the 1870s, then hauled to the new site in 1915. The fifteen-acre farmsite was acquired by the Bagg Bonanza Farm Historic Preservation Society in 1989; the society's ultimate goal: restore all the buildings and resume agricultural production, in order to demonstrate to the public this important chapter in the history of North Dakota and westward expansion. The facility is open Memorial Day through Labor Day on Tuesday through Friday from 11:00 A.M. to 5:00 P.M. and on weekends from noon to 6:00 P.M. Call (701) 274–8989 for more information. (You can spend the night at the nearby **Adams Fairview Bonanza Farm B&B.** Call 701–274–8262 for information and directions.)

In Fort Ransom, a pretty town on the wooded banks of the Sheyenne River (70 miles northwest of Wahpeton) that has gained repute as an arts center, visit the **Fort Ransom County Museum,** open afternoons May 1 through October. **Fort Ransom State Park,** a mile southwest of town, memorializes the site of old Fort Ransom, a 200-man military post built in 1867. The dry moat, once 8 feet deep, and building locations are readily discernible, but nothing remains of the fort buildings or its 12-foot-high log-and-sod stockade. The state park each year hosts the **Sodbuster Days** celebration in July, with wagon rides and horse-powered farming demonstrations. During late September's **Sheyenne Valley Arts and Crafts Festival,** the town turns into one large gallery, and the nearby state park hosts a **7th Cavalry Re-Enactment** horseback charge. Call (701) 973–4331 for more information.

Jamestown, at the junction of Interstate 94 and Highway 281, is home to the *World's Largest Buffalo,* a sixty-ton sculpture that commemorates the animal formerly so abundant in these parts that the earth trembled as herds thundered by. Nearby are the new **National Buffalo Interpretive Center,** featuring artifacts from the days of the buffalo hunters, and **Frontier Village,** where numerous old buildings have been moved in and visitors are entertained with live music and a herd of much smaller, living bison. The facility, located off Interstate 94 at exit 258, is open daily May through September from 9:00 A.M. to 9:00 P.M. Call (701) 252–6307 for more information about the attraction, which includes the Louis L'Amour Gallery among its finds.

The **Fort Seward Interpretive Center** (701–252–6682), also in Jamestown, is open daily. Its **Fort Seward Wagon Train** (701–252–6844), which creaks out of town and onto the prairie in late June, is as authentic in every detail as the organizers can make it. This weeklong outing has attracted participants from throughout the United States and several foreign countries. Registration is limited to the first 150 sign-ups. For more information on Jamestown sites and activities, call the Promotion and Tourism Center at (701) 252–4835 or stop by their office at 212 Third Avenue Northeast.

Southwest North Dakota

In Bismarck/Mandan, 100 miles west of Jamestown on Interstate 94, head to the **North Dakota Heritage Center** (701–328–2666), located on the State Capitol grounds. Open daily 8:00 A.M. until 5:00 P.M. (it opens at 9:00 A.M. on Saturdays and 11:00 A.M. on Sundays), it features a brilliant array of historical items that relate to the state and the northern plains in general. On display are frontier military and pioneer items, along with one of the world's premier collections of Plains Indian artifacts. Also visit the **North Dakota Railroad Museum,** north of Mandan, featuring Northern Pacific Railroad artifacts, and **Camp Hancock State Historic Site,** in downtown Bismarck at 101 West Main Street. The old log headquarters building, now disguised with clapboard siding, holds exhibits on local history and is open from May 16 to September 15 Wednesday through Sunday from 1:00 to 5:00 P.M. Call (701) 328–9664 for information.

A ride on either the **Fort Lincoln Trolley** from Mandan or the *Lewis & Clark* paddlewheeler out of Bismarck will deliver you to superlative, history-rich **Fort Abraham Lincoln State Park.** Gen. George Armstrong Custer was stationed here when he initiated the events that alienated the

Sioux Indians once and for all, in particular his exploratory mission into the Black Hills, the Sioux's most sacred place. It was also from Fort Lincoln that Custer, by many accounts an egomaniacal dullard, marched west to meet his maker at the Little Big Horn. Custer's home, recently renovated, is open for touring daily from 9:00 A.M. to 8:30 P.M. Memorial Day through Labor Day and by appointment the rest of the year.

In late June the **Frontier Army Days** gathering features a reenactment of military life at the post in 1874, presented by the Frontier Army of Dakota. Also at Fort Lincoln are a top-notch museum, which houses cavalry-era relics, a trading post, and the **On-A-Slant Mandan Village,** with eighteenth-century earth lodges that were reconstructed by the Civilian Conservation Corps (CCC) in the 1930s. The park is situated 5 miles south of Mandan on Highway 1806; call (701) 663–9571 for more information.

Big area events include the **Mandan Jaycee Rodeo Days** (701–222–4308), conducted over the Fourth of July, and the **United Tribes Powwow** (701–255–3285), held in early September. For an overnight possibility, check out the **White Lace Bed and Breakfast** (701–258–6877). For further information on Bismarck/Mandan sites and celebrations, call the Convention and Visitors Bureau at (701) 222–4308 or stop by the information booth on Highway 83 North.

Four miles west of Washburn, which is 40 miles north of Bismarck, visit **Fort Mandan State Historic Site,** where the Lewis and Clark Expedition spent the winter of 1804–05. Then head south of town to the **Cross Ranch Centennial State Park,** which encompasses a fine interpretive center, a network of trails, and the primitive Centennial Log Cabin. The cabin, which has neither electricity nor running water and is heated by a wood stove, is available for rent, sleeping ten (somewhat) comfortably. The cabin furnishings that aren't antiques are replicas, handmade by members of the Fort Lincoln Corral of the Westerners International, the group also responsible for gathering and identifying the donated antiques. For information and reservations call the park at (701) 794–3731.

Adjacent to the park is the 6,000-acre **Cross Ranch Nature Preserve,** which encompasses approximately half of the ranch developed late in the nineteenth century by A. D. Gaines. Bob and Gladys Levis bought the ranch in 1956, renaming it the Cross Ranch when they acquired Teddy Roosevelt's old Maltese Cross brand. The Nature Conservancy then purchased the Cross Ranch in 1978, in order to preserve a unique cross-section

With Custer at Fort Lincoln

I n the spring of 1874, a young George Bird Grinnell traveled west to join Gen. George Custer's Black Hills expedition as a naturalist. On this trip gold was discovered in the Black Hills, which led to events that precipitated the Battle of the Little Big Horn. Consider these passages from *The Passing of the Great West—Selected Papers of George Bird Grinnell*, edited by John F. Reiger (Winchester Press: 1972).

We left St. Paul for Fargo, where we spent the night, and the following day took a daylight train for Bismarck, Dakota, just across the river from Fort Abraham Lincoln, our destination. At the time Bismarck was the end of [the] track for the Northern Pacific Railroad. . . .

Custer did no shooting that was notable. It was observed that, though he enjoyed telling of the remarkable shots that he himself commonly made, he did not seem greatly interested in the shooting done by other people. . . .

Soon after crossing the Little Missouri . . . the abandoned camp was found of a great body of Indians. . . . In conversation that evening in front of General Custer's tent, . . . North [L. H. North, Grinnell's assistant] remarked that perhaps it was just as well the Indians had gone before the expedition got there, as there were a great many of them. Custer commented, "I could whip all the Indians in the northwest with the Seventh Cavalry."

(Grinnell went on to become Teddy Roosevelt's favorite conservation adviser, a founder of both the Boone & Crockett Club and the Audubon Society, and one of the greatest early authorities on the Plains Indians.)

of the Missouri River valley's diverse habitats, including upland prairie, brushy draws, and forested river bottom. As in an earlier day, bison—a large and growing herd of them—graze the unbroken prairie.

Near Stanton, 70 miles upstream along the Missouri River from Bismarck, the **Knife River Indian Village National Historic Site** memorializes one of the oldest sites of continuous occupation in North America. The National Park Service's multimillion-dollar Native American

Interpretive Center, designed in a style that echoes that of the surrounding earth lodges, explores the Mandan and Hidatsa people who resided here. The Corps of Discovery spent the winter of 1804–05 in the region with these people (see Fort Mandan State Historic Site, p. 416); it was here, in fact, that Lewis and Clark met Sacajawea (sometimes spelled Sakakawea or Sakagawea) and took her into the fold of the expedition. The visitor center, a half-mile north of Stanton, is open daily Memorial Day through Labor Day from 8:00 A.M. to 6:00 P.M. and from 8:00 A.M. to 4:30 P.M. the rest of the year. For information call (701) 745–3309.

Lewis and Clark also spent time with the Mandans and Hidatsas on their return trip from the Pacific Northwest in 1806, and the August presentation, **Lewis and Clark Among the Earthlodge People,** resurrects the events that unfolded during that visit. Call (701) 745–3309 for schedule information.

Nearby **Fort Clark State Historic Site** marks the location of one of three major fur-trading posts established on the upper Missouri early in the nineteenth century. Built in 1831 by James Kipp for the American Fur Company, the fort's primary goal was to enhance trade with the Indians who lived at the earth-lodge village that had sprung up at the site just a decade earlier. The whites traded iron tools, liquor, cookware, glass beads, and sheet metal—all hauled up-river in steamboats—in exchange for buffalo hides, corn, meat, and horses.

Things went relatively smoothly until June 1837, when the steamboat *St. Peter* delivered, along with its cargo, a scourge of smallpox. The disease decimated the Indians: It's estimated that the Mandan population of the village plummeted from 1,600 to 100 individuals by late that autumn. (The *St. Peter* also brought smallpox to upstream Fort Union that summer.) The historic site, 7 miles southeast of Stanton, is open daily April 1 through October 31 from 8:00 A.M. to 5:00 P.M. Call (701) 794–8832 for information.

The Knife River flint, quarried and shaped into tools by the earth-lodge people, was crucial to the Mandans' and Hidatsas' roles as agents of trade. An impressive display of the flint, which has been found at archaeological excavations as far away as the southeastern United States, is exhibited at the **Dunn County Museum** in Dunn Center, 60 miles west of Stanton. Ten miles northwest of Killdeer (which is just west of Dunn Center) the **Killdeer Mountain Battlefield State Historic Site** marker commemorates the July 28, 1864, battle fought between Gen. Alfred Sully's 2,200 troops and a village of approximately 6,000 Sioux. Sully's troops managed to scatter the village and kill between 100 and 150 Indians, while losing only five soldiers.

Dickinson, Queen City of the Prairies, hosts **Rough Rider Days** over the Fourth of July weekend—a whiz-bang Western fest that features a rodeo, dancing, and concerts. The community's **Joachim Regional Museum** includes changing displays that interpret the history of western North Dakota. Call (701) 225–5115 or 225–4988 for more information.

The **Logging Camp Ranch,** 14 miles northwest of Amidon, was established in 1884 as a horse-trading enterprise. Available for rent today are three hand-built, native-pine cabins with electricity (but no running water or bathrooms) and a larger lodge that sleeps eight, with showers, bathroom, and kitchen. Hiking and four-wheel-drive rides through the ruggedly eroded, red-scoria-accented Badlands are popular at the ranch, which has been in the Hanson family since 1904 and was opened to guests in 1983. For information and reservations call (701) 279–5501 or 279–5702.

Catch the Bully Spirit in Medora, North Dakota's most popular summer attraction, "Where City Slickers Become Rough Riders." Medora, 25 miles east of the Montana border on Interstate 94, is jam-packed with Old West sites and celebrations: For a beginning take in the **Dakota Cowboy Poetry Gathering** (701–623–4444), which brings top-notch local and national cowboy poets to town over Memorial Day weekend and also features a Western art show. The Burning Hills Amphitheater, nestled into a natural Badlands bowl, is home to the *Medora Musical*—an entertaining homage to Teddy Roosevelt and the cowboying way, whooped up amid an inspirational outdoor setting. After parking above the bowl, visitors are lowered seven stories down an escalator into the 2,800-seat amphitheater, where the Broadway-style show with an Old West twist is performed nightly, mid-June through Labor Day. For reservations call (701) 623–4433.

Shop for a spell or simply mosey about Medora's **Cowboy Boomtown,** with its Western-flavored stores, restaurants, swinging-door saloons, shooting galleries, and museums. The **Billings County Courthouse Museum,** open daily in summer, features top-notch displays on ranching, whereas the **Museum of the Bad Lands** brims with relics of life in general on the Western frontier.

The rugged, rough-hewn beauty of the Badlands cemented Theodore Roosevelt's rock-hard conviction for conserving the natural world. As

The Medora Musical *is performed every night from mid-June through Labor Day.*

president he signed into law the 1906 Antiquities Act, under which he set aside eighteen national monuments and also set the stage for the 1916 creation of the National Park Service, the agency that ultimately designated and continues to protect Roosevelt's namesake preserve, **Theodore Roosevelt National Park.** Bighorn sheep, elk, longhorn cattle, and bison roam the park, which is divided into a South Unit and North Unit. (The undeveloped Elkhorn Ranch Site, the location of one of T.R.'s two area ranches, lies along the Little Missouri River between the two; inquire at the visitor center concerning access.) The park's Medora Visitor Center, at the west end of town, includes a museum that displays some of Roosevelt's personal effects, along with artifacts of early ranch life and exhibits on the natural history of the Badlands. T.R.'s restored Maltese Cross cabin is situated behind the visitor center.

The **Chateau de Mores State Historic Site** details the origins of Medora and a chapter in the compelling life of Antoine de Vallombrosa, the dashing Marquis de Mores. The French nobleman founded Medora, naming it for his wife, and invested millions in his scheme to ship slaughtered

Teddy Roosevelt and the Badlands

T he nation's first dude ranch opened near Medora in the 1880s, during the period when Texas cattlemen were driving huge herds of longhorns into the region. Wealthy Easterners, such as Theodore Roosevelt, made pilgrimages to the Badlands, hoping to find adventure in the Wild West they had heard and read so much about.

Young Roosevelt first arrived in 1883, frail and asthmatic, to hunt buffalo; he so enjoyed the rugged outing and the time spent with guide Joe Ferris that he bought a cattle ranch 8 miles south of Medora. Roosevelt worked roundups and went hunting with free-spirited cowpokes on his Maltese Cross Ranch, experiences that would change him forever and mold his future. In a speech at Fargo in 1910, Roosevelt declared that it was in Medora "where I spent the happiest and most profitable years of my life. If it had not been for what I learned during these years . . . here in North Dakota, I would never in the world have been president of the United States."

cattle east from here in refrigerated railcars, in order to provide consumers with a fresher, better-tasting product. De Mores built a packing plant, bought cattle and rangeland, and employed a bevy of cowboys and slaughterhouse workers.

For three years the enterprise hummed, and De Mores expanded his business interests to include even a Medora-to-Black Hills stage line. But the meat-packing plan and the Marquis's empire collapsed in 1886, as a result of the public's growing taste for corn-fed beef, fierce competition from Chicago meat packers, and De Mores's often less-than-astute business practices. His never-say-die spirit still glows, however, as a symbol of the optimistic outlook of Western-frontier dreamers. The most graphic reminders of his one-time presence are the packing-plant smokestack (the plant burned in 1907) and the sumptuous twenty-seven-room hill-top château that his family donated to the state in 1936. The interpretive center and château are open daily May 16 through September 15 from 8:30 A.M. to 6:30 P.M.; call (701) 623–4355 for additional information.

You can make like a Roosevelt Rough Rider while in the Medora area by heading south 20 miles to the **Dahkotah Lodge** (800–508–4897) and taking part in one of their trail rides. Camping, cattle drives, and cabin overnights are all options at the lodge, where reservations are required. Closer to town, **Peaceful Valley Ranch** (701–623–4496) leads interpretive horseback rides through the spectacular badlands of Teddy Roosevelt National Park. For a unique badlands dining experience, take in the **Pitchfork Fondue,** a mouth-watering steak dinner served at Medora's Amphitheatre Picnic Site. Tickets are available at area motels and campgrounds and at the **Harold Schafer Heritage Center.**

For more information on Medora's sites, accommodations, and activities, including details on trail-ride outfitters, call the Convention and Visitors Bureau at (701) 623–4444 or stop by either the Theodore Roosevelt National Park visitor center at the west end of town or the information desk at the historic **Rough Riders Hotel** (701–623–4433), a hotel, incidentally, famous for its buffalo burgers and other Western fare, served daily from 7:00 A.M. to 9:00 P.M.

Northwest North Dakota

At **Fort Union Trading Post National Historic Site,** which straddles the North Dakota–Montana border, recent National Park Service excavations have unearthed a mother lode of artifacts that shed new light on the fort's past. Portions of the stone bastions have been reconstructed, as have the Indian trade house and the Bourgeois House, the imposing, purposely pretentious residence of the post commander. The exterior of the Bourgeois House appears much as it did in the 1850s; inside it holds a visitor center and reference library. Fort Union is open Memorial Day through Labor Day from 8:00 A.M. to 8:00 P.M. and the rest of the year from 9:00 A.M. to 5:30 P.M. Call (701) 572–9083 for more information.

The **Fort Union Trading Post Rendezvous,** slated for mid-June, resurrects a gathering from the fur-trade era. Participants rendezvous for four days of serious business and serious fun, donning clothing and residing in dwellings typical of the early 1800s. Competitions include tomahawk throws, buffalo-chip tosses, and frying-pan throws; blacksmithing and other primitive-skills demonstrations run continuously.

Fort Buford State Historic Site, location of the military post built literally with the remains of Fort Union, housed six companies of infantry and

Fort Union

White interest in the region that surrounds the confluence of the Missouri and Yellowstone rivers was kindled when William Clark, of the Lewis and Clark expedition, opined that whoever came to claim the confluence region would likely take control of the fur trade of the entire Northwest.

John Jacob Astor, of the American Fur Company, built Fort Union at the confluence in 1829, with the ruthless Scotch-Canadian Kenneth McKenzie serving as bourgeois, or superintendent. For twenty years thenceforth Fort Union was at center stage of the upper Missouri fur trade. Crow Indians from the south, Assiniboines from the north, and Blackfeet from the Missouri headwaters brought beaver plews (pelts) and buffalo hides to trade. Inhabitants and visitors included white and black Americans, Spaniards, Italians, Germans, Russians, Englishmen, Frenchmen, and others.

Demand for beaver waned in the mid-1830s, as European hat makers switched to silk as their preferred fabric. Simultaneously, however, the demand for buffalo hides increased, so trade remained strong at the fort until late in that decade, when a smallpox scourge arrived aboard the steamboat St. Peter. Trade diminished, was temporarily revived, and then slowed again when a second smallpox epidemic devastated the Indians in 1857.

By the time the Civil War exploded, Fort Union had seen its better days. The majority of the buildings were dismantled by the Army in the 1860s, and soldiers floated the logs downstream a mile for use in constructing the Fort Buford military post.

cavalry at its zenith. Its vital location at the confluence of the Missouri and Yellowstone rivers ensured that the soldiers stationed there saw plenty of action. Among the Indian-fighting units garrisoned at Buford were the black Buffalo Soldiers of the 10th Cavalry and 25th Infantry.

Nez Perce Chief Joseph was imprisoned at the fort for a spell, as were the Sioux leaders Gall, Crow King, and Sitting Bull. Today a museum housed in one of the original military structures relates the fort's history, and in June the 6th Infantry group stages a reenactment at the fort. The site is open daily May 16 through September 15 from 9:00 A.M. to 6:00 P.M. and the rest of the year by appointment; call (701) 572–9034 for information.

Where to Eat

Rough Riders Hotel, Medora, (701) 623–4433
Pitchfork Fondue, Medora, (701) 623–4433

Where to Stay

Adams Fairview Bonanza Farm Bed & Breakfast, outside Wahpeton, (701) 274–8262
White Lace Bed and Breakfast, Bismarck-Mandan, (701) 258–6877
Logging Camp Ranch, outside Amidon, (701) 279–5501 or –5702
Dahkotah Lodge, outside Medora, (800) 508–4897
Rough Riders Hotel, Medora, (701) 623–4433

Index